Books by Bruce Catton

The Coming Fury
Never Call Retreat
A Stillness at Appomattox
Terrible Swift Sword
This Hallowed Ground

Published by WASHINGTON SQUARE PRESS

BRUCE CATTON
A STILLNESS AT APPOMATTOX

WASHINGTON SQUARE PRESS
PUBLISHED BY POCKET BOOKS
New York   London   Toronto   Sydney   Tokyo

WSP

A Washington Square Press Publication of
POCKET BOOKS, a division of Simon & Schuster Inc.
1230 Avenue of the Americas, New York, N.Y. 10020

ISBN: 0-671-53143-3

First Pocket Books printing November 1958

30   29   28   27   26   25   24

WASHINGTON SQUARE PRESS and WSP colophon are
registered trademarks of Simon & Schuster Inc.

Printed in the U.S.A.

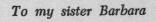

To my sister Barbara

Contents

CHAPTER IV

White Iron on the Anvil

CHAPTER V

Away, You Rolling River

CHAPTER VI

Endless Road Ahead

A STILLNESS AT
APPOMATTOX

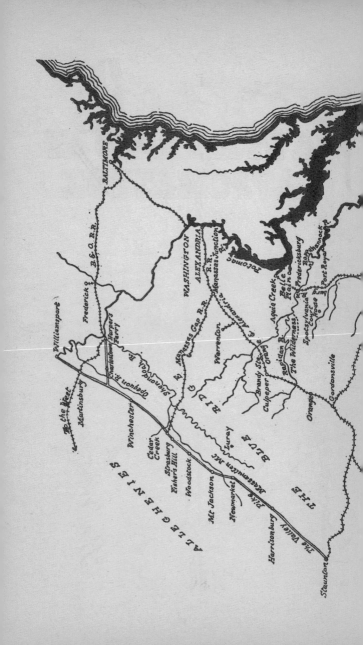

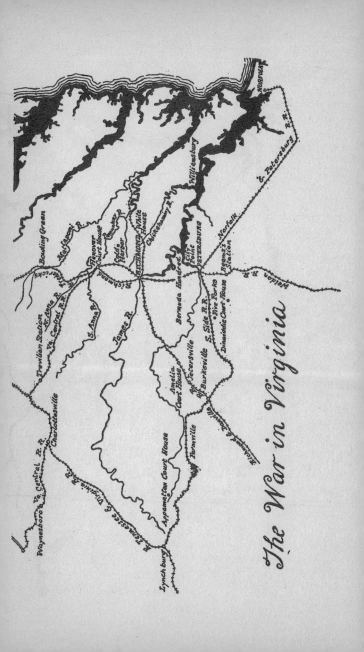

The War in Virginia

CHAPTER I

Glory Is Out of Date

---

1. A Boy Named Martin

EVERYBODY agreed that the Washington's Birthday ball was the most brilliant event of the winter. Unlike most social functions in this army camp by the Rapidan, it was not held in a tent. There was a special, weatherproof ballroom—a big box of a building more than a hundred feet long, whose construction had kept scores of enlisted men busy. Some of these had been sent into the woods to fell trees. Others had taken over and operated an abandoned sawmill, to reduce the trees to boards. Still others, carpenters in some former incarnation, had taken these boards and built the building itself, and it was pleasantly odorous of new-cut pine, decorated with all of the headquarters and regimental flags which the II Army Corps possessed. The flags may have been worth seeing. It was the boast of this corps that although it had suffered nearly 19,000 battle casualties it had never yet lost a flag to the enemy.

At one end of the ballroom there was a raised platform on which, to dazzle the guests, there was an idyllic representation of what the ladies from Washington might imagine to be a typical army bivouac—spotless shelter tents pulled tight to eliminate wrinkles, piles of drums and bugles, tripods of stacked muskets, mimic campfire with cooking kettles hung over it, and as a final touch two brass Napoleons, polished and shining until their own gun crews would hardly know them, reflecting the light of Chinese lanterns, as brightly festive as any instruments of pain and death one could hope to see.

Some of the guests—the wives of officers who had enough rank or influence to be attended by their womenfolk while in winter quarters—were more or less permanent residents of this highly impermanent camp. Others, who had come down from the capital by train just for this occasion, were quartered in wall tents, and since a woman in a hoop-skirted party gown could neither ride horseback nor walk on the muddy footways of an army camp, their escorts called for them in white-topped army ambulances.

The escorts were of course officers, both of staff and of line. They wore their dress uniforms, and they had their swords neatly hooked up at their belts, and even though they were to spend the evening dancing many of them wore spurs. It was remarked that both escorts and guests seemed to make a particular effort to be gay, as if perhaps the music and the laughter and the stylized embrace of the dance might help everybody to put out of mind the knowledge that in the campaign which would begin in the spring a considerable percentage of these officers would unquestionably be killed.

That knowledge was not easy to avoid. The war was just finishing its third year, the end of it was nowhere in sight, and what lay ahead was almost certain to be worse than what had gone before. Neither the officers who wore spurs and swords to the dance floor, nor the women who swirled their voluminous skirts to the music without regard for these encumbrances, retained any romantic illusions about this war. Yet they still had the ability—perhaps there was a necessity about it—to create illusions for the moment; and this evening there seems to have been a conscious effort to enter into the Byronic mood, an eagerness to see a parallel between this ball and the fabulous ball given in Brussels by the Duchess of Richmond on the eve of Waterloo. The dancers tried to act the parts which the romantic tradition called for, and while the music lasted—the brave music of a military band, playing the swinging little tunes that would keep reality at bay—they could maintain their chosen attitudes, changing tragedy into a dreamy unobtrusive melancholy that would do no more than highlight the evening's gaiety. It was at one of these dances that a young woman found herself chatting with a general officer whose only son had recently been killed in some outpost skirmish up the river. She offered her sympathy. The general bowed: "Yes, madame, very sad! Very sad! He was the last of his race. Do you waltz?" [1]

The dance lasted until the small hours, and at last the ambulances went off through the sleeping camp, and there was a final tinkle of chatter and laughter and so-glad-you-could-come under the frosty stars as the guests went to their tents. And the next afternoon everybody reassembled in and around a reviewing stand in an open field for a grand review of the II Corps, with the commanding general of the Army of the Potomac taking the salute as the long ranks of veterans went past.

Like the dance, the review was an occasion: a quiet reminder, if anybody needed one, that dances and bright officers and everything else rested finally on the men in the ranks, who went to no parties and who could be turned out to parade their strength for the admiration of the officers' ladies. It was noted that the major general commanding, George Gordon Meade, was in rare good humor. He was lean and grizzled, with a great hawk nose and a furious temper, and his staff had learned to read omens in his behavior. When the army was about to do something he gave off sparks, and those around him did well to step quietly and rapidly, but today the omens were good. He was lighthearted, making small jokes and telling stories, enjoying the review and the company of the guests, and acting the part of a major general who had nothing in particular on his mind. Staff observed and took heart; some weeks of quiet must lie ahead of the army. [2]

In this judgment the staff officers were wrong. There was a movement afoot, and General Meade did not wholly approve of it. He was at ease, perhaps, merely because the imminent movement would involve only a fragment of the army, and because it did not seem likely to have any great importance one way or the other. Visible sign that something was in the wind was the presence at this infantry review of the 3rd Cavalry Division of the Army of the Potomac, led by Brigadier General Judson Kilpatrick.

Kilpatrick was in his mid-twenties, young for a brigadier, a wiry, restless, undersized man with blank eyes, a lantern jaw, and an imposing growth of sand-colored sideburns; a man about whom there were two opinions. A member of Meade's staff wrote in his diary that it was hard to look at Kilpatrick without laughing, and the common nickname for him around army headquarters was "Kill Cavalry." His division fought well and paraded well—at this review it put on a noble mock charge, a thundering yelling gallop across the dead grass of the plain, troopers rising in their stirrups with gleaming sabers extended, all very stimulating for the visiting ladies—but its camp was usually poorly policed and in bad order, its horses were overworked and badly groomed, the clothing and equipments of the men had a used-up look, and its carbines were mostly rather dirty.

Yet the man had a quality, somehow. In combat he was valiant, and he was afraid of nothing—except, possibly, of the final ounce of the weight of personal responsibility—and he was slightly unusual among the officers of this army in that he neither drank nor played cards. At West Point he had been noted as a gamecock, anxious to use his spurs. Born in New Jersey, he was ardent for the Union and against slavery, and he had had many fist fights with other gamecock cadets from the South. William Tecumseh Sherman, with his genius for brutal overstatement, may have summed him up when, a bit later in the war, he asked to have Kilpatrick assigned to him for the march to the sea, explaining: "I know that Kilpatrick is a hell of a damned fool, but I want just that sort of man to command my cavalry on this expedition."

Kilpatrick had ambitions. It was his belief that if he survived the war he would become, first, governor of New

Jersey, and then President of the United States. At the moment, however, he was more concerned with the thought that he would presently become a major general, and various events hung upon this conviction.[3]

While the officers of the II Corps were having their ball, Kilpatrick had been having a party of his own—a lavish affair, held in a big frame house near Brandy Station, where Kilpatrick had his headquarters. The guests included a number of important senators—the Senate had to confirm the promotions of all general officers—and if the general did not drink he saw to it that any guests who did were taken care of. The party appears to have been loud, merry, and successful. One guest recalled that Kilpatrick had been "as active as a flea, and almost as ubiquitous." When the review was held on the following day Kilpatrick, who had arranged to have his cavalry take part, saw to it that his guests had places in the reviewing stand.[4]

But the senators were only part of it. In his reflections on the road to promotion Kilpatrick that winter had thought of two other points. One was the anxiety of Abraham Lincoln to extend friendship and amnesty to any citizens of the Confederacy who would return to their old allegiance to the Federal government. Mr. Lincoln had recently issued a proclamation offering such amnesty, and he greatly wanted copies of it distributed in the South. The other point was the relatively defenseless condition of Richmond, capital of the Confederacy, where there were confined many thousands of Union prisoners of war.

Putting these two points together, Kilpatrick had evolved a plan. A well-appointed cavalry expedition, he believed, under the proper officer (who might well be Judson Kilpatrick) could slip through General Lee's defenses, get down to Richmond before the Army of Northern Virginia could send reinforcements, free all of the Union prisoners, and in its spare time distribute thousands of copies of the President's proclamation. Having thought of this plan Kilpatrick managed to get word of it to Washington, and in the middle of February he had been formally summoned to the White

House to explain the scheme to Mr. Lincoln and to the Secretary of War, Edwin M. Stanton.

This summons Kilpatrick had obeyed gladly, amid mutterings on the part of his chief, Major General Alfred Pleasonton, who commanded the cavalry corps and who had a low opinion both of Kilpatrick's plan and of Kilpatrick's action in dealing direct with the White House. Pleasonton remarked tartly that the last big cavalry raid—Stoneman's luckless expedition, during the Chancellorsville campaign—had accomplished nothing of any consequence and had cost the army 7,000 horses. He added that if the President wanted his amnesty proclamation circulated in Richmond that could be done by regular espionage agents without taking a single cavalryman away from the army.[5]

But Pleasonton was not listened to and Kilpatrick was. He may have owed a good deal to Secretary Stanton, who had a weakness for fantastic schemes. He probably owed more to Mr. Lincoln himself, who was forever hoping that the seceding states could be brought back into the Union before they were beaten to death, and who, from long dealings with officers of the Army of the Potomac, had come to look with a kindly eye on those who were willing to display a little initiative. In any case the project had been approved at the very top, and orders came down from Washington to give Kilpatrick 4,000 troopers and let him see what he could do. Simultaneously, whole bales of pamphlets reprinting the amnesty proclamation arrived at Brandy Station.

The enthusiasm aroused by all of this at army headquarters was tepid. Army intelligence was well aware that Richmond was lightly held this winter. There were strong fortifications about the city, but hardly any troops occupied them, the chief reliance being on militia—and on the presence just below the Rapidan, far from Richmond but close to the Army of the Potomac, of the indomitable soldiers of the Army of Northern Virginia.

In theory, Richmond was open to a sudden grab. But headquarters could not help remembering that a plan not unlike Kilpatrick's had been cooked up a month earlier by the imaginative but incompetent Ben Butler, who commanded Federal troops around Fortress Monroe. Butler had proposed that the Army of the Potomac make a pretense of an offensive, to keep Lee busy, while Butler's own troops marched up the peninsula and seized Richmond, and after a good deal of correspondence back and forth the thing had been tried. The Army of the Potomac had done its part, getting into a smart little fight at Morton's Ford and suffering two or three hundred casualties, and with Confederate attention thus engaged the way had been open for Butler to do what he proposed to do. But somehow nothing much happened. Butler's troops advanced, encountered a broken bridge several miles below Richmond, paused to contemplate it for a while, and at last retreated, and everything was as it had been before except that Lee had been alerted and now held the Rapidan crossings in greater strength.

Major General John Sedgwick, unassuming and wholly capable, who commanded the army just then in the temporary absence of General Meade, commented indignantly on the business in his dispatches to Washington, but he succeeded only in ruining his own standing at the War Department.[6] The administration still believed that Richmond could be taken by a bold stroke, and an officer who disagreed was likely to be considered fainthearted and politically unsound. Also, there were all of those pamphlets to be distributed.

Orders were orders, in other words, and Meade dutifully set about obeying them. His part was to enable the cavalry to get through the Rebel lines along the Rapidan, and he devised a little stratagem: the army would make an ostentatious lunge toward the right, as if it meant mischief somewhere down the Orange and Alexandria Railroad, and while the Confederates were looking in that direction Kilpatrick's men could go slicing off to the left. If the trick worked, so that the expedition once got past Lee's army, the whole project might very well succeed.

It was all top secret, of course, for everything depended on taking Lee by surprise. As far as headquarters knew there had been no leaks. And then one day, just about the

time the ladies were gathering for the Washington's Birthday
ball, there came limping across the railway platform at
Brandy Station a youthful colonel of cavalry whose mere
presence here was proof that the story was all over Washington.

This officer was Ulric Dahlgren. In addition to a colonel's
commission, he possessed, at twenty-one, much glamor, a
wooden leg, and some extremely important connections. His
father was Rear Admiral John A. D. Dahlgren, a world authority on ordnance and one of the Navy's hard-case shell-
backs to boot. Inventor of the heavy bottle-shaped Dahlgren
gun which the Navy favored so much, he was also a good
friend of Abraham Lincoln. Currently, the admiral was in
charge of the fleet which was vainly trying to batter its way
into Charleston Harbor. A square-jawed, bony, tenacious
Scandinavian, lean and sharp-cornered, he rode in the front
line of action in a hot ill-ventilated monitor instead of taking
his ease in his admiral's suite on the flagship, and he was
deeply proud of the son who freakishly had forsaken the
Navy and sought fame in the hard-riding, headline-happy
squadrons of the cavalry corps.

Young Dahlgren was tall and slim and graceful, with a
thin tawny beard and much charm of manner. He was alleged
to be the youngest colonel in the Army, and an admiring
Confederate wrote of him that he had "manners as soft as
a cat's." Born in Pennsylvania, he had grown up in the
Washington Navy Yard, and when the war began he was
studying civil engineering. Early in 1862 he decided that it
was time for him to fight—he had just passed his nineteenth
birthday—and he was forthwith given an Army captaincy by
Secretary Stanton himself. A bit later he found himself on
the staff of General Joe Hooker.

He may have been commissioned by pure favoritism, but
he turned out to be a good soldier. In the fall of 1862 he
won distinction by leading a cavalry raid into Fredericksburg
—a stroke that accomplished nothing much but showed bold-
ness and leadership—and the next summer, during the Gettysburg campaign, Dahlgren made his reputation.[7]

While the fighting was beginning around Gettysburg, Dahlgren took a couple of troops of cavalry and went prowling far around in Lee's rear, and he captured a Confederate courier coming up from Richmond with dispatches. The capture was important, for the courier bore a letter from Jefferson Davis telling Lee that the government did not think it advisable to bring Beauregard and a new army up to the Rappahannock to add weight to Lee's invasion of the North. The letter was promptly sent to Meade, who was thus enabled to campaign in the secure knowledge that Lee was not to be reinforced.

A few days after this, Dahlgren's outfit got into a fight with Rebel cavalry at Boonsboro, Maryland, and Dahlgren was badly wounded. His right leg was amputated, and he spent the next few months convalescing at his father's home in Washington. Then, in November, a one-legged army officer on crutches, he went down to the fleet off Charleston and lived on his father's flagship, going ashore now and then with the Navy in small-boat expeditions of one kind and another. Early in the winter he returned to Washington to receive a colonel's commission and to have an artificial leg fitted, and just as this was done he heard about the Kilpatrick expedition. (The bar at Willard's was abuzz with it.) Dahlgren hurried down to see Kilpatrick about it, satisfied himself that he could ride a horse despite the handicap of a wooden leg, and shortly after the II Corps review he wrote to his father:

"I have not returned to the fleet, because there is a great raid to be made, and I am to have a very important command. If successful, it will be the grandest thing on record; and if it fails, many of us will 'go up.' I may be captured or I may be 'tumbled over' but it is an undertaking that if I were not in I should be ashamed to show my face again. With such an important command I am afraid to mention it, for fear this letter might fall into wrong hands before reaching you. I find I can stand the service perfectly well, without my leg. I think we will be successful, although a desperate undertaking. . . . If we do not return, there is no better place to '*give up the ghost.*'" [8]

Kilpatrick gave Dahlgren a key assignment. When the expedition moved there would be an advance guard of 500 troopers which would swing west to strike the James River some miles above Richmond. While the main body approached the city from the north and east, this group would cross the river and come up to the city from the south. With the attention of the defense centered on Kilpatrick, it was believed that this party could enter Richmond almost unopposed. It would seize the principal prison camp at Belle Isle, free the 15,000 prisoners there, lead them out on the north side, rejoin Kilpatrick's column there, and all hands would go romping back to the Union lines. And this advance contingent, on which the success of the whole movement would very largely depend, was to be commanded by Colonel Dahlgren.

So it was all arranged, and Kilpatrick got his formal orders on February 27. He was to "move with the utmost expedition possible on the shortest route past the enemy's right flank," and next day various cavalry commands were ordered to report at his headquarters, where the men were issued five days' rations and officers were ordered to see to it that all the horses were well shod and that the men's arms and equipments were in order. The troopers obeyed gleefully, for this sounded like a raid, and as one man remarked, "It is easier to get a trooper or even a hundred for a raid than to get one to groom an extra horse." [9]

Ponderously but surely, the army machine began to move. John Sedgwick took his VI Corps upriver toward Madison Court House, and flamboyant young Brigadier General George Armstrong Custer, with his gaudy uniform, his anointed curls, and his hard, expressionless eyes, took his cavalry division off on a dash toward Charlottesville—wondering, as he rode, whether he might not be cut off entirely and so be compelled to ride all the way to Tennessee to join Sherman's army. The bait thus dangled was taken, and the Army of Northern Virginia took thought for its left flank;

and on February 28, a fine starlit evening with a moon putting a shimmer on the waters of the Rapidan, Dahlgren and Kilpatrick took their men down to the river at Ely's Ford, rounded up the Rebel pickets there, and set off on their long ride.[10]

They were good men, and there was a chance that they might succeed. Yet they were pursuing a dream, because peace could not now be won by planting pamphlets about amnesty in the Confederate capital, and the thought that it might come so was essentially a romantic thought, however noble. This venture was a departure from reality, of a piece with the officers' dances at which men and women quoted Byron to themselves and borrowed, for their own beset lives, the tag ends of implausible poetry describing a bloodless bookish war. It was born of a romantic dream and it was aimed at glory, and glory was out of date, a gauzy wisp of rose-colored filament trailing from a lost world. Victory could no longer be imagined as a bright abstraction, lying like the sunrise at the end of a shining road. It was an ugly juggernaut that would crush and smash many values and many lives into the everlasting mud, and it was the only thing that counted nowadays. The longer the war lasted the more victory was going to cost, and a dazzling cavalry raid would not even be the small change of the final purchase price.

Still, for whatever it might be worth, the expedition rode on, and the men slipped safely past Lee's right flank, trotting at dawn through a sleepy crossroads town known as Spotsylvania Court House, where Kilpatrick reined in briefly to let Dahlgren's men go on ahead. The troopers were in high spirits, and they were in enemy country, and they reflected that the five days' rations issued to them did not include any meat, which indicated that they were expected to forage liberally on pasture and farmhouse. A Pennsylvania regiment came down a country road, and in a farmyard there was an old woman with a flock of geese, and it amused the soldiers to ride into the flock, sabers swinging, to see how they might decapitate the long-necked birds without dismounting or coming to a halt. The woman seized a broom and fought with them in frantic despair, and the men shouted and guffawed as they dodged her blows, and they advised her that "the Yanks are hell on poultry." At last all of the geese were killed, and the woman slammed the gate of her front-yard fence and screamed the protest of the defenseless civilian who lay in the path of war—"You 'uns are nothing but dirty nasty Yankees after all!" [11]

The column rode on, collecting foodstuffs as it rode, and a staff officer went through the regiments announcing that the Rebels had no troops in Richmond, no one but government clerks and bookkeepers to bar the way. It was a fine bright day and a pleasant war, and the march went on unbroken except for a very short breather now and then. But during the afternoon the sky grew cloudy, and when dusk came there was a cold, gusty wind driving icy rain into the men's faces. Twenty-four hours in the saddle, and no rest in sight, and the war began to look a little less like a rowdy picnic; and they came to Beaver Dam Station after dark, and while the rain turned to sleet, freezing on overcoats and scabbards and carbine barrels, the men set fire to station and freight house and boxcars and outbuildings, cavorting madly about their bonfire, pleased that they were laying a heavy hand on the republic's enemies, making strange prancing silhouettes against the red flames in the smoky night. Then they went on again, leaving their fires as a great meaningless beacon, and they followed narrow roads in Egyptian darkness, and men in the outside files lost their caps to the low branches of unseen overarching trees.

Dahlgren and his party were off to the west somewhere, presumably, making for the James River crossing, and from time to time a signal corps officer who was riding with Kilpatrick turned aside to send up a rocket as a signal to the detached party. The rockets sputtered and climbed the wet black sky and went out, futile signals from nowhere to nobody, and there was no way to tell where Dahlgren was or whether he ever saw them. The blind column went on and on, everybody cold and soaked and exhausted.

There were Rebel skirmishers adrift somewhere in the night, and at intervals these spattered the column with bursts of fire, carbine flashes winking ominously in the surrounding blackness. Up ahead there were parties cutting down trees to obstruct the road, and the progress of the column became a maddening succession of confused stops and blind gallops —sudden traffic jams as the regiments jangled to an unexpected halt, men swaying in their saddles with fatigue or clumping heavily to the ground to rest their horses, then going on again at top speed to catch up with the rest, and it began to be possible to see why the young general was known as Kill Cavalry. Horses foundered, and some of the troopers had to plod along on foot, carrying their saddles, getting help by clinging to a comrade's stirrup. The storm grew worse and no one could see anything, and whether a man collided with a tree or with his neighbor was entirely up to his horse.[12]

Sometime during the night there was a brief, unsatisfactory halt for rest. Then the column moved on, having more brushes with Confederate bushwhackers, and a gray cheerless dawn came in; and at last, around midmorning of Tuesday, March 1, the men came out on the Brook Pike within five miles of Richmond. Up ahead were the permanent fortifications of the capital, and by all information these could be held only by militia, and Kilpatrick flung out a dismounted skirmish line, brought up his six field guns, and prepared for his big moment.

Yet the war that morning seemed to be full of evil omens, and there was no way to tell where Dahlgren was. According to the plan, he should at this moment be in Richmond, followed by a multitude of released prisoners of war, and Kilpatrick opened with his guns to let Dahlgren know that the main body was where it was supposed to be. But there came no answering sign from Dahlgren. Instead there were Confederate guns which opened a brisk fire, and from somewhere Kilpatrick heard, vaguely, that veterans from Lee's army had entered the lines, and it began to seem to him that he was in trouble.

The skirmishers crept forward, peppering the Rebel lines and getting peppered in return. Kilpatrick rode to the front, and a soldier heard him complain: "They have too many of those damned guns; they keep opening new ones on us all the time." What had begun as the prelude to a smashing attack slipped imperceptibly into a sparring match, with everybody waiting hopefully for some indication that Dahlgren had got into Richmond and would presently get out again. But the gray skies and the bleak countryside gave no sign. The Confederate trenches lay half a mile away across a level plain, the fields heavy with cold mud, chilly mist, and smoke lying low over all. The Rebel fire grew stronger, and the day dragged on toward evening.

Kilpatrick had imagined this expedition, he had pulled wires to get it approved and to win command of it, and now he and his division were here at the gate of Richmond, and his advance guard was lost off beyond the smoky flats and someone a good deal tougher than government clerks seemed to be manning the Rebel guns. The quick victorious assault that had looked so possible back at Brandy Station seemed now an effort too great for worn-out unaided cavalrymen to make. At last the weight of responsibility was too much, and at dark—feeling that "an attempt to enter the city at that point would but end in bloody failure"—Kilpatrick called in his skirmishers, wheeled his command about, and headed back to the north side of the Chickahominy River. There, beyond the Meadow Bridge, the command went into bivouac.[13]

The bivouac was not a success, although the expedition had been without sleep for sixty hours. The men had no shelter tents, and the weather grew much worse. One trooper recalled their woes, in a breathless expressive sentence: "A more dreary, dismal night it would be difficult to imagine, with rain, snow, sleet, mud, cold and wet to the skin, rain and snow falling rapidly, the roads a puddle of mud, and the night as dark as pitch." He added that it was impossible to build fires to cook food, and anyway all of the poultry that had been taken so blithely had long since been consumed.

Late in the evening Kilpatrick partially recovered his grip on himself and determined to make one more try. He ordered two columns formed for a dash up the Mechanicsville Pike, but it took time to get exhausted men and horses into line in the consuming storm, and before the columns were half ready a swarm of Confederate cavalry—no militia, now, Wade Hampton's veterans from Lee's army—came pelting in through the slush and opened a heavy fire. Hampton had brought two fieldpieces with him, and these slammed case shot in at destructive range, and befogged soldiers found the inky woods full of flashes of fire and angry yells of "Git, you damned Yankees!" and there was great confusion and much shouting and fruitless cursing.[14]

In the end the attack was beaten off, but this clearly was no place to make a camp, and the troopers got on their horses again and went squelching off through the mud, with scattered Confederates following to prick them along with rifle fire from the dark. Finally, long after daybreak, the outfit made another camp some miles away from Richmond, and while the men got what sleep they could Kilpatrick waited for news of the missing Dahlgren.

He got it, late that day, when some 300 of Dahlgren's men came stumbling into camp, without Dahlgren. Their story made Kilpatrick no happier.

Dahlgren's 500 had got down to the James River on schedule, burning sundry gristmills and canal boats on the way, and they stopped briefly at a plantation owned by James A. Seddon, the cadaverous-looking aristocrat who was Secretary of War in President Davis's cabinet. Dahlgren went up to the big house, full of boyish charm and abundantly living the part of the dashing romantic cavalryman, and he found that Secretary Seddon was not at home. Mrs. Seddon was, however, and Dahlgren charmed her, and they sat in her drawing room and chatted. When he identified himself she confided, prettily, that his father the admiral had been a beau of hers, back in the old days, and now she and the admiral's son sat there and pledged each other in blackberry wine out of silver goblets, and apparently for the young man

and the older woman the war narrowed to the misty focus of
something by Sir Walter Scott. Then Dahlgren took his
leave, very knightly and courtly, and he rode down to the
river to make his crossing.[15]

At the river bank the knightly pose vanished. Earlier in
the day Dahlgren had picked up a young colored man, held
in servitude on some looted plantation, and this man had
said that he knew where and how the James River could be
forded, and he had been the guide who led the party to this
spot. But when the cavalcade came jingling down to the
river bank at the place the guide had chosen, the water was
deep and wicked-looking, swollen by rains and clearly not
to be crossed save in boats, of which the cavalry had none.
There was sudden wrath, a cry of treachery, and Dahlgren
decided—apparently rather hastily, but a raider as deep in
enemy territory as he was would hardly take a judicial view
of things—that the guide had maliciously misled him. He
immediately ordered the lad hanged to the nearest tree.

One can picture the business, after all these years: stern
young colonel, coldly furious at this mischance breaking in
on his bright dream of glory; befuddled guide, staring blankly
at a river all black and foaming where normally a man could
wade across; expectant staff, seeing death in the young colonel's eyes and whipping a picket rope from the nearest
saddle; oak tree with convenient branch overhanging the
bank, quick flurry of movement and smothered cry of protest, tanned hard faces looking on expressionless—and then
the finished deed, inert body dangling at the end of a taut
cord, and the law of war is hard and there is more to a
cavalry raid than laughing troopers splashing through the
shallows in winter moonlight, more to it even than a bright
young colonel drinking a toast to his father's old-time sweetheart with purple wine reflecting candleshine in a silver cup.
Some echo of the colonel's anger seems to have reached the
lower echelons, because the troopers went back and burned
Secretary Seddon's barns.[16]

Unable to cross the river, Dahlgren and his men went trotting toward Richmond on the north side, things vaguely going

wrong and the shadow of disaster rising on the cold dark sky. Far ahead they heard Kilpatrick's guns, and toward evening they got up close to the city's defenses. But it was too late now; Kilpatrick had seen too many Rebel guns and had retreated, the Confederates in Richmond were waiting for them, and Dahlgren was in a desperately bad spot—cut off from the main body, men and horses ready to drop, the whole country roused against him, safety many miles away.

Dahlgren did his best to get his men out of it. He rode at the head of the column, and he got the command away from Richmond and north of the Chickahominy in a driving sleet storm, and it seemed as if all the soldiers in the Confederacy were buzzing around like hornets to sting the invaders to death. For a time the command had to fight its way along the road—miserable fighting in the dark, nothing to be seen but a ragged line of fire as unseen infantry assailed the outriders, quick spat-splash of flying hoofs as the troopers charged up the road, jeering taunts from the fields as the Rebels slipped away—with the whole business repeated, as likely as not, a quarter of a mile farther on.

Somehow, in the night and the storm and the weird intermittent firing, Dahlgren's column broke in half, the separated halves losing touch and stumbling on as best they could. The 300 who had just come in to Kilpatrick's camp constituted one of these halves. The other half, with which Dahlgren himself had been riding, had vanished, and these survivors had no notion where it was or what had happened to it.[17]

Only one thing was clear, to Kilpatrick and to everyone else: the whole expedition was a flat failure, and there was nothing for it but to ride down the Virginia peninsula and get within Ben Butler's lines before disaster became absolute. This, at length, Kilpatrick did, and in the course of the next few days he learned about what had happened with Dahlgren.

Followed by some 200 troopers, Dahlgren had struck off for the northeast. All handicaps considered, his party made good progress, achieving a spectacular crossing of the Mattapony River, with Dahlgren remaining on the southern shore in personal command of the rear guard, firing his revolver at Rebel pursuers, while men and horses ferried themselves across on some scows they had found. Dahlgren crossed last of all, moved up to the head of the column, and resumed the march. But the state was aroused, and the march was not unlike the British retreat from Lexington and Concord, with every bush, barn, and tree seemingly sheltering a Confederate sniper.

The final catastrophe came at night. A body of Virginia cavalry had got around in front of the Dahlgren party, and these men and some home guards and embattled-farmer types laid an ambush in a forest. Dahlgren came along with his men trailing out behind him, his revolver in his hand, and in the blackness beside the road he heard men moving. He raised his weapon and shouted his challenge: "Surrender, you damned Rebels, or I'll shoot you!" For answer there was a heavy volley from encircling foes. Dahlgren fell from his horse, dead, with four bullets in him, and his command dissolved in a bewildering sequence of shots, cries, confused riding, and hand-to-hand grapplings. Most of the men who were not killed outright were quickly run down and captured.[18]

So that was that, and the raid was over. For achievements, the men could count a number of barns, flour mills, railroad buildings, and freight cars burned, and some incidental waste and ravage on a good many farms—there had been, for instance, the demonstration that an agile mounted man could behead a goose with his saber. Also, thousands of copies of the amnesty proclamation had been thrust into the hands of dazed bystanders, left in homes and shops and churches, stowed away in books on the shelves of manor houses, and generally left lying about so that any Confederate who felt like coming back into the Union might learn the terms on which his return could be negotiated. All of this, whatever it might amount to, had been done at minor cost, as such things were figured: one promising young cavalry colonel, 340 of other ranks, and about a thousand horses, plus some damage to prestige.

A fizzle, in other words, worth no more than a passing glance—except that the war had changed, and something hard and cruel and vicious was coming to the surface, and this raid was a dark ominous symbol of it, with bitterness and hatred visible behind it and growing out of it.

The men who killed Colonel Dahlgren (he himself had thought there was no better place to give up the ghost) had not been kind to his body. Someone cut off a finger to get at a ring he was wearing. Another took his artificial leg as a souvenir. Others got his watch, additional valuables, and his clothing. His body itself was carted off to Richmond in a pine box without a lid, and it went on display in a railroad station there, a show for the curious. And someone also took from his pockets the papers on which he had written down the objects of the expedition, and these papers seem to have been tampered with, so that they finally appeared to prove that his principal aim had been to burn and sack the city of Richmond and to murder Jefferson Davis and all his Cabinet; and these papers were openly published, to put a ramrod in the spine of Secession.

Braxton Bragg, chief military adviser to President Davis, forwarded them with an endorsement denouncing "the fiend-ish and atrocious conduct of our enemies," and Secretary of War Seddon sent them on to Lee, suggesting that since arson and assassination had been on the agenda the Yankees taken prisoner from Dahlgren's command ought to be hanged. Lee himself, who had sanity enough for three or four cabinet officers, agreed the papers were atrocious, but he doubted that executing the prisoners would help much. After all, he remarked, the projected murder and rapine had not actually taken place, the validity of the papers was in some question, and anyway the Federals held certain Confederate raiders who had looted a train along the upper Potomac and were considering accusing these men of plain highway robbery—and altogether if the business of hanging prisoners were started no one could be sure just how it would end. Lee sent the papers on to Meade under a flag of truce, with a note

asking, in effect: Is this the kind of war you are going to be
fighting from now on, and if so how about it? [19]

A sensation, indubitably: possibly offsetting the effect of
Mr. Lincoln's offer of amnesty and brotherhood. Kilpatrick
reported bitterly that the Confederates had used bloodhounds
to hunt down fugitives from Dahlgren's scattered command,
Northern publicists fumed and foamed over the mutilation of
Dahlgren's corpse, and the old admiral wrote to General
Butler to say that he would appreciate it if, by any flag of
truce negotiations, the body could be recovered and brought
north for decent burial. Meade wrote to Lee that neither
President Lincoln, he himself, nor General Kilpatrick had
ordered any cities burned or civilians killed, and a Richmond
newspaper acidly commented that the chief casualty of the
expedition had actually been "a boy named Martin, the
property of Mr. David Meems, of Goochland"—he whom
Dahlgren had incontinently hanged for leading him to a ford
that was not a ford.

The newspapers had a field day. The Richmond *Examiner*
urged its readers to realize that "we are barbarians in the
eyes of our enemies," and called for reprisals, saying that
the war now was "a war of extermination, of indiscriminate
slaughter and plunder on the part of our enemies." The
editor dilated on the wickedness of the Yankee design of
"turning loose some thousands of ruffian prisoners, brutalized
to the deepest degree by acquaintance with every horror of
war, who have been confined on an island for a year, far
from all means of indulging their strong sensual appetites—
inviting this pandemonium to work their will on the unarmed
citizens, on the women, gentle and simple, of Richmond,
and on all their property." The New York *Times*, in its turn,
exulted that the expedition had at least destroyed millions of
dollars in Rebel property, and spoke zestfully of what the
raiders had seen in war-racked Virginia—"the large number of
dilapidated and deserted dwellings, the ruined churches with
windows out and doors ajar, the abandoned fields and work
shops, the neglected plantations." It mentioned Martin, the
luckless colored guide, as a man who "dared to trifle with

the welfare of his country" and it approved his hanging as "a fate he so richly deserved." [20]

So in both North and South there was fury, and the propagandists righteously sowed the wind, and the war between the sections, which once seemed almost like a kind of tournament, had at last hardened into the pattern of total war.

Kilpatrick's cavalry got back to the Army of the Potomac, after a time, taking ship from Fortress Monroe and debarking at Alexandria. The men were supposed to have a few days of relaxation at the Alexandria rest camp, but there was an unfortunate incident. Alexandria was policed by colored troops just then, and the cavalry of this army had no use for Negroes in uniform, and one of the colored guards halted a Michigan trooper to enforce the rule that none but couriers, orderlies, and other persons on duty were permitted to ride through the town's streets. The Michigan soldier drew his saber and killed the man, on the spot, and punishment followed quickly: the whole command had to march back to its camp on the Rapidan at once, without a chance to rest or to draw new clothing.[21]

2. Turkey at a Shooting Match

The army had always been impatient of restraint, and even in its early days a provost guard which tried to arrest dashing cavalrymen had to make a certain allowance for breakage. Yet provost guards had not hitherto been cut down with sabers; nor had they ever before been men with black skins, recently elevated from property to manhood, wearing the national uniform and empowered to enforce the national will. The army was dubious about it. (A colored sergeant, about this time, given an argument by an unruly private, leaned forward and tapped the chevrons on his sleeve. "You know what dat mean?" he demanded sternly. "Dat mean guv'-ment!") [1]

The colored man had been part of the war from the beginning, to be sure, but in the old days nobody had to spend much time thinking about him. He was just Uncle Tom, or a blackface minstrel with a talent for slow humor, or a docile contraband who could be made to do chores for soldiers. If he was none of these things he was a mystery, and figuring him out might bring a headache.

A New York cavalryman remembered that back in 1862 he and a comrade made friends with a free colored man, an aged Negro called Uncle Jake, who had a log cabin not far from their Virginia camp, and one day the old man asked the two soldiers to come to dinner. They went, and found themselves in a neat little room with a dirt floor, dinner cooking at the fireplace, table set for two. They had never imagined a dinner at which host and hostess stood by and ate nothing while the guests sat and ate, so they insisted that Uncle Jake and his wife draw up chairs and dine with them. Uncle Jake flatly refused, and he appears to have been slightly scandalized. Never in his eighty years, he said, had he heard of a Negro sitting at table with a white man, and all of their entreaties would not move him. So the soldiers ate the dinner—a good dinner, the cavalryman recalled, with roast possum as the main course—and went away, puzzled and ill at ease about that queer line drawn between host and guest.[2]

But that had been in the early days. Nothing in all the world was the same now as it used to be—not the war, nor the army, nor for that matter the colored man himself. He was coming out of the shadows and a new part was being prepared for him, and although the army did not like the transformation it was nevertheless the army which had brought it to pass. For the army had created a myth and the myth held a kernel of truth, and no cruel misuse of sword or noose would quite kill it.

The myth rode with Custer's men, as they came sloping back from their stab at Charlottesville—rain frozen on weapons and uniforms, saddles creaking with ice, trees along the way all silver with frozen sleet, tinkling when the branches moved. They found themselves at the head of a strange procession.

As they went along the Virginia roads their bugles sounded down the wind like the trumpets of jubilee, and the slaves laid down their burdens and came out by the scores to follow. Before long the cavalrymen were leading an outlandish tatterdemalion parade of refugees, men and women and helpless children, people jubilant and bewildered and wholly defenseless, their eyes on the north star.

Some of these had carts and wagons, some of them rode on mules or oxen, and some stumped along on foot, carrying their few possessions. They took their place just ahead of the rear guard, and in the struggle to keep up they endured great hardships. When the Confederates assailed the retreating Yankees, Custer's officers would ride through, shouting and pleading and threatening, and there was general bedlam—bullets in the air, crying children, livestock grown either panicky or balky, creating fearful knots and tangles in the traffic, troopers swearing and women screaming, weaklings here and there falling out by the roadside and watching in despair as the column moved on without them. When they were not storming with rage the troopers were braying with laughter. It struck them as very funny to see a desperately frightened Negro riding a runaway mule, holding onto one of its ears with one hand and its tail with the other. Despite all difficulties most of the refugees kept going, and as they plodded along in the cold rain and mud one of the soldiers felt that the Union Army was "the representative to them of the great idea of freedom." [3]

For that was the myth that this army had created, and it had vitality, and it went like a bent flame down plantation roads and country lanes. When Kilpatrick's division crossed from Richmond to Butler's lines the colored folk greeted it with ecstasy, and the raid that accomplished so little was a light across the sky to many hundreds of people. As the division passed one big plantation house, forty or fifty slaves crowded down to the road to watch. A young woman suddenly sprang up on the fence, waving her sunbonnet and crying: "Glory! Glory hallelujah! I'se gwine wid you! I'se gwine to be free!"

The whole crowd came surging out in a moment, and Old Marster was running down from his veranda shouting fruitless threats, a helpless Canute berating an unheeding tide.[4] The scene was repeated, with variations, over and over, until presently the cavalrymen were surrounded and followed by thousands of slaves whom no one any longer owned and for whom no one in particular was likely to be responsible: a devoted shuffling multitude, men and women carrying bundles, tiny children trudging along big-eyed, gray-haired old folk leaning on canes, scores and hundreds of people coming out of the past into the unknown.

All of this was stimulating to tired soldiers, for it was pleasant to be hosannahed and wept over as bringers of freedom. But finally the men got to New Kent Court House, and there for the first time the cavalry saw colored soldiers—some of Ben Butler's men, trim and neatly uniformed, lining the roadside to greet the cavalry, cheering wildly as the head of the column came up, white eyes a chalkline in a long row of black faces. Cavalry returned the cheers, and one trooper wrote that "a mountain of prejudice was removed in an instant." Yet somehow there was a catch in it, and prejudice had not been removed so far that it could not quickly return. Late that night it began to rain again, and Kilpatrick's men were making a sodden bivouac without shelter, and they suddenly realized that these colored soldiers occupied a warm dry camp with wall tents standing. So along toward midnight the cavalry attacked the camp, driving the colored soldiers out into the cold with blows and angry words and taking the tents for themselves, and there was no further exchange of cheers.[5]

The soldiers were not the same men they had been three years ago, and they dimly realized the fact. An Ohio soldier looked back wistfully to the time when they had all been recruits, with knowledge ahead of them—to "those happy, golden days of camp life," when each regiment eagerly awaited its marching orders and the only worry was the haunting fear that the war might end before a man got his fair chance to fight.[6] In those days there was a great difference between regiment and regiment, and between man and man. Western regiments derisively yelled, "Paper collars!" at Eastern regiments, which they considered dressed up and dudish, and the Easterners retorted that the Westerners were uncouth backwoodsmen. The city man looked and acted unlike the man from the country, and even a casual glance would show the difference between Hoosier and Ohioan, between Pennsylvanian and down-East Yankee. Now the distinctions were gone, and all of the volunteers looked very much alike. An officer in a Maine regiment mused that the army was a great leveler, and he wrote how "rich men and poor, Christians from pious back-country homes and heathen bounty-jumpers from the slums of New York . . . would bathe in and drink from the same stream, whether prior or subsequent to the watering of the brigade mules." [7]

The army had put its stamp on all of its infinitely various members. It had produced a type, at last, and the volunteer had become the old-timer—rusty in a worn uniform, wearing his forage cap with its broken visor tugged down over his eyes, tolerant of high authority but not especially respectful toward it (one fussy brigadier was greeted on all sides as "Old Bowels"), taking eventual triumph for granted, but fully aware that he himself was the man who was going to pay for it.

Yet to say all of that is merely to say that the army had done to its members what armies always do to recruits. The men had changed and that was that, and if the gates of Eden had swung shut nothing had happened that does not happen to everyone sooner or later. But along with all of this, something had happened to the army itself. Once it had reflected what was left of frontier democracy, loose-jointed and informal, bound together by a sharing of traditions and ideals. Now it was becoming professional, and the binder was beginning to look like cold force. Old relationships had shifted, and the typical army campfire was no longer a little glow in the dark lighting the bronzed faces of sentimentalists singing sad little songs. Army life had an edge to it now. The word "comrade" was ceasing to be all-inclusive, and because that was so the gap between officer and man was ominously widening.

In the beginning this gap had not been very impressive. Most of the men had known their company and regimental commanders before the war. They had been neighbors then and they expected to be neighbors again, and although they were willing to obey any orders which seemed to be sensible they saw no reason for anyone to be stuffy about it. Government was mostly by consent of the governed and discipline was casual and haphazard, which sometimes led to odd happenings on the march and in battle. It was getting ever so much tighter and sterner now, partly because loose discipline irked the army command but chiefly because the situation in which the loose discipline of a volunteer army could be tolerated no longer existed.

Except for the old-timers, the Army of the Potomac was not really a volunteer army any more, and it could not be conducted as one. The men who were coming into the ranks now were for the most part either men who had been made to come or men who had been paid to come. The former—the out-and-out conscripts—sometimes made good soldiers, for their principal shortcoming (aside from a certain reluctance to volunteer) was poverty; a draftee with money could either hire a substitute and so gain permanent exemption, or pay a $300 commutation fee and at least win exemption until his name came up in some new draft call. Unfortunately, however, not many of the new recruits were conscripts. Most of them were men who had joined up only because they got a great deal of money for doing it, and in the great majority of cases these men were worse than useless.

The number of men to be drafted in any state, city, or county always depended on the number that had previously volunteered. If many had volunteered, few or none would be drafted. Since nobody liked the draft, it was to everybody's interest to promote volunteering, and this was done principally by the payment of cash bounties. By the winter of 1864 these were running very high. States, cities, and towns were bidding against each other—some were almost bankrupting themselves in the process—and the drafted man who wanted to hire a substitute was bidding against all three. The results were fantastic. The provision by which a drafted man could buy his way out of the service was a remarkably effective device for making young men cynical about appeals to their patriotism. When it went hand in hand with a system of bounties which often ran as high as a thousand dollars per enlistment, there was in operation an almost foolproof system for getting the wrong kind of men into uniform.[8]

This system had created the institution of the substitute broker—the man who for a fee would find potential soldiers and induce them to enlist. Some of these brokers may have been relatively honest, although there is nothing in any contemporary accounts to make one think so, but for the most part they seem to have inspired army authorities to some of the most glowing invective in Civil War annals. At times they operated precisely as waterfront crimps operated, making their victims drunk, getting them to sign away their bounty rights, and then rushing them through the enlistment process before they recovered. Now and then an authentic deep-sea sailor, congenitally disposed to being shanghaied, got caught in this net. Such men, when they came to, usually made the best of things and went on to become good soldiers.[9]

Most of the time the broker did not need to go to the trouble of drugging anybody. It was simpler to dredge in the backwaters of city slums and find human derelicts who, for a little cash in hand, would willingly assign their bounty rights and go and enlist. Hardly any of these men were physically fit to be soldiers, but the broker made such enormous profits that he could usually afford any bribery that might be necessary to get them past the examiners. Horrified medical officers in the Army of the Potomac were finding that new lots of recruits often included hopeless cripples, lunatics, and men far along in incurable disease. Of fifty-seven recruits received that winter by the 6th New York Heavy Artillery, seventeen were so completely disabled that even a layman could see it—some, for instance, had but one hand, and a few were out-and-out idiots. Of recruits received by the cavalry corps in March, 32 per cent were on the sick list when they reached camp.

A Federal enrollment officer in Illinois wrote that the substitute broker's business was conducted "with a degree of unprincipled recklessness and profligacy unparalleled in the annals of corruption and fraud." Rising to genuine eloquence in his indignation, he protested that it put the uniform "upon branded felons; upon blotched and bloated libertines and pimps; upon thieves, burglars and vagabonds; upon the riff-raff of corruption and scoundrelism of every shade and degree of infamy which can be swept into the insatiable clutches of the vampires who fatten upon the profits of the execrable business."

Helpless immigrants speaking no word of English, some still wearing their wooden shoes, were swept up from the docks at seaports and hustled off to the recruiting officers. A veteran in a Massachusetts regiment said scornfully that more than half of one draft of recruits his regiment got that winter came in under assumed names, and that most of these men forgot what names they had used and were unable to answer at roll call. He remembered that the last set of recruits in whom the regiment felt any pride was a detail that came to camp in the fall of 1862.[10]

Even worse than the gangs sent in by the brokers, however, were the professional bounty-jumpers. These often were out-and-out criminals, who had found that their familiar arts of burglary, highway robbery, and pocket-picking were much more laborious and less rewarding than the racket which was made possible by the high-bounty system. They made a business of enlisting, collecting a bounty, deserting at the first chance, enlisting somewhere else for another bounty, deserting again, and keeping it up as long as they could get away with it. Since the authorities never solved the problem of checking desertion, they were usually able to get away with it about as long as they wanted to keep on trying, and if a few of them were caught and executed now and then the hazards of the profession were, on the whole, no worse than the risks they normally ran with the police.

These men brought into the Army of the Potomac an element the army had never had before, and of which it could not possibly make the slightest use. In camp they were valueless, and early in 1864 the army command stipulated that no bounty men could be used on picket or outpost duty. "If those fellows are trusted on picket," remarked one veteran, "the army will soon be in hell." [11] The mere business of guarding them to see that they did not desert or plunder their honest comrades took time and effort that should have been used in other ways. In battle they were a positive handicap. Under no circumstances could they be induced to fight. If by tireless effort a regiment succeeded in getting any of them up to the firing line they would immediately desert to the enemy, and their utter unreliability made any regiment which had them in its ranks weaker than it would have been if it had received no recruits at all.

A New Hampshire soldier reported indignantly that "such another depraved, vice-hardened and desperate set of human beings never before disgraced an army," and he pointed out how the bounty-jumpers and substitutes, simply by their presence in camp, corrupted the relationship between officers and men in the veteran regiments:

"Before their advent, common toil, hardship and danger, for months and years, had made them a band of brothers. Between the officers and men there existed the most perfect confidence and friendship. Punishment was uncalled for, as disobedience, demanding it, was unknown; and camp guard had long been a thing of the past. The men came and went almost at their pleasure."

But as the new men came in this idyllic situation changed:

"No pleasure or privilege for the boys in camp any more, for the hard lines and severe discipline of military necessity apply with a rigidness never before applied." [12]

A Connecticut soldier called the 300 recruits his regiment got that winter "the most thorough-paced villains that the stews of New York and Baltimore could furnish—bounty-jumpers, thieves and cutthroats, who had deserted from regiment after regiment in which they had enlisted under fictitious names, and who now proposed to repeat the operation. And they *did* repeat it." Two hundred and fifty of the 300, he said, ran away within a few weeks.[13]

In three years of war the soldiers of the Army of the Potomac had seen many things, but they had never seen anything like the habits and morals of these new comrades in arms. One veteran remembered listening, dumfounded, to the tales the new men told: "They never tired of relating the mysterious uses to which a 'jimmy' could be put by a man of nerve, and how easy it was to crack a bank or filch a purse. They robbed each other as freely as they did others. We noticed on their arrival that nearly every man had his pocket cut."

The bounty-jumpers had plenty of money, and when they were not picking one another's pockets they spent their spare time gambling. Poker had always been a favorite diversion of the private soldier, but the games that developed now were played for huge stakes, with professional cardsharps sitting in: "Thousands of dollars would change hands in one day's playing, and there were many ugly fights indulged in, caused by their cheating each other at cards." A man in the 13th Massachusetts wrote indignantly:

"We often talked over, among ourselves, this business of filling up a decent regiment with the outscourings of humanity; but the more we thought of it, the more discontented we became. We longed for a quiet night, and when day came we longed to be away from these ruffians." [14]

Some of the new men found army life pleasant—three meals a day, lodging taken care of, plenty of chance to loaf—and instead of deserting they became old soldiers, in the traditional army meaning of the term, pretending to be sick or disabled so that they could avoid drill and take their ease in the hospital tents. Some claimed to have rheumatism so badly that they could not bend their knees. The doctors would chloroform such men, and while they were unconscious would manipulate their legs. If this indicated that nothing was actually wrong, the men when they came out from under the anesthetic would be sent back to camp on foot, guards walking close behind ready to jab them with bayonets if they faltered. An Illinois soldier recalled a man who spent weeks in hospital, insisting that one of his hip joints was crippled by some obscure malady. In desperation the hospital stewards one day strapped him to his cot and applied red-hot pokers to the hip. After the third application the man cried out in pain and admitted that he had been shamming. He was allowed to stay in hospital until the burns healed and then was sent back to duty.[15]

An immense amount of work was required by the mere task of getting the new recruits from the enlistment centers to the army camps. Details of veterans were sent north to do guard duty at the recruit camps, and they quickly found that nothing but prison discipline would do.

In Boston Harbor there was an island on which new recruits were housed, uniformed, given some rudiments of drill, and assigned to different regiments. Men from the 22nd Massachusetts were sent up to guard this camp, and they found the work irksome. Day and night, every foot of the island's shore had to be patrolled to foil desertion. The shore was rocky and in winter the rocks were icy, and sentinels slipped and fell and wished fervently that they were back along the Rapidan. One man wrote fondly: "Large portions of Virginia are absolutely free from rocks." The veterans guarded the steamers which brought recruits to the island, and at the wharf they had to search all of the new men as they came ashore, seeing to it that no liquor or weapons were smuggled into camp. They took each recruit's money from him and deposited it with the provost marshal's clerk, for delivery when the man finally reached his regiment. It was held unwise to let the men have any money while they were on the island, for fear they would bribe their way to freedom.

One of the men who performed this guard duty wrote that "Some of the most noted, hardened and desperate villains in this country" were to be found among the recruits, and he said that to smuggle money past the guards these men would hide hundred-dollar bills in anything from hollow coat buttons to the inside of their ears.[16] A soldier who guarded a similar rendezvous at Riker's Island, New York, wrote: "As for the conscripts, they were unspeakable," and asserted that many of them had to wear the ball and chain while they were waiting for assignment to combat regiments. An artillerist from the IX Corps, guarding replacements at a camp in Kentucky, wrote that he and his fellows "preferred to go into an engagement with the enemy rather than guard such a rabble," and a New Hampshire veteran who guarded recruits at Point Lookout, Maryland, said that "there were many desperate and dangerous criminals among them who would not hesitate to commit any crime that passion, avarice or revenge might incite them to." He remembered with glee one group of six which got hold of a rowboat and tried to escape in it. For punishment, four of the men were compelled to carry the rowboat around camp all day long, while their two fellows sat in it and industriously rowed in the empty air.[17]

A steamship transporting these recruits from New York or Boston to Virginia was usually a floating bedlam. The steamer's civilian crew, more often than not, would be in league with the bounty-jumpers, and sometimes the officers likewise had been bribed, and whisky would be hidden in coal bunkers, in staterooms, and in odd corners below decks. Winter storms being common, hatches were usually battened down as soon as the vessel sailed, and the hold was jammed with desperate unwashed men, most of them seasick and the rest of them drunk, high-stake card games going on in the smoking light of swaying lanterns, bitter fights taking place as the more defenseless recruits were openly robbed. Some fairly important money would be involved, on these trips; a draft of a few hundred men each carrying his bounty might easily have a quarter of a million dollars in cash in its collective possession. Sometimes a group of these replacements would try to mutiny, and then the veterans with loaded muskets and fixed bayonets would go into action. When the steamers came up Chesapeake Bay or the Potomac, and land was not far away, men would spring from the decks to swim ashore, and at such times the guards would coolly fire, reload, and fire again until the swimmer sank out of sight in a little swirl of bloody water.[18]

Early in this winter of 1864 a teen-ager in upstate New York enlisted in a battery of field artillery—a veteran battery on duty in Virginia which had sent back for a few replacements—and to his amazement as soon as he had signed the papers he was put in a penitentiary building at Albany, the army having chosen this place as the only suitable depot for its new recruits. He found approximately a thousand draftees and bounty-jumpers there, closely guarded by double lines of sentinels, and he appears to have been about the only man in the lot who had joined up for love of country.

"If there was a man in all that shameless crew who had enlisted from patriotic motives, I did not see him," he wrote afterward. "There was not a man of them who was not eager to run away, not a man who did not quake when he thought of the front. Almost to a man they were bullies and cowards, and almost to a man they belonged to the criminal classes."

In due time orders came to send 600 of these men down to the Army of the Potomac. After roll call there was a frantic scurrying for cover. Some men cut open their straw mattresses and crept inside to hide. Others hid under bunks, or in latrines. One man was fished out of a huge garbage can in the mess hall, where he had burrowed down under coffee grounds and other oddments. He was kicked down a flight of stairs and prodded out to the parade ground with bayonets. When the detail at last was formed, an officer stepped out and announced that any man who tried to run away during the trip would be shot.

The officer's word was good. Three men were shot dead as the crowd marched through Albany to the steamboat wharf. Two more, who jumped from the steamer as it went down the Hudson, were shot in midstream. Four more were shot in New York, as the men were marched from one pier to another. After the steamer finally unloaded its consignment at Alexandria and the men were put on freight cars to go to the front, five men tried to escape from the moving train and were shot dead. All in all, the young recruit said that his associates were "as arrant a gang of cowards, thieves, murderers and blacklegs as were ever gathered inside the walls of Newgate or Sing Sing." [19]

Recruits like these helped to spoil some men who were already in the army and who might otherwise have behaved fairly well. Every regiment had its quota of scapegraces who were always on hand at mess call but who worked or fought only under compulsion. They tended to follow the lead of the worst elements in camp, and the worst elements now were about as bad as they could be. A veteran in one of Phil Kearny's old regiments left his own classification of the different varieties of worthless soldier to be found in the army:

"I will explain here and make a few remarks about shirks, bummers, sneaks and thieves, all called camp followers. The first is a man that when the army comes up, and is expecting that every man will do his duty, now that we are ready to meet the enemy, he looks around to see if any of his comrades are watching him and *drops* to the rear—deserts his comrades in time of danger. He then becomes a bummer, and prowls around, and will do anything to keep himself away from danger in the ranks. He then becomes a sneak and tries to get an ambulance to drive, or 'sich.' After that he becomes the thief, and will steal from friend and foe alike, and is devoid of all principle. Reader, look around you, and see if there is such men in your midst. Shun them as you would a viper, and show to them that they are despised in private life by their neighbors as they were in the army by their comrades." [20]

There undoubtedly is exaggeration in some of these accounts. The old-timers in the Army of the Potomac disliked conscripts and utterly despised high-bounty men, and in writing about such people they were not likely to remember anything good about them if they could help it. Certainly the army that winter did get some recruits who made good soldiers. One veteran, admitting that the army as a whole was not as good as it had been a year earlier, asserted that the old battalions were still superb even when they had absorbed fairly large numbers of replacements. Some states sent down whole new regiments, and while these "high-number" regiments were never accounted the equals of the ones with lower numbers, which had enlisted in 1861 or 1862, several of them made excellent records. The Irish Brigade brought its five regiments up to full strength early in 1864, and it got fighters. Most of the IX Corps regiments filled their ranks during the winter—the corps had been serving in Tennessee, and when it was brought East the regiments were given a chance to go home and do their own recruiting—and the corps does not seem to have lost its old fighting quality with the transfusion. It would undoubtedly be a strong overstatement to say that all of the men brought in by draft and bounty were useless.[21]

Yet if there is exaggeration in the complaints there is not very much exaggeration. The testimony about the evils which the high-bounty system caused is unanimous, and it comes from high officers as well as from private soldiers. The provost marshal general of the army, in a report written at the end of the war, said flatly that "the bounty was meant to be an inducement to enlistment; it became, in fact, an inducement to desertion and fraudulent re-enlistment." He pointed out that the states paying the highest bounties were precisely the ones with the largest proportion of deserters, and emphasized that desertions all through 1864 reached the astounding average of 7,300 each month. Not only was this a prodigious rise over all former figures; it meant that in the long run the army lost nearly as many men through desertion as it lost in battle casualties.[22]

For a long time the Confederate authorities made a distinction between Federal deserters who voluntarily came into their lines and soldiers who were captured in battle, and to the former they offered jobs in war plants and freedom from restraint. In the spring of 1864, however, they concluded that it was no go. The deserters were pure riff-raff, of no more use in a Richmond factory than in the Union Army, and one day the Richmond papers announced that henceforth all such would be locked up in prison camps along with soldiers taken in action. The colonel of a Connecticut regiment got a copy of a paper containing that announcement, and waved it happily in front of his men, declaring:

"The colonel commanding hopes that all the scoundrels who

desire to desert to the enemy after swindling the government out of heavy bounties have already left us"; but in case a few still remained he would read the Confederate announcement, which he did, adding that a prospective deserter ought to realize that "neither army considers him fit to be trusted anywhere, or able to earn his living." Since prisoners of war were subject to exchange, the colonel reminded his men that deserters might some day find themselves back with their regiment. If that happened, he said, they would be shot.[23]

What all of this meant was that the Army of the Potomac had to take on Regular Army discipline. The Regulars were used to hard cases and knew how to handle them. In ordinary times a Regular regiment would expect to lose perhaps a fourth of its men through desertion, but it could turn the rest into fighters. Now the volunteer regiments were following suit, caste lines were hardening, and discipline was enforced by brutality.

The artillerists led the way. The volunteer batteries had always had more of a Regular Army flavor than the infantry regiments, possibly because in the early days General McClellan had taken pains to brigade one regular battery with every three batteries of volunteers, and the force of example had been strong. In any case, the gunners this winter were pounding their recruits into shape, hurting them with cold ferocity when they needed correction. Their favorite punishment centered around the fact that every artillery caisson carried a spare wheel, mounted at the rear of the caisson a couple of feet off the ground at a slight angle from the vertical. An insubordinate artillerist was made to step on the lower rim of this wheel, and then he was spread-eagled, wrists and ankles firmly lashed to the rim. This done, the wheel was given a quarter turn so that the man was in effect suspended by one wrist and one ankle. He would be left in this position for several hours, and if he cried out in pain—as he usually did, before long—a rough stick was tied in his mouth for a gag.

Even worse was being tied on the rack. At the rear end of every battery wagon was a heavy rack for forage—a stout wooden box, running across the end of the wagon and protruding a couple of feet back of the rear wheels. The man who was up for punishment was made to stand with his chest against this rack while his wrists were tied to the upper rims of the wheels. Then his feet were lifted and tied to the lower rims, so that he was left hanging with all of his weight pressing against the sharp wooden edge of the rack. He was always gagged first, because not even the toughest customer could stand this punishment without screaming. The man generally fainted after a few minutes of it, and some men were permanently disabled. One gunner recalled that men sentenced to the rack sometimes begged to be shot instead.[24]

The infantry had no spare wheels or forage racks, but it had its little ways. Commonest punishment was the "buck and gag." The erring soldier was made to sit on the ground, his knees drawn up to his chin and his hands clasped over his shins. After his wrists were bound together a heavy stick was thrust under his knees and over his arms, and a gag was tied in his mouth. He was then left to sit there for some hours, suffering no extreme of pain but utterly helpless and voiceless, enduring cramps, thirst, and the jibes of unfeeling soldiers. It was also found effective to tie a man by his thumbs to the branch of a tree, pulling him just high enough so that he could keep his thumbs from being torn out of joint only by standing on tiptoe.

In a way there was nothing new about all of this. Brutal punishments had always been on tap, but hitherto they had hardly amounted to more than the army's backhanded way of cuffing the ne'er-do-wells and misfits who had found their way into the ranks. Now the harshness was becoming central. An important number of soldiers responded to that sort of language, and therefore it was being addressed to all of the soldiers. There was a new tone to the army. The old spirit had been diluted and the old ways had changed. The veterans drew closer together, seeming almost to be aliens in the army which they themselves had created.

And the great danger now was that the veterans might presently get out of the army altogether and leave everything to the newcomers. Under the law they might do this, and nobody could stop them, and if that happened the war was lost forever, because conscripts and bounty men could not make Robert E. Lee's incomparable soldiers even pause to take a deep breath.

Federal regiments in the Civil War enlisted, usually, for three years. There had been a number of nine-month regiments, earlier, and some had come in to do a two-year hitch, but the three-year enlistment was the rule. Now the time was running out. The old 1861 regiments had just about finished their terms. In May and June and July and August they would come to the end of their enlistments, and under the law there was no way to compel their members to remain in service if they did not choose to remain.

Fighting was expected to begin in April or May. The prospect, therefore, was that just as the campaign got well under way the army would begin to fall apart. The army authorities could see this coming but there was nothing on earth they could do to keep it from happening except go to the veterans —hat in hand, so to speak—and beg them to re-enlist.

The big thing was to get them to re-enlist as regiments, and inducements were offered. If three fourths of the men in any regiment would re-enlist, the regiment could go home as a unit for a thirty-day furlough, and when it got back to camp it would keep its organization, its regimental number, its flag, and so on. In addition, the veterans would be cut in on some of this bounty money. Adding state and Federal bounties together, the average soldier who signed on for a second enlistment would get about $700, on which he might have quite a time for himself during that month's furlough. So the authorities put on a big campaign, and the old regiments were called together and cajoled and orated to, and the men observed that on such occasions a good deal of whisky seemed to be available for the thirsty.

Now the high command was talking to men who had had it.

The record of these three-year regiments contained the whole story of the war in the East, down to date—Bull Run and the Seven Days, Antietam and Fredericksburg, Chancellorsville and Gettysburg, plus the mean little skirmishes and minor battles in between, the hard marches in dust or mud, the dreary months in unsavory camps. Whatever there could possibly be in war to make a man say, "Never again!" these soldiers knew about it. There were in the North thousands upon thousands of young men who had had no part in the war, and the veterans knew all about them and knew that if they themselves re-enlisted these men would remain civilians, with every night in bed and nobody shooting at them. They knew, too, that the thousands of recruits who were coming in now were corrupting the army and giving it little of value. When the fighting began again the load would have to be carried by the old-timers, the men who had survived many terrible battles and whose numbers, by the mere law of averages, must be about due to come up. The veteran who was asked to re-enlist had a good many things to think about. A man in the 3rd Michigan wrote:

"After serving three years for our country cannot we go home, satisfied that we have done our share toward putting down the rebellion, and let those who stayed at home come and give their time as long; the country is as dear to them as us."

A man in the 25th Massachusetts noted that few of his comrades were signing up, and he spelled out his own feeling:

"I shall not re-enlist, and my reasons are, first, I have no desire to monopolize all the patriotism there is, but am willing to give others a chance. My second reason is that after I have served three years my duty to my country has been performed and my next duty is at home with my family."

A member of the 13th Massachusetts noted that his regiment "listened with respectful attention" while officers urged re-enlistment and extolled the valor of old soldiers, but he added: "It was very sweet to hear all this, but the 13th was not easily moved by this kind of talk. The boys knew too well what sacrifices they had made, and longed to get home again and, if possible, resume the places they had left." In the end the 13th refused to re-enlist, except for a handful who signed up for places in another regiment.[25]

Altogether, there are few facts in American history more remarkable than the fact that so many of these veterans did finally re-enlist—probably slightly more than half of the total number whose terms were expiring. The proffered bounty seems to have had little influence on them. The furlough was much better bait. To men who had not seen their homes for more than two and one half years, a solid month of freedom seemed like an age. A member of the 5th Maine said that it actually seemed as if the war might somehow end before the furloughs would expire, and he wrote of the men who re-enlisted: "What tempted these men? Bounty? No. The opportunity to go home." [26]

It was not hardship that held men back. The 100th Pennsylvania had been marooned in eastern Tennessee for months, cut off from supplies and subsisting on two ears of corn per day per man, but when the question of re-enlistment came up only 27 out of the 393 present for duty refused to sign. In the 6th Wisconsin, which had done as much costly fighting as any regiment in the army, it was noted that the combat men were re-enlisting almost to a man; it was the cooks, hostlers, clerks, teamsters, and others on non-combat duty who were holding back. And the dominant motive, finally, seems to have been a simple desire to see the job through. The government in its wisdom might be doing everything possible to show the men that patriotism was for fools; in the end, the veterans simply refused to believe it. A solid nucleus did sign the papers, pledging that the army would go on, and by the end of March Meade was able to tell the War Department that 26,767 veterans had re-enlisted.[27]

The men signed up without illusions. A company in the 19th Massachusetts was called together to talk things over. The regiment had left most of its men on various battlefields, in hospitals, and in Southern prison camps, and this company now mustered just thirteen men and one wounded officer. These considered the matter, and one man finally said: "They use a man here just the same as they do a turkey at a shooting match, fire at it all day and if they don't kill it raffle it off in the evening; so with us, if they can't kill you in three years they want you for three more—but I will stay." And a comrade spoke up: "Well, if new men won't finish the job, old men must, and as long as Uncle Sam wants a man, here is Ben Falls."

The regiment's historian, recording this remark, pointed out that Ben Falls was killed two months later in battle at Spotsylvania Court House.[28]

3. From a Mountain Top

On the tenth day of March, 1864, Lieutenant General Ulysses S. Grant came down to meet General Meade and to have a look at the Army of the Potomac.

They made an occasion of it, and when Grant reached headquarters they turned out the guard. The guard included a Zouave outfit, 114th Pennsylvania, which had seen much hard fighting before the luck of the draw pulled it out of combat ranks and assigned it to headquarters, and it was natty with baggy red pants, white leggings, short blue jackets, and oriental-looking turbans. With the guard came the headquarters band, also of the 114th Pennsylvania; a melodious group, distinguished from most of the other army bands by the fact that all of the players were always sober when time came to make music. It had learned to play the kind of music Meade liked—something soft and sweet, usually—and it tootled away vigorously today, quite unaware that the lieutenant general was completely tone-deaf, disliked all music rather intensely, and could not for the life of him tell one tune from another.[1]

The meeting between Grant and Meade was brief. Meade suggested that it might suit the new general in chief if the commander of the Army of the Potomac quietly retired, and Grant quickly rejected the offer—and wrote that he was favorably impressed by the way it was made. Mostly, the two men seem to have spent their time sizing each other up, and each man liked what he saw. They would appear to have made an odd picture, standing together. Grant was five feet eight, stooped, unmilitary in his gait, with creased horizontal wrinkles across his brow giving him a faintly harassed look, and for once he was togged out in dress uniform, black sugar-loaf hat set squarely on his head, sash about his waist, straight sword of a general officer belted at his side. Meade was taller, skinny, and bearing something of a patrician air, harsh lines cutting down from the corners of his nose. He spoke of the army as "My people," and he wore a felt hat with peaked crown and turned-down brim which gave him a Tyrolean appearance.[2] They had their talk, and then the Zouaves presented arms and the band played ruffles and flourishes, and Grant went away. He came back, a little more than a fortnight later, and from that moment on, in spite of fact and logic, the army was known as "Grant's army."

Grant made his headquarters in a plain brick house near Culpeper Court House, with tents for his staff pitched in the yard, and he got down to work. He was commander of all of the armies of the United States—counting everything, he had twenty-one army corps and eighteen military departments under him, for a total of 533,000 soldiers—and he had a diversity of jobs to do, from winning the war down to keeping the politicians from running the Army of the Potomac, and he had very little time for small talk.[3]

Ulysses S. Grant was a natural—an unmistakable rural Middle Westerner, bearing somehow the air of the little farm and the empty dusty road and the small-town harness shop, plunked down here in an army predominantly officered by polished Easterners. He was slouchy, round-shouldered, a red bristly beard cropped short on his weathered face, with a look about the eyes as of a man who had come way up from very far down; his one visible talent seemingly the ability to ride any horse anywhere under any conditions. These days, mostly, he rode a big bay horse named Cincinnati, and when he went out to look at the troops he set a pace no staff officer could match, slanting easily forward as if he and the horse had been made in one piece, and his following was generally trailed out behind him for a hundred yards, scabbards banging against

the sides of lathered horses, the less military officers frantically
grabbing hats and saddle leather as they tried to keep up.

Somewhere within the general in chief there hid the proud,
shy little West Point graduate who put on the best uniform
a brevet second lieutenant of infantry could wear when he
went home to Ohio on furlough after graduation, and who got
laughed at for a dude by livery-stable toughs, and who forever after preferred to wear the plain uniform of a private
soldier, with officer's insignia stitched to the shoulders. He
had three stars to put there now—more than any American
soldier had worn except George Washington and Winfield
Scott—and he had little eccentricities. He breakfasted frequently on a cup of coffee and a cucumber sliced in vinegar,
and if he ate meat it had to be cooked black, almost to a crisp:
this author of much bloodshed detested the sight of blood,
and was made queasy by the sight of red meat. When he prepared for his day's rounds he accepted from his servant two
dozen cigars, which were stowed away in various pockets,
and he carried a flint and steel lighter with a long wick, modern style, so that he could get a light in a high wind.

He received many letters asking for his autograph, but, he
admitted, "I don't get as many as I did when I answered
them." He was not without a quiet sense of humor; writing
his memoirs, he told about the backwoods schools he went to
as a boy, saying that he was taught so many times that "a
noun is the name of a thing" that he finally came to believe it.
As a man he was talkative but as a general he was close-
mouthed. When the crack VI Corps was paraded for him and
officers asked him if he ever saw anything to equal it (hoping
that he might confess that the Army of the Potomac was better drilled than Western troops, which was indeed the case)
he remarked only that General So-and-so rode a very fine
horse; the general in question, a brigade commander, having
recently invested $500 in a fancy new saddle of which he was
very proud.[4]

Nobody knew quite what to make of him, and judgments
were tentative. One of Meade's staff officers commented that
Grant's habitual expression was that of a man who had made

up his mind to drive his head through a stone wall, and Uncle John Sedgwick, canniest and most deeply loved of all the army's higher officers, wrote to his sister that he had been "most agreeably disappointed" both with the general's looks and with his obvious common sense. (As it happened, "common sense" was the expression most often used when men tried to say why they liked Sedgwick so much.) Sedgwick was a little bit skeptical. He said that even though Grant impressed him well, it was doubtful whether he could really do much more with the army than his predecessors had done, since "the truth is we are on the wrong road to take Richmond." [5] Having unburdened himself, Sedgwick retired to his tent to resume one of his everlasting games of solitaire, leaving further comment to other ranks.

Other ranks had their own ideas, which did not always approach reverence. A squadron of cavalry went trotting by one day while Grant sat his horse, smoking, and one trooper sniffed the breeze and said that he knew the general was a good man because he smoked such elegant cigars. Two privates in the 5th Wisconsin saw Grant ride past them, and studied him in silence. Presently one asked the inevitable question: "Well, what do you think?" The other took in the watchful eyes and the hard straight mouth under the stubbly beard, and replied: "He looks as if he meant it." Then, reflecting on the problems which politics could create for a general, he added: "But I'm afraid he's too near Washington." The first soldier said that they would see for themselves before long, and remarked contemplatively: "He's a little 'un."

One man said that while the soldiers often saw Grant he was always riding so fast that they could not get a good look at him, and another commented: "After the debonair McClellan, the cocky Burnside, rosy Joe Hooker and the dyspeptic Meade, the calm and unpretentious Grant was not exciting anyway." He felt that the most anyone really saw was "a quiet solidity." [6]

If the general had solidity he would need it, because he was under great pressure. Hopes and fears centered on him, not to mention jealousies. The country at large believed that he was the man who at last was going to win the war, possibly very quickly. The day when men easily expected miracles and hoped to find another Napoleon under the newest general's black campaign hat had died out long ago, but if miracles were out of order ruthless determination perhaps would do, and that much seemed to be visible.

Over in the Army of Northern Virginia, James Longstreet was quietly warning people not to underestimate this new Yankee commander: "That man will fight us every day and every hour till the end of the war." [7] Nobody in the North heard the remark, but the quality which had called it forth had not gone unnoticed. Here was the man who looked as if he would ram his way through a brick wall, and since other tactics had not worked perhaps that was the thing to try. At Fort Donelson and at Vicksburg he had swallowed two Confederate armies whole, and at Chattanooga he had driven a third army in headlong retreat from what had been thought to be an impregnable stronghold, and all anyone could think of was the hard blow that ended matters. Men seemed ready to call Grant the hammerer before he even began to hammer.

Yet if there were many who uncritically expected much, there were some who had corrosive doubts. Congress had passed an act creating the rank of lieutenant general, knowing that if the act became law no one but Grant would be named, knowing that in passing the act it was doing only what the situation and the country demanded. Yet Congress had had one worry all the while it was acting—a worry expressed in the simple, vulgar question: If we turn the country's armies over to this man, will he stay sober?

The question was never debated publicly and never forgotten in private. Never before had there been anything quite like this uneasy concern that the nation's survival might hang on one man's willingness to refrain from drinking too much. Along with the legend of victory, there had arisen about Grant this legend of drunkenness—bad days in California, forced resignation from the army, hardscrabble period in Missouri and Illinois, surprise at Shiloh. All of these were items in the legend, and men who knew nothing whatever about it had at least heard of President Lincoln's offhand crack that he would like to buy for his other generals some of Grant's own brand of whisky. Men looked at Grant and saw what they had been led to see. Some saw quiet determination, and others, like Richard Henry Dana, saw "the look of a man who did, or once did, take a little too much to drink," and considered that there was an air of seediness and half pay about the fellow.

The question had finally been resolved in Grant's favor, of course, but not without much soul searching on the part of those who had to resolve it. And as a hedge against a chancy future, Congress had created for the lieutenant general the post of chief of staff, and into this post there had come the thin, impassioned, consumptive little lawyer from Illinois, John A. Rawlins.

Rawlins knew no more about military matters than any other lawyer, except for what had rubbed off on him through three years with Grant, but that did not matter. He ran Grant's staff capably enough, although high policy sometimes got away from him and he was hesitant about asserting himself where officers of the Regular Army were concerned, but what was really important about him was the fact that he had a mother hen complex. He was devoted to the Union with a passion that was burning the life out of him, but he was even more devoted to U. S. Grant, and his great, self-chosen mission in life was to guard the general's honor, well-being, and sobriety. In elevating Grant the government had in effect elevated Rawlins as well. Unformulated but taken for granted was the idea that he was the man who would save the man who would save the country.[8]

There was a good deal of needless worry in all of this. Grant was no drunkard. He was simply a man infinitely more complex than most people could realize. Under the hard, ruthless man of war—the remorseless soldier who hammered and hammered until men foolishly believed him raw strength incarnate—there was quite another person: the West Point cadet who hated military life and used to hope against unavailing hope that Congress would presently abolish the military academy and so release him from an army career; the young officer who longed to get away from camp and parade ground and live quietly as a teacher of mathematics; a man apparently beset by infinite loneliness, with a profound need for the warm, healing, understanding intimacy that can over-leap shyness. Greatly fortunate, he found this intimacy with his wife, whom he still loved as a young man loves his first sweetheart, and when he was long away from her he seems to have been a little less than whole. On the eve of every great battle, after he became a famous general, with the orders all written and everything taped for the next day's violence, and the unquiet troops drifting off into a last sleep, he would go to his tent and unburden himself in a long, brooding letter to this woman who still spoke of him, quaintly, as "Mister Grant."

So it could happen badly with him, when he was alone and cut off and the evils of life came down about him. Marooned in California, far from his family, tormented by money prob-lems, bored by the pointless routine of a stagnant army post under a dull and unimaginative colonel, he could turn to drink for escape. He could do the same thing back in Missouri as a civilian, working hard for a meager living, all the luck breaking badly, drifting into failure at forty, Sam Grant the ne'er-do-well. Deep in Tennessee, likewise, sidetracked by a jealous and petty-minded superior, the awful stain of Shiloh lying ineradicable on his mind, his career apparently ready to end just as it was being reborn, the story could be the same. There was a flame in him, and there were times when he could not keep the winds from the outer dark from blowing in on him and making it flicker. But it never did go out.

In any case, the Army of the Potomac was hardly in a posi-tion to look down its nose on officers who drank. It had an abundance of them, and they had been seen in every level from army commander down to junior lieutenant. There had been times when the sleep of enlisted men had been broken by the raucous noises coming from the tents of drunken of-ficers. There had been one notable occasion this past winter when a famous corps commander got drunk, walked full-tilt into a tree in front of his tent, and was with difficulty restrained from court-martialing the officer of the guard on charges of felonious assault. A little Quaker nurse in a II Corps hospital, commenting on the fact that both a corps and a division commander had been drunk during a recent battle, wrote bitterly: "I don't care what anyone says, war is humbug. It is just put out to see how much suffering the privates can bear, I guess." Perfectly in character was the tale told of a major who commanded an artillery brigade, a heavy drinker despite the fact that he came from prohibitionist Maine. This man had a birthday coming up and he wanted to celebrate, and he called in his commissary officer and asked how much whisky they had in stock. The officer said there might be as much as two gallons, and the major was indignant.

"Two gallons!" he repeated. "What is two gallons of whisky among one man?" [9]

To do the army justice, it did not worry about Grant's drinking. A general who never got drunk was a rarity—so much so that his sobriety was always mentioned in his biography, as a sign that he stood above the common run. What troubled the officer corps—and, to an extent, the enlisted man as well—was the fact that Grant came from the West. The West seemed to be a side show where a general could win a reputation without really amounting to much. (After all, there had been John Pope.) Federal troops in the West were thought to be an undisciplined rabble. Also—which was what really mattered—they had never been up against the first team. They had never had to face Robert E. Lee.

Lee was the one soldier in whom most of the higher officers of the Army of the Potomac had complete, undiluted confidence. Among the many achievements of that remarkable man, nothing is much more striking than his ability to dominate the minds of the men who were fighting against him. These men could look back on several years of warfare, and what they saw always seemed about the same—the Army of the Potomac marching south to begin an offensive, well-equipped and full of confidence, and, within days or weeks, fighting doggedly and without too much confidence to escape annihilation. Twice the army had won a defensive battle, letting its enemies go away unmolested afterward, but when it took the offensive it invariably lost the initiative. Its own plans never seemed to matter, because sooner or later both armies moved by Lee's plans. Grant was untried. His record probably meant nothing. Just wait until he tried tangling with Lee! [10]

As it happened, this attitude worked both ways; if soldiers in the East had a low opinion of soldiers in the West, the Westerners returned the feeling with interest. A Federal general in one of the Western armies, reading the sad news from Chancellorsville the preceding spring, had remarked that "we do not build largely on the Eastern army," and continued: "When we hear, therefore, that the Eastern army is going to fight, we make our minds up that it is going to be defeated, and when the result is announced we feel sad enough but not disappointed." Westerners believed that the Army of the Potomac had never been made to fight all out and that when all was said and done there was something mysteriously wrong with it. The Westerners had had no Antietam or Gettysburg, but they had had a Shiloh and a Stone's River, and they felt that they had seen the Confederates at their toughest. When the IX Corps was sent to Tennessee in the fall of 1863, Western troops greeted the boys with the jeering question: "All quiet along the Potomac?" and announced caustically: "We'll show you how to fight." [11]

So there were mutual doubts, and the effect was unfortunate. The officers of this army not only viewed Grant's advent with strong skepticism; in many cases this skepticism verged on outright hostility, so that it was ready to burst out with a bitter, triumphant "I told you so!" if the new general should run into trouble. Grant's presence here was an implied criticism of the army's prior leadership and strategy. Through him, the administration was striking its final blow at the whole complex of emotions and relationships which had come down from McClellan—and McClellan remained, next to Lee, the man in whom most of the veteran officers still had implicit confidence.

Among the private soldiers there was mostly a great curiosity. It was noticed that of a sudden the enlisted man had become a student of newspapers and magazines, reading everything he could find about the new general in chief. Men made themselves familiar with Grant's campaigns, and it was not uncommon to see campfire groups drawing maps in the dirt with sticks to demonstrate how Vicksburg and Chattanooga had gone. At the worst, there was resigned acquiescence. One man summed up his company's opinion by saying: "He cannot be weaker or more inefficient than the generals who have wasted the lives of our comrades during the past three years." He concluded that "if he is a fighter he can find all the fighting he wants." [12]

Ohio and Pennsylvania soldiers, huddling together on a picket post, talked it over:

"Who's this Grant that's made a lieutenant general?"

"He's the hero of Vicksburg."

"Well, Vicksburg wasn't much of a fight. The Rebels were out of rations and they had to surrender or starve. They had nothing but dead mules and dogs to eat, as I understand."

The men nodded, and one said that Grant could never have penned up any of Lee's generals that way. Longstreet or Jeb Stuart "would have broken out some way and foraged around for supplies." [13]

An impressionable newspaper correspondent might describe Grant as "all-absorbed, all-observant, silent, inscrutable," a man who "controls and moves armies as he does his horse," but the enlisted man wanted more evidence. He liked the fact that Grant went about without fuss and ceremony, and he was ready to admit that "a more hopeful spirit prevailed," but for the most part he went along with the company officer who said that only time would tell whether this new general's first name was really Ulysses or Useless. [14]

Yet there was a change, and before long the men felt it. There was a perceptible tightening up, as if someone who meant business had his hands on the reins now. Orders went forth to corps and division commanders to make a radical cut in the number of men who were borne on the returns as "on special, extra, or daily duty," and attention was called to the discrepancies between the numbers reported "present for duty" and those listed as "present for duty, equipped." In brigades and divisions the inspectors general became busy, and where equipment had been lacking it suddenly materialized. Long trains of freight cars came clanking in at Brandy Station, to unload food and forage, uniforms and blankets, and shelter tents and munitions. Men found that they were working harder now than in the past. Subtly but unmistakably, an air of competence and preparation was manifest.

Cavalry found that a new day had dawned. The Pleasontons and Kilpatricks were gone, and at the top there was another Westerner—a tough little man named Phil Sheridan, bandy-legged and wiry, with a black bullet head and a hard eye, wearing by custom a mud-spotted uniform, flourishing in one fist a flat black hat which, when he put it on, seemed to be at least two sizes too small for him. Like Grant, he rode a great black horse when he made his rounds and he rode it at a pounding gallop, and it was remarked that he "rolled and bounced upon the back of his steed much as an old salt does when walking up the aisle of a church after a four years' cruise at sea."

Cavalry's camps were better policed, the endless picket details were reduced, and it appeared that Sheridan was going to insist on using his corps as a compact fighting unit. When Sheridan was taken to the White House to meet the President, Lincoln quoted the familiar army jest—"Who ever saw a dead cavalryman?"—and it was obvious that Sheridan was not amused. Meeting a friend at Willard's a little bit later, Sheridan said: "I'm going to take the cavalry away from the bobtailed brigadier generals. They must do without their escorts. I intend to make the cavalry an arm of the service."

One trooper complained that people now were checking up on all routine jobs, so that a man grooming his horse had to put in a full sixty minutes at it: "There is an officer watching you all the time, and if you stop he yells out, 'Keep to work, there!'" With all of this came businesslike new weapons: seven-shot Spencer magazine carbines, made regulation equipment by a recently revived Cavalry Bureau.[15]

Artillerists were put through endless maneuvers, wheeling back and forth in the dust and mud to become letter-perfect in such intricacies as "changing front to the right on the first section," and banging away in constant target practice. Batteries were taught to come galloping up to a line, halt and unlimber, completely disassemble their pieces until wheels, guns, gun carriages, and limber chests lay separate on the ground, then at a word of command reassemble the whole business and go galloping away again. One gunner declared that a good gun crew could perform the whole maneuver in several seconds less than one minute, and another grumbled that all of this "was of as much practical use to us as if we had been assiduously drilled to walk on stilts"; and whether it was useful or otherwise the drill was repeated over and over and the gun crews got toughened up for the approaching campaign.[16]

None of this, naturally, missed the infantry. There were unending drills, and much target practice. The army command had caught on to the notorious fact that some soldiers simply did not know how to shoot. On every battlefield, ordnance officers had collected hundreds of discarded muskets containing anywhere from two to a dozen unexploded cartridges. In the heat of battle men failed to notice that they had not pulled trigger, and reloaded weapons which had not been fired; or, indeed, they were so untaught that they did not even know enough to cap their pieces and so pulled trigger to no effect, failing to realize in all the battle racket that they had not actually fired. A circular from headquarters decreed that every man in the army should be made to load and fire his weapon under supervision of an officer, since "it is believed there are men in this army who have been in numerous actions without ever firing their guns." [17]

The bark of the drill sergeant echoed across the hardtrodden parade grounds where new levies were being put into shape. (In the Irish Brigade, an irate non-com was heard shouting: "Kape your heels together, Tim Mullaney in the rear rank, and don't be standing wid wan fut in Bull Run and the other in the Sixth Ward!") Transportation was cut down

—one wagon to a brigade was the rule now—and many wagon drivers came back to the ranks and shouldered muskets. One of these passed a wagon train one day and heard a mule braying. Fixing his eye on the beast, the man retorted: "You needn't laugh at me—you may be in the ranks yourself before Grant gets through with the army." All in all, it was as a New England soldier wrote: "We all felt at last that *the boss* had arrived." [18]

There were many reviews: no McClellan touch now, with pomp and flourish, but a businesslike marshaling of troops to be seen by the general in chief, who rode by always at a gallop, sometimes on Cincinnati, sometimes on a little black pacer named Jeff Davis, and who for all his speed always seemed able to look each man in the ranks squarely in the eye. The general did not appear to care whether anyone cheered or not. The Iron Brigade was drawn up one day in line of massed battalions, a cold drizzle coming down, and as Grant came along the line regiment after regiment gave him a cheer. Grant was preoccupied, studying the faces of the hard fighters in this famous brigade, and he neglected to give the customary wave of the hat in response, and so the colonel of the 6th Wisconsin at the far end of the line told his men not to cheer but simply to give the formal salute. They obeyed, and as Grant came along he noticed the omission and slowed to a walk. The colors were dipped, and Grant took off his hat and bowed. The Wisconsin boys were pleased, and after the parade broke up they said that "Grant wants soldiers, not yaupers." [19]

What the soldiers liked most of all was the far-reaching hand with which Grant hauled men out of the safe dugouts in Washington and brought them into the army.

The Washington fortifications had been manned for two years with what were known as heavy artillery regiments—oversized regiments mustering around 1,800 men apiece, trained both to act as infantry, with muskets, and to man heavy guns in the forts—and these regiments never had any trouble keeping their ranks filled, because men could enlist in them in full confidence that they would have to fight very little and march not at all. They led what the Army of the Potomac considered an excessively soft life, with permanent barracks, no trouble about rations, and every night in bed.

Their possessions were many, because infantry commands leaving Washington for the front always discarded (or could be quietly despoiled of) much property, and so the "heavies" had extra blankets, stoves, civilian-type bedsteads, and good table equipment. Their hospitals boasted white sheets and pillowcases, and some regiments even maintained regimental libraries. Certain regiments actually kept pigs, feeding them on swill from the company kitchens and dining frequently on fresh pork. One outfit of mechanically minded Yankees set up a little machine shop, and before inspection they would take their muskets in and have the barrels turned in lathes to take on a dazzling gleam and polish, with machine-driven buffers to put a glossy sheen on the stocks. These men had been enjoying a very comfortable war, and the combat troops had been resenting it (and envying them) for a long time.

Now, without warning, these huge regiments left their happy homes, marched down to the Rapidan, and began to pitch their shelter tents in the mud just like everybody else, and the infantry was jubilant. Veterans would line the roads, whooping with delight, calling out all manner of greetings—asking the new regiments why they had not brought their fortifications along, referring to them derisively as "heavy infantry," inquiring when their guns would arrive, and offering instruction about various aspects of the soldier's life. These heavy artillery regiments were many times as large as the veteran infantry outfits—the colonel of the 12th Massachusetts was protesting just now that his regiment could muster only 207 enlisted men for duty—and the veterans would make heavy-handed remarks on the fact; when a new regiment came in they would ask what division this was.[20]

Certain cavalry commands met a similar fate, and got just as much sympathy. Some of these had been in camp at Washington for a refit, waiting with perfect resignation for the slow processes of government to provide them with remounts. These abruptly found themselves deprived of sabers, of carbines, and of all hope of new horses, given infantry muskets instead, and sent down to the Rapidan on foot. A Connecticut heavy artillery regiment, meeting such a command of dismounted Maryland cavalry, asked incautiously: "Where are your horses?" A Marylander replied sourly: "Gone to fetch your heavy guns." The Official Records contain a plaintive and quite useless protest by an outraged colonel, who recited that he led a spanking new regiment of Pennsylvania cavalry into Washington that spring—1,200 men, well mounted, disciplined, drilled, and equipped—only to be ordered to turn in his horses and weapons, draw muskets, and consider his command infantry thenceforward.[21]

All of this pleased the infantry greatly, cavalry in general not being too popular with foot soldiers, and there was admiration for the general who had brought it all to pass. With this admiration came a dawning respect for his power. Pulling the heavy artillery and the dismounted cavalry down to the Rapidan meant that Washington was being left almost defenseless. In earlier times, White House and War Department had insisted on keeping 40,000 men or more within the Washington lines, even though no enemies ever came within miles of them. If this new general could override that insistence he must have prodigious strength. Apparently he could have things just about the way he wanted them, and the army would move with greater power. At the very least, it seemed that the country's strength was going to be *used*. When he rode the lines, a soldier wrote that the men would "look with awe at Grant's silent figure." [22]

Not all of the changes were popular. One which was bitterly resented by thousands of the best soldiers in the army was a shake-up which consolidated the five infantry corps into three. Actually, this was none of Grant's doing, Meade having put it in the works before Grant took over, but it was announced while all the other changes were taking place and it was generally accepted as part of Grant's program. Meade seems to have made the move partly because he felt that the army would work better with fewer and larger units, and partly because there were not as many as five qualified corps com-

manders in the army anyway. The consolidation enabled him
to shelve several generals who had been withering on the
vine—the best of them, probably, crusty and slow-moving
George Sykes, famous because of the work his Regulars had
done in the early days.

What made this shake-up unpopular with so many men was
the fact that the I Corps and the III Corps ceased to exist,
their brigades being distributed among the three corps which
survived. These two corps had been famous and their men
had been cocky, wearing their corps badges with vast pride,
and they were brought almost to the verge of mutiny by the
change. (One army historian, writing more than twenty years
later, asserted that "the wound has never yet wholly healed in
the heart of many a brave and patriotic soldier.")[23] The two
organizations had been wrecked at Gettysburg and it had
never been possible, somehow, to repair the damage and
bring them up to proper strength. Yet the consolidation was
unfortunate. Heretofore, each corps had had its own indi-
viduality and its own tradition, and these had done much for
morale. Just as the three which remained were striving to
digest the miscellaneous lot of new recruits which were coming in, they were given the unhappy brigades and divisions
from the two corps which had been abolished. The result was
that nobody quite felt that his old outfit was what it used to
be. There was also the possibility that the great increase in
the size of each corps would put a new strain on the corps
commanders.

In the midst of all of this reshuffling the army almost lost
John Sedgwick. Sedgwick had never felt it necessary to as-
sure Washington that he hated Democrats and loved emancipation, nor had he ever concealed his admiration for Mc-
Clellan, and these things had made him suspect with Secretary
Stanton. Early this winter Sedgwick had bluntly told the War
Department that Butler's poorly handled attempt to capture
Richmond had done the Union cause more harm than good,
and since Butler was a pet of the radical Republicans—a standing test of the other generals' allegiance to the cause, so to
speak—this was remembered where it would hurt. In Febru-

ary Sedgwick wrote to his sister that the army grapevine was predicting a reorganization "to get rid of some obnoxious generals," and he admitted that he himself might be on this list. It would not bother him much, he said, if this turned out to be true: "I feel that I have done my part of field duty. . . . I could even leave altogether without many regrets."

So when Meade began to make changes Stanton told him that it would be well to find some other place for Sedgwick, and after some argument back and forth it had finally been agreed to put Sedgwick in command up in the Shenandoah Valley. It would have been an odd sort of demotion, for the valley command was destined to be very important, but it was all upset at the last minute when Mr. Lincoln unexpectedly gave the job to Franz Sigel, and in the end Sedgwick remained in command of the VI Corps.[24]

With the men of this corps he was very popular. One day in this winter of 1864 Wheaton's brigade of the VI Corps came in to camp after several months of detached service in western Virginia. The brigade detrained in a miserable cold rain, and since all of the good camp sites had been taken it appeared that they would have to pitch their tents in a muddy field, with no shelter from the elements and the nearest source of wood for campfires several miles away. There was a fine grove near by, to be sure, but some brigadier and his entourage had long since pre-empted it. While the men stood disconsolate in the wet, a burly horseman in a muddy cavalry overcoat came splashing up—Sedgwick. He took in the situation at once, rode over to the little grove, told the brigadier and his henchmen to pack up at once and move to some other place, and ordered Wheaton to have his brigade take over the vacated camp site.[25]

Winfield Scott Hancock led the II Corps. He had been badly wounded at Gettysburg and the wound still bothered him, but he came back at the end of the winter with all of his old gusto and the men were glad to see him. He was a vivid, hearty sort of man—his chief of staff, with strong understatement, remarked that he was "absolutely devoid of asceticism" —and it was believed that he could conduct a long march with less straggling and more professional competence than any other officer in the army. He differed from most Regular Army officers (including Meade himself) in that he liked volunteer soldiers and did his best to make them feel that they were as good as Regulars, and his army corps repaid him for that attitude.[26] The corps badge was a trefoil, and when the men went into action they had a way of yelling: "Clubs are trumps!"

To the V Corps, in place of the departed Sykes, came one of the most baffling figures in the army—Major General Gouverneur Kemble Warren.

Warren was thirty-four, with long jet-black hair and a mustache which he was fond of twirling; a slightly built man with sallow complexion, looking not unlike an Indian, well liked by the troops because he displayed great bravery under fire. (No officer could be popular in this army unless he could show a spectacular contempt for danger.) He was a queer mixture of the good and the ineffective—a fuss-budget with flashes of genius, a man engrossed in detail and given to blunting his cutting edge by worrying over trifles which a staff captain ought to have been handling. He had never heard of delegating authority, and he had a certain weakness for setting his own opinion above that of his superior officer's.

He had had two great days. One was at Gettysburg, when as an engineer officer on the commanding general's staff he had stood on Little Round Top, had seen the coming danger, and by a hair's thin margin had got Union troops there in time to save the day. The other was at Mine Run, in December, when half of the army had been given to him for a mighty assault that was to destroy the Rebel army and make General Warren a national hero. At the last minute General Warren had discovered that the Confederate line was far stronger than had been supposed: so strong, indeed, that the attack could not possibly succeed and would be no better than a second Fredericksburg. With no time to refer matters to the army commander he had had the moral stamina to call things off, let Meade's wrath descend entirely on himself, and take whatever rap might be coming.

He came from Putnam County, New York, and as a young

man he was a sobersides, not to say a bit of a prig. He can be
seen, at twenty-two, a very junior second lieutenant, writing
home to his mother telling her how to rear the eleven other
children she had borne: "You must dress them warmly and
give them the best of shoes to keep their feet dry. . . . Put
flannel underclothes on them all. Cold fingers and cold ears
are not much account, but cold feet is the cause of a great deal
of sickness. If Edgar is still troubled with that tickling in his
throat, put woollen underclothes on him, place a plaster on his
chest, keep his feet warm and dry, and I know it will disappear." Yet he would not merely give advice: "I have money
to spare, if that is lacking."

An engineer officer, he had worked on Mississippi River
flood-control projects, and under Harney he had fought the
Sioux Indians. He had an unmilitary ability to be sensitive to
human suffering. The worst thing about fighting Indians, he
wrote, was that one shot a good many women and children,
and when it came time to dress their wounds afterward one
discovered that they were just like any other women and children and not at all like howling savages. He had filled in for
Hancock in charge of the II Corps, this past winter, and now
he had a corps of his own. It included many good fighters and
contained some of the best of the troops from the departed
I Corps, and what it might do would depend a good deal on
General Warren.[27]

So the army had been made over, with familiar organizations broken up and familiar faces gone, and what nobody
could miss was the fact that it was being made larger and at
the same time harder and more compact. The three rebuilt
army corps were grouped more closely together. The detached troops which had been spending dreary months guarding the line of the railroad back to Alexandria were all called
back into camp. To replace them there appeared an old familiar figure from the unhappy past—Major General Ambrose
E. Burnside, dignified and friendly and incurably addicted to
fumbling, short jacket belted tightly around his tubby figure,
bell-crowned hat shading his incomparable whiskers.

His IX Corps had been brought up to full strength again

(it now contained a solid division of colored troops, who had gone wild with enthusiasm when they were paraded past Abraham Lincoln in Washington) and it was coming down from its rendezvous at Annapolis to occupy the line of the railroad. The corps was not formally a part of the Army of the Potomac. It was to act with the army, receiving direct orders from the general in chief; meanwhile it was on the railroad, and its arrival meant that the army could operate as a unit, none of its manpower wasted guarding the line of supply.

Imperceptibly, a new spirit was appearing. Competence and confidence had arrived, neither one obtrusive, both unmistakable. Yet the soldier lived at the bottom of the pool, in a dim greenish light in which no outlines were very clear. He had seen army commanders come and he had seen them go, and he was going to take very little for granted. The only certainty was that the campaign ahead was going to be very rough, and the men frankly dreaded it—more on account of the marching, they said, than of the fighting. The viewpoint was aptly expressed in a letter which a Pennsylvania private wrote at the end of April: "If Congressmen at Washington, or the Rebel Congress at Richmond, were required to endure the hardships of a soldier's life during one campaign, the war would then end." [28]

Army life went on, despite shifts in command. There were baseball games, as spring dried the fields—the 13th Massachusetts beat the 104th New York one day by a score of 62 to 20—and there were the endless chores of army routine. An Illinois cavalry regiment came to camp after a spell of provost guard duty in Washington, reporting that it had been policing upwards of a hundred houses of prostitution, and a trooper confessed that "this work, although it amused the men for a time, and was arduous to perform, did not satisfy those who longed for more active service." There were the age-old attempts to wangle furloughs. An Irish private one day went to his regimental commander, explaining that his wife was ill and the children were not well and that it was necessary for him to make a short visit to his home. The colonel fixed him with a beady eye and said: "Pat, I had a letter from your wife this morning saying she doesn't want you at home; that you raise the devil whenever you are there, and that she hopes I won't grant you any more furloughs. What have you to say to that?"

Quite unabashed, the soldier replied that there were "two splendid liars in this room" and that he himself was only one of them: "I nivir was married in me life." [29]

Perhaps the abiding reality this spring was the unseen army across the river, the Army of Northern Virginia. A fantastic sort of kinship had grown up in regard to that army. There was no soft sentimentality about it, and the men would shoot to kill when the time for shooting came. Yet there was a familiarity and an understanding, at times something that verged almost on liking, based on solid respect. Whatever else might change, these armies at least understood one another.

Physically, they were not far apart, and the pickets often got acquainted. One Federal picket detail, which was ordered to hold certain advanced posts by day but to pull in closer to camp at night, discovered that a deserted log hut which it was using by day was being used by Rebel pickets at night, the Confederate arrangement here being just the reverse of the Federals'. Two groups of rival pickets met at this hut one morning, the Confederates being tardy in starting back to camp. There was a quick groping for weapons, a wary pause, then a conversation; and the Southerners said that if the Yanks would give them a few minutes to saddle up they would get out and the old schedule might go on. It was so arranged, with a proviso that each side thereafter would leave a good fire burning in the fireplace for its enemies.[30]

The enlisted men knew their enemies better than the officers did. Cedar Mountain was just inside the Union lines, and there was a signal station on top of it, and one day, with marching orders imminent, two officers from a Maine regiment climbed this mountain to take a glimpse of the Rebel country. Far below them, in rolling broken fields and woods, they saw the storied land of the Rapidan—"grinning," as one of them wrote, "with dreadful ghosts," for many men had died in the fighting along this river during the last three years. Today everything looked peaceful, and spring was on the land, and through telescopes they could see a Confederate camp. There were men lounging about in shirt sleeves, some of them smoking their pipes and washing their clothes, others playing ball. The two officers stared at them for a long time, getting their first look at Confederate soldiers off duty. At last they put down their telescopes, and one officer turned to the other.

"My God, Adjutant," he said. "They're human beings just like us!" [31]

CHAPTER II

Roads Leading South

---

1. Where the Dogwood Blossomed

IT WAS the fourth day of May, and beyond the dark river there was a forest with the shadow of death under its low branches, and the dogwood blossoms were floating in the air like lost flecks of sunlight, as if life was as important as death; and for the Army of the Potomac this was the last bright morning, with youth and strength and hope ranked under starred flags, bugle calls riding down the wind, and invisible doors swinging open on the other shore. The regiments fell into line, and great white-topped wagons creaked along the roads, and the spring sunlight glinted off the polished muskets and the brass of the guns, and the young men came down to the valley while the bands played. A German regiment was singing "John Brown's Body."

Beside the roads the violets were in bloom and the bush honeysuckle was out, and the day and the year had a fragile light that the endless columns would soon trample to fragments. The last campaign had begun, and a staff officer sat on a bank overlooking the Rapidan and had a curious thought: how odd it would be if every man who was to die in the days just ahead had to wear a big badge today, so that a man watching by the river could identify all of those who were never coming back!

The men of this army left books and letters behind them, and in these there is a remarkable testimony that the men who marched away from winter quarters that morning took a last look back and saw a golden haze which, even at the moment of looking, they knew they would never see again. They tell how the birds were singing, and how the warm scented air came rolling up the river valley, and how they noticed things like wildflowers and the young green leaves, and they speak of the moving pageant which they saw and of which they themselves were part. "Everything," wrote a youth from Maine, "was bright and blowing." It would never be like this again, and young men who were to live on to a great age, drowsing out the lives of old soldiers in a land that would honor them and then tolerate them and finally forget them, would look back on this one morning and see in it something that came from beyond the rim of the world.[1]

Cavalry took the lead, moving down through the busy camps to the historic Rapidan crossings, Germanna and Ely's fords. Foot soldiers watched them go, and called out, in what they conceived to be the idiom of their Southern foes: "Hey there! Where be you-all going?" Jauntily, the troopers called back that they were on their way to Richmond. But although the army felt that this campaign was going to be better than previous ones it still was skeptical, and cavalry needed to be put in its place anyway, so the infantry cried out: "Bob Lee will drive you-all back just as he has done before." [2]

The troopers pushed on and crossed the river, and they left the sunlight behind and went up the winding woods roads that led into the Wilderness.

This was a mean gloomy woodland, a dozen miles wide by half as deep, lying silent and forbidding along the southern bank of the river. Its virgin timber had been cut down years ago, mostly to provide fuel for small iron-smelting furnaces in the neighborhood, and a tangled second growth had sprung up—stunted pines, innumerable small saplings, dense underbrush, here and there a larger tree, vines and creepers trailing every which way through dead scrub pines with interlaced spiky branches; there were very few places in which a man could see as far as twenty yards. The soil was poor, and there were hardly any farms or clearings, and the land under the trees was like a choppy sea, broken by ridges and hillocks and irregular knolls.

There were dark little streams that never saw the sun, and these had cut shallow ravines, some of which had very steep banks. These water courses wandered and twisted and turned on themselves, soaking the low ground into bush-covered swamps, and the thickets covered their banks. Once in a great while there would be a house—paintless, sometimes made of hewn logs, looking gaunt and forsaken like the forest itself, with a hopeless corn patch and weedy pasture around it—and there were a few aimless lanes, hardly more than tracks in the jungle, which did not seem to go anywhere in particular.

It was the last place on earth for armies to fight, and the entire Army of the Potomac was marching straight into it.

Actually, the high command had little intention of fighting here. The two armies had been facing each other, with the Rapidan between them, a number of miles upstream from the Wilderness, and when Grant made his plans he had two choices. He could move by his right flank, sliding along the line of the Orange and Alexandria Railroad in the general direction of Gordonsville, swinging past Lee to the west, and forcing him to fight in open country; or he could go by his left, slipping quickly through the Wilderness, heading for a position behind Lee's right—where, as in the other case, there could be fighting in the open.

He had taken the second choice, for reasons which seemed good to him. Chief reason was the matter of supply. Counting everybody, he would be taking some 116,000 men with him, and more than 50,000 horses, and it seemed improbable that the single-tracked railway line could supply all of them adequately. Furthermore, the railroad led through country infested with guerillas—John S. Mosby's famous irregulars, mostly, who attacked Yankee supply lines and outposts so viciously and effectively that the region between Brandy Station and Alexandria was commonly known as "Mosby's Confederacy." If the Federal army dangled at the end of a hundred miles of railroad, these men would have a field day, and so would Jeb Stuart's far-ranging cavalry, and half of the army would have to be left behind to cope with them. So the army was going to the left, where if it made progress there would be seacoast bases, with a short roadway for the enormous wagon train.

There might have been a third choice: McClellan's old route of 1862, putting the army on boats and going down by water to the tip of the Virginia peninsula, with a landing at Fortress Monroe and a quick march toward Richmond between York and James rivers. That way, the army could get up within shooting distance of Richmond without trouble, and the long overland hike with exposed supply lines and hard fighting at every crossroads would be avoided. Before he got to Brandy Station Grant felt that that was the way to go, and soldiers as good as John Sedgwick agreed. Why fight one's way to Richmond when the army could travel most of the way by water and come up to the doors of the Rebel capital fresh and unbloodied?

The trouble was that it was not that kind of war any more. Meade's soldiers had noticed many changes this spring, but what they had not seen was the fact that the role of the Army of the Potomac itself had changed. The goal now was not to capture Richmond but to fight the Army of Northern Virginia—to begin to fight it as soon as possible and to keep on fighting it until one side or the other could fight no more.

Whatever happened, Lee must never again be allowed to take the initiative. It might or it might not be possible to beat him, but it was all-important to keep him busy. It must be made impossible for him to detach troops to oppose Sherman, who was breaking his way into Georgia with the contemptuous remark that when you pierced the shell of the Confederacy you found hollowness within. Also, Ben Butler was advancing toward Richmond on the south side of the James, and if the Army of the Potomac spent the first month of the campaign getting on and off of steamboats Lee could concentrate against Butler, destroy him and his army, and thus win a dazzling victory at comparatively low cost.

For all of these reasons, then, the Army of the Potomac had one paramount responsibility: it must get close to the enemy as soon as possible and it must stay close until the war ended. If it did that, victory would come. It might not come in Virginia, and the price paid for it might be terribly high, but it would come in the end.[3]

So the army was heading down into the Wilderness, hoping to cross that unwholesome area quickly and to get the Army of Northern Virginia by the throat immediately thereafter. It was a good enough plan. The difficulty might lie in the fact that Lee was notoriously averse to fighting battles when and where his enemies wanted to fight them.

Some of the soldiers felt this, and as they crossed the river they were vaguely uneasy. A cavalry regiment got over in the middle of the night, drove off the Rebel pickets at the crossing, and went jogging up the sandy roads into the black forest. As they rode the men talked, and one man said that he never thought "the army went hunting around in the night for Johnnies in this way." A comrade explained: "We're stealing a march on old man Lee."

They thought that over briefly, and someone suggested: "Lee'll miss us in the morning."

"Yes," said another, "and then look out. He'll come tearing down this way ready for a fight." [4]

Lee was on Grant's mind, too, that day. At noon Grant crossed the Rapidan and made temporary headquarters in a deserted farmhouse overlooking the ford, and a newspaper correspondent brashly asked him how long it would take him to reach Richmond. About four days, said Grant soberly; then, as the newspaperman goggled at him, he went on—four days, provided General Lee was a party to the agreement. If not, it would probably take a good deal longer.

Grant had ridden past the troops in midmorning, his ornamented staff trotting at his heels. Riding beside him there was the lone civilian amid all those thousands of soldiers—

Congressman Elihu B. Washburne of Illinois, Grant's personal friend and political sponsor, a headquarters visitor for the opening days of the campaign. Washburne wore civilian clothes of funereal black, and when the soldiers saw him they asked one another who this character might be. A staff officer heard one rear-rank wit telling his mates that it was simple: the Old Man had brought along his private undertaker.[5]

For the first twenty-four hours nothing happened. Warren and Sedgwick got their men over the river at Germanna Ford and headed south. The day was warm, and in the hollow roads no air was stirring, and before long the roadside was littered with packed knapsacks, overcoats, extra blankets, and other bits of gear which sweating soldiers found too heavy to carry. The veterans wagged their heads: all of that stuff was a sure sign that there were lots of recruits in the ranks—no old-timer would load himself down with excess baggage at the beginning of a march.

Artillerists gloated, and scampered about collecting loot; they had an advantage over infantry, in that gun carriages and caissons offered handy places to carry such extras. The more experienced gunners warned their mates not to be hasty. If they waited for heat and fatigue to become a little more oppressive, some of the straw-feet would begin discarding even their haversacks, and those must be collected at all costs. If this march was like most others, they would leave the supply trains far behind, and it was important to lay in a surplus of food.[6]

The road wound and climbed slowly for several miles, and at last it came out into an open space by a crossroads. Off to the left there was a run-down, abandoned stage station, still known as Wilderness Tavern, a ruinous place with its yard full of weeds, half hidden by scraggly trees. Behind it was a meadow where, just a year ago, the Confederates had had a field hospital during the battle of Chancellorsville, and in that field the doctors had amputated the arm of Stonewall Jackson.

A general who came down from Germanna Ford and

stood here by the deserted tavern facing south was practically in the middle of the northern fringe of the Wilderness. To get through the Wilderness he could turn right, turn left, or go straight ahead, and no matter which way he went he had about six miles of Wilderness to cross. Squarely across his path lay the region's principal east-west highway, the Orange Turnpike, which ran from Fredericksburg through Chancellorsville to Orange Court House. Two or three miles to the south there was a companion road roughly parallel to the Turnpike, the Orange Plank Road, a narrow track with a strip of planking running beside a strip of dirt. (The rule in the old days was that a loaded wagon was entitled to stay on the planking; unloaded wagons had to yield the right of way and turn off into the mud.)

The road south from Germanna Ford crossed the Turnpike, slanting off toward the east as it went south, crossed the Plank Road, and finally got to the southern border of the Wilderness and the open country beyond. About halfway between the Turnpike and Plank Road crossings it became known as the Brock Road. The names of these three highways were presently to be written in red on the annals of the Army of the Potomac.

Thus, of the three main highways here, two ran east and west and one went north and south. Interlaced across them were various minor roads and lanes, mapped imperfectly or not at all, giving the appearance of going nowhere and, often enough, actually doing it. Only on the three main roads was any sense of direction to be had. All of the minor roads just wandered.

Somewhere to the west lay the Army of Northern Virginia. Presumably it was moving south, in order to get below the Wilderness and head the Yankees off. If by any chance it proposed to make trouble here in the Wilderness, the Turnpike and the Plank Road were the avenues by which trouble would come. Hence before the army halted for the night it was important to picket those roads, and late in the afternoon of May 4 it was so arranged, with cavalry riding west on the Plank Road and infantry solidly planted on the Turnpike.

While Warren's and Sedgwick's troops were making their bivouac along the Germanna Road and around the Wilderness Tavern, Hancock and the II Corps were making camp half a dozen miles to the east. They had crossed the Rapidan at Ely's Ford, and their route had led them to the historic Chancellorsville crossroads, where the ruins of the old Chancellor house lay charred amid the vines and the creepers, and where the bones of many unburied dead men took on a pallid gleam in the dusk. According to the plan, Hancock's men were to move on in the morning, swinging south and west in a wide arc, getting far down on the lower edge of the Wilderness. They could have gone farther this day, and it might have been well if they had done so, but the belief was that the army had the jump on its enemies. So Hancock's men camped in a haunted gloaming, where Hooker's men had fought a year earlier, and eerie omens were afloat in the dusk.

The army was spraddled out over a wide expanse of country. Burnside's IX Corps was coming down to the Rapidan from the north, the great wagon trains were trundling up behind Hancock at Chancellorsville, and scores of silent guns were parked by the Turnpike. There was something uncanny and foreboding in the air, and when night came seeping up out of the blackness under the low trees the camps were invaded by memories and premonitions.

It was the last night for many young men—the last night, in a sense, for the old Army of the Potomac, which had tramped down many roads of war and which at last was coming up against something new. The men were bivouacked on the sharp edge of a dividing line in the war, and it appears that somehow they sensed it. After tonight, everything was going to be different. The marching and the fighting were going to be different, and the comradeship around the campfires was going to be thinned out and changed, and nothing they had learned was going to help very much in the experience that lay just beyond the invisible treetops, where a wind made a stir and rustle in the branches.

In a New York regiment, in Warren's corps, it was remembered that the ordinary songs and campfire chat were missing, and the men were uneasy. They felt that they were far down in the enemy's country, and this dank Wilderness did not seem a good place to be, and they carried "a sense of ominous dread which many of us found it almost impossible to shake off." In one of the cavalry regiments the chaplain brought a group together for divine service, and he read a text about buckling on the whole armor of God and urged the men to "be prepared to stand an inspection before the King of Kings," and the usually irreverent troopers listened in silence, standing with firelight flickering on brown young faces, and some of them wept.[7]

In Hancock's artillery park the gunners found many unburied skeletons from last year's fight, and the old-timers recalled the horror of that fight, where men with broken backs or shattered thighs lay in the underbrush and watched the flames that were going to burn them alive creep closer and closer. One man predicted that "these woods will surely be burned if we fight here," and others said that they did not fear being killed nearly as much as they feared being wounded and left helpless for the forest fires. A soldier stood by a campfire and abstractedly prodded a grinning whitened skull with his toe: moved by a gloomy impulse, he turned to his comrades and cried: "This is what you are all coming to, and some of you will start toward it tomorrow." Off in the woods the whippoorwills began their remote mournful whistling, and near Wilderness Tavern pickets in the dark wood could hear a dull featureless rumbling far away to the west and they knew that somewhere in the night the Rebels were moving in great strength.[8]

Morning came in clear, with a promise of warmth later in the day, and the army began to move before sunrise. Warren's corps was to go south, sidling toward the west as it went, with Sedgwick's men following close behind and Hancock's corps swinging around farther to the left, and the troops got under way promptly. As they moved, Warren sent one division west on the Turnpike, just to make certain the flank was protected, and the colonel who had the advanced skirmish line in this division rode to the top of a rise and looked westward. The roadway here was like an open glade pointing straight toward Lee's army, its dusty white floor lying empty in the dawn, shadowy woods on either side; and far down this avenue the colonel dimly saw a column of moving troops, with men filing off into the forest to right and left, and he sent a courier hustling back to his division commander with the message: Rebels coming this way! [9]

His division commander was Brigadier General Charles Griffin, a lean man with a big walrus mustache and a knack of exuding parade-ground smartness even when he was un-buttoned and dirty: an old-time Regular Army artillerist and, like many such, a hard case. His troops liked him very much—once when he came back from sick leave the men pulled him off his horse and carried him to his tent on their shoulders, which did not often happen to generals—and he had very advanced notions about getting his guns well to the front in battle. It was said that in one fight a battery commander whom he was sending forward looked at the approaching enemy and protested: "My God, General, do you mean for me to put my guns out on the skirmish line?" To which Griffin answered impatiently: "Yes, rush them in there—artillery is no better than infantry; put them in the line and let them fight together." [10] So this morning, with Rebel skirmishers approaching, Griffin pulled a section of guns out of the nearest battery and sent it rolling west on the Turnpike to support his own skirmishers. He had the rest of his division form a line of battle astride the Turnpike, and when the line was formed he ordered it to advance. If the Confederates wanted to start something here he would find out about it soon enough.

This was mean country for a moving line of battle. One hundred feet from the Turnpike a man lost sight of the road entirely, and there seemed to be no other landmarks whatever. No regiment could see the troops on its right or left unless an almost literal elbow-to-elbow contact was main-tained, and no general could see more than a small fraction of his troops, or control them except by sending aides and couriers stumbling off through the woods—amid which, in most stretches, it was quite impossible to ride a horse. The going was tough, with scrubby thickets and clumps of saplings breaking the lines apart and all manner of tangled dry stuff underfoot, but the men struggled along and by and by they heard scattering shots from the skirmishers in the woods ahead.

They overtook their skirmish line, at last, and there seemed to be a substantial number of Confederates in front of them. The firing grew heavier, and it turned into regular volley firing, and a rank fog came in as the battle smoke was trapped under the low branches. To right and left and in front the dark woodland began to glow fitfully with savage, pulsating spurts of reddish light.

Keeping their formation as well as they could, the men stumbled on. They could see nothing of what lay in front of them, but the firing grew heavier every minute. The Rebels obviously meant to make a regular fight of it; the firing line was a mile wide, and everyone was shooting desperately into a gloom where moving figures were glimpsed only at rare intervals. Griffin wheeled his two guns a little farther along the road—there was no way to get them off into the woods because nothing on wheels could possibly leave the highway—and they fired straight down the Turnpike, and what had begun as an affair of the skirmishers developed into a full-dress battle.

Griffin sent men back with the news. It was very hard for him to tell what was going on more than a few rods from where he stood, but it seemed obvious that he had had a head-on collision with a Rebel assaulting column fully as big as his own, and the high command had better know about it right away. Meade got the word in his headquarters in a field near Wilderness Tavern, and it seemed to him that Lee must have left a rear guard here to hold the road while he took his main army farther south. He prepared to get other troops up to help Griffin push the rear guard out of the

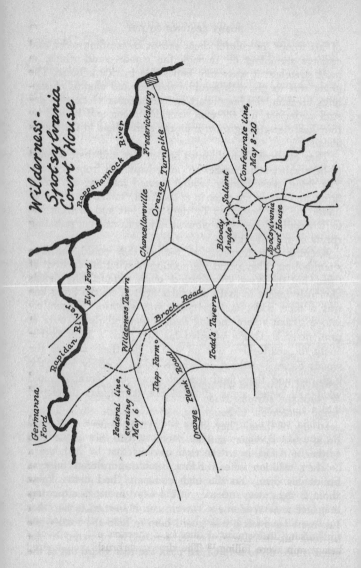

Wilderness-
Spotsylvania
Court House

Rappahannock River
Rapidan River
Germanna Ford
Ely's Ford
Fredericksburg
Chancellorsville
Orange Turnpike
Wilderness Tavern
Brock Road
Tapp Farm
Orange Plank Road
Todd's Tavern
Bloody Angle
Confederate Line, May 8-20
Spotsylvania Court House
Federal line, evening of May 6

way, and he sent an officer spurring back toward Germanna Ford to tell Grant about it.[11]

In a few minutes Grant came up. He talked with Meade and Warren, and listened to the firing, which kept getting heavier and heavier, and word was sent out to stop the movement south: if Lee really wanted to fight here the whole Army of the Potomac would accommodate him. Sedgwick had better bring his men up as fast as he could and Hancock must start back from his thrust below the Plank Road.

Grant's people pitched his headquarters tents in a little meadow in the southwest angle of the crossroads and Grant himself rode up on a knoll just south of this meadow. He dismounted, sat on a stump, lighted a cigar, drew out a pocketknife, picked up a twig, and began to whittle. A staff officer remembered that Grant was all dressed up this morning, wearing his best uniform with the frock coat unbuttoned, a sash about his waist, sword at his side; he was wearing tan cotton-thread gloves which he forgot to remove, and his work with the twigs and the pocketknife began to snag the fingertips of these gloves and before long they were ruined.[12] Grant was sitting here quietly, whittling like a Yankee, and as he smoked without ceasing he issued the orders that would feed more and more troops into this fight.

The fight kept growing bigger. Griffin's men were advancing but it was very slow going, and as the rising wind whipped wisps and streamers of powder smoke through the treetops the advance came to a halt. The Confederates were being reinforced, although hardly any of the Federals had seen any of them. They knew of their presence only as the firing grew stronger, and as bursts of rifle fire came from farther and farther to the right and left.

The smoke intensified the forest gloom and made it opaque. Splinters and tiny branches came down as the bullets clipped through the trees, and only in the rare clearings could any man get a glimpse of his enemies. A Maine regiment came up to a little field, and the bullets were hitting the dried soil and raising little spurts of dust as if the first big drops of a heavy rain were falling.[13] The dry underbrush and matted duff underfoot began to take fire, here and there, so that malicious little flames ran along the battleground.

It was like fighting blindfolded. Here they were, in a woodland so dense that even in peacetime maneuvers a division would have been unable to keep its alignment; now there did not seem to be any alignment at all, and what was supposed to be a battle line was nothing more than a sprawling, invisible series of groups and individuals, each one firing into the woods and the smoke as if it was the Wilderness itself that was the enemy and not the men in it. A company or a regiment would crouch in the underbrush and fire manfully, taking losses but holding firm; then a sudden swell of firing would be heard off to one side or toward the rear, and for all anyone knew the rest of the army had run away and the Rebels were taking over, and men would begin to retreat, firing as they went, looking for some place where they could feel that they were part of an ordered line.

The battalions of Regulars in Griffin's division were ordered forward, and they found the undergrowth all but literally impassable. One company commander reported afterward that in order to get forward at all he had to hack through the vines, creepers, and bushes, breaking a trail so that his company could follow in single file. When a more open space was reached the men would form company front, but in a few moments they would have to return to single file. Inevitably, men lost touch with their comrades, whole regiments disintegrated, and scores of men blundered into the Confederate lines and were made prisoner. There were regiments which could not even learn the direction from which the musketry that was destroying them was coming. Nothing whatever could be seen but trees and brush and blinding smoke. As one man said, it was "a battle of invisibles with invisibles." [14]

So the line crumbled and came back, and the wild noise of battle was a high-pitched, nerve-racking tumult, and at last Griffin found his men back where they had started from, Rebels on both flanks and things getting worse instead of better. Griffin knew that some of Sedgwick's men had been ordered up on his right and some of Warren's men on his left, but they seemed to have gone astray somewhere and as far as he could learn his division was all alone. He got his line stabilized somehow, and put his men to work improvising breastworks, and then he went back to headquarters, an angry man all fuming. He galloped up to Meade on the knoll where Grant was whittling and he threw himself from his horse and bitterly denounced the generals who were supposed to be helping him but whose troops were not appearing.

Griffin swore and shouted and then hurried back to his troops. Grant had heard him, and he was not used to brigadiers who publicly and profanely denounced their superiors, and as Griffin stormed off Grant—who somehow had not quite caught his name—went over to Meade and asked: "Who is this General Gregg? You ought to put him under arrest."

For once in his life Meade was calm and not irascible. He stood facing Grant, towering head and shoulders over him, and he murmured gently: "His name's Griffin, not Gregg, and that's only his way of talking"; and as he spoke he leaned forward and buttoned up Grant's uniform coat for him, for all the world like a kindly father getting his son ready for school.[15] Then Grant went back to his stump and his twigs and his cigars, and couriers dashed off with orders, and in the trackless forest the support troops shouldered their muskets and tried to go forward through the midday twilight.

It was becoming increasingly obvious that this was no rear guard the Federals were fighting. (As a matter of fact, it was Confederate General Ewell's whole army corps: far from looking for a battleground to the south, Lee was making his fight right here, and if the Federals got one foot of Wilderness ground they were going to have to pay for it.) One of Sedgwick's divisions went stumbling up a cow track in the woods, and at what seemed to be a suitable place the men tried to form a proper battle line and go on to close quarters. But the trees and the undergrowth were too thick. A battle line could not advance, could not even be formed, and at last the separate regiments went blindly forward in column, giving up the formation in which they could fight for a formation in which they could at least move. They reached ground that had been fought over, and around them was the pungent smoke of a forest fire, and they plowed through burnt-over spaces where their feet kicked sparks and smoke puffs out of the matted ground. Dead men lay in these cinders, their bodies charred and partly consumed, and a fearful stench lay in the air.[16]

There was no enemy to be seen anywhere. A brigadier made his way to his division commander and asked where he should put his men. "Move," said the commander grandly, "to the sound of the heaviest firing." This was no help at all, because as far as the brigadier could tell the firing came from everywhere, and the only way to find the Rebel battle line was to blunder into it. The smoke became heavier and heavier as the men advanced, and the sound of rifle fire and shouting men and crackling flames grew louder, and the bullets came faster and more deadly. A Wisconsin soldier wrote that the men in his regiment, quite unable to see where they were going or whom they were shooting at, simply knelt in the twilight and "fired by earsight."

There was a high wind, and it whipped the little flames in the underbrush into big flames, and its roar in the treetops mingled with the roar of battle as if some unimaginable tempest were lashing this dark forest. Men who fought were aware that all about them wounded men were pathetically trying to drag themselves along the ground away from the fires.

In one place the soldiers came to a swampy ravine, all overgrown with scrub pines. The ravine was not a hundred yards wide, but the farther bank was completely invisible. There were Rebels there in plenty, as the men could easily tell; some of them were shooting, and others were using axes to cut trees for breastworks, and the wild racket told just what was going on, but from first to last there was no one to be seen. So the men of the VI Corps piled up logs and scooped up earth for breastworks of their own and hung on in the twilight, trading death with enemies they never saw, and at times the noise of musketry all about them swelled up to a clamor such as they had never heard before in any of their battles. There was no sound of artillery, because guns could not be advanced or fired in this jungle—Griffin had long since lost the two guns he had pushed along the open Turnpike— but thousands upon thousands of men were firing their muskets as fast as they could load, until the whole Wilderness seemed to throb with the endless concussion.[17]

These VI Corps men were coming up on the north side of the Turnpike. South of it, Warren was hurrying about through the woods, trying to get his other divisions up on Griffin's left. Grant was still sitting on his stump on the little knoll behind the lines, but his staff officers were ranging far and fast through the tangle, and the orders they carried were infusing something of the bearded little general's relentless drive all down the army's chain of command. Nobody had planned to fight here but here was where the fight was, and if in the past the Army of the Potomac had never quite managed to get all of its men into action that fault was not going to be repeated now.

There had never been a fight like this before. Things were clear enough on the map, and Grant had an uncanny way of studying a map once and then carrying it in his memory, but neither he nor anyone else had ever tried to fight a battle in a place where nobody could see anything at all. The armies were visible neither to their enemies nor to their own commanders. It would do no good for the commanding general to ride out along his lines, because there was quite literally no place where as many as a thousand men could be seen at one time, and in any case where the men were fighting the forest was so dense that riding was impossible. There were no adequate roads, and the Federal maps were very imperfect anyway, and the most careful directives could come down to a matter of saying—The enemy is over there somewhere; go and find him and fight him.

Warren cantered along a farm lane and came up to one of his trusted division commanders, Major General James Wadsworth—white-haired, crowding sixty, an old man as ages were reckoned in the army—and Warren told him to get his men into action just south of the Turnpike. Wadsworth was a stout fighter, much admired by his men; he was very wealthy and he was serving without pay, and they honored him for it, and they remembered how on the weary march to Gettysburg he had seized civilians who stood cheering by the roadside and had taken their shoes for his own men to wear. He was quite willing now to go in and fight beside Griffin's division, but he did not know where Griffin's division was and he asked Warren. Warren pulled out a pocket compass and studied it—tactics here were as much a matter of navigation as anything—and he told him to march straight west. Wadsworth's division fell into line, crossed an open field, and plunged into the wood.[18]

The division marched quickly into trouble. Either Wadsworth had no compass or it was defective, or perhaps in that incomprehensible undergrowth it was not humanly possible to move any body of troops in a straight line. In any case the men swung round toward the north, and instead of coming in beside Griffin's men they came in on an angle, presenting their left flank to the Confederates just at the moment when the Confederates were sending in reinforcements for a counterattack. The noise of the firing swelled to a terrible new pitch as enormous rolling volleys came out of the woods to break regiments and brigades to bits.

No one could remember anything very distinctly, afterward. Some regiments found that they had got in behind other regiments that were supposed to be far off to one side. Others knew they were near the Rebels only when they found themselves being shot at—shot at with deadly aim, they noticed: the Confederates were hugging the ground and firing low, and if they could not see much of their target they were hitting it with murderous efficiency.

There seemed to be whole acres where the musketry had cut the saplings in two a few feet from the ground, so that the tops lopped over drunkenly to make progress even more impossible. Wadsworth tried hard to swing his division around to face the flanking fire, but it could not be done

Troops could not be maneuvered in this ground. Companies fought by themselves, lone squads by themselves sometimes, and the fact that no connected battle line could be seen seemed to give a new terror to the fighting. Some regiments broke and fled, not because they were being punished but because the crash of battle suddenly sounded beside or behind them and the panic cry: "We're flanked!" was raised.

Beyond Wadsworth, Warren had found his division of Pennsylvania Reserves. The Reserves were famous veterans—Meade's own division, once upon a time, the division whose command the governor of Pennsylvania once offered to George B. McClellan in the springtime of the war. It was led by a former army surgeon, Brigadier General Samuel W. Crawford, a member of the original Fort Sumter garrison: "a tall, chesty, glowering man, with heavy eyes, a big nose and bushy whiskers," as one of his men remembered him, who "wore habitually a turn-out-the-guard expression." Crawford tried to bring his men in beside Wadsworth's, but he had even more trouble than Wadsworth had had. One regiment blundered straight into the middle of a Confederate brigade and was captured almost entire, and the others stumbled around in the underbrush, lost all sense of direction and contact, and knew only that they were constantly being shot at from the most improbable directions by men they could not find. It seems that the Reserves were just a trifle lukewarm about things, anyway, this day. Most of them had refused to re-enlist, and the division was fully aware that it had only twenty-seven more days to serve before it would be sent home. Understandably, this tempered enthusiasm: who wanted to get shot, so near the end of his time as a soldier? [19]

The whole Wilderness seemed to be boiling and smoking, with dense clouds going up to blot out the sunlight. From the rear, Warren pushed the rest of his corps into the fight, and there is no coherent story to be told about any of it: it was all violent confusion, with occasional revealing glimpses to be had in the infernal clogged mist.

The Iron Brigade went forward and was routed, and for

once in their history the men of this famous command ran
for the rear, all organization lost—to be rallied, somehow,
half a mile back, just in time to fix bayonets and check the
rout of another brigade which came streaming back over
them. A New York regiment crossed a weedy little field, got
into more of a fight than it could handle, and ran back to
the other side of the field, leaving many wounded men in
the open space. The woods were on fire, and the flames were
driven by the wind across the dried growth in the field
where the wounded men lay, and the New Yorkers looked
on in paralyzed horror as the flames reached these helpless
men and ignited the paper cartridges in the boxes at their
waists. (One man remembered how the noise of these exploding cartridges—which made dreadful wounds in the sides of
the wounded men—made quite a cheerful-sounding pop-pop-
pop which could be heard despite all of the surrounding
din.) For a moment the fighting around this field ceased, and
Northerners and Southerners alike went out into the open
to try to drag the men to safety.

The smoke blew down across the field, and all around to
right and left there was the unending sound of rifle fire, and
the log breastworks the Confederates had built took fire and
sent heavy yellowish white smoke billowing out in choking
clouds, and the living and dead bodies that lay under it
were burned beyond recognition.[20] And all of this was a
part of the fight to see which side could hold its ground
astride the Orange Turnpike.

This was one battle. Two miles to the south of it, along
the Plank Road, there was a wholly separate battle, just as
desperate, drawing men in as the first battle had done, a
battle which for a time was a fight by the Army of the
Potomac for simple survival.

Key point here was the place where the Plank and Brock
roads crossed. A thin line of cavalry had been patrolling the
Plank Road, and while Griffin's men were going into action
along the Turnpike this cavalry found Confederate infantry
pressing up the Plank Road. The infantry began to seem very
numerous and determined, and it drove the Yankee cavalry

away, and if the Confederates could seize the crossroads the Federal army would be cut in half, with Hancock's corps isolated off to the south, the rest of the army fighting west of Wilderness Tavern, and the Rebels planted squarely in between. So the cavalry sent couriers riding frantically off to headquarters, men who rode with crumpled envelopes held in their teeth, one hand for the reins and the other for the carbine.

Back on his knoll, Grant read these dispatches and he reached out for the nearest troops. These happened to be Brigadier General George W. Getty's division of the VI Corps —6,000 soldiers as cool and as tough as any, including in their number a Vermont brigade which is still remembered as one of the two or three best in the army. Getty was told to get his men over to the Plank Road at top speed and clear the Southerners out of there. At the same time gallopers were sent off to Hancock to tell him to double back on his tracks and get to that vital crossroads as fast as he could.

Getty made it with seconds to spare. He rode ahead of his troops, his staff and mounted orderlies trotting at his heels, and the last of the cavalry had gone and the advancing Confederates were clearly visible. It would be a few minutes before the Federal infantry could get up, so Getty coolly planted himself and his mounted people in the middle of the road, to make it look as if cavalry reinforcements or artillery or somebody of consequence was making a stand here. The bluff worked, briefly; the advancing Confederates slowed down and sent skirmishers creeping forward to find out what was going on, and in the minutes that were bought Getty was able to get his leading regiments into line of battle and start them moving west.[21]

There was enough to keep them busy. The Confederates here belonged to A. P. Hill, and he had a way of piling his men in fast and hard, and the rival battle lines ranged deeply into the woods and fired as fast as they could handle their muskets. Getty could see that he was outnumbered, and he wanted to fight at long range and wait for help. But Grant felt that the day was made for fighting, and he sent down

word to wait for nothing—pitch in and attack, and if any reinforcements show up we'll send them to you.

So Getty's bugles sounded, high and thin over the noise of
the firing, and the Federal battle line went crashing forward
through the timber. It got to close quarters at once, and in the
pathless tangle on both sides of the Plank Road there was an
enormous shock and crash of battle, Federals and Confederates shooting at each other at fifty paces, artillery on both
sides firing down the narrow road and making it a place where
no man could live.

One officer noted that this was like no fight he had ever
heard of. Usually, he said, when two rival lines of infantry met
at close range the fight was quite brief, one line or the other
quickly giving way. But here there was no giving way whatever. The men simply lay on the ground or knelt behind logs
and stumps and kept on firing, and the very intensity of their
fire pinned both sides in position—the only chance for safety
was to crouch low or lie flat; if a man stood up either to advance or to run away he was almost certain to be shot.[22]

In a way, the fact that the men could rarely see what they
were shooting at made it even worse. They simply pointed
their rifles into the rolling smoke and the thick stunted trees
and blazed away, shooting low by instinct, and a sheet of
flame swept over the desolate intricate woodland, hitting anything that stood three feet off the ground. So this fight went
on for no one knew how long—an hour, two hours, an eternity
—and the battle zone grew wider and wider as Confederates
came groping blindly forward on the flanks. The woods took
fire, just as they had done farther north, and the crackle of
flames mingled with the wild yelling and cursing of men and
the swinging, whacking crash of rifle fire, and the dense forest
seemed to trap the roar of battle and press it close to the
ground so that the noise became unendurable, more terrible
than anything that had ever been heard before. Getty had
all of his men in action and there were not enough of them,
not by half, and the Vermont Brigade hung on with a thousand of its men killed or wounded, and the terrible little flames
came snaking forward through the dead leaves and dry pine

thickets. Wounded men were seen to load and cap their
muskets so that they could shoot themselves if the fire reached
them.[23]

Somewhere to the north old Wadsworth was ordered to
swing his battered division around and come down to help.
He was in a good spot to land on the Rebel flank and he was
only a mile away, but his regiments and brigades were trying
to wheel around in the densest part of the Wilderness and he
was taking a good deal of care because he did not want to
drift into battle by the flank a second time—and, all in all, he
might as well have been north of the Rapidan. By prodigious
effort he got his men faced south and they started to move,
but they could reach no one but isolated Confederate skirmishers. They stood squarely in front of a great gap in the
Confederate line, but they could not come close to finding it,
and they drifted down through the blinding forest like a hulk
gone out of control, to run aground at last a few furlongs away
from the place where they were needed.

In the rear, Hancock's men were at last coming up the
Brock Road. Hancock was in the lead, shoving the winded
men out of column and into line in the miserable second
growth, prudently putting some of them to work building a
log breastwork at the edge of the road for use in case anything went wrong.

There was a nightmare slowness about it all. The Brock
Road was no better than a narrow lane, bordered closely by
all but impenetrable woods—it had taken Stonewall Jackson
two mortal hours to form a battle line in this area, just a year
ago—and the road was clotted with artillery and confused
moving troops and men felling trees and piling up log barricades. The day grew old and the sun was going down, the
western light coming all red and tarnished through the blowing clouds of heavy smoke, and Getty's exhausted line was
about ready to fall clear out of the war; and at last Hancock
got a couple of brigades lined up and he sent them in to the
attack.

When they hit they hit hard—they were veterans, and they
believed that when Hancock told them to charge he meant

for them to keep on going—and as Hancock slid new troops in behind them and on both sides they swept into the littered woods like a tornado. They overran Getty's tired men and bent the Confederates back, and now it was the enemy's turn to feel that they were outnumbered, outflanked, and forsaken. But if the Yankees had one of their crack combat outfits in here, so did the Confederates, and in these murky woods any little knot of determined men could cause much trouble, and there was a titanic wrestle in the darkening woods, and it is possible that in all the war the men of the North and the South did no more desperate fighting than they did right here, on the two sides of the Plank Road.

The Federals had had much close-order drill, and they were used to fighting in solid ranks, where each man could see his comrades at his side. This was not like that at all. It was Braddock and his British Regulars fighting the Indians all over again, and the scrub pines, the brush piles, and the massed saplings broke the advancing lines apart, leaving fragments that felt isolated and alone. As one veteran recalled it, "the troops were so scattered and disorganized by the straggling way they had got forward that there was no central discipline to bind the men together." So this advance was no triumphal march; it had wide gaps in it, and terrible routs and defeats, and desperate deeds of bravery and of cowardice which no one ever knew about. The veteran 1st Massachusetts, shock troops if there ever were any, was cut up into squads and platoons, and the fragments came up toward a little rise of ground and got a close-range volley from Rebels lying prone just beyond the ridge, and broke and ran for it in wild fright. Their panic spread to right and left, for cohesion and spirit were gone, and in a moment a whole division was running away—Gershom Mott's men, who had been Joe Hooker's division long ago, famous as one of the stanchest divisions in the army, shattered and useless now.[24]

But Hancock had more men than Hill had, and in the end they made their weight felt. The fugitives lost their panic when they got back to the log breastworks by the Brock Road, and the men who had not run kept on advancing, and the Confederates along the Plank Road were on the edge of final disaster when night and sheer breathlessness and muscle weariness at last came down and stopped the fighting. The armies did not draw apart. They simply stopped where they were, and regiments and brigades lay all over the Wilderness, facing in every direction, nobody knowing where he or his neighbors or his enemies might be. Northerners and Southerners were all intermingled in the dreadful night, so close together that men were constantly blundering into the wrong camp and being made prisoners. Skirmishers were awake, firing at any sound or movement, and afterward it seemed to some men that the battle really went on all night without much letup. Deep in the woods many fires sparked and smoldered.

There were horrors in the night. An officer from a New England regiment, out hunting stragglers, groped through the fathomless dark and somewhere far in the rear a wakeful battery sent over a casual, unaimed shell. It burst near him, and its sudden flare lit up a dogwood tree right before him, white blossoms waxen and mystically motionless in the quick red light. Half blinded, the officer moved on in the succeeding darkness, missed his path, stumbled, and kicked a heap of smoldering leaves into flame; and the flame caught in the hair and beard of a dead sergeant lying in the path, lighting up a ghastly face and wide-open sightless eyes.[25]

2. Shadow in the Night

Never before had there been a night like this one. A reek of wood smoke, powder smoke, and the dreadful odor of burned bodies hung in the air, soiling the night and dimming the stars. There was no silence. Pickets and skirmishers were nervous, firing at everything and at nothing, and from the rear there was a steady rumble and murmur as troops marched up to take new positions. From miles of scorched ground, up front, there was an unceasing crying of wounded men.

Usually wounded men on the battlefield did not make a great deal of noise. The bad pain generally came later on, and while men here and there might moan and cry out and call for water, most of them took what they had to take in a stunned, half-dazed silence. But this night was different. The underbrush was aglow with stealthy fires, and the ground was matted with dead leaves and dry pine needles, and the terror of the flames lay upon the field so that men who could not move screamed for comrades to come and help them. On both sides, stretcher-bearers tried to do what they could; but it was very dark and the woodland was a creepy maze, and anyway a man who went out to help the wounded was very likely to be shot. A Federal wrote that "the Rebels were fidgety and quick to shoot," and a Confederate officer said the Yankee skirmishers made it impossible for his troops to help wounded men who lay only a dozen paces outside of their lines.[1]

Behind the front there was ceaseless movement: steady tramp of long columns getting into place for the next day's fighting, and a confused coming and going of stragglers and broken squads and companies hunting their proper commands. In all of this, too, there was a restless stirring by veteran soldiers who were operating a strange, unofficial, and highly effective little system by which the enlisted man kept himself informed about things.

After every battle, men by twos and threes would slip away from their bivouacs and wander up and down the lines, visiting other campfires to exchange information. They were always welcomed, and they were always watched quite closely, because they were notoriously light-fingered and would steal any haversacks that were within their reach. The army called these men "news walkers," and they were in fact amateur and self-appointed reporters, hunting the information by which they could judge how the battle was going, what army morale was like, and what the prospects were for the morrow. They were on the prowl tonight, and one of Hancock's gunners told how he and his mates would look up from their campfires to see "shadowy forms hurrying rapidly through the woods or along the roads." The gunner described their method of operation:

"Frequently these figures would halt, and then, seeing our fire with men around it, they would issue forth from the woods and join us. They would sit down, filling their pipes, light them with glowing coals, and then, with their rifles lying across their knees, ask for the Second Corps news, inquire as to our losses and whether we had gained or lost ground, and what Confederate command was opposed to us. They would anxiously inquire as to the truth of rumors of disaster which they might have heard during the day. They would listen attentively to what we said, and it was a point of honor not to give false information to these men. And they would briefly tell the Fifth or Sixth or Ninth Corps news, and quickly disappear in the darkness."

So it went tonight, with the smoky tainted air heavy under the trees, and men who had fought all day were hiking for miles to find out what had really been happening. Their system was effective. It was notorious that no headquarters announcement was believed unless it jibed with what the news walkers picked up. Often enough the soldiers had a better line on the situation than the generals had, and when they criticized strategy or tactics they usually knew what they were talking about. As the movement finally died out and the men turned in for such sleep as they could get, the army had a pretty fair notion of what had been happening and what was apt to come next.[2]

What would come next, indeed, was fairly obvious: a big attack along the Plank Road, where the disordered pieces of A. P. Hill's Confederate corps lay crisscross in the darkness. Lee had fought with part of his army missing, and the missing portion—Longstreet's corps—would not be up until midmorning or later. What was in the cards therefore was a hard smash at Lee's right, to overwhelm it before Longstreet's rough veterans could get on the scene, and the fighting was apt to begin as soon as the first faint light broke over the eastern sky.

Grant wanted the attack made at four o'clock, but the corps commanders were having much trouble getting their disordered divisions sorted out and Meade persuaded the general to allow a postponement. Burnside's IX Corps was south of the Rapidan now, and Burnside was under orders to get his men down to the Plank Road and join in the assault. Meanwhile, by a little after five in the morning, Hancock got his own troops and Getty's thinned division from the VI Corps lined up for action, and he immediately sent them west on both sides of the Plank Road.

They ran into action at once. Hill's Confederates had hardly so much as tried to straighten their lines during the night—all of the ordinary difficulties of moving troops in this jungle were infinitely intensified in the darkness—and they were not in the best shape to meet an attack. But they were very tough characters and they started firing as soon as the first Yankee skirmishers came crashing through the underbrush, and beneath the low branches the gray half-light of dawn became spectral with wispy layers of smoke. The skirmishers waited to let the main battle line catch up with them, and then everybody went plunging forward and the battle of the Wilderness was on again.

Hancock was a driver, and he sent his men on like a flood tide. From their dark bivouac north of the road, Wadsworth's division from the V Corps fell into line and came tramping down at an angle, flanking some of Hill's men and knocking them out of the way. The Federal battle line was more than a mile wide and it moved with enormous weight, overrunning the islands of stubborn resistance and shooting down the Rebels who were groping for new positions, and an unearthly racket of musketry went rolling up the sky.

Back by the crossroads Hancock was elated. The wound he had received at Gettysburg still hurt him, and he had official permission to go about in an ambulance if he chose, but he was astride his horse today and as reports came back he felt that everything was going as it should. To one of Meade's staff officers he called out gaily: "We are driving them, sir—tell General Meade we are driving them most beautifully!"

He was robust and handsome and the joy of battle was on him, and to look at him as he sat his horse in this moment of triumph was to understand why the war correspondents liked to tag him "Hancock the superb."

Yet even as he exulted in his success he was beginning to fret. Burnside's men were coming down much more slowly than had been expected. They were supposed to take part in this big attack and they should be here now, but they were not showing up and Hancock began to worry. He told Meade's man that with their weight added to his own column of attack "we could smash A. P. Hill all to pieces!" [3]

Yet things were going well, regardless. Two miles west of the crossroads where Hancock was waiting, the cheering Federals were sweeping in on the edge of a meager little clearing around the Widow Tapp's farm, where Lee himself stood among his guns and tried to patch up a dissolving battle line. Just beyond him the white tops of the Confederate wagon trains were visible, and if Hancock's men could just go driving on across this clearing Hancock's goal would be won.

And there was a moment, just here by the Tapp farmstead, with dawn coming up through the smoke and the Northern advance breaking out of the trees, when the authentic end of the war could be glimpsed beyond the ragged clearing. If Hancock's men could go storming on for another half mile, Lee's army would be broken and it would all be over. It may be that the Army of the Potomac never came nearer to it than this—neither above the Antietam, nor at Gettysburg, nor anywhere else—and final victory was just half an hour away. But the magical half hour flickered and was lost forever, and if any Northern soldier saw victory here he saw no more than a moving shadow distorted by the battle smoke.

Confederate artillery was massed in the open ground, and the guns fired before the last fugitive Rebels had time to get out of the way, and for a moment the pursuing Federals were knocked back into the woods. Then west of the clearing there rose the high, quavering scream of the Rebel yell, and Longstreet's men—here at last!—came running in, gripping their rifles in their tanned fists. Lee was in their midst, swinging his hat and trying to lead them until they made him go back (for they knew that the Confederacy could live no longer than that man lived) and there was a staggering shock as the Northern and Southern assault waves dashed together. Above and below the Plank Road, far off into the dark murky wood, the fighting swelled and rolled as more and more of Lee's last-minute reserves came running into action, and the counter-attack broke the force of the Federal charge.[4]

But the charge was still on. Back by the Brock Road Hancock was still driving reinforcements forward. Almost half of the army was under his command this morning, and he proposed to use every man who had been given him. Wadsworth's men struggled out of the jungle at last and the Plank Road lay across their way, and they surged forward in a great crowd, yelling mightily. They got into the path of Getty's division, which was driving west along the road, and there was a heavy traffic jam, two divisions all intermingled, men swearing, officers thwacking about with swords, and the disordered mob sagged off toward the south; and Lee's guns in the Tapp farm clearing caught the right flank of Wadsworth's uneven line and blasted it with fearful effect. Wadsworth was galloping desperately up and down the Plank Road, his old Revolutionary War saber in his hand, trying once again to get his line wheeled around so that it could face the firing instead of getting it all in the flank. Back to the right and rear the leading division of Burnside's corps was at last creeping down through the woods, and far to the north by the Orange Turnpike Warren's and Sedgwick's soldiers opened a hot fire on Ewell's men, to keep the Confederates from sending help from their left to their right.

The focus of it all was the narrow Plank Road and the deadly woods on both sides of it. Never before had the Army of the Potomac thrown so many men into one assault as were thrown in here. Twenty-five thousand soldiers were moving up in one stupendous charge, and most of them were battle-trained veterans. Yet what they had learned in other battles seemed to be of little use here, and in the Wilderness numbers did not seem to count. They were fighting a strange, desperate fight, without color and without drama. The whole thing was invisible. It was smothered down out of sight in five miles of smoking wilderness, and even men who were in the storm center of it saw no more than fragmentary pictures—little groups of men moving in and out of a spooky, reddish luminous haze, with rifles flashing indistinctly in the gloom, the everlasting trees and brush always in the way, the weight of the smoke tamping down everything except the evil flames that sprang up wherever men fought.

In other battles these soldiers had known the fearful pageantry of war. There was none of that here, for this was the battle no man saw. There was only the clanging twilight and the heavy second growth and the enemies who could rarely be seen but who were always firing. There was no more war in the grand style, with things in it to hearten a man even as they killed him. This was all cramped and close and ugly, like a duel fought with knives in a cellar far underground.

Up from the forest came a tumult such as none of the army's battles had made before. It had a higher pitch, because so little artillery was used, but more rifles were being fired than ever before and they were being fired more rapidly and continuously, and the noise was unbroken, maddening, beyond all description. A man in the VI Corps called it "the most terrific musketry firing ever heard on the American continent," and a New Yorker said that from the rear it sounded like "the wailing of a tempest or the roaring of the ocean in a storm." Groping for the right superlative, another soldier wrote that "the loudest and longest peals of thunder were no more to be compared to it in depth or volume than the rippling of a trout brook to the roaring of Niagara." Far back by Wilderness Tavern Meade's chief of staff tilted a professional ear and commented that the uproar "approached the sublime." [5]

Always the little flames sprang up, as the blast from rifle muzzles hit the dried leaves and the brittle pine twigs, and the fear of these flames haunted every soldier. Often, when they were hit, men cried at once for help—anything was better than to lie in a firetrap and wait for the flames. It may be that the heavy blanket of stifling smoke that drifted on ahead of these fires was a mercy, for there were men who believed that it often suffocated the wounded, quickly strangling the life out of them before the fire could torture them to death.[6]

Behind the lines, far to the rear where the smoke-fog and the noise came rolling down the wind, there was a constant movement of walking wounded looking for field hospitals. Some came alone, using muskets as canes or crutches. Others came in little groups, supporting each other, the halt leading the maimed and the blind. All of them were bloody. Cavalry patrols ranged all approaches to the rear areas and when a straggler appeared their curt demand was: "show blood!" The man who could not do it was arrested as a runaway.

The wounded came back with tight, bloodless lips, and in most cases their clothing was disarranged. Unless he was totally disabled, the wounded man's first act, usually, was to tear his clothing open and look at his wound, to see whether it was going to be mortal. The examination over, some men would look relieved, confident that they had little to worry about. Others would turn pale and stare blankly at nothing, convinced that they could not recover. These men had seen many gunshot wounds, and they were pretty fair diagnosticians.

On this day the wounded brought discouraging tales back to the dressing stations. They said the fighting was not going well, and one man remarked glumly that "the Confederates are shooting to kill, this time." Hospitals were alive with rumors of disaster: the right wing had crumbled, Lee had seized the Rapidan crossing, the army would soon find itself surrounded. The adolescent drummer boys had been pressed into service, along the firing lines, as stretcher-bearers. Properly, this was not drummer boys' work, but as one man said, "It was in the Wilderness, under Grant," where "even boys counted." [7]

Along the Plank Road there was complete pandemonium. The narrow lane was choked with moving men—regiments and bits of regiments trying to re-form, hundreds of Confederate prisoners who had been disarmed and told to hike to the rear and who were trying hard to get back out of range, stretcher-bearers and walking wounded moving along with the same idea in mind, dazed stragglers and lost men hunting in vain for their regiments or for some quiet place to hide or for a safe road to the back country. There was such a tangle in every great battle, of course, and during every attack there were places just behind the front where it looked as if the army were coming apart. Yet the confusion in the Wilderness this morning was something special.[8] The commanders behind the lines—Grant, smoking and whittling and noting all the dispatches, Meade near him talking busily with staff officers, Hancock at the crossroads ordering men forward—they had no conception of what was really going on up in front. They could not have one. The battle was out of their control, fighting itself, a great curtain of distance and forest and choking smoke cutting them off from contact and knowledge. Things were going wrong, and they could not know about it—nor, if they did know, could they do anything about it.

In this forest it was almost as bad to win as to lose. Either way, a battle line was certain to get thrown into hopeless disorder. Along five miles of fighting front there was hardly one brigadier who could really control his own line, because there was hardly one brigadier who could put his hand on more than a fraction of his own command. The lines had been jumbled as they had never been jumbled before. Divisions and brigades were all divided. Along the zone of the heaviest firing there was not a single regiment which had on either flank a regiment which so much as belonged to its own army corps.[9]

Commands were broken into moving fragments which floated blindly about trying to reassemble without the faintest idea where their comrades might be. Reinforcements lost their way as they tried to go forward and made the trouble worse, so that instead of adding weight to the attack they crippled it. In one place, men would be standing ten ranks deep, and a few hundred yards to right or left there would be a complete gap in the line, with nobody at all to hold the ground and only the bushes and the blinding haze to keep the Confederates from seeing what an opening lay in front of them. Brigades got in behind one another and shot blindly into the ranks of their own friends.[10]

One of Hancock's best brigadiers was ordered to move up the road and support Getty's division, but before he could get started Getty's division had been crowded over to some other part of the battlefield, so that the support troops moving in without skirmishers ran head on into a Southern battle line, which opened a deadly fire before the Federals realized that they were anywhere near the enemy. The brigadier did not know whether he was within half a mile of the place where he was supposed to be—nor did he know what he was supposed to do, now that he was wherever he was, except fight, which he could not help doing with Rebels all around him. Long after the war he wrote that he still did not know what had been expected of him. What he had actually done was to get several hundred of his men shot to no purpose at all, and it seemed improbable that that was quite what Hancock had wanted.[11]

Near the road, Wadsworth was still moving his regiments about so that they could renew the attack. The old man was tired and he felt unwell, and he told an aide that he really ought to turn command of the division over to someone else and go to the rear, but there was too much to do just now and he would wait for a lull. Somewhere behind him, men from the IX Corps were pushing forward; the men said afterward they made the final fifty yards of their advance crawling on hands and knees through a pine thicket, and when they got through the thicket they had a terrible hot fight with some Rebels behind a fence-rail breastwork. South of Wadsworth's division, soldiers said that all morning long they had seen neither a general officer nor a staff officer to tell them what to do. They were without commanders, and each regiment was fighting entirely on its own.[12]

This sort of thing could last just so long before something gave way. Nobody knew what was happening because nobody could see 100 feet in any direction, but suddenly, without any warning, the sprawling line across the Plank Road began to come to pieces. Out of the smoke came men who had stopped

fighting and were unhurriedly going back out of action, and
nothing that anyone said to them seemed to make the slightest difference. One of Wadsworth's soldiers said it was the
strangest sight ever seen: the men pressing to the rear did not
seem to be demoralized or scared, and yet they did not quite
look like organized troops retreating under orders, either.
They were just going back, looking like "a throng of armed
men who were returning dissatisfied from a muster." One of
Meade's staff officers noticed that the men were not running,
and were neither pale nor frightened, nor had they thrown
away their weapons: "They had fought all they meant to fight
for the present and there was an end to it." A New Jersey soldier noted the same baffling traits and said the only explanation he could make was that "a large number of troops were
about to leave the service." [13]

Whatever had happened, there it was—an unpanicked but
irreversible retreat by the army's shock troops, thousands of
men turning their backs and sauntering calmly toward the
rear. Wadsworth's men caught the infection, and as they
turned to go the Rebels hit them with hard volleys that
turned the retreat into actual rout, and the whole division dissolved, thousands of men streaming off through the woods.
Wadsworth stormed along trying to rally them, but a Confederate bullet killed him and for the time being his division
simply went out of existence; of 5,000 men who advanced
with it in the morning, fewer than 500 could be rallied that
evening, the rest all scattered over five square miles of un-
plumbed forest. (It might be noted that 1,100 of the 5,000
had been shot.) [14]

So the whole advance crumbled, and back by the Brock
Road it looked as if this half of the army had broken up. Hundreds of men were pouring down the Plank Road, and other
hundreds were breaking out of the woods, and the whole
Wilderness seemed to be leaking beaten Yankees. Hancock's
inner thoughts just then were not recorded, but he must have
thanked the god of battles that the evening before he had
had his men build a stout log breastwork all along the western
side of the Brock Road, a heavy fence of piled-up saplings

standing three feet high and running north and south for two miles or more.

It was just the dike that was needed to check this retreat. Disorganized men who reached it looked about them, fell in behind the barricade, loaded their muskets and peered into the blank woodland from which they had just emerged. Shattered regiments and brigades, crawling over this rude fence, managed to form new ranks on the east side of it, and stood there waiting for orders, their panic gone. Off to the north the roar of battle continued, for Burnside's men at last were making their presence felt, but they had come in too late and their attack was not heavy enough, and nothing that they could do could change the situation on the south side of the Plank Road.

What had happened was perfectly simple, and it had turned into catastrophe largely because nobody could see what was going on.

When Hancock made his advance that morning he had been plagued by a report (which happened to be false) that some or all of Longstreet's men were apt to come up into action from the south. On his extreme left, therefore, he held one division out of action as flank guard. All sorts of wild rumors about approaching Confederates had been circulating that morning, and the result was that some 8,000 of Hancock's best soldiers had been immobilized. Furthermore, as the rest of the corps advanced along the Plank Road, a gap two miles wide had opened between the assaulting column and this reserve division.

Eventually Hancock decided that all of the rumors were false, and he sent word to this idle division to advance so as to come up on the left flank of the men who were making the attack on the Tapp farm. If this had been done, Longstreet's counterattack would probably have been blunted. But all of Hancock's messages seem to have gone astray—couriers hit by stray bullets, or captured by Confederates, or just plain lost in the battle turmoil—and John Gibbon, the highly competent soldier who commanded the reserve division, never got the orders. So the division stayed out of action, and when the

Federals began to fight with Longstreet's troops in the wild chaos two miles to the west their southern flank was unprotected.[15]

Longstreet discovered this, and mounted a cunning flank attack. This hit the left end of the Yankee firing line and broke it just at the moment when the confusion of the whole line was at its worst. The effect was like tipping over the first in a row of dominoes. The men who were driven in by the flank attack went north, toward the Plank Road, retreating across the immediate rear of all the troops that were in line. Blind and bewildered, and quite unable to see anything, the men in front knew only that the troops on the left were running away; and in the invisibility out of which they had emerged there sounded much musketry and the jeering, triumphant sound of the Rebel yell. The fight had not been making much sense for half an hour or more; now it was ceasing to make any sense at all, and one after another the men headed back for the Brock Road—not panicky, for the most part, but not doing any more fighting just now, either.

For a while there was a lull. The Confederates were as much disorganized by their victory as the Federals had been by their own a little earlier. In the confusion Longstreet was shot by his own men, and he was carried to the rear coughing blood, out of action for months to come, and it was going to take an hour or more to get his brigades unscrambled so that the advance could be resumed. So Hancock was given precious time to organize his defenses along the Brock Road, and when the Rebel attack was at last renewed the men were ready for it.

Not too ready, possibly: the men had fallen in behind the log barricade willingly enough, yet it was noticed that in some places they simply cowered close to the earth, pointed their muskets up toward the treetops, and maintained a fire that could hurt no one except birds. Yet by this time the forest fire was just about taking charge, anyway. The Rebel battle line that charged up to the Brock Road came splashing through little pools of fire, and here and there the log breastworks themselves caught fire and blazed up hotly, so that neither side could hold possession, and attackers and defenders stood a dozen yards apart and fought each other through a sheet of flame. In some places cannon had been put into line, their muzzles protruding out over the logs, and the gunners tried to work these in spite of the fire. Some of these men were horribly wounded when cartridges were exploded at the guns' muzzles.[16]

In a few places the Rebels came through the line. But there were reserves to deal with them—Samuel Carroll's brigade, which had driven Jubal Early's men out of the guns on Cemetery Hill at Gettysburg, on the night of the second day's battle there—and these men rammed the attackers back. The Southerners finally retreated out of sight through the burning woods, and all that had been accomplished—about all that was possible, under the circumstances—was to increase the casualty lists on both sides.

Grant had spent most of his time on the knoll over by the Turnpike, and there had not been much that he or anyone else could do to control this insane battle that slipped out of sight every time the fighting lines went into action. Yet somehow he had created a new atmosphere around headquarters, and around noon he sent word to Hancock to put on a new offensive, early in the evening, with the same men who had been driven back in the morning. The Rebel assault on the Brock Road had of course canceled this plan, but if anyone cared to make a note of it, there it was—the commanding general's only reaction to news of a reverse had been to call for another attack.[17]

It had been somewhat the same, once that day, when Ewell's men bent the Union line back near the Turnpike and got some guns far enough forward to shell the very knoll where Grant was sitting. An anxious staff officer came up and asked if it would not be prudent to move the whole headquarters setup back out of range until they knew whether this position was going to be held. Grant took a quiet drag on his cigar and said that it would be even better to wheel some guns of their own up on the knoll and make certain that the position was held; so the guns were brought up, and the gen-

eral kept on whittling twigs—completing the ruination of his
tan gloves, in the process—and the Confederate attack was
beaten off.[18]

Now and then the grim news that came back from the firing
lines had a personal touch. An aide came over from Hancock's front once to tell Grant that the Rebels had killed Brigadier General Alex Hays—red-haired, coarse-grained, hard-
drinking, and hard-fighting, who had spent three years with
Grant at West Point, had served in the old 4th Regulars with
him after graduation, and had been with him in Mexico,
where Hays had marveled at Grant's ability to get his supply
train through in spite of all obstacles. Hays commanded a
brigade in the II Corps, and he had helped to beat off Pickett's
great charge at Gettysburg, and now a bullet had found him
in the wild mix-up along the Plank Road. Grant took the news
quietly, saying that he was not surprised to learn that Hays
had been in the front line of action when he was killed: "It
was just like him." [19]

Dusk came at last, with smoke and a muffled crying in the
air, and still the battle was not over. Lee had a pugnacity to
match Grant's, and just a year ago on the edge of this Wilderness he had flanked a Federal army quite as large and as confident as this one and had sent it scurrying back across the
Rapidan in utter defeat. Now, as the day ended, one of Lee's
brigadiers pointed out that up north of the Turnpike the right
flank of John Sedgwick's line was exposed, and in the gathering dark a Confederate striking column came whooping down
on this naked flank and drove it headlong.

As so often happened, the Confederates had found a soft
spot. The Union flank here was held by Sedgwick's 3rd Division, two brigades which had not been with the VI Corps
very long. Their earlier experience had mostly been in the
Shenandoah Valley under the command of a flamboyant and
remarkably inefficient general named Milroy, who had led
them to a number of defeats. The rest of the corps dubbed
them "Milroy's weary boys," and considered them something
less than full-fledged members of the club.

They had been posted in the woods facing west, with sev-

eral miles of unoccupied country between the end of their line
and the Rapidan River, and during the day Sedgwick had
worried about them. He had sent a cavalry regiment over to
keep an eye on the flank—a regiment of recruits, unfortunately,
which failed to do its job—and a bit later he had a staff officer go on a long scout to make sure that the Rebels were not
up to anything sinister. Everything had been quiet at the
time, but now at dusk the Confederates broke these two luckless brigades into splinters, and throngs of disorganized excited men went rushing through the thickets past Sedgwick's
headquarters.

Sedgwick was on his horse at once, galloping over to the
scene of the disaster, and he sent his staff flying along the
dark woods trails to bring up reinforcements. The men who
had run away kept on running, and before long they were
scudding back past army headquarters, bearing wild tales of
ruin and collapse, while a mighty sound of musketry and
cheering went up from the woods to the north.[20]

The news that came to Grant and Meade had an alarming
sound. Sedgwick held the army's extreme right, and if the
Confederates once broke his line and got well around it the
whole army was cut off and utter disaster might be in the
cards. A couple of Sedgwick's brigadiers who tried to rally
the defeated troops were captured, as were several hundred
of Milroy's weary boys, and at one time Grant and Meade
were told that Sedgwick himself had been captured and that
his whole corps had gone to pieces. Various officers from the
beaten brigades, their nerve wholly gone, had wild tales to
tell, but Grant and Meade seemed quite unshaken.

Meade was coldly furious with two staff officers who came
rocketing in to tell him that all was lost. "Nonsense!" he
shouted. "If they have broken our lines they can do nothing
more tonight"; and he sent the Pennsylvania Reserves over to
stem the tide. Another officer came up to Grant, crying that
he had seen this sort of thing before and that he knew just
what was happening: Lee was getting around to where he
could cut the army's communications, and if something
weren't done about it they were all in a terrible pickle. Grant

heard him out, and then he blew up, ceasing for once to be the phlegmatic sphinx of legend. He was sick and tired, he declared with heat, of being told about what Lee was going to do: "Some of you always seem to think he is suddenly going to turn a double somersault and land in our rear and on both our flanks at the same time." As for the panicky officer himself, Grant had a curt order: "Go back to your command and try to think what we are going to do ourselves, instead of what Lee is going to do!" [21]

Sedgwick, meanwhile, was competently busy. He pulled unshaken troops out from the left of his line and without fuss or apparent haste got them faced north and sent them in to halt the triumphant Rebels. (One of these soldiers remembered how his own colonel, taking his cue from Sedgwick, went along the line telling the men: "Don't be in a hurry, boys —let them come well up before you let them have it!") The Confederate attack was checked, at last, at substantial cost, and once things were stabilized Sedgwick put in the rest of the night drawing a new line more to the right and rear and getting troops into it so that the army's flank could be more firmly anchored. Just at dawn, with the job finished, the Vermont Brigade came tramping up from the scene of its two-day fight along the Plank Road, and as the column came by Sedgwick the soldiers let out a wild cheer. Sedgwick waved his hat, and a staff officer noticed that he "blushed like a girl" with pleasure at the cheering.[22]

There had been some anxious moments at headquarters, for all of the outward calm. After the needful measures had been taken, and there was nothing to do but wait for an hour or so to see whether those measures would work, Grant went into his tent, lay down on his cot, and had a very bad ten or fifteen minutes of it. One of his staff wrote later that Grant went to sleep at once and slept as quietly as a baby, but that was just part of the legend. The army had rubbed elbows with sheer catastrophe that night and Grant knew it, and when he was alone he could be as much tormented by suspense as anyone else.[23]

Yet the catastrophe had never materialized, and on the

morning of May 7—forty-eight hours after the battle began—
the two armies were just about where they were at the start.
It was a foggy morning, and there was heavy smoke from the
brush fires, and officers on reconnoissance could see very little, even on the roads or in clearings. Along the Turnpike,
rival skirmishers had little spats now and then, although nobody seemed ready to bring on a real fight.[24] On the Plank
Road the Confederates had drawn back—the burnt-over acres
where there had been so much fighting the day before were
no place for a battle line—and the hot day wore away with
little active contact between the armies.

From end to end of the Union line there were breastworks
—stout affairs of piled logs, on the Brock Road; lighter con-
structions of heaped wood and earth, deeper in the forest—
and the men made themselves as easy as they could behind
these works and speculated about what was likely to happen
next. They did a great deal of talking about it, and mostly it
boiled down to the simple question: Had they just fought a
second battle of Chancellorsville?

The two battles were very much alike. They had been
fought in very nearly the same place. Each time, a Union
army with a great advantage in numbers had plunged into a
forest where numbers did not help much, had seen its flanks
broken in, and had had very heavy losses. (The toll for the
two days in the Wilderness was more than 15,000 casualties,
about equal to Chancellorsville.) After Chancellorsville, the
army had admitted defeat and had gone back across the river.
Would it do the same thing now?

In the Philadelphia Brigade the men were cynical. They
agreed that by all precedents the army would retreat, would
grant furloughs lavishly to restore morale, would spend weeks
reorganizing and ordering new equipment, and—after getting
reinforcements—would probably think about making some
new move. That afternoon the wagon trains got under way,
creaking slowly off toward Fredericksburg. A Massachusetts
soldier admitted that "most of us thought it was another
Chancellorsville, and that next day we should recross the

river," and a cavalryman said his comrades "supposed they were on another skedaddle." [25]

Night came at last, and couriers sped to corps and division headquarters, and the men in Warren's corps—unspeakably weary, after two days of fighting and practically no sleep—left their trenches, fell into column, and started marching. They found themselves on the Brock Road, and in the darkness they were filing south immediately in rear of Hancock's men, who still held their charred log barricades; and as they marched the men realized that they were not heading toward the river crossings at all but were going south toward the lower edge of the Wilderness. The road was crowded, and nobody could see much, but as the men trudged along it suddenly came to them that this march was different. Just then there was a crowding at the edge of the road, and mounted aides were ordering: "Give way to the right!" and a little cavalcade came riding by at an easy jingling trot—and there, just recognizable, was Grant riding in the lead, his staff following him, heading south.

This army had known dramatic moments of inspiration in the past—massed flags and many bugles and broad blue ranks spread out in the sunlight, with leadership bearing a drawn sword and riding a prancing horse, and it had been grand and stirring. Now there was nothing more than a bent shadow in the night, a stoop-shouldered man who was saying nothing to anyone, methodically making his way to the head of the column—and all of a moment the tired column came alive, and a wild cheer broke the night and men tossed their caps in the darkness.

They had had their fill of desperate fighting, and this pitiless little man was leading them into nothing except more fighting, and probably there would be no end to it, but at least he was not leading them back in sullen acceptance of defeat, and somewhere, many miles ahead, there would be victory for those who lived to see it. So there was tremendous cheering, and Grant's big horse Cincinnati caught the excitement and reared and pranced, and as he got him under control Grant told his staff to have the men stop cheering because the Rebels were not far away and they would hear and know that a movement was being made.[26]

It was the same on other roads. Sedgwick's men back-tracked to Chancellorsville, and as the men reached that fatal crossroads the veterans knew how the land lay and knew that if they took the left-hand fork they would be retreating and if they turned to the right they would be going on for another fight. The column turned right, and men who made the march wrote that with that turn there was a quiet relaxing of the tension and a lifting of gloom, so that men who had been slogging along quietly began to chatter as they marched. Here and there a regiment sang a little.[27]

Back by the wagon trains one of Sedgwick's officers came upon Burnside's division of colored soldiers, so dust-colored the men looked white. They were heading south like everyone else, and the officer saw a big colored sergeant prodding his men on with the butt of his rifle and ordering, "Close up dere, lambs." [28]

3. All Their Yesterdays

This was the night when everybody was dog-tired. The whole army was on the march, the wood smoke hung in the still air on the windless roads, and the only noise was the endless shuffle and scuffle of feet in the dirt, and now and then the clank of bayonets rattling against canteens. The men were drunk with fatigue, and nerves were as frazzled as muscles. The dust rose in choking clouds, so that blue uniforms looked gray when the columns passed campfires, and the men in the ranks staggered against each other and tripped on one another's heels. Looking back on it afterward, a man in the VI Corps felt that the whole night was "a medley of phantasmagoria," and the one sustaining thought was that at the very least they were going to get out of the Wilderness.[1]

The main road south was the Brock Road, and Warren's

men had the lead. They came around midnight to an obscure crossroads where Todd's Tavern was situated, and there they ran into an insane traffic tie-up. This had many causes, most of which could be blamed on the attempt to make a forced march, along inadequate forest roads, with an army that was almost out of its head with weariness; but it was one of the most expensive traffic tie-ups in American history, because in the long run it cost many lives.

It was a bad time for delay. Off to the southeast was the tiny hamlet of Spotsylvania Court House; a sleepy village where a few stores and houses stood grouped about a little park containing a brick box of a building with Greek-revival pillars across the front, the whole place as insignificant and as unknown to the world at large as Chickamauga and Antietam creeks had been a year or so earlier. Now the village was about to take on a sinister and enduring fame, because in this region of meandering unpaved highways it was an important road crossing. The outcome of the war might depend on which army got there first. If the Army of the Potomac could win the race, it would stand between Lee's army and Richmond, and the outnumbered Confederates might be forced to destroy themselves attacking Yankee breastworks. Thus there was need for haste, and the march was pressed.

But it was like moving in a nightmare. The road was narrow and the darkness was absolute, and the men dozed stupidly as they walked. Somewhere off to the right was the Confederate army, a moving presence which every man could feel and which made itself physically known, now and then, through a spat-spat of skirmish fire somewhere ahead. Rebel cavalry had been ranging these parts and it had cut down trees and left them lying across the road, and men with axes had to go forward and cut these logs apart before the army could pass.

Yankee cavalry was moving about in the night, too, and it was even more of a trial than the Confederates. It clogged the roads, and at Todd's Tavern it seemed to be all bunched up, overflowing the highway and making a murmur of talk and clumping hoofs and clanking gear, and the infantry came to a halt and waited for someone to clear the way.

Headquarters had gone on in front, as was proper, and headquarters included various detachments of enlisted men who had troubles of their own. Among the escort troops was the 3rd Pennsylvania Cavalry, a veteran regiment which despised all recruits and had learned to look out for itself; and it happened that in the thick midnight the escort troops took a wrong turn and went off down a lane which would have landed them inside the Confederate lines if someone had not discovered the mistake and called a halt. The Pennsylvanians pulled up presently and began marching back toward the main road, troopers all very irritable. Nothing would have come of it if the Pennsylvanians had not been followed by a brand-new regiment of cavalry which had just come down from the Giesboro Point depot in Washington, brave with unused equipment and neatly groomed, unwearied horses—a regiment which, simply because it was new, the Pennsylvanians held in deep contempt.

In the countermarch, then, the Pennsylvanians had to pass the long column of recruits, and as the two regiments overlapped it occurred to the veterans that a cavalryman, all in all, was no better than his horse, that their own horses were worn out and in bad order, and that the horses of the recruits were fresh and vigorous. Nobody said anything in particular, but just as the two regiments were stretched out side by side on a pitch-dark road the Pennsylvanians by a common impulse sprang to the ground, pushed the rookies off of their horses, sprang into the vacant saddles, and thus obtained remounts in the twinkling of an eye.

The rookies had never been warned about this sort of thing, and for the vital seconds that really mattered they were too dazed to resist. They came to fast enough, once the exchange had been made, and a tremendous fist fight boiled up in the middle of the forest—men on foot trying to grapple with mounted men, nobody able to see so much as his clenched fist in front of his nose, the fight streaming out along the byway and spilling over into the main road and turning into a complete unregimented riot which nobody but the 3rd Pennsylvania understood and which nobody on earth could quell.

It went on for an hour or more, and the advance of the whole Army of the Potomac came to a halt, infantrymen falling asleep in the dust while Yankee cavalry fought Yankee cavalry and the noise of the combat went up to the unheeding sky. It ended at last, with the Pennsylvanians getting away on their new horses and the rookies doing their grumbling best on the beaten nags they had inherited. Next morning the officers of the 3rd Pennsylvania looked their men over and remarked, sagely: "The horses look remarkably well after the night's march," and the first sergeants innocently said, "Yes sir," and that was all there was to it. But the army had lost a couple of hours on the road to Spotsylvania Court House.[2]

The escort troops were got out of the way at last, and cavalry skirmishers were trotting on in front, and in the gray of earliest dawn the infantry saw puffs of smoke rising from fields and woodlots up ahead where Confederates disputed the right of way. The column halted, while officers went forward to see how the land lay, and the 12th Massachusetts had the advance, followed by the 9th New York. As they stood in the road a solitary horseman came back from the skirmish line and began ordering the regimental officers to deploy their men on the left of the road. The horseman was undersized and swarthy, and he wore a funny flat felt hat with a floppy brim, and he talked as one having authority, and the infantry colonels bluntly asked him: Who are you, giving us orders like this?

The horseman flipped up the brim of his hat so that his face could be seen—olive-dark face with heavy mustaches and hard eyes—and he barked out his name: "Sheridan!" He added that Rebel infantry was just ahead, strung out behind brush piles and cowsheds in the rolling farm land, and it was time for Yankee infantry to go in and chase them out. So the New Yorkers and New Englanders filed off the road, deploying into fighting formation, and Sheridan kept saying: "Quick! Quick!"[3]

Presently the lines were formed, and their officers told the infantry that nothing but dismounted cavalry lay in front, and the battle line went forward in the hazy dawn. It went for a mile or more, ground very rough, Rebels withdrawing very slowly, and a great many Federals fell out of ranks from sheer exhaustion. Those who kept on found the enemy resistance pretty stiff to be coming from any dismounted cavalry, and as the light grew and they could see better one man turned to his mates and grumbled: "Pretty dismounted cavalry—carrying knapsacks!" They pulled up at last on a wooded knoll, discarding their own knapsacks—they were at the last pitch of weariness, and the loads were heavy—and while the men caught their breath their division commander, bushy-bearded General John Robinson, rode forward and tried to make out what was in front of him.

From the foot of the knoll the ground ranged down into a little valley, with the road to Spotsylvania Court House cutting squarely across it. A quarter of a mile away, on the far side of the valley, there were woods on the rising ground. These woods were not as dense as those in the Wilderness, and in them the general could see a fairly long line of Rebel soldiers, working feverishly to throw up a low breastwork of fence rails and earth. Most of his own division was trailed out behind him over several miles of road and he had just one brigade in line, and it seemed to him that he should let the men rest, wait for the rest of the division to come up, and then if he had to fight go in with everybody together. But then Warren came up, all eager and impetuous, and Warren told him to keep going.

It was hardly seven o'clock but the morning was hot already, and Robinson did not think his beaten-out men could make it. He asked for more time, so that he could at least mass his division for the assault, but Warren was impatient and told him to go ahead without waiting. Orders were orders.

Robinson took a last look at the Rebel position—it looked pretty strong, with the trench line stretching along the crest of the opposite hill—and he consoled himself by thinking that if the attack were made now the Rebels at least would not have time to bring up artillery and make the job completely impossible. So he gave the word, and his men got to their feet and went down into the valley.

There was a chance that they might make it. The Confederates had marched all night, too, and were in no better shape than Robinson's men, and they were still busy trying to finish their trenches. A mile beyond them lay the courthouse and the vital road crossing, and a rattle of carbine fire came faintly over the treetops from a dispute the rival cavalry patrols were having there. If Robinson's men could push this one line of Confederates out of the way, the town and the crossing belonged to the Union and Lee was cut off, and the war would take a very different turn.

But the going was very hard, and there were mean little gullies cutting across the ground, and the Confederates began to lay down a scorching fire of musketry, so that the advancing brigade took heavy losses. The men forced their way through an entanglement of felled pines, started up the farther slope, found the Rebel fire too heavy, and hugged the ground in lee of a steep little bank that gave some protection, waiting for the support troops to come up.

Looking back, they could see Robinson's second brigade, Maryland troops, mostly, falling into line on the knoll and starting forward, and for a moment they took heart. But more Confederates had come up, and these fired over the advanced brigade's heads and hit the Marylanders hard, so that the support wave fell into confusion and began to break for the rear. Robinson himself came along the slope to rally them, but a bullet hit him in the knee and he went down with a wound that would cost him his leg and take him out of the war for keeps. The Maryland brigade ran away and the rest of the division had got into a fruitless fight off to the right somewhere, too far away to lend any help here.

The Federal attacking line hung on for a while, and then a new Confederate brigade appeared off to one side, driving in a fire that went lengthwise along the huddled line and killed men who crouched flat against the slope, and it was too much. The men made a final, desperate attempt to charge the

Rebel line, and a few of them reached the breastworks and got into a leaden-armed bayonet fight with men as weary as themselves. Then at last they gave up and ran—a queer, slow, stumbling flight, because they were simply too tired to run fast, even when discipline was gone and they were running for their lives.

The brigadier commanding these troops wrote later that he himself very much wanted to run at top speed, but could do no more than hobble along using his unsheathed sword as a cane. He fell in a field before he got very far, and he was carried off, unconscious, and the Rebels kept on firing as the men retreated. The remnant of Robinson's division at last regrouped itself back of the knoll from which it had started. Its division commander and every brigade commander had been put out of action, more than 2,000 enlisted men had been shot, there were stragglers all over the place, and there was no more fight left in anybody. The division had fought its last fight. A day or so later army headquarters broke it up and assigned its remnants to other units.[4]

The rest of Warren's corps came up, followed by Sedgwick's, and the fight that had begun as an advance-guard scrap for possession of an insignificant little ridge spread all across both sides of the little valley and began to pull two whole armies into it. The troops which had been racing for Spotsylvania Court House were running a dead heat to this rolling, half-wooded area a mile west and north of the hamlet, and as fast as the men came up they were strung out on the firing lines, each line unrolling to north and south as more troops arrived. Batteries were brought up, their gun crews glad to see open ground again in place of the impossible Wilderness tangle, and the guns took position on the high ground and began hammering.

It was a confused fight that grew by what it fed on, with separate regiments colliding briefly here and there as they struggled for favorable positions. There was a whole series of little assaults and counterassaults which cost lives and drained away reserves of strength and endurance but which were buried in the reports as incidental to the general process of getting the battle lines established. Toward evening, though, Grant felt that there were enough men on hand to make a real fight of it, and the Federals staggered forward for an attack.

Gruff General Crawford got his Pennsylvania Reserves ahead so that they overlapped the right end of the Confederate line and for a moment it looked as if they might break something loose, but the men were simply too exhausted to drive their attack home. Also, at the last minute they collided with Robert Rodes's division of Confederates, which had just come on the scene in a state of equal exhaustion. For a time the worn-out troops blazed away at each other at short range, and then the Pennsylvanians pulled back and the day ended with the rival armies spread out in a great crescent, the concave side to the east, with Spotsylvania Court House nestled on the Confederate side of the curve. Sedgwick's and Warren's men were in line side by side, and Hancock was coming up behind and Burnside was bringing his corps down through the night from somewhere off to the north.

The infantry lines were restless as the darkness came down, and patrols and skirmishers were forever prodding at one another and firing sharply at the sight or sound of movement, and now and then the chat-chatter of their firing provoked the artillery to add its own voice. Farther back, the immense column of Yankee cavalry was all astir. It was taking off on a ponderous move that might turn into a very big thing, and while there were certain military reasons for the move the controlling factor in all of it was the fact that two very hot-tempered men had just had a violent argument.

George Gordon Meade commanded the Army of the Potomac, and when he rebuked a man he did it with angry words that struck sparks. On this day he was furiously dissatisfied with the job of his cavalry. The tangle which his own escort troops had kicked up was the least of his worries. What bothered Meade was that the cavalry corps itself, Sheridan's command, had failed in the early morning hours to clear the road from Todd's Tavern down to Spotsylvania. Sheridan had issued certain orders for this movement, and Meade had canceled some of them without bothering to tell Sheridan, and it appears that neither man had planned the business very well anyway. The upshot had been that the army was delayed and missed a big chance. So when Sheridan came to Meade's headquarters, around noon, Meade greeted him with angry words that resounded all over the place, loudly denouncing him for letting his cavalry get in infantry's way.

Phil Sheridan was an uncomplicated man whose chief trait, for good or for evil, was a driving combativeness, and he replied in words just as hot. It was Meade's fault, he shouted, because Meade had countermanded his orders; he was fed up with it, and if he could just pull his cavalry together and use it the way cavalry ought to be used, he could go out and whip Jeb Stuart out of his boots. So it went, back and forth, with staff and orderlies pretending to be deaf and drinking it all in, and at last Meade stalked off to tell Grant about it.

Back of this row was something more than a mere clash of temperaments. Meade was correct in blaming most of the delay on Sheridan, but Sheridan did have a proper complaint. Army headquarters still held more than a trace of the crippling old theory that the cavalry corps after all was pretty much a staff outfit like the signalers, its commander in effect ranking as a member of the general's staff rather than as a leader of combat troops. McClellan had seen it so, and only the departed Hooker had disagreed with him. Sheridan wanted to use his men the way Stuart used his—as a hard, compact, striking force—and it was not possible. What the generals were really arguing about was whether cavalry was to be regarded as a fighting corps or as a collection of train guards, scouts, and couriers, and Grant saw the point as soon as Meade began to talk to him.

When Meade reported how Sheridan had said he could whip Stuart if he could take his men and go off on his own, Grant looked up.

"Did Sheridan say that?" he asked. "Well, he generally knows what he is talking about. Let him start right out and do it." [5]

So the cavalry corps had been collected in one imposing

mass—13,000 mounted men, plus horse artillery, a sinewy column such as this army had never before mustered; and presently it set out on a wide swing that would carry it clear away from the camps and battle lines and take it down cross country on a beeline for Richmond. Stuart would not dare ignore it, the way he had ignored Stoneman's raid in the Chancellorsville campaign, for if he did it had weight enough to go straight into the capital, or to work ruinous damage in the army's nexus of transportation and supply. He would have to follow it and bring it to bay and get into a stand-up fight with it, and then it would be seen what came of it all.

When it set out the cavalry did not go jingling off at a trot, pressing for stray minutes and wearing out its horses. It moved at a walk, conscious of its power, as if it had all the time in the world. Once the advance guard brushed into a Rebel skirmish line, and sent a few squadrons forward to tap the line and see what it was made of. The firing grew brisk and the squadrons came tumbling back. Up came Sheridan, hotly asking what was the matter here. Too many Johnnies up ahead, the men told him.

"Cavalry or infantry?" he demanded. Cavalry, he was told.

"Keep moving, boys—we're going on through," he ordered. "There isn't cavalry enough in all the Southern Confederacy to stop us."

The men cheered, and Sheridan waved his hat, and they broke through the skirmish line and the column kept on going—slow, remorseless, powerful.[6]

On their swing away from the army the troopers went back across the Wilderness, and on the Plank Road they met a great wagon train of wounded men, heading east toward Fredericksburg. It was a dreary procession. There were not ambulances enough to carry all of the men who had been wounded in the Wilderness, and empty ammunition wagons, ration wagons, and similar vehicles had been put into service. These wagons had no springs, and the roads were very rough, and a steady, monotonous sound of moaning and screaming went up from the long train and could be heard far away, long before the wagons themselves came into sight. For miles the wagons filled the road, so that the cavalry had to get off to the side and go trampling through the underbrush.

Between and beside the wagons were the walking wounded, and these men begged for water as the cavalrymen went by, so that the column was slowed while troopers hastily offered their canteens. They were not supposed to do this, but as one trooper wrote, the calls of the wounded men were "an appeal that could not be denied. . . . We had water in our canteens and we took time to dismount and hold them to the lips of the thirsty comrades." The wagons jolted on, an enormous cloud of dust lying in the air above and all around, and now and then the train would halt while some wounded man who had died was taken out and laid in the woods.[7]

Never had the wounded men had it any worse. The fighting in the Wilderness had caused more casualties than Antietam itself had caused, and the medical corps was snowed under. First orders had been to send the trains northwest back across the Rapidan to a spot on the Orange and Alexandria Railroad, so thousands of men had been loaded in wagons and started in that direction. But when the army moved down toward Spotsylvania those orders had to be changed, because the old route by Germanna and Ely's fords was no longer being guarded and Mosby's raiders would unquestionably capture any hospital train that tried to use it. So it had been decided to send the wounded over to Fredericksburg, and the clumsy procession had countermarched (giving the men an extra twenty-four hours in the graceless wagons) and new trains were made up to carry more of them, and thousands upon thousands of wounded were now making the agonizing trip to Fredericksburg.

The medical corps that was taking charge of all this was fearfully shorthanded, because the army had marched off to fight new battles and most of its doctors, hospital attendants, and loads of medical supplies had to go along. A few could be spared for the men in the trains, but nobody knew what would happen when they finally reached Fredericksburg because that was a firmly secessionist town badly ravaged by war and it was not currently occupied by any Federal troops.

An abundance of stretcher-bearers had been detailed, a party from each regiment, but most of them were quite useless. Human nature being what it is, the average colonel picked out for this detail the men who were least likely to be of any help if they remained with the regiment, the inevitable consequence being that the worst loafers and thieves in the army had been appointed to help care for the wounded. Doctors noticed that the pockets of nearly all of the dead men and most of the helpless wounded men had been slit open for the easier removal of purses and watches.

The surgeons had done what they could. They began by sorting the wounded men into three classes—those who could probably walk back, those who had to be carried, and those who could not be moved at all and so would have to remain in field hospitals in the Wilderness, which was still smoldering and which stank to the highest heavens, what with thousands of unburied bodies. A very few doctors could be spared to remain with these men—four of them, two regular hospital stewards, and twenty of the priceless detailed attendants, as it was finally worked out, for about a thousand totally disabled men.

When the wagons were loaded there had been a further sorting out. Some of the men could sit up, and empty ammunition boxes were supplied for them to sit on, so that sometimes six or ten could ride in one wagon. With the amputees there was a different classification. It was quickly discovered that men took up less room if they lay on their sides than they required when they lay on their backs, so the leg cases were grouped accordingly: if each man in an ambulance had lost his right leg, each man could lie on his left side—for however many terrible hours the trip might last—and they could fit together nicely, like so many spoons, and it was so arranged.[8]

It was about one in the morning of May 9 when the head of this great caravan of misery came creaking down into sleeping Fredericksburg, a wrecked, half-lifeless town that lay across the path of war, which had seen much suffering and now was to see more.

It had been a drowsy pleasant place, once. In the old days

the tubby English merchant ships drifted lazily up the river and moored here, and the grave men in knee breeches and silk stockings who traded in them had built formal homes of red brick on the quiet streets, and back of the town on the heights they had put up mansions with white pillars, so that an eighteenth-century air of order and certitude had given the place a special flavor. But the old days were long dead and now there was a bitter new flavor, and the very name of the town had taken on a hard ring, and in many homes North and South it was a name of death and deep shadows: a sinister word, carrying a shudder with it, one of the homely American place names made dreadful by war. The town had known violence and gunfire and screaming, and the meadows beyond had seen naked corpses turning blue under a frozen moon, with guns flashing from the hilltops and the wreckage of old houses littering the streets. All of that, earlier in the war, and now this: seven thousand wounded men coming in at one in the morning, with no one riding on ahead to announce their coming or to get things ready for them, and not one sullen resident owning the slightest desire to help the Army of the Potomac in any way whatever.

A regiment of dismounted cavalry had come along as train guard, and it sent men scurrying about to knock the town awake and find places to put the wounded. Churches were taken over, and warehouses, mills, public buildings, and the larger private homes, and all through the night the wagons were laboring up to these doorways and unloading. In some cases, wounded officers of rank were quartered with Fredericksburg families, and these men got along well enough. Nobody in town had any sympathy for Yankees, but the people were not brutal or callous, and so a very fortunate few of the wounded got into real beds.

Most of them were simply laid on the floor—any floor that was handy. Many buildings were still half-wrecked from Burnside's bombardment of December 1862 and contained puddles of stagnant rain water that had come in through gaping holes in the roof, and men were dumped down in this seepage so that the pools became bloody. One warehouse which had contained leaky barrels of molasses had a quarter inch or more of gummy treacle all over the floor. No straw was available for bedding. There was nothing for it but to put the men on the bare floor—in rain water, half-dried syrup, or whatever—and hope that they could make the best of it.

The best was not very good. Washington had had no warning that this move was coming, and so no supplies had been sent down. There were just thirty army doctors on hand to look after the 7,000 wounded, all of whom by now needed attention very badly; needed at the very least to be bathed and given fresh clothing and hot soup, and to have their bandages changed. Practically none of these things could be done, partly because of a woeful shortage of help and partly because the medicines, fresh dressings, and food that were on hand were strictly limited to the little that had been carried in the wagons. The man who got so much as a hardtack and a drink of water that day was in luck. It took more than twenty-four hours just to get the men out of the wagons. A good many of them died, which meant that some of the attendants had to ignore the living and serve on burial details.[9]

The doctors did their best, and some of the stretcher-bearers finally turned out to be fairly useful, and it might not have been so bad if they could once have got the situation stabilized. But the army kept pumping new streams of wounded men in on them faster than the ones they already had could be cared for, and although the men who were trying to cope with this in-gathering of misery worked until they were gray-faced and stupid with fatigue, they kept falling farther and farther behind. It was as if war, the great clumsy machine for maiming people, had at last been perfected. Instead of turning out its grist spasmodically, with long waits between each delivery, it was at last able to produce every day, without any gaps at all. Since the medical service had never been up against anything like this before—had never dreamed of anything like it, in its wildest hallucinations—there was bound to be trouble.

One doctor wrote that for four days in a row—including most of the intervening night hours—he did nothing whatever but amputate arms and legs, until it seemed to him that he could not possibly perform another operation. Yet hundreds of cases were waiting for him, and wounded men kept stumbling in, begging almost tearfully to have a mangled arm taken off before gangrene should set in. "It is a scene of horror such as I never saw," he cried. "God forbid that I should ever see another." A day or two later he had found no end to it: "Hundreds of ambulances are coming into town now, and it is almost midnight. So they come every night." [10]

For the fighting at Spotsylvania began before any of the men who had been wounded in the Wilderness had been got back to Fredericksburg. The job of cleaning up after one battle had barely been begun when a brand-new battle was opened. Robinson's men had their bloody fight for the approaches to the courthouse crossroads while the army's ambulances were still full of men who had been hurt two or three days earlier, and these ambulances were getting farther and farther away from the army right when the army was developing an urgent new need for them. Some 1,500 men were wounded in Robinson's fight, and they were collected at dressing stations not far behind the front. This collection was made easier by the fact that the army was having an unprecedented amount of straggling. Medical directors estimated that from two to four able-bodied men were leaving the ranks with each wounded soldier, and while that made it almost impossible for the army to fight successfully, it did solve momentarily the problem of getting wounded men back out of danger. The trouble was that very few of these volunteer helpers of the afflicted went back to their regiments afterward. They faded away, following wagon trains north or simply dematerializing in the general confusion, and most of them showed up sooner or later in Fredericksburg.

And so that tragic little city, already completely swamped with wounded men, became equally swamped with men who wandered about on foot, stole food, got in everybody's way, and in general succeeded in doubling the size and complexity of the problem which existed here at the Rappahannock crossing. The stragglers mingled with the walking wounded.

A great many of them picked up bloodstained bandages and put them on so that they could pose as wounded men and, if their luck held out, get aboard the hospital steamers and ride back to Washington. Some of them carried realism even farther, and the harassed doctors eventually discovered about a hundred cases of self-inflicted wounds.

Up at the front, Meade was desperately trying to find more ambulances. Most general officers had commandeered one or more ambulances for personal use. They made comfortable living quarters, as a matter of fact, and generals were using them much the way auto-trailers were used in the 1940s, and now Meade ordered all of these turned over to the army's medical director at once. From general headquarters and from the three army corps upwards of fifty ambulances were thus acquired, and with these and with empty ammunition and forage wagons a regular shuttle service back to Fredericksburg was established.[11]

Just in time to avert complete chaos, the first steamers from Washington came down the Potomac. These could not come around to Fredericksburg yet—guerillas made the Rappahannock unsafe, and the Navy was sending a couple of light-draft gunboats to see about it—and they tied up at the old Potomac River landings, Aquia Creek and Belle Plain. These landings were twelve or fifteen miles from Fredericksburg, via villainous corduroy roads, which meant an extra spell in purgatory for any wounded man who made the trip. (A ride in a springless wagon over a corduroy road was about as bad as anything war had to offer.) Yet once a man was put aboard one of the steamers the worst was over, and in a few hours he would be in a regular hospital around Washington: a poor enough place, perhaps, by modern standards, but paradise itself compared with lying unfed and unattended in a springless wagon or on the wet gummy floor of a half-roofed warehouse.

There was a good deal of a jam at the river landings, for the piers were inadequate, and before the boats could take wounded men aboard they had to unload their own cargoes, and usually the narrow makeshift dock that was to receive the cargo was crammed with long lines of stretchers and a huddled mass of walking wounded. The stragglers and malingerers got in the way very badly, and the good civilian doctors who came down with the hospital ships could be imposed on by these men as regular army surgeons could not have been, so that transportation needed by suffering men was often preempted by men whose only trouble was a desire to get away from the zone of fighting. The army caught on to this, eventually, and in a few days no man could get aboard any of the steamboats until he had been examined by a hard-boiled army doctor who knew all of the dodges.[12]

The steamers brought down the things the impromptu Fredericksburg hospitals needed—foods, medicines, bandages, doctors, and hospital attendants—and they came just in time to keep the situation from becoming completely impossible. But mostly they brought down supplies for the army itself. The emphasis was on the job ahead, not on the wreckage that was being left behind, and it was obvious to everybody that the army was not going to stop to lick its wounds. If the lot of the wounded men could be made endurable, that would be fine, but the only thing that really mattered was the fighting.

The wounded men themselves realized this, and they took a sardonic pleasure in the sight of reinforcement troops moving south through Fredericksburg. One day a heavy artillery regiment, fresh from the Washington barracks, came marching through—muskets polished, uniforms neat and unfaded, band playing in front—and the wounded men on the sidewalks and in doorways set up a derisive cheer. One man called out: "Go it, Heavies—old Grant'll soon cut you down to fighting weight!" Another man sourly eyed the band and cried: "Blow —you're blowing your last blast!" [13]

Days after full steamboat connection with Washington had been established, a nurse in a II Corps hospital in Fredericksburg wrote that the wounded men were still getting nothing to eat but hardtack and coffee, and when she contemplated the lot of the average private she exploded: "O God! such suffering it never entered the mind of man or woman to think of!" What she saw in Fredericksburg, she added, was worse than what she had seen in the hospitals at Gettysburg, the sole improvement here being that most of the men were at least under cover.[14]

The men at the front were given no time to worry about what happened behind the lines. For a long time they had told one another that the one thing they wanted (aside from an end to the war) was a fighting general in command. Now they had him, and they were learning that there were elements in the bargain on which they had not counted. The trench lines in the country around Spotsylvania Court House grew longer and longer, and as they did so the men began to see that the heavy fighting had hardly so much as started, and that what had begun in the Wilderness was to go on and on with no end to it. There was no more maneuvering for position, no more tapping a line cautiously to find a soft spot. Men were simply lined up and sent forward, and sometimes it was like the Wilderness fighting all over again, rival lines colliding drunkenly in the dusk of pine thickets, no order or plan to the battle, armies fighting like infuriated mobs.

There was an obscure bit of ground here called Laurel Hill, and both sides wanted it, and a man in the 20th Maine recalled how they fought for it:

"The air was filled with a medley of sounds, shouts, cheers, commands, oaths, the sharp reports of rifles, the hissing shot, dull heavy thuds of clubbed muskets, the swish of swords and sabers, groans and prayers. . . . Many of our men could not afford the time necessary to load their guns . . . but they clubbed their muskets and fought. Occasionally, when too sorely pressed, they would drop their guns and clinch the enemy in single combat, until Federal and Confederate would roll upon the ground in the death struggle." [15]

John Sedgwick had brought his corps up into action, and after he got the men to the spot where Robinson's luckless men had made their attack his staff officers felt that the general was gloomy and depressed. One of them recorded a general impression "of things going wrong, and of the general exposing himself uselessly and keeping us back, of Grant's coming up and taking a look, of much bloodshed and futility."

Yet no mood of depression ever lasted very long with Sedgwick. He had had all the war he wanted, to be sure, and in his letters to his sister in Connecticut he was writing longingly of the day when he could get out of the army and come home to stay—"Can any spot on earth be as beautiful as Cornwall Hollow?" he asked her—but he never let gloom get the better of him for long. The morning after he got his corps to the front he was up early, and when he called briefly at Grant's headquarters, men there remembered that he seemed especially cheerful and hopeful. Grant had compliments for the way he had been handling his troops, and Sedgwick presently returned to his own tents, which were pitched on a little hill close to the place where Robinson's men had formed for their fight the day before. When he got there Sedgwick found that random shots from Rebel sharpshooters were causing trouble, so he sent his young Major Hyde to advance the pickets a little, to end this nuisance.

Major Hyde came back, after a while, and Sedgwick was seated on a cracker box under a tree; and Sedgwick had the major sit down by him, and pulled his ears for him, and joked with him while Hyde reported on his mission. Then Sedgwick walked over to an artillery emplacement to give the battery commander some directions, and the sharpshooters' bullets were pinging around and the gunners were ducking, and Sedgwick laughed at them and told them not to worry—the sharpshooters were so far away "they couldn't hit an elephant at this distance."

A minute after this there was a sharp cry from the gun pits —"The General!" The headquarters people ran over and there was Sedgwick on the ground, a bullet hole under the left eye, killed by one of the sharpshooters whose aim he had derided. They put his body in an ambulance and carried it back to army headquarters, where it was laid in an evergreen bower with the Stars and Stripes wrapped around it. When Grant was told, he seemed stunned. Twice he asked, "Is he really dead?" Later he told his staff that to lose Sedgwick was worse than to lose a whole division of troops.[16]

Washington was many miles away, and little was known there about how the fighting was going, except that the army was constantly calling for more men and more food and ammunition. But the real storm center was the White House. Here was Lincoln, sleepless and gaunt and haggard, his tough prairie strength tried now as never before. He had once characterized another man, who could see no wrong in human slavery, by musing that he supposed that man did not feel the lash if it were laid on another man's back instead of on his own. That kind of insensitivity he himself did not have, and the fact that he lacked it was his greatest asset and his heaviest cross.

He could feel what hit somebody else, and however remote the quiet rooms in the White House might be from the fearful jungles below the Rapidan, all of the lines led back here, because here was held the terrible power to still the tempest or make it go on to the very end. Lincoln could pardon condemned soldiers who fell asleep at their posts, or who broke and ran for it in the heat of action—he called these latter his "leg cases," saying that a brave man might be cursed by cowardly legs which he could not keep from bearing him back out of danger—and he was the man who with a word could have stopped all of the killing, and he had to will that the killing go on.

Now John Sedgwick was dead, and the great wagon trains were lumbering down to Fredericksburg, every day and every night, and the white ash and charred twigs of the Wilderness were dropping on disfigured bodies which no one would ever name, while long columns of weary men went blindly into new fights that would be worse than what they had just come away from; and Lincoln sat late at night with a volume of Shakespeare's tragedies, and to a friend he read the lines of Macbeth's despair: [17]

> *Tomorrow, and tomorrow, and tomorrow*
> *Creeps in this petty pace from day to day*
> *To the last syllable of recorded time,*
> *And all our yesterdays have lighted fools*
> *The way to dusty death.*

This was in the White House. The young men of the Army of the Potomac had had many yesterdays to light their dusty way, but they did not talk about them. They simply lived by the remembered light those days had given them, and the days were various, and nobody can say just where all of the light came from or what it finally meant. (Take a morning in Ohio, for example. The land is flat, and when dawn begins there is a thin mist everywhere, and it glows with the first light so that the green trees begin to come out black in the distance, and the earth rolls gently off to meet them, and the truth about many things lies not quite veiled in the hollow places where the mist lies the longest; and a man who sees it knows something, but what sort of light is that for a soldier?)

One of the things these men had got out of their long yesterdays was a toughness and a jaunty humor. On the morning after the Laurel Hill fight, Grant came riding past the littered slopes to a new place that had been picked for his headquarters. A fife and drum corps was somewhere about, and when the musicians saw the general they suddenly, on inspiration, struck up a rollicking little tune.

Many soldiers were near, and when they heard the tune they looked about them and saw Grant, and then they all began to cheer and laugh. Grant noticed it, and he was quite unable to tell one tune from another—he had a feeble jest, to the effect that he knew just two tunes: one was Yankee Doodle, and the other wasn't—and he asked an aide what the band was playing to cause all of this commotion. The aide explained that it was playing a popular camp-meeting ditty which the whole army was familiar with: a little number entitled, "Ain't I glad to get out of the wilderness!" [18]

4. Surpassing All Former Experiences

There were many young men in the army and one of them was a colonel named Emory Upton. He was thin, wiry, freckled, with unruly hair and a trim goatee and mustache; an intense, passionate man, a Regular Army officer who was impatient with the army's way of doing things and especially with the ways of its higher officers. None of these, he said contemptuously, knew how to lead men. They commanded the best soldiers in the world but they did not know what to do with them.

Like John Sedgwick, in whose corps he served, Upton poured out his thoughts in long letters to his sister. To her he spoke his mind about generals:

"I have never heard our generals utter a word of encouragement, either before or after entering a battle. I have never seen them ride along the lines and tell each regiment that it held an important position and that it was expected to hold it to the *last*. I have never heard them appeal to the love every soldier has for his colors, or to his patriotism. Neither have I ever seen a general thank his troops after the action for the gallantry they have displayed."

Having written this, young Colonel Upton added that when he meditated on all of the incompetence in starred shoulder straps, and then considered his own qualifications, "there is no grade in the army to which I do not aspire."

Upton was the son of a New York farmer. He had spent a couple of his teen-age years at Oberlin, in Ohio, just in time to absorb the fervid religious and abolitionist sentiments that yeasty place was germinating then. He was a sober youngster, worrying about his soul, about the Union, about slavery, about his own health—at one stage he refused to sleep on a pillow for fear it would make him round-shouldered—and he entered West Point in 1856 and was graduated shortly before the war began, number eight in his class. He could have gone into the engineers, the army's *corps d'élite*, but for some reason he chose artillery instead. He had various staff and line appointments in the early days of the war, and then went over into the volunteer service and became colonel of the 121st New York, whose boys found him stiff on the matter of discipline but, on the whole, a man they could like.[1]

Because he was a good leader of men and also a thoughtful scientific soldier, he had risen to brigade command, although (and the fact irked him) he had not yet been made a brigadier general. In the fall of 1863, when Meade and Lee maneuvered fruitlessly back and forth across the Rapidan country, Upton had led a surprise attack on a Confederate fort at Rappahannock Station, winning a sparkling little victory and capturing more than a thousand prisoners. Now he was restlessly observing what happened when the army butted up against the solid trenches that appeared like magic whenever the Rebels drew their lines, and it seemed to him that there was a better way to do things.

Upton, in short, felt that he knew how to break through those Rebel entrenchments, and he spoke up about it, and on the afternoon of May 10 they gave him twelve picked infantry regiments, his own 121st New York among them, and told him to go ahead.

There was much fighting that day. The opposing lines lay in a great rambling curve, and off toward the Federal right some divisions from Hancock's and Warren's corps made a savage and costly assault on the Rebel trenches, coming up through a grove of spiky dead pines as tangled as anything in the Wilderness and being rebuffed with heavy loss. Half a mile or more north and east of the place where they fought, Upton massed his twelve regiments late in the afternoon.

The spot that had been picked for him was not promising. Upton's men faced east, looking toward a wood. There was a little road going off through the trees, and it came out into a field which sloped up for 200 yards to the enemy's works, which were formidable. Out in front there was a heavy abatis of felled trees, the sharpened branches pointing toward the Federals, and the main trench line was several dozen paces beyond. This trench was solidly built of logs and banked-up earth, and along the top there ran a head log, blocked up a few inches above the dirt so that Confederate riflemen could stand in the trench, aim and fire their pieces through the slit under the log, and enjoy almost complete protection. Heavy traverses—mounds of earth running back at right angles from the main embankment—had been built at frequent intervals as a protection against enfilade fire. This line was strongly manned with first-rate troops, and a hundred yards in the rear of it there was a second line, not yet wholly completed but also held by good troops. Here and there along the front line there were emplacements for artillery, so that all of the slope out in front could be swept both by rifle fire and by canister.

The obvious fact here—at least it was obvious to Upton—was that an assaulting column's only hope was to get a solid mass of riflemen right on the parapet as quickly as possible. If the men stopped on open ground to exchange volleys with those thoroughly protected Confederates they would be destroyed in no time. So Upton formed his men in four lines, three regiments side by side in each line, and he issued explicit orders: every man was to have his musket loaded and his bayonet fixed, but only the men in the three leading regiments were to cap their muskets. (To "cap" a Civil War musket was to put a copper percussion cap in the breech so that it could instantly be fired. With uncapped weapons, the men could not fire as they charged but would have to keep on advancing and so would reach the trench with loaded muskets which could then very quickly be capped for close-range firing.) When the first three regiments reached the trench they were to fan out to right and left and drive the defenders off down the line, while the second wave swarmed in behind them to open fire on any reinforcements that might try to come up from the Confederate second line. The remaining two lines were to lie down just short of the trench for use as they might be needed.

Officers were taken out to the edge of the open space and were shown the ground, everything was carefully explained, and then the twelve regiments moved forward. They got to the edge of the woods, Upton took them out into the open, and they set out up the slope on a dead run, yelling like maniacs.

A sharp fire greeted them, and getting through the abatis was tough, but the solid column kept on going and swept up to the trench without a halt. At the parapet there was brief, desperate, hand-to-hand fighting. As Upton remarked in his report, the Confederates "absolutely refused to yield the ground," and the first Yankees who got up on the parapet were shot down or bayoneted. Others pitched their bayoneted rifles over the parapet like deep-sea harpooners spearing whales, or held their pieces out at arm's length, pointing downward over the parapet, and fired. Then men began to jump over into the trench, clubbing and stabbing, the weight of numbers began to tell, the defenders were killed or driven away, and Upton's leading regiments swept down the line to right and left while the next wave dashed across the open ground and seized the second trench. All in all, the thing had worked, and the twelve regiments had broken the Confederate line wide open right where it was strongest, taking prisoners and waving their flags and shouting with triumph.[2]

But to break the line was only half of it. Upton's men were three quarters of a mile away from the rest of the Union army, and the Rebels were bringing up strong reinforcements and opening a heavy fire from in front and from both flanks. Now the twelve regiments must hold on while their comrades in the rear came up to exploit the break-through.

This had been arranged for. On high ground off to the left and rear Mott's division from the II Corps was lined up ready for the word, and it was sent forward as soon as Upton's men got their grip on the Rebel position. But Mott's was an ill-fated division, and most of the fire was burnt out of it. Its morale had been ruined when it was transferred from the defunct III Corps, early that spring, and in the Wilderness fighting it had been shot up and driven in panic, and Mott seems not to have been the officer who could pull the men together. In addition, the division had to advance down a broad open glade, half a mile long and 400 yards wide, and at the end of the glade the Confederates had twenty-two cannon in line, waiting. These guns had a direct line of fire down the glade, and they could not miss, and they broke Mott's division before it got fairly started. Better troops might have got farther, but the artillery would probably have taken charge anyway, and this assault went entirely awry and never got within a quarter of a mile of the Rebel line.[3]

Down to the right were the troops which had made the unsuccessful attack earlier in the day, and it was resolved to send them in again. The men had just succeeded in re-forming their lines after their repulse when a staff officer came galloping up, riding from brigade to brigade with orders for a new attack. One of the men who had to make this charge wrote afterward that "there was an approach to the ridiculous" in the way in which these orders were given. He specified:

"No officer of higher rank than a brigade commander had examined the approaches to the enemy's works on our front, and the whole expression of the person who brought the message seemed to say, 'The general commanding is doubtful of your success.' The moment the order was given the messenger put spurs to his horse and rode off, lest by some misunderstanding the assault should begin before he was safe out of range of the enemy's responsive fire." [4]

That kind of spirit never broke any Confederate lines, and this charge was beaten before it was made. The men moved out sluggishly, convinced that their job was hopeless. After a brief advance they halted and opened fire, but before long they seem to have concluded that there was no sense in it, and everybody turned and ran for the rear. Rebel fire followed them, and the dead pines in the thicket took fire, and what began as a fairly orderly retreat ended as a rout. The soldier who wrote so bitterly about the way the charge was directed confessed that some of the best men in the army "not only retired without any real attempt to carry the enemy's works, but actually retreated in confusion to a point far in the rear of the original line and remained there until nearly night." Staff officers sent to recall them found the men quietly grouped around their regimental flags, making coffee.[5]

So Upton's regiments were left out on a limb, with a good part of the Rebel army gathering to destroy them and no help coming up; and the young colonel at last had to lead his men back to their lines, with a thousand of them left dead or wounded on the ground. They brought a thousand prisoners back with them, and they had made an authentic break in a formidable line, but in the end it had all been a failure.[6]

Yet when night came down the high command felt that the general picture was encouraging. These cruel trenches were not invulnerable, after all, and what twelve regiments had done could perhaps be repeated with a bigger force. An Ohio cavalryman who was serving as orderly at Grant's headquarters saw Grant talking with Meade about it, puffing his cigar as he talked, and he heard Grant say: "A brigade today—we'll try a corps tomorrow." A little later the new commander of the VI Corps, General Horatio Wright, came in. Wright was stocky and bearded, slow-moving, competent rather than brilliant, not beginning to fill the place in the soldiers' affections that Sedgwick had filled; but he was the man Sedgwick himself had once designated as his successor, and he felt that the whole trouble today had been failure of the supporting troops. He said earnestly to Meade: "General, I don't *want* Mott's troops on my left; they are not a support; I would rather have no troops there." [7]

In the end, the generals concluded that Lee's army might be utterly defeated if Upton's technique were used on a larger scale, properly supported, and Meade's staff immediately went to work to plan an enormous blow that would send Hancock's entire corps through the lines and would bring all of Wright's and Burnside's men up as supports.

It would take time to mount an attack of this size, and it could not be done overnight. So on May 11 the troops held their lines, and another great train of wounded was started back toward Fredericksburg. Yet although the front was comparatively inactive there was a steady firing all day long, and the toll of killed and wounded on both sides crept constantly higher. In midafternoon it began to rain—a sullen, persistent drizzle that looked as if it might go on for days—and when the sun went down the air turned chilly, and the battlefield was smoldering with little brush fires and wreathed in flat layers of smoke that hung low in the rain. When night came it was dull and starless, and long after dark there began a tramping of great columns of troops as the men followed obscure roads to their new positions.[8]

More than half of the army was on the move. Grant and Meade had chosen a new spot for their break-through—the very spot that Mott's men had so ingloriously aimed at, made inviting in spite of its banked-up cannon by an accident of geography.

The Confederate lines covering Spotsylvania Court House were uneven and they did not run in straight lines for more than a few rods at a time, but in general they formed two tangents—a long one, opposite the Federal right, facing roughly toward the north, and a shorter one somewhat to the east of this facing northeast and east. These two lines did not intersect. Instead, they were joined by a great loop of entrenchments that bulged out toward the north to cover some high ground: a huge salient nearly a mile deep and half a mile wide, dubbed by the Confederates, from its outline on the map, the Mule Shoe. It was the western side of this salient that Upton had attacked on May 10, and the guns that had broken up Mott's dispirited formation were placed at the northernmost tip of the salient where the lines of the Mule Shoe came to a blunt angle.

If this salient could be broken, Lee's army would be cut in half. By military teaching, the point of a salient was a hard place to defend, since the fire from the defenders on the two sides of the point tended to diverge. It was for that reason that the Confederates had stacked up so many guns at the broad tip, and since there was a clear field of fire in front of this place the guns were extremely effective. But it was believed that if a solid corps of infantry made a sudden rush at the very moment of daybreak—a rush patterned after Upton's,

with no firing and no stopping until the parapet was reached
—the men could overrun the tip of the salient before the guns
could hurt them very badly. Then, with the end of the salient
punched in, the support troops could come piling in on either
side—and there, it might be, was the recipe for victory.

So Hancock's corps was to take position three quarters of a
mile north of the tip of the salient, and at the first light of day
it was to go into action. On Hancock's left Burnside's corps
was in line, and Wright's corps was lined up on Hancock's
right, and they were to come in the moment Hancock's men
needed help. On the extreme right of the army was Warren's
corps, and it was to be on the alert also, ready to smash the
Confederate left down below the salient. Thus virtually all of
the troops would be thrown into the offensive, which was a
new note: never before had the army tried to put its entire
weight into one co-ordinated smash.

There have been worse battle plans, and although neither
Grant nor Meade realized it they were helped by a thumping
piece of good luck. During that rainy afternoon of May 11,
Rebel scouts had seen Federal trains moving off toward the
northeast, and it seemed to Lee that Grant was beginning to
shift around the Confederate right. It would be necessary to
move fast to meet the shift, and during the evening Lee ordered that all artillery which was posted where it could not
move quickly should be pulled out of the line and held in
readiness for a quick start. This applied principally to the
twenty-two guns in the nose of the salient, and sometime before midnight all of these guns were limbered up and taken
back to the rear. General Ewell, who commanded the Confederates who held the salient, was left without his ace of
trumps.[9]

A good plan, then, and unexpected good luck to go with it;
and yet, as that black wet night unrolls its story, one gets the
impression of a queer, uncertain fumbling, as if there mysteriously existed in the army a gap between conception and
execution which could never quite be bridged. Meade's chief
of staff was General Andrew A. Humphreys, and Humphreys
was very capable; the column of attack belonged to Han-

cock, who was by all odds the army's best corps commander; but with good men to plan and lead, and ample staffs to aid them, what finally came out of it all was a blundering lunge which hit the right spot largely by accident and which missed turning into an incredible disaster only because those twenty-two guns had been taken away.

Never before had the soldiers and their leaders gone into action so completely ignorant about where they were supposed to go and what they were going to find when they got there. Hancock wrote that he had sent a couple of staff officers out the afternoon before, with an officer from Grant's staff, to look the ground over, "but owing to the uncertainty as to the exact point to be attacked no very definite information was obtained." [10] He tried to use Mott's dejected soldiers to drive in the Rebel picket line so that he could get a better view of things, but the attempt was a flat failure and when it came time to move the corps up to the jump-off point the best corps headquarters could do was to lay a map on a farmhouse table and study it. Here where the troops were forming there was a house, clearly shown on the map; off to the south the map showed another house, which seemed to be approximately in the middle of the Rebel salient; draw a line, then, from house to house on the map, see what compass point the line hits, and give that to the division commanders for a guide.

It was done so, by lamplight, while the rain came down in sheets outside, and the division commanders got their instructions, which were vague—the attack was supposed to hit the Rebel flank, it was a move of more than ordinary importance, and if it succeeded the country would owe a great debt to the officers responsible; that was about it, as men who were present recalled it. No one knew anything about the strength of the enemy or even about the enemy's position, except that it was off to the south. When it was time to move, staff and engineer officers would be on hand to take the men to the spot where they were to begin their charge.[11]

Hancock gave the lead to his first division, which was led by Brigadier General Francis Barlow. Barlow had been a New

York lawyer before the war, knowing nothing about military matters, and after Fort Sumter he had joined a militia regiment as a private. He had a knack for leadership, and he liked to fight, and in the reshuffle that followed Bull Run he became a colonel. He had been badly wounded at Antietam and again at Gettysburg, and he was a slight, frail-looking man with no color in his cheeks, a loose-jointed unsoldierly air about him when he walked, with deadly emotionless eyes looking out of a clean-shaven face, and when he spoke his voice seemed thin and lackluster.

To all appearances he was no soldier at all, but the man who went by Barlow's appearance was badly deceived. He was hard and cold and very much in earnest, a driving disciplinarian who began by making his men hate him and ended by winning their respect because he always seemed to know what he was doing and because the spirit of fear was not in him. When he wrote his reports he often lapsed into legalistic jargon: his troops moved "on or about" a certain hour, and after various experiences they took "the aforesaid hill" or wood lot or whatever, and through it all there is the echo of a lawyer's clerk preparing a deposition; but underneath everything there was a ferocious fighting man who drove himself and his men as if the doorway to Hell were opening close behind them.[12]

Barlow got his men together in the dripping night. Upton's example had struck home, and the division was put into a solid mass one regiment wide and twenty or thirty ranks deep, everybody elbow to elbow and each line right on the heels of the line ahead. Orders were to advance in complete silence, nobody yelling or touching the trigger of his musket until they reached the Rebel trenches. On Barlow's right, invisible in the inky wet, was the division led by General David Bell Birney, a pale, ascetic-looking man with a wispy beard and a Puritanical devotion to his duty, and somewhere back of these men were John Gibbon and his division, with Mott's unhappy warriors still farther to the rear waiting to be called on if needed. Altogether, there were more than 15,000 men grouped together here in the leaking dark, their clothing as wet as if they had all fallen in a river, nothing ahead of them but the silent night and the loom of indistinct hills and forests in the downpour. Barlow was the guide, to take them up to the tip of the Rebel salient.

After much blind galloping by couriers and staff officers, the immense mass of soldiers began to move, mud clinging to heavy feet at every step. Barlow had his compass points straight, and he set out confidently enough, with two staff officers beside him for guidance. But as they moved he learned that these officers knew no more than he did about what lay ahead of them. Indeed, they were complaining bitterly about being sent to conduct a move when they knew nothing whatever about it. They staggered and stumbled on—by Barlow's orders all horses were left behind, and division commander and all other officers were tramping along on foot—and nobody could see anything and nobody knew anything, and presently the whole situation began to strike General Barlow as very funny in a horrible sort of way.

At his side was Hancock's chief of staff, and this man, Barlow wrote, was "a profane swearer" who as they plodded on kept making pungent remarks about the conduct of the war. As this officer made the high command's utter ignorance about everything connected with this venture more and more obvious, Barlow asked him finally, and in straight-faced jest, if he could at least be sure that there was not an open canyon a thousand feet deep between the place where they then were and the place where the Confederates had built their trenches, and the officer frankly confessed that he had no such assurance; upon which firebrand Nelson Miles, one of Barlow's brigadiers, voiced his disgust so loudly and bitterly that Barlow had to tell him to shut up. The rain stopped, and the sky began to grow dull and pale, and a thick clammy fog floated up from the lower ground. The vast column oozed along down a slanting field, and Barlow at last told the staff people: "For Heaven's sake, at least face us in the right direction, so that we shall not march away from the enemy and have to go round the world and come up in their rear." [13]

This much the staff officers could do, and at some point or

other in the predawn grayness they called a halt, and they gestured brightly toward the fog ahead and said that the enemy was off there somewhere, although they confessed freely that they did not know how the enemy's works were built or how many enemies were in them or what the ground in front of the enemy's position might be like. Barlow had a mental picture of a crude map which an officer in the 16th Massachusetts had scratched on a kitchen wall for him, an hour or two earlier, and he tried to keep that in mind. Then the staff officers went away, and Barlow was on his own, and he ordered his men forward and the big assault was on.

Not all of the men knew that they were actually beginning an attack. So hazy were the arrangements that some of them supposed they were simply making a routine change of position, and at the rear of the divisional column there were officers' servants, camp cooks, and so on, leading mules loaded down with spare tents, cooking equipment, and provisions. Out in front of the blind column the 66th New York had been deployed in a dense skirmish line, and presently this line rolled over the Rebel pickets, coming in out of the milky obscurity so suddenly that the pickets had no time to sound the alarm. The pickets were disarmed and sent to the rear and the division plodded on.[14]

It broke through a thicket and approached a little ridge, and the men thought this ridge was the Rebel line and they raised a sudden cheer and everybody broke into a run. As they ran, the troops lost all formation and became a dense, crowding mass. They passed over the ridge, finding no Confederates on it, and swept down across a broad hollow, the dim light slowly growing brighter, and in the hollow they ran into the heavy abatis their foes had prepared for them. They sprang on this entanglement and tore it apart hand by hand, working in frenzied haste, and the Confederate line was not a hundred yards beyond. The racket had roused the defenders, and the trenches began to spit flame as the men who stood in them opened fire.[15]

As the Federals ran forward there was a careening rush just behind the Confederate line, and the twenty-two missing

guns came back over the muddy ground on a spattering gallop. The Confederate command in the salient had sniffed
trouble during the night and had sent desperate appeals for
the return of these guns, and now they were coming up to
the rear of the trench line just as the Northerners were coming up to the front of it. If the guns had been in position, the
piled-up division that was coming up the slope would have
given them the kind of target gunners dream about, and Barlow's men would have been murdered, but the Yankees' luck
was in and the guns did not quite make it.

Two or three guns did manage to swing into the gun pits
and fire a round or two—one shell went sailing over the combat men and smashed into one of the misguided headquarters
details that were stupidly coming along in the rear, dismem-
bering a pack mule and filling the air with frying pans, sides
of bacon, and other matters—but it was too late. The massed
Federals went flooding over the trenches as if a dam had been
broken, stabbing with their bayonets and cheering to split
their throats, and the whole end of the salient was broken in.
Twenty of the guns and three or four thousand Confederate
infantrymen were captured en masse, and the yelling soldiers
went streaming on into the foggy woods and ravines beyond
the trenches.[16]

They were on their way—somewhere, no one knew where,
impelled by a rush that was both powerful and fragile. The
ground was rough and the trees and thickets were obscure
in the wet hazy light, and no one knew a thing except that
the Rebel line had been smashed and that the thing to do was
probably to keep on running. The different regiments and
brigades were as thoroughly scrambled as if the whole division had been tossed in a giant's blanket. What ran down
the open space inside the Mule Shoe was not the hard spearhead of an army corps but simply an excited mob, wholly
confused and without any vestige of organization or control.
It would be an irresistible flood tide up to the moment when it
ran into something solid. Then it would turn into foam and
the wave would recede.

Midway down the Mule Shoe the something solid appeared

—an ably led division of Confederate veterans bent on driving the Yankees back to where they came from. Lee himself was among them, getting them set for a counterattack, trying to lead it himself until the Southern Army's sure instinct for self-preservation forced him to the rear. These Southerners formed a battle line and tilted their muskets down and came charging up the salient, and they hit the disorganized Yankees and sent them running. There were wild moments of confused fighting in the misty woods and up across the little fields and hollows, and then the Federals came pelting back to the captured trenches. Here they stopped running and turned around and dug in to hold onto what they had gained, while the high command sent fresh troops up from the rear to exploit the break that had been made.

For half a mile or more, all along the toe of the salient, the men of the II Corps held the Confederate trenches. These were wide and deep, with so many traverses built back from them that they were like a series of adjoining cellars, and their walls were made of piled logs and banked-up earth, the ground at the bottom all muddy and covered with inches of filthy rain water. In this long jagged ditch the Federals suddenly went on the defensive, while the Rebels came storming out of the woods to wrest the line away from them.[17]

Practically all of Hancock's corps was up now, and there was not room for nearly all of the men to get on the firing line. In places they were jammed forty ranks deep, outside of the trenches, trying to crowd their way forward so that they could shoot Confederates. They had seized the captured guns and swung them around, but there were no gunners among them and few of the infantrymen knew much about handling cannon. One man remembered how they loaded these weapons with any bits of metal they could find, including broken muskets, and fired them helter-skelter, endangering themselves about as much as their enemies. An Irish private was gleefully fitting a primer into the breech of one of the guns, and a comrade tried to tell him that the weapon was elevated for extreme long range, so that it would shoot far above the oncoming Rebels. "Never fear!" yelled the Irishman, jerking the lanyard and firing the piece. "It's bound to come down on somebody's head!" [18]

The Federals were here in overwhelming numbers, and their very numbers were a handicap. Barlow tried desperately to get the men re-formed, so that an organized attack could be resumed. There was no point in trying to go down the open ground in the middle of the salient. The recipe for victory now was to organize an advance that would sweep along the trench lines to right and left, flanking the Confederate defenders and widening the breach until it was past mending. But as fast as Barlow could get a few elements sorted out and put into line a new mass of reinforcements would come loping in from the rear, and the line would vanish.

Things had happened too fast. What sketchy planning there had been was based on the theory that a great deal of sheer muscle would be needed to break the Rebel line. What actually happened, however, was that the line broke at the first touch, and what was needed immediately thereafter was quick footwork rather than brute strength. But the muscle was still coming in and there was no way to stop it and footwork was quite out of the question. There was nothing for it now but for everybody to get together and shove.

Both sides were shoving at once, and in the same place, and the result was the wildest, bitterest in-fighting of the entire war.

In effect each side was making a charge and repelling a charge at the same moment and with the same troops. The Confederates were fighting with a last-ditch fury. Far to their rear Lee was building a new trench line across the throat of the salient. It would be an all-day job and until the line was finished the men up front must at any cost whatever either drive the Yankees out or at least keep them from coming in any deeper. That meant close-range fighting carried out without any letup. The battle front was a mile wide by now, with Burnside's men fighting their way through the woods on the east and Wright sending his VI Corps in on the west, and in no place along this front were the rival firing lines more than a few yards apart.

It began to rain again, and the men in the trenches stood to their knees in bloodstained water, and the ground outside the trenches, trampled by massed thousands of men, turned into a stiff gumbo in which bodies of dead and wounded men were trodden out of sight. From the rear Barlow could see an immense mass of Federals lying flat in this muck, twenty or thirty ranks jammed together in a formless crowd, the men in the rear passing loaded muskets forward to the men in front. An orderly brought Barlow his horse and the general galloped back to Hancock to beg that no more men be sent forward.

Never before on earth had so many muskets been fired so fast on so narrow a front and at such close range. About all that kept the two armies from completely annihilating each other was the fact that most men were firing too rapidly to aim. A whole grove of trees behind the Rebel line was killed by shots that flew too high, and the logs of the breastworks were splintered and, a Confederate officer said expressively, "whipped into basket-stuff." Bodies of dead and wounded men were hit over and over again until they simply fell apart and became unrecognizable remnants of bloody flesh rather than corpses. There were big charges and little charges, with bayonet fighting when the men came to close quarters, and at times Union and Confederate flags waved side by side on the parapets, with bullets shredding them into tattered streamers.[19]

A few hundred yards to the east of the blunt tip of the salient there was a place where the Rebel trench line made a little bend to the south, and right at this bend a spirited Confederate counterattack regained part of the breastworks. On the Yankee side of the works there was a ditch, and as the Southerners retook their trench, men of the VI Corps came charging in and occupied the ditch, and for a distance here the rival battle lines were literally face to face with only the log breastwork between them.

Men fired at one another through chinks in the logs, or stabbed through the chinks with their bayonets, or reached over the top to swing clubbed muskets. Where the Vermont

Brigade was fighting, men were seen to spring on top of the logs and fire down on their enemies as fast as their comrades could pass loaded muskets up to them. Each man would get off a few rounds before he was shot, and usually when one of these men fell someone else would clamber up to take his place. Dead men fell on top of wounded men, and unhurt men coming up to fight would step on the hideous writhing pile-up.[20]

Emory Upton had his thinned brigade in beside the Vermonters. He was riding his horse back and forth just behind the firing line, the only mounted man in sight, going unhurt by some miracle—every man on his staff was either killed or wounded. He was proud of the way his men were fighting, but he felt that they would do even better if they had the help of some artillery, and he sent back for a section of guns. In a few moments two brass fieldpieces from a regular battery came splashing madly up through the rain, wheeling about to unlimber within literal whites-of-their-eyes range—artillery charging entrenched infantry, as if all roles were reversed in this mad war.

The gunners sent double charges of canister plowing through the Confederate ranks, and at this close range the effect was fantastic. Inspired by it, the gunners laid hands on their pieces and ran them forward until they touched the very parapet, and then they resumed firing and kept it up as long as the guns could be manned, which was not very long. When the guns at last fell silent they could not be removed because all of the horses were dead, and of the twenty-four men who came on the field with them only two were on their feet unwounded.[21]

There had been hand-to-hand fighting before, but it invariably reached a quick climax and then ended, one side or the other breaking and running away. Here nobody broke and nobody ran. The fighting did not stop for a moment, and the unendurable moment of climax hung taut in the air and became fixed, a permanent part of some insane new order of things. Some regiments sent details a dozen paces to the rear to clean muskets; men were firing so continuously that their weapons became foul with burnt powder and could not be loaded. Amazingly enough, as the day wore on exhausted men from time to time would stagger a few feet away from the firing line, drop unhurt in the mud, and fall sound asleep. Now and then men had to stop fighting and lift the bodies of dead and wounded comrades out of the wet ditch and drop them in the mud outside. There were so many bodies they interfered with the fighting.[22]

This was the Bloody Angle, the place where a trench made a little bend, and where the two armies might have clasped hands as they fought; and it was precisely here that the war came down to its darkest cockpit. It could never be any worse than this because men could not possibly imagine or do anything worse. This fighting was not planned or ordered or directed. It was formless, monstrous, something no general could will. It grew out of what these men were and what the war had taught them—cruel knowledge of killing, wild brief contempt for death, furious unspeakable ferocity that could transcend every limitation of whipped nerves and beaten flesh. There was a frenzy on both armies, and as they grappled in the driving rain with the smoke and the wild shouting and the great shock of gunfire all about them this one muddy ditch with a log wall running down the middle became the center of the whole world. Nothing mattered except to possess it utterly or to clog it breast-high with corpses.

There was no victory in all of this and there was no defeat. There was just fighting, as if that had become an end in itself. A Massachusetts soldier wrote that the firing continued "just so long as we could see a man," and a Pennsylvanian agreed that "all day long it was one continuous assault." A man in the Iron Brigade probably spoke for every man in the army when he called this fight at the Bloody Angle "the most terrible twenty-four hours of our service in the war." An officer in the VI Corps, trying to describe the fight afterward, wrote that he had only confused memories of "bloodshed surpassing all former experiences, a desperation in the struggle never before witnessed." Trying to sum up, he concluded: "I never expect to be fully believed when I tell what I saw of the horrors of Spotsylvania, because I should be loath to believe it myself were the case reversed." [23]

The fighting went on all day long and it continued after dark—there were men on the firing line who said they had fired more than four hundred cartridges apiece, from start to finish. Finally, somewhere around midnight, it died out. The Confederates had at last finished the cutoff line at the base of the salient, and they slipped quietly back to it, and in the darkness the entire salient disappeared. The exhausted Federals got a drugged sleep in the rain, and in the morning they went cautiously forward to take a look at the ground they had won.

There was nothing remarkable about it, except that the region around the Bloody Angle offered the most horrible sights of the war. In places, the trenches held corpses piled four and five deep, and sometimes at the bottom of such a pile a living wounded man would be found. The firing had been so intense that many bodies had been hit over and over again and were mutilated beyond any chance of identification. One of Wright's staff officers remembered that once during the previous day he had ordered some guns up to an advanced position, and he could not remember having heard anything from them thereafter, so he went out to look. The two guns, he found, had reached the designated position, and each piece and caisson was wheeled halfway around, but the guns had never got into battery. A burst of Rebel fire had caught them in mid-turn and every man and horse had been killed, "and they lay as if waiting the resurrection." [24]

Clearly, the ground that had been won was not worth what it cost, either from an esthetic or a military standpoint. The Rebel line had been broken but it had been mended again, and the armies were just about where they were before. The Federals had gained a square mile of quite useless territory at the price of nearly 7,000 casualties. Rebel losses, to be sure, had been heavier, but that was cold comfort. The big push had been made and it had not quite worked.

Yet perhaps all of that did not really matter. Something inexorable was moving, and old words like victory and defeat had lost their meaning. The slouchy little man with the stubbly red beard meant to keep going, and the entire war was one continuous battle now, and if one blow failed another one would immediately be struck. The day after the Bloody Angle fight new orders came down, and that night Warren drew his V Corps out of its place at the extreme right of the Federal line and marched it around in an enormous circle, behind the rest of the army, to a place on the extreme left. It was a cruel march, for the rain was still falling and the roads were knee-deep in mud, and the soldiers were as nearly dead with fatigue as living men can be, so that when Warren reached his destination in the morning he had only about 1,000 men with him. But the laggards came up later and there was a hard, wearing, inconclusive fight, and the next day there was another fight, and the army kept sidling around to its left, forcing Lee's army to shift to meet it.[25]

A week went by, with a battle of some sort fought every day, and the Union army which had been directly west of Spotsylvania Court House on May 8 was directly east of it on May 19, and every unit in the army had fought as it never had fought before. There had not been an hour, day or night, in all that time when there had not been firing somewhere along the front. Every day the wagons went back to Fredericksburg with wounded men, and every day other wagons came up to the front with supplies so that the endless fighting might continue.

On this nineteenth of May the Confederates made another of their patented blows at the Yankee flank. Ewell's corps went out beyond the Union right and came down through the woods heading straight for a road where the vast wagon trains were unloading, and all that stood in the way was an untested division made up of some of those heavy artillery regiments which had been uprooted from their comfortable berths in the Washington forts.

The veterans had not been kind to these men. As they were marched up to go into their first fight, the ex-artillerists passed a batch of wounded men who were awaiting medical attention. These men exhibited their wounds, some of which were pretty ghastly, and pointed out that the heavies would very soon be getting hurt as badly as this or even worse. Some called out, "Dearest, why did you leave your earthworks?" Others pulled a covering blanket from a dreadfully mangled corpse that lay by the road and invited the green soldiers to look at what happened to combat soldiers. There was nothing for the heavies to do but swallow hard and keep marching, and before long they formed line of battle and went off through the underbrush to fight with Lee's veterans.

The heavies knew nothing about fighting, but they were willing to learn. For an hour or more they had it out with Ewell's men, back and forth across a series of wooded hollows and little ravines, and at the end of that time the Confederates were in full retreat, with 900 dead and wounded left on the ground. About an equal number of the heavies had been shot, and when a newspaper correspondent asked how they had behaved, one of their officers explained: "Well, after a few minutes they got a little mixed and didn't fight very tactically, but they fought confounded plucky." It is recorded that ever after that the Army of the Potomac had no more jeers for heavy artillerists but admitted them to full comradeship.[26]

A day or so after this the army began to move again. It was not just edging a little farther around the Confederate flank, this time, but was really taking to the road, heading south. The soldiers' spirits rose with the move—the Spotsylvania area was one any soldier would be glad to leave—and although a light rain was falling, it merely served to lay the dust, and as they marched a number of the battle-thinned regiments did what veterans rarely did: they began to sing while they marched.

Yet moods could change fast, and the singing did not last long. A regiment would be trudging down the road, singing as if all of war's trials were far away. Then, inexplicably, the song would come to a sudden stop. There would be a brief silence, and then from one end of the regiment to the other, spurred by a common impulse, the men would yell: "I want to go home!"[27]

CHAPTER III

One More River to Cross

---

1. The Cripples Who Could Not Run

THE drama no longer lay in the great events that took place down by the footlights. At the back of the stage there was a silent unbroken procession of young men who looked old and tired, wearing uniforms much the worse for weather and hard wear: a procession that moved eternally out of life and into death or mutilation, compelling the attention simply because there were so many men in it that it was hard to think about anything else. Lincoln had to see it, and he paced the halls of the White House without sleep, a grotesque lanky figure who could feel the lash on another man's back, and he considered the sound and fury which Macbeth had heard on his own stage and he listened for something beyond it. If that something was there it would come out someday, and if it was not there then the sooner the idiot's tale was told and finished the better for everyone. Always the silent procession kept moving, and there were off-stage sounds of hoarse cheers, and bursts of musketry and the thudding of the guns, and the maddening imperious command of the bugles.

In the old days there would have been a lull. There had been continuous fighting or marching for more than two weeks, and the soldiers had neither taken off their clothing nor had an unbroken night's rest since they crossed the Rapidan. Losses had been appalling. Many brigades were no bigger than regiments ought to be, and any number of regiments were down to normal company strength. Two whole divisions had been cut up so badly that they had to be discontinued, the remnants consolidated with other units. Behind the army there was a litter of broken human bodies extending all the way back from Fredericksburg to the crowded hospitals around Washington.

The casualty lists told a story. The army moved south from Spotsylvania Court House a little more than a fortnight after it had crossed the Rapidan. In that time more than 33,000 men had been lost. Averaged out, this meant that 2,000 men were being killed or wounded every twenty-four hours. Fredericksburg and Chancellorsville together had taken no such toll as this. Now, instead of pulling back for a breathing spell, the army was going to plunge even more deeply into action, with every prospect that the killing would go on and on without a respite.

Grant had had to change his plans, for this move south had not been on his program. In the heat of the fighting around the little courthouse town he had told Washington that he would fight it out along this line if it took all summer, and when he said it that promise made sense. Lee's army was smaller than the Army of the Potomac, and in the fighting thus far the two armies were losing just about the same percentages of the numbers engaged. If they were applied long enough these percentages meant certain doom for the weaker army. The mathematics were ugly but inexorable: sooner or later, Lee's army would be too thin to stand the hammering.

But the picture had suddenly changed, and instead of forcing a decision where it was, the Army of the Potomac now had to march for the open country, trying to get into such a position that Lee would have to stop digging invulnerable trenches and come out to attack. Those deadly percentages would work for the Federals only as long as Lee was deprived of reinforcements. Grant had made certain arrangements to bring that deprivation about, and those arrangements had unexpectedly collapsed.

In the Shenandoah Valley there was a little Union army

under Franz Sigel, moving south to close that granary and highway of war to the Confederacy, and south of the James River Ben Butler was leading two army corps up toward the Rebel capital. It did not really matter very much whether either of these generals actually reached his goal, so long as both of them kept diligently trying to reach it. But both men had failed.

Sigel met a scratch Confederate army at a town called Newmarket and was driven back in wild rout, a devoted and unskilled soldier failing in a task he should never have been given. (How differently John Sedgwick might have done it, if the demotion Stanton had planned had been accomplished!) Butler had done no better. With much ceremony and scheming he managed to let inferior numbers drive him into a broad peninsula jutting out into the James. The Confederates promptly dug in across the neck of the peninsula, leaving him locked up as securely as if he and all his soldiers had been in prison.

With these two disasters, everything came unstitched. Grant got the bad news while he was still hammering at the Spotsylvania lines, and the evil part of it was the certain knowledge that, because Sigel and Butler had been beaten, the Confederates who had been fighting them would immediately move up to reinforce Lee. That meant that to "fight it out along this line" was no longer a good move. The Confederates had had heavy losses in the past fortnight—in the first week of the action, 7,000 Rebel prisoners had been sent north, and more were coming in—and up to now the terrible percentages had been working for the North. But now the defeats along the James and the Shenandoah meant that Lee's losses would all be made good. In effect, the Army of Northern Virginia was going to be about as strong after three weeks of fighting as it had been before the fighting began. Plans which had been based on the assumption that it would be a great deal weaker would have to be changed.

So Grant sat down at his field desk and wrote orders for another move by the left flank: a move like the one which took the army out of the Wilderness, a shift east and south, maneuver in place of continued fighting. In a way this might be playing Lee's game, but there was no help for it. Reinforced, Lee could hold his Spotsylvania lines indefinitely. If there was such a thing as a road to victory, it led around those trenches, not over them.[1]

As the army began to move, Grant and Meade studied the casualty lists together. They were in contrast, those two soldiers. Men who had long since lost their enthusiasm for generals looked at them curiously when they appeared side by side. There was a gunner who remembered how his battery was brought forward one day to beat in some Rebel strong point which was holding up an infantry advance. Shortly after the guns opened Grant and Meade rode up and posted themselves under a nearby tree to watch the fight. Meade was nervous, moving about, constantly stroking his beard, fretting when the fight went badly. Grant stood quietly, a cigar in his teeth, his face utterly expressionless in its wreath of tobacco smoke, and he seemed like a man forced to watch something that did not interest him at all. The fight failed, and the open field in front was stained with blue bodies, and the two generals mounted and rode off, Grant still looking as if he had seen nothing in particular.

"The enlisted men looked curiously at Grant," wrote the gunner. "And after he had disappeared they talked of him, and of the dead and wounded men who lay in the pasture field; and all of them said just what they thought, as was the wont of American soldiers."[2]

Yet the contrast between the two generals was not quite what it seemed to be. Grant was the stolid, remorseless killer and Meade was the sensitive man who sparred and drew back and tried at all times to conserve the lives of his men; yet of the two it was Grant who winced in agony at the price men were paying for the fighting. It was he and not the other man who felt the compulsion to look at the unbroken column moving across the back of the stage, the men who marched from life to death and carried the war on their bowed shoulders. It seems that the thought of this wrung some kind of outcry from him—*must* there be all of this killing?

It was Meade who laconically gave him such comfort as could be given.

"Well, General," said Meade, "we can't do these little tricks without losses." [3]

The whole army had grasped this point, accepting it without enthusiasm but with a minimum of complaint. Yet the burden of the losses lay everywhere, and now and then it caused an outcry, unheard at the moment, echoing faintly down the years. In a Wisconsin regiment a devout chaplain somehow found a quiet hour and managed to hold divine services, and to the tanned veterans who were grouped about him in the firelight he preached a thumping sermon full of hell-fire and eternal punishment, predestination darkly illumined by grace abounding, and the regiment's colonel was rubbed where it hurt. He called the chaplain to his tent after the services and told him off.

"I don't want any more of that doctrine preached in this regiment," said the colonel sternly. "Every one of my boys who fall fighting this great battle of liberty is going to Heaven, and I won't allow any other principle to be promulgated to them while I command the regiment." [4]

A Michigan infantryman, looking back on the fighting, noted in his diary that General Lee must be a great strategist. No matter where the army went, the Rebels were always there in front of it, and the Rebel line always seemed to hold firmly no matter how hard it was hit. And the soldier mused: "Now what is the reason that we cannot walk right straight through them with our far superior numbers? We fight as good as they. They must understand the country better, or there is a screw loose somewhere in the machinery of our army."

Commenting on the Bloody Angle fight, the same soldier was moved to a protest:

"Surely, we cannot see much generalship in our campaign so far, and the soldiers are getting sick of such butchery in such a way. Half the time the men are fighting on their own responsibility, and if there is anything gained so far it is by brute force and not by generalship." [5]

Whatever the ins and outs of it might be, the soldier had

touched on a basic point. The only value that seemed to amount to anything any more was the simple courage of the enlisted man. In different ways the various units of the army recognized the fact and reacted accordingly, and the soldiers found their own direct and brutal ways to punish the men who did not measure up.

In a Pennsylvania regiment which fought at the Bloody Angle there was one man who ran from the fighting and found safety in the rear. He was fished out of his transient security, and next day the colonel devised a horrible punishment. He had the man bucked and gagged and deposited him, trussed up and helpless, in front of regimental headquarters. Then he had the man's own company march past him in single file, and as they did so the colonel ordered them to spit in the face of the man who had run away. The men obeyed without a quibble and felt that the punishment was simple justice.

A New York battery had a different system. This battery was in the IX Corps line during hard fighting to the east of the Bloody Angle, and a general who came by in the heat of the battle found one wriggling man tied up between two trees near the guns, a helpless target for all of the Confederate bullets. The general asked about it, and was told that the man was a notorious shirker, present for duty only when it was time to draw rations; the men had caught him this time and had spread-eagled him under fire, hoping that he would be hit. The general laughed and told the battery commander to keep the man tied up until sundown, and an infantry major who happened by burst out: "I'll bet he is a big-bounty man. Keep the --- ------ --- -- - ----- there and get him killed, if possible, for the good of the service!" In some miraculous way (for the Rebel fire was very heavy) the man escaped all harm. He was released at night and he vanished in the dark and the battery never saw him again.

A Massachusetts soldier wrote that a straggler in his regiment was taken to the colonel, given a drumhead court-martial, and immediately shot to death—an event, he said, which noticeably discouraged straggling in the regiment thereafter.

A company of Regular sharpshooters was paraded one evening, between fights, to see a runaway comrade drummed out of service in the old manner. The man's head had been shaved and the buttons of his uniform had been cut off, and he was marched down between the facing rows of his fellows, each man standing with lowered musket and fixed bayonet; and a squad came along just behind the man with more bayonets to prod him on his way. As the scapegrace shaven figure shambled along, the fife and drum corps piped the "Rogue's March":

> Poor old soldier—poor old soldier—
> Tarred and feathered
> And then drummed out
> Because he wouldn't soldier.

At the end of the ceremony the man fled into the woods, and the men saw no more of him.[6]

Yet, if the soldiers would readily kill or humiliate cowards, they could also laugh at them. A standard army joke was the story of the notorious slacker who bragged that when the battle was at its worst he could always be found where the bullets were thickest—far to the rear, safely hidden under an ammunition wagon. The army also liked the story about the Irish private (a good story was always pinned on an Irishman in those days, if possible) who used as his own means of escape from action the shopworn excuse that he had to help a wounded comrade to the rear. In one battle, according to this story, the soldier undertook to help a comrade who cried that his leg had been shot off. Bending down, he got the wounded man over his shoulder and started out. As he stumbled along a cannon ball came out of nowhere and took off the head of the man he was carrying. After a time the Irishman got to a dressing station and offered his burden to the doctors, who asked him what he expected them to do for a man who had no head. Dumfounded, the soldier looked at the corpse and cried indignantly: "The deceiving creature—he told me it was his leg!" [7]

Sometimes the army's stories were told on Confederates. The Philadelphia brigade claimed that at Spotsylvania a ragged Rebel jumped out of the opposite trench and came running toward the Union lines. Just as he reached his goal a bullet hit him, and when the Federals came to pick him up he gasped: "I'm sorry you shot me—I was coming over to take the oath of allegiance." His captors confessed that they had no copy of that famous oath, but one of them remarked that they did have a canteen with a little whisky in it. Reviving, the Confederate sat up and said eagerly: "That will do just as well." [8]

The mail service caught up with the army just as it was leaving the Spotsylvania Court House area, and for the first time since they crossed the Rapidan the men got letters from home. They also got newspapers, which they read with eager curiosity, and as they read these papers they discovered anew that the war as it was described for people back home bore very little resemblance to the war which they themselves were actually fighting. In a Massachusetts battery the men hooted at newspaper accounts which proclaimed that Lee's army was "utterly routed and fleeing in confusion." One of the gunners remarked disgustedly that this, "like so much of the trash published by the papers during the war, would have been decidedly important if true." [9]

It did not really make much difference, for there was nothing the outside world could tell these soldiers anyway. The army's world was enclosed by cavalry patrols and moving skirmish lines, and in the obscurity beyond those boundaries there was the Rebel army, sometimes out of sight but never out of touch. The normal state of all previous armies—the state in which most of the soldier's time was spent—was neither marching nor fighting but quiet life in camp, barracks, or garrison. An army might march far and fight furiously, but when all of its days as an army were added up it would be found that most of them had been dull, monotonous days of inaction. But from the moment the Army of the Potomac crossed the Rapidan on May 5 to the end of the war, eleven months later, there was no inaction whatever.

Instead there was marching or fighting every day, and very often both together, and physical contact with the enemy was never wholly broken.[10] The final grapple had begun, and the war had become a war of using up—using up men and emotions and the wild impossible dreams that had called the armies into being in the first place—and everything that Americans would ever do thereafter would be affected in one way or another by what remained after the using up was completed.

The armies were moving on parallel lines. They were never far apart, and they bumped and jostled each other as they moved, a fringe of fire running up and down the lines, with cavalry patrols fighting for the possession of lonely road crossings, artillery defending the fords and bridges at streams, infantry skirmishers colliding on plantation fields. By day and by night there was always the chance that any of these little tussles might develop into a full-scale battle.

There were many wearing night marches, and the men were very tired, and one soldier said long afterward that the very appearance of the army had changed, as if everything that had happened looked out of the faces of the marching men: "The men in the ranks did not look as they did when they entered the Wilderness: their uniforms were now torn, ragged and stained with mud; the men had grown thin and haggard; the experience of those twenty days seemed to have added twenty years to their age."

This soldier remembered that there was much straggling in these marches, and yet it was not the familiar business of sloughing off the fainthearts who always dropped out of ranks when the army moved. Now good men who wanted to keep up were dropping by the roadside because they could not take another step, and the nightly bivouacs had a strange appearance. An average company might have fifteen men present when it grounded arms for the night. Five of these would promptly be detailed for picket duty. Of the ten who remained, at least half would fall to the ground, too exhausted to collect wood or water or build campfires or do anything else. The men who remained on their feet would hunt fence rails or sticks to make a fire, and would collect canteens to get water, and in one way or another would provide a meal for the company. The sure sign that the men who lay inert and did nothing were not shirkers was the fact that these men would cook coffee and meat for them.

No night's rest was ever unbroken. There would always be picket firing, or some unexplained call to arms at midnight, and if nothing else happened there was a constant trickle of tired laggards going through the camp waking up those who slept to ask where their own regiments might be.[11]

If infantry and cavalry happened to bivouac together, dawn would reveal an oddity. Cavalry was always awakened by bugle calls, but the morning summons to infantry was the long roll beaten on the drums. The cavalrymen would sleep soundly through the beating of the drums but would rouse instantly when their own bugles sounded, while it was just the other way around with infantry—bugles would not awaken them, but they got up at once when the drums began to beat. Sometimes a wakeful battery would fire a few salvos in the night, and get answering salvos from an unseen Rebel battery, and the troops would remain asleep. But the same men would come out of their blankets at once, fumble for their muskets, and fall into line if a few musket shots were fired by their own pickets.[12]

Yet if everybody was tired, morale was good. The country the army was in now had never been touched by war and it looked clean and open and prosperous, with houses that had neither been pillaged nor abandoned and fields where good crops were growing. For all the toll taken by hard marching, a newspaper correspondent wrote that there were fewer stragglers and less grumbling than when the campaign first began, and a New York officer agreed that "the men never marched with so little complaining or so little straggling." If the white inhabitants were all stanchly secessionist, the plantation colored folk were strongly inclined in the other direction, and men's spirits rose when a teen-age colored girl stood by a fence corner waving her sunbonnet and calling out gaily:

"I'se right glad to see you, gen'l'men, I'se right glad to see you."

There were abundant fence rails for campfires, and army authorities made no more than a pretense of enforcing the standing rule against destroying fences. In one regiment it was remembered that when the column halted for the night, with the men eagerly spotting the wealth of rails in the nearest field, the colonel, before they broke ranks, would sternly call out: "Now, boys, I don't want to see one of you touch a rail." He would then face in the opposite direction, keeping his gaze fixed on the distant hills, resolutely seeing nothing while his men took the fences completely to pieces.[13]

Now and then the private soldier would encounter the aristocratic spirit of the Old Dominion in all of its pristine freshness. As the army got down to the North Anna River, a regiment was sent across at Jericho Ford, and hostile Confederates were believed to be very near, so the regiment formed line of battle in a well-tilled garden just behind a pleasant country house. As the men fell into place in this garden, examining muskets and cartridges to see if they had been dampened by the ford, an elderly woman came out of the house to lodge a dignified protest:

"Gentlemen, why have you come? Mr. Lee is not here. You are spoiling my garden."

The men chuckled and paid little attention until the colonel finally ordered: "Boys, keep between the rows." [14]

The inevitable foraging on defenseless civilians seems to have been kept to a minimum. There were dairy herds in this area, however, and the men did want fresh milk, and they occasionally tried to get it for themselves. (The average soldier in those days knew how to milk a cow.) This did not always work out very well. A Massachusetts soldier explained why: "To hold a dipper with one hand and milk with the other, particularly when three other hands were endeavoring to do the same thing on the same cow, and she unwilling to stand still, required a degree of skill that few of us possessed." [15]

The farmers' worst troubles probably came because both

armies had by now acquired the habit of digging trenches the moment they halted. Any position where a brigade stopped might easily become the scene of a fight, and the great virtues of an entrenched position had by now become visible to everyone. It was rarely necessary for an officer to tell the men to entrench. Usually they began digging even before they started to boil their coffee.

Every division carried axes and spades in its ammunition wagons, but the men rarely waited for these to be brought forward. They would begin the work by themselves, using bayonets, sharpened pieces of wood, and any small tools they might carry with them. All of this digging did not improve the farmers' fields very much, and a Philadelphia veteran reflected on the loss that was involved. One day, he said, his division fell into line on a well-cultivated farm and put in several hours digging a long, deep trench, tearing down a barn and several outbuildings that stood in the way. No sooner was this finished than the presence of Rebel forces was reported off on the flank, so a new trench was dug at right angles to the first. By the time it was finished the enemy had changed front again, and so a third line was constructed—after which orders to move were brought in and the division marched away, leaving the luckless farmer with fields that were completely crisscrossed by deep ditches. What the farmer ever did about it the soldier was quite unable to imagine.[16]

The Confederates had learned about digging trenches, too —had in fact learned it before the Federals did. It was an axiom by now that if the Rebels had half a day in any given position they would build good fieldworks, and if they were given an extra twenty-four hours they would get dug in so completely that they could not possibly be pushed out. The private soldier was getting war-wise, and if he was called on to attack an entrenched position, he could usually tell at a glance whether the attack had any chance to succeed. It was commonly said in the army that the heavy artillerists had suffered heavy losses in the Spotsylvania fight largely because the men were so green: they had advanced to attack the enemy in solid ranks, worrying about keeping their alignment and fussing over parade-ground details, and thereby had presented a target the Southern marksmen could not miss. Veteran troops would have spread themselves out, going forward in short rushes, lying down between volleys and protecting themselves as they fought.[17]

For a number of days the army's existence consisted of a series of attempts to get around Lee's flank so that there could be fighting after the old manner, with nobody hidden in trenches and every Rebel out in the open where he could conveniently be shot. This never quite happened, since Lee could move just as fast as Grant could move, and the Confederates knew the country better; and there was a confused, meaningless series of little fights for river crossings and road centers—little only by comparison with what had gone before, big enough for the men directly involved, in their casualty lists and their drain on energies.

As always, the pickets made close contact, and one day across a stream some Confederates asked Wisconsin soldiers why they had come down to steal the slaves of men who had done them no harm. The Westerners replied that they did not care about slavery: all that concerned them was to save the Union.

"You-all aren't Yankees," cried a Confederate. "You 'uns and we 'uns ought to go together in this war and let the Yankees go by themselves!"[18]

Strange new names were entered on the army's annals—Ox Ford and Quarles Mill and Jericho Ford, and the other crossings of the North Anna River; roads down to the Pamunkey, places like Hawes's Shop and Bethesda Church, and the rambling network of highways that led to a desolate crossroads known as Cold Harbor. In all of these places there was fighting, and before and after each fight there was a forced march, and the army neither won nor lost as it moved on. It added to its knowledge and to its losses, and it got deeper and deeper into Virginia, but it never quite got around the end of the Rebel army and the big showdown was always somewhere ahead.

The army had conquered nothing and it possessed not a foot of Virginia soil except the ground on which it actually stood. All the way back to the Rapidan, Virginia was still Confederate territory, and the men who strayed past the army lines to the rear were quite as likely to be shot or captured as if they had strayed out to the front. Rebel cavalry roamed far and wide, and it was assisted by pestiferous bands of guerillas—informal groups of semiofficial mounted men, who were peace-loving farmers half of the time and blood-thirsty raiders the rest of the time. These bands covered all of the rear, and no wagon train could pass between the army and the river bases north of Fredericksburg without a strong escort.

Grant scorned to look behind him. To keep a safe supply line open all the way back to Belle Plain and Aquia Creek on the Potomac would take too many fighting men away from the front, so he simply refused to try. When the army left Spotsylvania the bases on the Potomac were closed. For the time being a new base was opened at Port Royal, downstream from Fredericksburg on the Rappahannock. That was closer to the army, and as soon as the distance back to Port Royal became too great a new base could be opened at White House, on the Pamunkey. Later, if things went well, there could even be a base on the James River itself. Whatever happened, the army would no longer be tied to the Potomac by a long, cumbersome wagon train.

There was significance in this, for names can be important. At the beginning of the war the army had been named the Army of the Potomac, and the overtones of that name had never been forgotten. Above everything else, the army had been the shield of Washington, standing near the Potomac River to defend the capital. Now the ties had been cut. The army had left the river from which it took its name, and it was not going to see that river again while the war lasted. It was going south—going glacially, destroying itself as it destroyed other things, but moving with inevitability. Except in its name, which it wore proudly, like a battle flag prized all the more because weather has stained it and bullets have cut it, it was no longer the Army of the Potomac. The Potomac had become a backwater. Hereafter the rear was going to have to take care of itself.

That meant problems for the rear echelon, and these problems were borne largely by a strange little detachment of hopelessly crippled men who did not seem to think that mere physical disability need keep a man out of the army. These men, officially, were members of the 18th Regiment of the Veteran Reserve Corps, and they made up as unusual a fighting force as the United States ever armed and equipped for action.

Sometime earlier the authorities had meditated on the great loss of manpower involved in the discharge of wounded veterans who were still sound enough for light duty behind the lines, and they had organized a body which they called the Invalid Corps, which was recruited in army hospitals. Any wounded man who was permanently unfit for field service but who could still be moderately active might, if he chose, enlist in this Invalid Corps. Some thousands of wounded men joined up, and they were scattered all over the North—guarding prison camps and arsenals, acting as hospital guards, doing provost guard duty at draft offices, and so on. It was a sound idea, but it got off to a bad start. The name "Invalid Corps" grated on everybody, and the field troops poked a good deal of fun at it, and members of the corps asked to be sent back to the front or discharged outright rather than bear the title "Invalid." Also, the authorities in their wisdom had devised a uniform of delicate robin's-egg blue, which nobody liked. After a time, therefore, the organization was renamed the Veteran Reserve Corps and given regular army uniforms, and it settled down to do useful work.

There were different classifications within the corps. The most nearly fit men were enlisted in what was called the First Battalion, which meant that they could be used for noncombat garrison and guard duty. Below them came the Second Battalion, whose men were too crippled or enfeebled to carry muskets or move about freely on their feet and who accordingly were designated for the lightest kind of duty.

The 18th Regiment was composed of six companies of Second Battalion men—nearly 500 men, altogether—and ordinarily they would have had no business within fifty miles of the Potomac River bases. But Grant was running things these days and he had stern ideas about making use of army manpower, and so in mid-May the 18th Regiment was put on a transport in Washington and told to guard a batch of the priceless bounty men who were being shipped down to the army.

The colonel in charge of the 18th Regiment was dubious. He pointed out that his men were supposed to be too infirm to carry muskets at all, and that they certainly could not march. However, he supposed they could fire at deserters, if they had to, and so the men were lined up and equipped as regular infantry and they got on the boat and set sail. They were not very military-looking. Some of them were crippled in such a way that they could carry their muskets only on the right shoulder and some could carry them only on the left, and some could not wear cartridge boxes and had to stuff their ammunition in their pockets. Most of them were not hearty enough to carry the regulation forty rounds anyway, and could take only five or ten.

They disembarked, finally, at Belle Plain, where they were put on guard duty. They were badly needed. There were incoming drafts of recruits to look after, and there was a steady stream of Confederate prisoners to be guarded and sent north, and there was a vast accumulation of stores to watch over and keep safe from marauding guerilla bands. Ordinarily a few regiments of front-line troops would be detached for this work, but Grant had other uses for these and there was nobody to do the job but the cripples.

As long as they stayed at the base things were not too bad. To be sure, these disabled men had no pup tents or any other kind of shelter, and the weather was very rainy. Somebody had forgotten to supply them with any blankets, and they had no surgeon or medical stores. But they did their job, reporting proudly that they successfully guarded nearly 3,000 Rebel prisoners—two of these escaped, and one other tried it and got shot—and that all of the recruits and army stores were guarded without loss. Their real troubles began when the base was shifted to Port Royal.

By land, Port Royal was twenty-five miles away. The army liked to have its men go places under their own power if possible, and so when moving day came the regiment was lined up for inspection, to see how many men could make the march. Of the 474 men present, the doctors reported that 166 might possibly be able to do it, provided that they carried no knapsacks. (All of the officers reported themselves fit and refused to let the doctors examine them.) The rest were put on a transport to go down by water, and the shaky 166 set out on foot in a driving rainstorm.

Somehow, they made it. The column's best speed was one mile an hour. The road was infested with guerillas, and a general at Port Royal sent back an anxious message to the colonel of the 18th: Can your men fight, if the guerillas attack them? Back came the reply: "Tell the general that my men are cripples and so they can't run away." Fortunately, they did not have to fight. They plodded and staggered along, marching for fifteen minutes and then resting for ten, with officers going up and down the line pleading and coaxing all day long. After two days they finally got to Port Royal. The next morning, only 42 of the 166 were able to get on their feet and answer at roll call.

Later on, they actually did have a fight, one time when Wade Hampton took Confederate cavalry up for a wild swipe at the Federal base, and they made out very well, helping a handful of sound men to beat the raiders off. The rest of the time they did guard duty. By special dispensation, those who could not walk were allowed to sit down as they guarded their beats. After a month of it a medical board got a look at the regiment and reported in horror that four fifths of the men were not only unfit for any kind of duty but were actually unfit to be out of hospital beds. So the 18th Regiment of the Veteran Reserve Corps was finally sent back to Washington, leaving its brief record as testimony that it was a hard war that was being fought nowadays.[19]

A hard war, bringing changes, and there was no road back

any more. The only roads that were left led on into more fighting, and the army that followed these roads looked less and less like the army that had crossed the Rapidan a few weeks earlier. Famous old organizations were vanishing and famous old names were disappearing. What had once been Joe Hooker's division no longer existed, and the Iron Brigade was no longer recognizable. The 3rd Michigan, Phil Kearny's pet in the early days of the war, was going off the army roster, and the 12th Massachusetts would do likewise in a few days— it had taught the army and the nation to sing "Glory, Glory Hallelujah!" and to date it had had 792 battle casualties. The great 2nd Wisconsin, being reduced to fewer than 100 rank and file and having lost all of its field officers, was recalled from combat duty and assigned to the provost guard.[20]

After the war was over someone asked crusty Brigadier General Romeyn Ayres if his famous old division of Regulars was still in service at this time. Ayres replied that the Regulars had mostly been killed.

"I had regulars—what were known as the regular division— before I went into the battle of Gettysburg," he said. "I left half of them there, and buried the rest in the Wilderness. There were no regulars left." [21]

2. Judgment Trump of the Almighty

The rivers of eastern Virginia slant down toward the sea from the northwest. Some of them are wide and deep and some are quite insignificant except during time of heavy rains, but each one can be a barrier to a moving army. In the spring of 1864 the Army of the Potomac had to cross all of them, and the crossings could be made only where there were no defenders. These facts shaped the route of the army, and all through the month of May it moved in a series of wide zig-zags.

Wanting to go due south, the army was forever going

southeast in order to find a good place to cross a river. Having crossed, it would turn southwest to get back on the route, and presently it would run into the Confederate army and there would be a fight. Since the Confederates could not be driven away from one of these spots where they elected to make a stand, the Federal army after a time would move southeast once more, sagging away from the direct road to Richmond but sooner or later crossing another river and cutting back to the southwest again. It moved like a ponderous ship tacking against a strong wind—a long slant to the left, a short leg to the right, another beat to the left and another slogging drive to the right; and if progress was slow it was steady.[1]

Many rivers had been crossed—the Rapidan and the Ny, the North Anna and the Pamunkey. If the Army of the Potomac was constantly being pushed toward the east, it was also gaining ground toward the south. The Confederate army always stood between it and Richmond, but the distance to Richmond was growing shorter and shorter. As May came to an end, the two armies were facing each other in a flat, featureless country of little streams and low ridges and small farms, spotted here and there with bogs and interlaced by narrow, winding roads. There was just one more river to cross —the Chickahominy, which ran across the Confederate rear just five miles away. Five miles beyond the Chickahominy was Richmond itself.

It was good to be this close to Richmond, and although they had packed more fighting and hard marching into the last month than they usually saw in half a year, the men were feeling hopeful. They seemed to be getting somewhere, at last, and a Massachusetts soldier reflected that "no backward steps were being taken," which, he remarked, was a brand new experience. He went on: "The Army of the Potomac having been unaccustomed to the sunshine of victory, rejoiced at the change and became buoyant with hope. The discouragement that hitherto attended us vanished as our confidence in Grant increased." He remembered that his regiment marched by a railroad siding one day and saw Grant, his uniform all dusty and worn, perched on a flatcar gnawing at a ham bone; the men cheered, and Grant casually waved the bone in acknowledgment and went on eating.

One officer insisted: "Never were the men more hopeful or in better spirits, more willing for marching, more ready to fight, than at this time," and he said they had "an idea that we were still advancing, that there was a plan that would be carried out successfully." Another officer wrote that "the men cannot help feeling that the worst is over, now that our great leader has pushed the enemy almost to the wall," and a new recruit who joined up just after Spotsylvania wrote home that the veterans with whom he talked "place unbounded faith in General Grant." A man in the IX Corps, recalling that his regiment lost its flag in the fighting east of the Bloody Angle, told how the men talked about the loss and agreed finally that it was cause for pride rather than for shame, since it proved that they had been in a very hot place; and he added stoutly, "Be it considered a disgrace by whom it may, that does not make it one." [2]

Looking back on the campaign, men remembered a series of pictures which, as one soldier said, were "like the fragments of a half-forgotten dream, distinct in themselves but without any definite connection as to time or place." He sketched in a few of these fragments: "I see a long column of weary soldiers, winding along over hill and valley, in the night, gliding past a stately mansion, with beautiful grounds and shaded walks, and everywhere the freshness and fragrance of spring. Again I see a line of battle stretching out across an open field, the men resting lazily in the ranks. A little to the left, near some shade trees, stands a battery ready for action, the guns pointing toward some unseen enemy beyond. It is noon, and the sunlight is pouring down upon the scene, bright and clear." [3]

If they were close to Richmond at last, and feeling good about it, the Rebels were always in front of them, ready for business. Furthermore, the field of maneuver was growing very narrow. The army could no longer swing back and forth in wide arcs, going twenty miles to one side in order to get

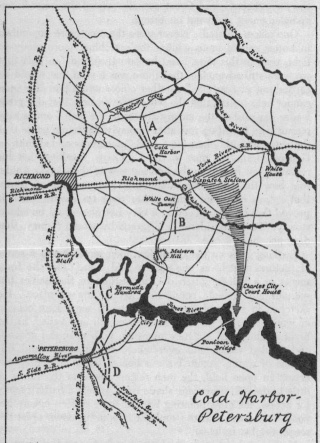

Dotted lines show opposing Union-Confederate lines
A   At Cold Harbor. Arrows indicate attacks of June 3
B   Federal cavalry and V Corps screening move to the James from Lee's army
C   Bermuda Hundred lines, where Ben Butler was bottled up
D   Attack on Petersburg, June 15-18
Broad shaded arrow shows movement of Army of the Potomac to James River

five miles forward. This was coffin corner, and there was little room to sidestep. Any road that was taken now had to lead to Richmond, and all of the roads to Richmond were blocked by pugnacious Southerners, who had trenches and gun pits wherever there was high ground.

Right now the Confederates were dug in behind the headwaters of Totopotomoy Creek, an insignificant watercourse whose turns and swampy banks offered good defensive ground. The chance of breaking this line looked no better than in the Wilderness or at Spotsylvania. It was better to go around the line than to try to go through it, and to go around it would be harder here than it had been before.

Down below the Federal left, within a mile or so of the Chickahominy, there was another of those seedy taverns that dotted the Virginia landscape—a quiet place at a sleepy crossroads, the name of it Cold Harbor, perched unobtrusively on a highway that wandered up from the Federal supply base, back at White House on the Pamunkey, and went on to cross the Chickahominy and go to Richmond.

This war went by a queer script of its own, and it had a way of putting all of its weight down on some utterly unimportant little spot that no one had ever heard of before—Shiloh Church, or Chancellorsville, or some such—and because armies contended for them, those place names became great and terrible. Now there was Cold Harbor, a wide spot on a lonely dusty road, set in a broad plain that was furrowed by tedious ravines and went rolling off to a chain of low hills on the south and west.

The weather was hot and the landscape looked barren, and a Federal officer who visited the place wondered how it had ever got its name. There was no harbor within miles, and the place was far from cold—was, in fact, as he reflected, very much like a bake oven—and the roads were ankle-deep in powdery dust that hung in low, choking clouds whenever a marching column went by, and it seemed that no man in his senses would ever want to come here. Years afterward, a veteran remarked that of all of the battlefields of the war, Cold

Harbor was the one spot he had never heard any old soldier express a desire to revisit.[4]

Cold Harbor lay beyond the flanks of the armies. If the Federals were going to side-step once more they would have to come through here. Conversely, if the Confederates planned a countermove of their own this was a good spot for them to take, because if they held this crossroads they would be closer to the Yankee base at White House than the Yankees were themselves. So as May came to an end the storm clouds of the war drifted down to Cold Harbor, with a hurricane of fire to sweep the dreary plain, and the name of the run-down little tavern became a name to remember forever.

The cavalry got there first. Phil Sheridan had led his horsemen back to the Army of the Potomac a week earlier after a wild, eventful swing that took him to the very edge of Richmond. He had destroyed a good deal of Confederate property, he had released certain captured Yankees who had been on their way to the Richmond prisons, he had had a big fight with the Confederate cavalry—and he had done one of the grim things that had to be done if the Confederacy was to die: he had killed Jeb Stuart. Now the raid was over and cavalry was back on the job again, and on May 31 Sheridan brought two mounted divisions cross country, shook them out into a line of battle, and drove them yelling and clattering over the crossroads.

Confederate troops were already there. Lee and Grant had simultaneously realized the need to occupy this spot, and Rebel cavalry stiffened with infantry had come on the scene just in time to meet Sheridan's hard drive. Sheridan's men forced them out—they had at last turned from mere raiders into hard men of war, these cavalrymen, and their magazine carbines gave them prodigious fire power at close range, and they got off their horses and fought on foot and got a grip on the flat land around the crossroads, sending the Confederate advance guard back in defeat.

Lee was not going to take this meekly, and he sent in a fresh division of infantry to drive Sheridan's troopers out. The troopers hung on, working the levers of their carbines fast and kicking up the dust with low-flying bullets, and when evening came Sheridan sent back word that he did not think his men could stay where they were. He was told to stay anyway because Federal infantry would be up shortly, and while the dismounted cavalrymen dug in their heels and fought, couriers rode northeast to where General Wright had his VI Corps, on the right end of the Yankee line, and told him to get his men around to Cold Harbor as fast as they could travel.[5]

The Army of the Potomac had moved by its left many times in this campaign, but it always did it in reverse order; if the army had simply faced to its left and started marching it would have invited a ruinous flank attack. On a shift to the left, the first troops to move were always those on the extreme right. They would fade back, move around behind the army, and come up on the other end of the line.

So it was today. The VI Corps held the right; now it left its trenches and during the night and early morning it went slogging along through choking dust which raised a foul, strangling cloud over every regiment and made it impossible to see the length of a company. Intermittent messages kept coming from Sheridan—hurry up, hurry up, cavalry alone can't hold this position much longer—and one of Wright's staff officers who rode on ahead to Cold Harbor found Sheridan "the most nervy, wiry incarnation of business, and business only, I had yet met." The men remembered this march as about the worst they ever made, and when they got to Cold Harbor in mid-morning of June 1, dirt-caked and completely worn out, they were happy to find that the firing had died down. They formed line of battle, an empty echoing plain before them, and most of the men dropped in their tracks and fell into a drugged sort of sleep.[6]

Reinforcements were coming. Down on the James River Butler's army was huddling ingloriously in its haven at Bermuda Hundred, and Grant had notified Butler that if he could not fight there he could at least send some of his men up to help the Army of the Potomac. So General Baldy Smith put 16,000 men on transports and took them down the James, around Point Comfort, and up the Pamunkey to White House. He was under orders to get down to Cold Harbor as fast as he could, and he should have reached the place while Sheridan's fight was going on, but there had been a mixup in his orders and he made a wearing, useless march up the river before higher authority caught up with him and put him on the right track. Late in the afternoon of June 1, Smith's men came down to the crossroads by the tavern and began to file into line on the right of the VI Corps—very tired, short of ammunition and artillery, with a great many stragglers wandering about on the lost roads somewhere off to the rear.[7]

The plain was covered with dust raised by the marching men, and the dust hung in the air like a gritty cloud bank. The artillery began to hammer at the Confederate works, half a mile away, and the smoke mingled with the dust and the setting sun looked dull-red and enormous through the haze. As the reinforcements moved in, Wright's men roused themselves reluctantly. A Connecticut soldier tugged the arm of a sleeping comrade and told him: "Jim, there's a pile of troops coming. I guess there's going to be a fight." Jim blinked and declared: "I don't care a damn. I wish they'd shoot us and be done with it. I'd rather be shot than marched to death."[8]

It was remembered later that the men seemed stupid with weariness as they formed line of battle, and the feverish excitement that often ran through a body of men lining up for a charge was missing. The road from Cold Harbor toward Richmond led off between fields and little plots of woodland toward the rising ground where the Rebels were waiting, and the road served as the guide line for the attack, with Wright's troops on the left of it and Smith's on the right. The men got under way at last, and where the ground began to rise they came on the entanglement of felled trees and sharpened saplings which the Rebels had put thirty yards in front of their firing line. As the Federals began to tear this apart the Southern riflemen opened fire with one long, rolling volley—"a sheet of flame, sudden as lightning, red as blood, and so near that it seemed to singe the men's faces," one survivor described it. Up and down the front of the two army corps the attacking lines wavered, and here and there men turned and ran for the rear. Then the lines surged forward again, and on the slopes near the Richmond road Ricketts's division and some of Smith's men broke into the Rebel works, taking prisoners and sending the rest of the defenders flying.

Ricketts's men were out to redeem themselves. They were Milroy's weary boys from the valley, the ones who had broken and fled in panic in the Wilderness fight, and the rest of the VI Corps had let them know that they were accounted second-rate soldiers not worthy of belonging to a good fighting corps. Ricketts had been nursing them along ever since, and he seems to have pulled them together and made soldiers out of them, and on this evening their division was the only unit in the VI Corps that gained its objective. To right and left the Confederate line held firm, and as the evening deepened into a wild twilight there was a furious fire fight.

Emory Upton had his brigade up close to the enemy, as usual—he had just learned that he was being promoted brigadier general because of his feat at Spotsylvania—and in line with the gospel he had been preaching he was on the firing line personally, helping his men to beat off a sharp Rebel counterattack. One of his regiments, the 2nd Connecticut Heavy Artillery, began to waver, and Upton galloped into the middle of it, shouting: "Men of Connecticut, stand by me! We *must* hold this line!" The wavering stopped and the regiment held, and one soldier remembered seeing Upton, dismounted, standing in the front rank firing an infantry musket. When one disheartened officer came up to report that he did not think his command could drive the Rebels back, Upton snarled at him: "If they come there, catch them on your bayonets and pitch them over your heads!" [9]

Darkness came at last and the fighting died away, and the Federals dug in where they were and counted their losses. These were fairly heavy—a total of some 2,200 for the two army corps—but the Confederates had had substantial losses, too, and 750 Southern prisoners were on their way back to the provost marshal's stockade. All in all, the day's action had been a success. The Confederates had been driven out of Cold Harbor and the Federal grip there was secure. Also, it appeared that this might be a good jumping-off point for a major attack.

Cold Harbor was not far from the Chickahominy, and there was no more room for shifting to the left. But the place was right on the Confederate flank, and while Lee had sent a good many troops down here they had been kept very busy and it did not seem probable that they could have built a strong defensive line. If there was any place along the line where an attack might succeed, it was right here, and success here would be dazzling because the Chickahominy ran across the Confederate rear and a beaten army trying to retreat fast across that river would be in dire trouble. Here, perhaps, was where the blow that would end the war could be struck. On top of these considerations there was the obvious fact that a blow could not very well be struck anywhere else. It was either fight here or develop a whole new campaign.[10]

These points had great weight, and Grant considered them and decided accordingly—which is to say that he ordered an all-out attack for daylight the next morning, with Wright's and Smith's corps to be reinforced by the twenty-odd thousand in Hancock's command, and with the rest of the army throwing its weight in where it was. Yet between a decision by the lieutenant general commanding and the ultimate appearance on the firing line of the soldiers who must make that decision effective there were many separate steps, and at Cold Harbor all of these were steps leading down into great darkness. There is a house-that-Jack-built quality to the tale: this went wrong because that went wrong, and that went wrong because of what happened just before, and that in turn. . . . Attitudes of mind and habits of thought formed when Cold Harbor was as remote as the mountains of the moon were still at work, each one affecting what was going to happen next, all of them put together forming a recipe for disaster.

Whatever was going to be done would have to be done very quickly. The whole idea was that at half-past four on the morning of June 2 the Confederates facing Cold Harbor would be off balance, unprepared to resist a solid blow. That assumption might well be correct; and yet it was as certain as anything could be certain that the Confederates would not stay off balance or unprepared very long, and that what was possible at dawn might be utterly impossible by midafternoon. The big attack that was set for dawn, in other words, had better take place at dawn and not at some other time.

But the reflexes of the chain of command in the Army of the Potomac had never yet been trained for speed. There was power here, and bravery, and simple determination— but the furious, implacable insistence on doing simple things quickly was not there at all. It had been bred out of the army in the leisurely days of 1862, when half a month one way or the other did not seem to make very much difference and the delay of a mere day or so did not make any difference at all, and nothing that the tough little man from the West had been able to do had changed things very much.

In all the history of this army, no general had yet been disciplined for being just a little bit late. Back of almost every defeat there was the story of chances lost because some commander had not done what he set out to do with the necessary vigor and speed. The assumption always seems to have been that the man on the firing line would somehow make up for all slackness and all delays.

In other ways, too, the generals had been brought up wrong. The tradition they had learned was that of close-order fighting in open country, where men with bayonets bravely charged a line of men firing smooth-bore muskets. That used to work well enough, because the range at which defenders could begin to kill their assailants was very short. Between the moment when charging men got into that range and the moment when they actually reached the enemy line, the defenders could fire no more than one or two shots apiece. Given a proper advantage in numbers, a charging line was bound to get to close quarters provided the men could just stand the gaff during the last hundred yards of their advance.

But the rifle came in and it changed all of that. The range at which charging men began to be killed was at least five times as great as it used to be, which meant that about five times as many of the assailants were likely to be hit. Furthermore, men on the defense had learned how to dig deep, solid trenches instead of standing up unprotected in the open; and the trench and the rifle put together meant that the old tradition was as dead as Hannibal. A few men, like young Colonel Upton, sensed that new tactics were called for, but most men could not quite get the idea. The way to beat the enemy was to pile into him head on, and if a great many men were killed that way it could not be helped because to get killed was the soldier's hard fate and it would never be any other way.[11]

The hard fact was that by 1864 good troops using rifles and standing in well-built trenches, and provided with suitable artillery support, simply could not be dislodged by any frontal assault whatever. This fact had been visible on many previous occasions, if anyone had thought about it. At Gettysburg, Slocum's brigades held solid log trenches on Culp's Hill, and in the reports their officers submitted after the battle there is evident a sort of dazed bewilderment that the men had been able to wreck a whole Rebel army corps at comparatively small cost. One Union general found 1,200 dead Southerners in front of his line, estimated that four times that many had been wounded, and noted that the trenches "rendered our casualties surprisingly incompatible with so terrible and prolonged an engagement." The same thing had been true, with the shoe on the other foot, at Spotsylvania. Meade's chief of staff assessed the fighting there and wrote that behind trenches "the strength of an army sustaining an attack was more than quadrupled"; then he revised his estimate upward and said that "there is scarcely any measure by which to gauge the increased strength" conferred by good earthworks.[12]

Yet although this lesson was obvious it was not being applied. A subtle weakness infected the system of command. Something was always going wrong, someone was forever leaving something undone, the loose ends were never quite tied up in time. The experience at Spotsylvania was the classic example. When the big attack on the salient was made no one really knew where the enemy was, how the land lay, or what the defenses were like. The man who had to lead the charge was at last forced to ask, in bitter jest, that someone at least point him in the right direction so that he might not miss the Rebel army entirely.

Taken as a group, the generals on whom the army's success depended so greatly seem to have slipped back during the campaign; or perhaps they simply stood still while the war moved on ahead of them. They were used to a war of successive broad panoramas, in which a corps commander could always find some spot from which he could get a fairly good general view of his whole line. Now there were no more panoramas and it was never possible for anyone to see more than a fraction of the field. If a general rode up front for a closer survey there was nothing for him to see but the backs of a few of his skirmishers. Trench warfare was new to everybody and it provided unheard-of complications for an army acting on the offensive. What used to be done visually had to be done nowadays with maps. (Just to make things worse, practically all of the maps owned by the Federal commanders contained very bad errors.)

In effect, the army was fighting blindfolded and most of the generals knew little more than the men in the ranks knew. A IX Corps soldier wrote that the whole campaign was confusing: "Of the previous movements we had been able to form some conception; but the operations since crossing the Pamunkey, conducted rapidly in jungles, swamps and labyrinths of forest; in storm and darkness; by marches and counter-marches, advances and withdrawals—all seemed

to us to be conducted without consistent plan or purpose."
The generals could have said the same thing. Indeed, Meade
did say it, complaining that in this country he had to fight
a regular battle just to conduct an ordinary reconnoissance.[13]

Meade's temper was getting worse than ever. At Cold
Harbor on June 1 he was denouncing Warren and Wright
—the one for moving without orders, the other for moving
too slowly with orders—and he was complaining angrily that
the corps commanders ought to act for themselves and not
lean constantly on army headquarters. At this untimely moment, one of Baldy Smith's staff officers came in to report
that Smith had arrived with his troops but had brought
little ammunition and no transportation and considered his
position precarious.

"Then why in hell," demanded Meade, "did he come at
all?" [14]

The big job on the evening of June 1 was to get Hancock
and his II Corps around to Cold Harbor in time for the
dawn attack, and the orders breathed unusual urgency:
"You must make every exertion to move promptly and reach
Cold Harbor as soon as possible. . . . Every confidence is
felt that your gallant corps of veterans will move with vigor
and endure the necessary fatigue." An engineer officer was
sent to lead the march, and just after sunset the movement
began.

The II Corps had no better luck with its guide here than
at Spotsylvania. Since the march would be long the engineer officer undertook to lead the corps on a short cut along
an unmapped woods road, and this road was not good.
There was profound darkness under the trees, and the dust
rose in unbelievable clouds, and the road grew narrower
and narrower until it was no more than a path and the corps
artillery finally got jammed in between the trees and could
go neither backward nor forward.

The long column piled up, and in the dusty darkness
regiments and brigades intermingled, and the still air was
very hot. Officers rode back and forth, colliding with trees
and falling down invisible banks, and it was too dark for

anyone to identify them or for them to see the troops they were trying to straighten out, and organization dissolved completely. Eventually, most of the troops had to countermarch by another road, and what was supposed to be a ninemile hike turned out to be fifteen miles.[15]

The corps was to be in position to assault at daybreak, which at that time of year meant around 4:30 in the morning, but by seven o'clock it was just beginning to come up to Cold Harbor, blue uniforms all Rebel gray with dust, stragglers strewn all over the line of march, everyone too blown to do more than put one heavy foot ahead of another. One of Meade's staff commented that a fifteen-mile march at night was more tiring than a twenty-five-mile march by daylight, and he added that these soldiers were all worn out before the march even began: "Our men no longer have the bodily strength they had a month before; indeed, why they are alive I don't see." [16] To make an immediate attack was plainly out of the question, and Meade ordered the fight postponed until four in the afternoon.

But in the afternoon things looked no better. The battered VI Corps was in place along the Richmond road, ready to go, but General Smith on the VI Corps' right was telling headquarters that what with battle losses and heavy straggling he had only 9,000 men in line of the 16,000 soldiers he had brought up from Bermuda Hundred, and if the Rebels should attack him he was not sure that he could hold his position. "An attack by me," he added, "would be simply preposterous." Beyond Smith's men, innumerable adjustments had to be made in the positions of Warren's and Burnside's corps, and they were doing a good deal of marching to and fro to get into new positions—being considerably pestered, the while, by intermittent Confederate stabs and thrusts—and it began to seem best to have those two corps act on the defensive and hold their positions while the fight was made at Cold Harbor.

At last, unable to get the unwieldy machine moving properly, headquarters ordered another postponement and fixed the hour of attack for daybreak on June 3. Darkness came, and there were bursts of rain, turning now and then into hail. All along the disordered lines the men dropped off to sleep, lying face down on the ground in the wet, glad that it was raining because it would lay the dust and cut the heat, dimly conscious that a good many things had been going wrong.[17]

Much had gone wrong, and what mattered most was that the attack was going to be twenty-four hours late. An assault at dawn on June 2 might possibly have succeeded, since on that morning the Rebels in front of Cold Harbor had not had time to get set for it. An assault at dawn on June 3 would not have a chance in the world to succeed, and the felony was compounded by the fact that nobody in particular had thought to study the lay of the land and the position of the Confederate defenses.[18] The Union army had spent the twenty-four hours of delay chiefly in wearing itself out; the Confederates had used the time with enormous industry and clever engineering skill to build a network of trenches, gun emplacements, and skirmishers' pits like nothing the Army of the Potomac had ever encountered before.

It was no simple line of breastworks that the army was going to attack in the morning. From the Chickahominy swamps all the way to the Totopotomoy, the Confederate line on the morning of June 3 was cunningly and elaborately designed to take advantage of every ravine, knoll, and hillock, every bog and water course, every clump of trees and patch of brambles, so that unending cross fires could be laid on all possible avenues of approach. A newspaper correspondent wrote of these lines: "They are intricate, zig-zagged lines within lines, lines protecting flanks of lines, lines built to enfilade an opposing line, lines within which lies a battery . . . a maze and labyrinth of works within works and works without works, each laid out with some definite design either of defense or offense." [19]

The ground was deceptive. The Confederate works lay on an uneven chain of low hills and ridges, none of them high enough to look frightening, all of them just high enough to be ideal for defensive purposes. There was hardly a spot

on the front which could not be hit by rifle fire and artillery
fire from dead ahead and from both sides. The very pickets
and skirmishers were dug in, and to make matters worse the
Union front at Cold Harbor bowed out slightly, so that
advancing units would follow diverging paths and would
expose their flanks to heavy fire.[20]

Neither Grant nor Meade had ordered anybody to make
a detailed survey of the ground. Apparently they assumed
that the corps commanders would do that as a matter of
routine. The assumption was wrong, since corps routine in
the Army of the Potomac did not extend to such matters,
and so nobody knew anything of any consequence about
what lay ahead. All that was certain was that 40,000 men
in three army corps were to begin marching toward Richmond at dawn. What they were going to run into along the
way was something they would have to find out for themselves.

The rain stopped just before dawn, and as the sky grew
lighter it was clear, with a promise of heat. Gunners in the
Federal gun emplacements could just see and hear the infantry columns moving forward in the dim light. A moment
later they saw orderlies come back, leading riderless horses,
by which they knew that the regimental and brigade commanders were going in on foot. The light grew stronger, and
half a mile ahead the men could see the main line of Confederate works—an uneven tracing of raw earth across the
fields and through the groves, looking empty but somehow
ominous. Then couriers came spurring up to battery commanders, and on the II Corps front one cannon was fired
as a signal, and along three miles of gun pits the men ran
to their places.

A gigantic crash of artillery broke the morning quiet just
as the crackle of skirmishers' fire began. Suddenly the
empty-looking Rebel trenches were dotted with black slouch
hats and thousands of musket barrels, long sheets of flame
ran from end to end of the trench lines, an immense cloud
of smoke blotted out the sight of them, and the rocking
volume of sound dazed men who had been in the war's worst

battles. One of Hancock's gunners wrote, in awe: "It had the fury of the Wilderness musketry with the thunders of the Gettysburg artillery super-added. It was simply terrific." [21]

This was the army's major offensive, the culmination of a month's bloody campaigning, and it was not one fight but many fights: a conglomeration of charges by individual brigades rather than one massed assault. There was no one line of battle, wide and deep, each part supporting all the rest. Instead there were many separate assaults, all going forward at once, each one more or less isolated from the others, so that every unit felt that it was advancing unaided into the very center of the strongest enemy line it had ever seen.

Hancock had three divisions of infantry, and he sent two of them in with the third held back for support. The divisions promptly separated. Barlow took his men in with two brigades in front, and these swept across a sunken road, beating down the Southern skirmishers who held it, and charged on and broke into the main line of Confederate works, capturing several hundred prisoners and three guns and, for an incredible instant, making it look as if they were going to win an amazing success. Yet the ground just behind them was swept by a terrible cross fire from Confederates off to the right and left, and when the support troops tried to come forward they were broken and driven back, and Barlow's two leading brigades were isolated.

From both sides Rebel gunners were sending shell and solid shot plowing the length of the captured trench with murderous effect, and from the ground ahead of Barlow's men, massed infantry plastered them with an unbearable volume of musket fire. The men stayed there as long as they could, but it was not very long, and in a few minutes they ran back, crouched down behind a low swelling in the ground, and with bayonets and tin cups began frantically to dig in. They had done their best, and instead of retreating to the starting place they were valiantly hanging on within a few rods of the Confederate line, but they had not opened the road to Richmond.

On their right, Gibbon's division had even worse luck. It set out bravely enough, the veterans knowing full well that they were going into a death trap but setting their teeth and going forward anyway. As the lines moved into range of the Confederate fire the color-bearer of the 19th Massachusetts was shot, and the regimental commander told Corporal Mike Scannell to pick up the flag and carry it. Mike promptly declined, explaining: "Too many corporals have already been killed carrying colors." The commander blinked at him, and then promised: "I'll make you a sergeant on the spot." "That's business," said the corporal. "I'll carry the colors." So he picked up the flag and the regiment went on.[22]

Two hundred yards from the starting point Gibbon's division hit a deep swamp whose existence nobody had known about, and the swamp split the line in two, half of the men going to one side and half to the other. The swamp grew wider as the men advanced and the separated halves of the line could not rejoin, and in the swamp there were many snipers who took a heavy toll, and in the end two separated brigades went staggering up to the invulnerable trenches. One of these brigades got onto the Rebel line very briefly —there is memory of a colonel standing on the parapet, swinging his sword and shouting to his men to come on. But the colonel went down, his lifeless body draped across the parapet, and he was hit thereafter by so many stray bullets that when a truce was declared a few days later he could be identified only by the buttons on his sleeve. The other men who got up to the line did not fare much better than he did, and the attack collapsed a few seconds after it had touched the breastworks. The other brigade never reached the line—partly, it was said, because it contained many new troops who went charging in with great dash and much cheering, anxious to prove themselves, and who made such excellent targets of themselves that they were destroyed before they got within fifty yards of their enemies.

Gibbon tried to bring his rear brigades up to help, but orders got mixed somehow and the men were sent in wrong,

and in any case the Confederates had an artillery cross fire
that made it impossible for them to advance, and one brigade retreated with no surviving officer of higher rank than
captain. Inside of twenty minutes Gibbon's whole attack was
a flat failure, with more than a thousand casualties. A staff
officer noted with admiration that the beaten men did not
run for the rear, as usually happened when an assault failed.
Like Barlow's soldiers, they simply found places where the
ground offered a little protection and began to scrape out
foxholes for themselves, keeping up such fire as they could,
while far to their rear the Federal artillery thundered and
crashed in a vain effort to beat down the Confederate fire.[23]

On Wright's front the story was about the same, except
that the lines of attack were repelled more quickly. The
men found themselves advancing into what seemed to be
a semicircle of Rebel trenches, with guns a mile away smiting their flanks with shell while the everlasting riflemen in
front fired as if they all owned repeaters. The VI Corps by
now was accounted the stoutest fighting corps in the army,
but it could do nothing whatever. Along most of the corps
front no more than ten minutes elapsed from the moment
the men began their charge to the moment when those who
had not been hit started to burrow for shelter. Dense thickets and impassable briar patches, and little bogs which no
man could cross, broke the lines into fragments, and the
commands were all disconnected. "And all the time," one
soldier remembered, "there was poured from the rebel lines,
which we could not see, those volleys of hurtling death." [24]

If it was possible for anything to be worse than what was
happening to Hancock's and Wright's men, it was what was
happening to Smith's undermanned brigades. At the right
and left of his line Smith had found the ground so bad that
a major assault hardly seemed possible, but in the center
a shallow ravine offered some protection and he put the
weight of his attack there. The men ran out of the sheltering hollow in column of regiments, with the 12th New
Hampshire in front, its colonel waving a ramrod for baton
in place of his sword, and like the other columns the men

felt that they were charging into the center of a great flaming crescent, with guns and musketry hitting them from three sides at once.

A New Hampshire captain confessed afterward: "To give a description of this terrible charge is simply impossible, and few who were in the ranks of the 12th will ever feel like attempting it. To those exposed to the full force and fury of that dreadful storm of lead and iron that met the charging column, it seemed more like a volcanic blast than a battle, and was just about as destructive." A sergeant said that the men involuntarily bent forward as they advanced, as if they were walking into a driving hailstorm, and he related that they fell "like rows of blocks or bricks pushed over by striking against one another."

One man remembered that as he ran forward he suddenly saw all of his comrades drop to the ground, and he thought that someone had passed the order for everyone to lie down, so he did the same. His company commander came over, indignant, and began prodding the prostrate men with his sword, trying to get them to rise and resume the charge. He got nowhere, because they were all dead, and as another officer remarked, "nothing but the judgment trump of the Almighty would ever bring those men upon their feet again." Another man, marching forward at the right of his company, glanced to his left, saw no comrades, and assumed he had fallen a few paces behind. He hurried forward, only to find himself in another company; everybody else in his own line had been shot down.

In the dust and the smoke the men of this assaulting column never once saw their enemies, although they were charging across open ground. They saw nothing but a line of flashing fire and billowing smoke that seemed almost to close behind them as they advanced, and the musketry fire was so unbroken that it seemed "like one continual crash of thunder."

Altogether, it took the Confederates rather less than a quarter of an hour to break this attack and destroy the attacking column, and it is quite conceivable that in this particular fight the Rebels lost no men whatever. A few days later, when men met between the lines during a truce to bury the dead, a Confederate officer told one of the New Hampshire men: "It seemed almost like murder to fire upon you." [25]

And this, strangely and terribly enough, was the battle of Cold Harbor—a wild chain of doomed charges, most of which were smashed in five or ten minutes and none of which lasted more than half an hour. In all the war, no attack had ever been broken up as quickly or as easily as this, nor had men ever before been killed so rapidly. The half hour's work had cost the Union army 7,000 men.[26]

Yet if the attack was quickly over, the fighting did not end. For the most amazing thing of all in this fantastic battle is the fact that all along the front the beaten men did not pull back to the rear. They stayed where they were, anywhere from 40 to 200 yards from the Confederate line, gouged out such shallow trenches as they could, and kept on firing. Behind them the artillery continued to hammer away relentlessly, and all day long the terrible sound of battle continued. Only an experienced soldier could tell, by the sound alone, that the pitch of the combat in midafternoon was any lower than it had been in the murky dawn when the charges were being repulsed.

The fighting went on and on, only now it was carried on by men who had just taken the worst beating of the war, men who lay on their bellies in the dust, a sheet of Rebel bullets just overhead, piling little mounds of earth in front of them, rolling behind these to load, and firing as best they could. Now and then orders came up from the rear—brought by officers or couriers who crept across the open on their hands and knees—to renew the assault. When such orders came the men would fire a little faster than before, but no one would get up to charge. They were not being mutinous about it; getting up was simply impossible.

The long day wore away, and the heat and the flaming guns seared the great plain, and wounded men between the lines were hit and broken apart by the flying bullets and the exploding shell. One of Grant's staff officers rode up on a little hill and looked forward through his field glasses. An officer of a battery of field artillery posted on the hill asked him, sarcastically, if he could see Richmond. The staff man said that he could not, but that he expected to be able to do so very soon.

"Better get the barrels of that glass rifled, so they'll carry farther," said the gunner.

That night a private in the VI Corps wrote to his parents:

"If there is ever again any rejoicing in the world it will be when this war is over. One who has never been under fire has no idea of war." [27]

3. Secondhand Clothes

Life began with the darkness. All day long the men out in front huddled close to the ground, dust in their teeth, a glaring sun pressing on their shoulders. To peer over the rim of earth that lay between the firing line and the enemy was to ask for a bullet, and it was almost certain death to try to go to the rear for any reason at all—to have a wound dressed, to get food, to fill a canteen with muddy warm water, or to attend to a call of nature. Death was everywhere, its unspeakable scent in every breath men drew, the ugly whine of it keening through the air over the flat whack of the sharpshooter's rifle. On distant elevations, obscure in the quivering haze, there were the guns, cleverly sited, and the gunners were prompt to fire at anything that moved. From one end of the army to the other, men endured heat and thirst and nameless discomforts and waited for night.

At night the front came alive. Along the lines men took the shovels and picks and axes which details brought out to them and worked to make their trenches deep and strong. Where there were trees, they cut them down, put the slashed branches out in front for an abatis, and used the logs to make the breastworks solid. They dug their trenches deep, so that a man could stand erect in them without being shot, and they cut zig-zag alleyways through the earth back toward the rear, so that they might go to and from the front without being killed.

Being very human, the soldiers on both sides often dug their trenches so deep that while they offered almost perfect protection against enemy fire they were quite useless for fighting purposes. In each army it was found that there were long stretches of trench in which a man could not possibly point his musket toward the enemy, and from both blue and gray headquarters orders went out to front-line commanders warning that there must always be fire steps on which riflemen could stand to shoot their foes.[1]

Along much of the line the trenches were so close that the men could hear their enemies chatting together. In many places the lines were not far enough apart to give the pickets proper room, and in these places there was constant skirmishing all the way around the clock. Even where there was a decent distance, the lines were seldom quiet. Half a dozen shots from the skirmish lines could bring great rolling salvos from the guns, so that at times it sounded as if an immense battle were rocking back and forth over the desolate bottom-lands. Most of this cannonading did no great harm, for the men in the deep trenches were well protected against missiles fired with relatively flat trajectory, and fuses were so imperfect that even the best gunners could rarely explode a shell directly over a trench. To get around this difficulty the artillerists brought up coehorn mortars—squat little jugs of iron that rested on flat wooden bases and pointed up toward the sky, which could toss shells in a high arc so that they might fall into a distant slit in the earth. At night the fuses from these shells traced sputtering red patterns across the sky.[2]

The infantry hated the mortars, regarding them, as one veteran said, as "a contemptible scheme to make a soldier's life wretched." The weapons were usually out of sight behind a bank of earth, and when they were fired the men in the trenches could neither hear the report nor see the flash and puff of smoke. They had no warning: nothing but the hissing spark that rose deliberately, seemed to hang in the air high overhead, and then fell to earth to explode. Even more than the mortars, however, the soldiers hated sharp-shooters. They had a feeling that sharpshooters never really affected the course of a battle: they were sheer malignant nuisances, taking unfair advantages and killing men who might just as well have remained alive. One artillerist wrote that the sharpshooters would "sneak around trees or lurk behind stumps" and from this shelter "murder a few men," and he burst out with the most indignant complaint of all: "There was an unwritten code of honor among the infantry that forbade the shooting of men while attending to the imperative calls of nature, and these sharpshooting brutes were constantly violating that rule. I hated sharpshooters, both Confederate and Union, and I was always glad to see them killed." [3]

So much of the killing these days seemed to be meaningless. In a great battle men died to take or defend some particular point, and it could be seen that there was some reason for their deaths. But there were so many deaths that affected the outcome of the war not a particle—deaths that had nothing to do with the progress of the campaign or with the great struggle for union and freedom but that simply happened, doing no one any good. There was one day when a Federal battery took position in the yard of a farmhouse and began to duel with a Confederate battery a mile away. The firing grew hot, and the people who lived in the farmhouse huddled inside in desperate fear; and presently a poor colored servant in the house, driven beside herself with terror, sprang up in a lunatic frenzy, scooped up a shovelful of live coals from the hearth, ran to the doorway, and threw the glowing coals out in a wild swing. The coals landed in an open limber chest, which blew up with a mighty crash. Two or three gunners were killed outright, two or three more were blinded forever, the woman was quite unhurt—and there were more names for the casualty lists, testifying to nothing except that war was a madman's business. [4]

Now and then higher authority considered making a new assault. One day a note from II Corps headquarters came up to General Barlow, asking if he thought that the works in his front could be carried. Barlow was one of the few general officers in the army who actively enjoyed a good fight, but this time he advised against an attack, explaining that "the men feel just at present a great horror and dread of attacking earthworks again. . . . I think the men are so wearied and worn out by the harassing labors of the past week that they are wanting in the spirit and dash necessary for successful assaults." [5]

The men had become very war-wise. They knew better than anyone else the impossibility of carrying the Rebel trenches, and as Hancock said, when they were ordered to attack "they went as far as the example of their officers could carry them"—no farther. Officers who could persuade them to do the impossible were becoming scarce. There had been more than a month of fighting, and the best company and regimental officers were getting killed off. The best officers were always going into the most dangerous places, and there had been dangerous places without number in the past month, and the law of averages was working. The famous II Corps had lost noticeably in efficiency, not merely because its best enlisted men had been shot, but also because it was no longer officered as it had been. A brigade which was commanded by a lieutenant colonel, its regiments led by captains, and its companies commanded by junior lieutenants and sergeants, just was not able to do the things it had done before. The old leadership was gone. [6]

There were veteran outfits, of course, in which the men more or less led themselves. Yet the enlistments of many of these were about to expire, and the men were becoming very cautious. Every man in the army knew the exact date on which he would be released from service, and as that date drew near he resented being asked to run risks. Members of a Rhode Island battery complained that on their last day of service they were thrown into an exposed position and compelled to keep up an expensive artillery duel, and the battery's historian exploded in anger: "It was clear to everyone's mind that some mean, malignant villain, not worthy of wearing shoulder straps, had got the battery into this dreadful position purposely, for our term of service expired the next day, and we had long range guns, while short range guns were fired a quarter of a mile in our rear, the shells exploding over our heads instead of reaching the enemy's works." [7]

A week passed after the day of the disastrous assaults, and another week began, and as far as the men could see there was no change; perhaps they were to remain here at Cold Harbor forever, fixed in impregnable trenches that could never be captured and would never be abandoned. The trench system imposed its routine, which was not pleasant. These sandy ditches caught and held all of the sun's heat, so that the scanty supply of water in canteens became hot and distasteful, and the men tried to rig little awnings out of shelter-tent halves and cowered under them, hot and unwashed and eternally thirsty. A New Hampshire soldier predicted that trench life by itself "would soon become more dangerous to the Federal army than rebel bullets," and a Pennsylvanian remembered that what his outfit wanted most in those days was a complete issue of new clothing—what they wore had got beyond washing, and there was no water to wash it in anyway.[8]

When Cutler's division was briefly taken out of the line on June 8 for a short stay in the rear, its commander noted that this was the first day in more than a month in which no man in the division had been reported killed or wounded. One of his colonels wrote that he had had neither an unbroken night's sleep nor a change of clothing since May 5, and another remarked that he was so groggy with fatigue that it was impossible for him to write an intelligent letter to his family: "I can only tell my wife I am alive and well. I am too stupid for any use."

And General Warren, sensitive and high-strung, turned to another officer one day and burst out:

"For thirty days it has been one funeral procession past me, and it is too much!" 9

Warren was showing the strain, and both Grant and Meade were noticing it. He had been a good friend of Meade for a long time, and Grant had been favorably impressed by him. When the army crossed the Rapidan, Grant even made a mental note that if anything should happen to Meade, Warren would be a good man to put in command of the army. But somehow he was not bearing up well. Details engrossed him, and he seemed to have a stiff pride which made it hard for him to accept direction and counsel. Worst of all, he was never quite able to get his corps moving promptly. It was felt that he was slow in bringing his men into action the first day at Spotsylvania, and when the attack was made at the Bloody Angle and Warren was supposed to hit the Confederate left there had been a three-hour delay—a costly thing, which led Grant to tell Meade to relieve Warren of his command if he delayed any longer. Meade replied that he was about to do it without orders, but Warren finally got his corps in motion just in time to save his job.10

As a matter of fact, corps leadership throughout the campaign had been a good deal less than distinguished. Even Hancock seemed uninspired; it may be that the wound he got at Gettysburg, which was still very far from healed, was slowing him up more than anyone realized. John Sedgwick was gone, and Wright was not yet fully tested. He was obviously brave and diligent, but there were signs that he might be stiff and slow. Burnside was no more expert than he had ever been, and his relations with Meade were delicate. His IX Corps had at last formally been made a part of the Army of the Potomac. He ranked Meade, and was touchy about taking orders from him, and Meade was not a tactful person who would try to smooth down his ruffled feathers. Smith had served with Grant at Chattanooga and had won his confidence there, but he was not fitting smoothly into the Army of the Potomac.

Looking back on the Cold Harbor assault, a staff man in the VI Corps wrote scornfully that "its management would have shamed a cadet in his first year at West Point." [11] Emory Upton went into more detail in a bitter letter to his sister:

"I am disgusted with the generalship displayed. Our men have, in many instances, been foolishly and wantonly sacrificed. Assault after assault has been ordered upon the enemy's entrenchments when they knew nothing about the strength or position of the enemy. Thousands of lives might have been spared by the exercise of a little skill; but, as it is, the courage of the poor men is expected to obviate all difficulties."

Reflecting further on the matter, he wrote a few days later:

"Some of our corps commanders are not fit to be corporals. Lazy and indolent, they will not even ride along their lines; yet, without hesitancy, they will order us to attack the enemy, no matter what their position or numbers. Twenty thousand of our killed and wounded should today be in our ranks." [12]

Grant was well aware that there were grave shortcomings in command, but they were not too easily identified by a man who was looking down from the top rather than up from underneath. To Grant's tent one day came young Brigadier General James H. Wilson, leader of one of Sheridan's cavalry divisions, earlier in the war a member of Grant's own staff and therefore a man with whom Grant might talk frankly. Wilson was one of the young, fire-eating, just-out-of-West Point officers, like Upton, who studied the older men with the eyes of impatient perfectionist youth. Also, he had served in the Western armies, where Grant had had lieutenants like Sherman and Thomas and McPherson.

In the privacy of his tent, Grant asked the young brigadier:

"Wilson, what is the matter with this army?"

Wilson replied that a good deal was the matter—so much that it would hardly do to go into detail—but he said that he could easily suggest a good remedy. One of Grant's staff officers was Colonel Ely Parker, swarthy and massive and black-haired, a full-blooded Indian of the Iroquois persuasion. Give Parker, said Wilson, a scalping knife and a tomahawk, fill him full of the worst commissary whisky available, and send him out to bring in the scalps of a number of major generals.

Grant chuckled mildly and asked which ones. That did not really matter much, said Wilson; just tell Parker to attack the first ones he came to and not to quit until he had scalped at least half a dozen. After that Grant would have a better army.[13]

The soldiers themselves were not complaining a great deal. They felt toward their officers about as private soldiers usually do, but there is little to show that Cold Harbor affected that feeling very much. Their complaints were usually like the one voiced by the Michigan private, who inquired grumpily: "Who is putting down this monster rebellion? Is it the officers?" These, he noted, had servants to wait on them, and good food in their baggage wagons, whereas "the poor wearied soldiers who do the fighting" got nothing but dry hardtack to eat and had to sleep in the mud.[14]

Clearly enough, the soldiers hated Cold Harbor and the trenches and the dust and the heat, and most of them would have agreed with the New York private who wrote: "A fellow sufferer very truly remarked that we are in a very bad state—the state of Virginia." [15] Yet there is nothing to show that they had had any especial loss in morale. What the men left in writing shows weariness and a longing to get away from the sound of gunfire for a while, but nothing more.[16] If the generals were clumsy, most of them had always been that way and there was no reason to expect them to be any different. The Army of the Potomac seems to have spent more time talking and thinking about its opposite number, the Army of Northern Virginia, than about its own high command.

Its relationship with the Confederate army was unusual, a queer blend of antagonism and understanding. At times the feeling between the two armies was downright savage. A man in Smith's corps complained bitterly that long after the June 3 attacks had ended, Confederate riflemen amused themselves by shooting at the wounded men between the lines. Sometimes, he said, they even fired at corpses. There was a wounded New Hampshire officer who lay, helpless, twenty yards in front of the Union trenches, and all day long the Confederate sharpshooters kept anyone from going out to help him. One man was killed in the attempt, and after that the Union soldiers tried throwing canteens of water and bags of hardtack out to the wounded man, but nothing effective could be done for him as long as the Rebels could see to shoot. After dark, men dug a shallow trench out to where the officer lay, and after three hours' work they managed to get him back to safety. All of the soldiers in the line set up a cheer when the officer was brought in, and the cheer promptly drew a volley from the Confederate rifle pits.[17]

That was one side of the coin. For the other side, there was the fact that the pickets constantly arranged informal truces, meeting between the lines to trade knives, tobacco, newspapers, and other small valuables, and as they traded they talked things over. One of these peaceful meetings, unhappily, broke up in a row. A Confederate asked a Yankee who was going to win the Northern presidential election, and the Yankee said that he reckoned he himself would vote for Old Abe.

"He," said the Southerner, "is a damned abolitionist."

This immediately brought on a fist fight, and officers had to come out to break it up. Still, men who felt enough at home with each other to argue about politics and fight with their fists over it were hardly, at bottom, sworn enemies estranged by hatred.

A Massachusetts soldier on the II Corps front told how his regiment made friends with a Confederate regiment opposite it and worked out a fairly extended cessation of hostilities, and he said that if the enlisted men of the two armies had the power to settle the war, "not another shot would have been fired." The friendly Confederate regiment was at length moved away from there, and just before it left a Rebel soldier stood up on the rampart and called out a warning: "Keep down, Yanks—we 'uns are going away." As soon as the replacements came in the firing was resumed. When the V Corps was shifted around to the left of the Union line, so that it faced the Confederates across the Chickahominy River, the 118th Pennsylvania and the 35th North Carolina put in the day sitting on opposite banks of the narrow stream, fishing and chatting.

A soldier in a New York heavy artillery regiment wrote that it seemed, now and then, as if an increasing number of Confederates were willing to slip over to the Union side after dark and surrender, yet he added wryly that "when it comes to fighting, one would not suppose that any of them had the faintest idea of surrendering." Between fights, he said, Northerners and Southerners talked things over, concluded that peace would be a very fine thing, and agreed that "if a few men on both sides who stayed at home were hung, matters could easily be arranged." [18]

Yet the soldiers were only a part of it, and what happened to them out along the rifle pits amid the choking dust was having a queer reverse effect on men back home who would never know what it was like to charge a line of riflemen in the smoky twilight, gun butt raised to crush a human being's skull. For this was the year when the shadow of death lay all across America, and grotesque shapes moved within the shadow and laid hold of men's hearts and minds. The soldiers at the front could look ahead to peace without seeing it through a veil of hatred, and if they talked lightly about the need to hang a few stay-at-homes, they spoke as men who had seen so many killings that a few more might not make much difference. Yet there were quiet civilians who were talking of hangings, too, these days. They were men of years and peace, who might inspire violence but who had never actually seen any of it, and the war had worked upon them until they could feel that death and heartbreak were positive goods.

Some were men who had always lived by the sword, and they were beginning to see in this war a chance to reach a monstrous goal, with an undying fire blazing across a wasteland which had once been peopled by men who disagreed with them. But others were moderates, not usually given to thoughts of vengeance and reprisal, carried away now by the fury of war.

There was Gideon Welles, for instance, Secretary of the Navy, a white-whiskered, brown-wigged man, God-fearing and humorless and gossipy, a good Connecticut editor and politician who lived austerely, fathered a large family, and worshiped at the shrine of the Union. While the worst of the Cold Harbor fighting was going on, Welles communed with himself in his diary, seeing death and suffering as abstractions, remarking sagely that no man had been prepared for the extraordinary changes the war had brought. It often came to him, he wrote, that "greater severity" might well be invoked against the South—yet the thought had to be dealt with cautiously, for "it would tend to barbarism." And in his quiet study, where the night's peace was broken by no sound worse than the clatter of horse-drawn cabs on the paving stones outside the curtained windows, Welles reflected on the business of hanging one's enemies:

"No traitor has been hung. I doubt if there will be, but an example should be made of some of the leaders, for present and future good."

To be sure, the Southern leaders could be imprisoned or exiled, once the war was safely won, but that might not answer. People would try to rescue them, and parties would form to uphold their principles, and in the end these principles might revive and grow strong again. Perhaps ideas and emotions could be destroyed forever, if the men who held them were destroyed; and the thought led Mr. Welles to set down his conclusion:

"Death is the proper penalty and atonement, and will be enduringly beneficent in its influence."

But perhaps hangings would not be possible, since there is in man a deep tendency toward softness of heart. In such case, Mr. Welles felt, the Rebel leaders could at least be stripped of their wealth and their families impoverished. The effect of this (wrote the good family man) would be wholesome. Yet it did not really seem likely that any of these stern things would be done, and he concluded regretfully: "I apprehend there will be very gentle measures in closing up the rebellion." [19]

Mr. Welles might be wrong about the inevitability of gentleness. In this year when blood-red fantasies danced against the clouded moon of war, men who had never seen the grotesque indignity of violent death could talk easily about the good fruits that might grow at the foot of the gallows tree, and devout Christians could wonder if something precious might not slip too easily through the loose meshes of Christian charity. At this moment, when casualties in the Army of the Potomac had averaged 2,000 men a day for a solid month, Abraham Lincoln was waging the hardest fight of his life to uphold the dream that peace could finally be made decently and justly, without malice or a desire to have revenge.

For of all the men who controlled and directed the war, Lincoln was the one who most deeply shared the spirit that moved across the steaming trenches at Cold Harbor—fight to the limit as long as the fighting has to go on, but strike hands and be friends the moment the fighting stops. Before the war even began, in that haunted springtime when its dark shape was rising, Lincoln had tried to warn North and South that they could never travel on separate roads. Win or lose, someday they would have to get along with each other again, and whatever they did before that day came had better be done in such a way that getting along together would still be possible. The soldiers had got the point perfectly, and they expressed it very simply: Hang a few troublemakers and we'll all go home. Mysteriously, the fighting seemed to be bringing them mutual understanding, and they may almost have been closer to each other, in spirit, than they were to their own civilians back home. Yet there was nothing they could do about it. They had not made the war and they would not end it. They could only fight it.

And the men who had made the war—the sharp politicians and the devoted patriots, the men who dreamed the American dream in different ways and the other men who never dreamed any dreams at all but who had a canny eye for power and influence—most of these, by now, were prisoners of their own creation.

The hospitals in Washington were full as never before, and every day steamers came up the river with more broken bodies to be unloaded, and it was easy for those who watched this pathetic pageant to be embittered by what had happened to these men rather than inspired by what they had dreamed of. It was hard to think clearly, and the act of embracing unmitigated violence could be a substitute for thought.

There was a colonel on Grant's staff who typified the trend perfectly. He could see that Southern resistance was still very strong, although he did not seem to be able to see anything else very clearly, and he was going about the tents these days smiting an open palm with a clenched fist and growling: "Smash 'em up! Smash 'em up!" [20] As a tactical slogan this had its faults, since logically it led to nothing better than Cold Harbor assaults, but it was a perfect expression of the growing state of mind behind the fighting fronts. Smash 'em up: the war cannot be settled, it can only be won; smash 'em up—and afterward, on the pulverized fragments, we can sit down quietly and decide what we are going to do next.

If the war was to be won, it was important that it be won soon. It had been born of anger and misunderstanding and it was breeding more as it went along. It was pushing men to the point where vengeance seemed essential, driving even a man like Secretary Welles to think well of the process of dangling a political opponent by the neck, with convulsive feet kicking at the unsustaining air. The longer the war lasted, the harder it was for people to think beyond victory, the more probable that victory when it finally came would have to be total and unconditional. What Lincoln and the soldiers wanted was a dream, and 2,000 casualties a day created an atmosphere in which dreams could not live.

So a Cold Harbor stalemate was unendurable, and among the people who saw this was General Grant. He had been commissioned to break the fighting power of the Confederacy, and he still hoped that it could be done by one bold stroke rather than by a slow process of grinding and strangling and wearing out. Before he even bothered to seek a truce so that dead men might be buried and wounded men brought back within the lines—they lay there, untended, for several days, bullets flying low above them—he set things in motion for a new move. The network of trenches grew deep and strong, but even as they took on their air of grim permanence the army that crouched in them was given a new objective.

From the moment he crossed the Rapidan, Grant's ruling idea had been to go for Lee's army without a letup—to keep that dangerous body of fighting men so everlastingly busy that it could never again seize the initiative, to compel it to fight its battles when and where Grant chose rather than by Lee's selection. The chance for decisive victory lay that way, and in the past month's fighting the army had come tolerably close to it two or three times. To stay in the Cold Harbor lines would be to give up all hope of decisive victory, for if anything was clear, it was that no offensive at or near Cold Harbor could possibly succeed. General Halleck was clucking like a worried mother hen, urging that the army stay put and conduct a siege, running no risks and counting on time and general military erosion to wear the enemy down.[21] But even though Grant had given the Army of the Potomac more trench warfare in a month than it had had in all of its earlier existence, he still believed in a war of movement. He had taken Vicksburg by maneuver and he had one maneuver left, and now he would try it.

Grant had a basilisk's gaze. He could sit, whittling and smoking, looking off beyond the immediate scene, and what he was looking at was likely to come down in blood and ashes and crashing sound a little later. Right now he was looking all the way across the James River to a peaceful, sleepy Virginia city named Petersburg, which lay on the southern bank of the Appomattox River, twenty-odd miles south of Richmond, near the point where the Appomattox flows into the James.

What Grant saw when he stared off through the mists to-

ward Petersburg was the Confederates' problem of supply.
The immediate vicinity of Richmond did not begin to produce
enough food and forage to support either Lee's army or the
Confederate capital. An important part of this material came
down from the Shenandoah Valley, over the Virginia Central
Railroad and the James River Canal. Even more important,
however, was what came up from the Deep South, and most
of this came by railroads which ran through Petersburg. If
the Federal army could seize Petersburg, the Army of Northern Virginia and the civil government which supported it
would go on starvation rations. If, at the same time, the connection with the Shenandoah Valley could be broken, Richmond could no longer be defended.

Yet it was not Richmond itself which Grant wanted. He
wanted to destroy Lee's army, and to do that he had to get
it out of its trenches. The one way to compel it to move was
to cut off its supplies. So he made his plans: seize Petersburg,
block the line to the Shenandoah, and let hunger drive Lee's
army out into the open. Once that happened there could be
a finish fight, under conditions in which the Federal army's
advantage in numbers ought to be decisive.

Within forty-eight hours of the failure of the June 3 assaults Grant was writing his orders, and by June 7 Sheridan
had two of his cavalry divisions on the road, heading west for
Charlottesville. At Charlottesville Sheridan was to meet an
army under Major General David Hunter, who had replaced
Sigel after that general's inglorious defeat at Newmarket.
Hunter had the troops that had been Sigel's, another division
which General George Crook had led east from West Virginia, and a good body of cavalry under Averell. With these
men he had marched up the Valley to Staunton, crushing a
small Confederate force which tried to delay him, and at
Staunton he was turning east, burning and destroying as he
came. Grant's idea was that Hunter and Sheridan would join
forces and come down toward Richmond together, taking the
Virginia Central Railroad apart as they came and rejoining
the Army of the Potomac somewhere below the James River.[22]

Meade's engineers were building an inner line behind the

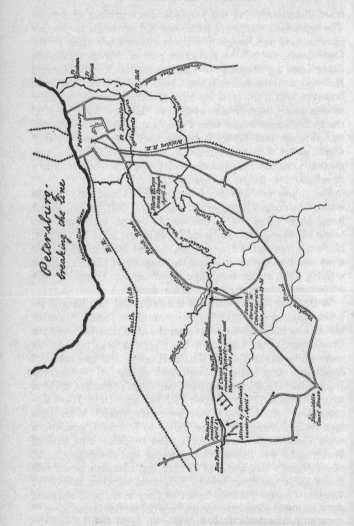

Petersburg.
breaking the Line

front at Cold Harbor, and the army as a whole was shifting slowly to its left, with Warren's corps lining up along the Chickahominy. A fleet of transports had come up the Pamunkey to the base at White House, and warships, transports, barges, and a great number of pontoons were being assembled at Fortress Monroe, ready to go up the James on order. The arrangements were intricate but they were well directed, and finally, late in the afternoon of June 12, Grant and Meade struck their headquarters tents and rode down the north bank of the Chickahominy, past Despatch Station, to make a new camp beside a cluster of catalpa trees in a farmhouse yard. As night came on, the hot air was filled with dust as 100,000 soldiers began moving out of the positions which they had occupied for the better part of a fortnight.

It was risky business. This was no mere repetition of the sidestep which had been done so many times on the march down from the Rapidan. This time the whole army was marching directly away from its foes, gambling that it could disappear completely even though the two armies were in intimate contact along a five-mile front, their lines nowhere more than a few hundred yards apart. Once it got clean away—if it did —the Federal army had to make a fifty-mile hike and cross a tidal river which was half a mile wide and fifteen fathoms deep: a river which, unlike all of the little streams which had been crossed earlier, bore on its surface a number of formidable ironclad Confederate gunboats. There were Yankee gunboats, to be sure, to keep these in check, but if even one Southern warship managed to slip past these defenders, it could turn the projected river crossing into disaster.

Much worse than the danger of the gunboats, however, was the chance that Lee would find out what was going on and would move out to interfere. If he should catch the Army of the Potomac in the act of turning its back on him and marching down to the James River, what he and his soldiers might do to it would hardly bear thinking about. Two years ago he had detected McClellan making the same move on the same ground, and only the utter greenness of his staff and command arrangements had kept him from destroying Mc-

Clellan's army. The greenness had long since been corrected.

Yet in making this move Grant was not simply gambling that Lee could be hoodwinked. Lee or any other general could be fooled briefly, in this country of obscure roads and concealing swamps and woods, but it was not likely that he could be fooled for very long. What Grant was really banking on was the belief that the terrible pounding of the last six weeks had taken something out of the Army of Northern Virginia—that it was no longer the quick, instantly responsive instrument that had made such deadly thrusts in the past, and that it would not lash out today as it had done in 1862, when it discovered its opponent in the act of making a flank march across its front. Those tawny gray legions were still unconquerable behind trenches, but they had lost the incomparable offensive power of the old days: that, in essence, seems to have been the bet Grant was really making.[23]

The different Federal moves were intricate, this night of June 12, but the timing was good. Hancock and Wright took their men back to the inner trench line as insurance against accidents. Smith led his XVIII Corps back to White House, where the transports were waiting. Burnside followed, turning off a few miles short of White House to follow a road down to the James. Wilson's cavalry, left behind by Sheridan, moved down to a Chickahominy crossing at Long Bridge—the bridge had long since been destroyed and the name merely designated a place—and went splashing across the river in the midnight dark, laying a pontoon bridge immediately afterward. Warren's V Corps promptly crossed on this bridge and marched boldly in the direction of Richmond along the fringe of historic White Oak Swamp.

By dawn of June 13 there was nobody left at Cold Harbor. Even the inner line was empty, for it needed to be held only long enough to protect the withdrawal of the rest of the army, and by daylight the VI Corps was following Burnside's men and Hancock was taking his corps down over the Long Bridge crossing. When Confederate skirmishers crept forward across the strangely silent rifle pits they found nothing but empty trenches and the indescribable unseemly refuse left behind by a departing army. Since the Yankees did seem to be moving toward Richmond below White Oak Swamp, Lee pulled his own army out of its lines and moved down to cover the capital, occupying roughly the ground that had been fought over so hard during the McClellan retreat in 1862, from Glendale to Malvern Hill. Meanwhile, Warren withdrew his own corps—he had moved forward simply to protect the rest of the army during the early stages of the march—and headed for a spot known as Charles City Courthouse, close to the James. Wilson's cavalry remained behind, holding all of the road crossings and driving back the inquisitive Rebel patrols. A curtain was drawn between the two armies, and for the first time in a month and a half Federal and Confederate infantry were out of contact.

Thoroughly delighted to get away from Cold Harbor, the men of the Army of the Potomac were also deeply surprised. For once, no camp rumor had warned of the move, and up to the last the men had been busy elaborating their trench system as if they were to stay there all year. Things had changed, one veteran mused, "and it was not now the custom to inform the rank and file, and the newspapers and the enemy, of intended movements." Another man was reminded by this march down to the river of the similar march two years earlier, under McClellan, and it seemed to him that everything was much better now than it had been then. Cold Harbor had been terrible, and what led up to it had not been much better, but morale was good and the men proved it by their looks and actions. On the earlier march they felt that they had been beaten, and were depressed; now they felt that they were on the way to victory, and they stepped out with a springy step.[24]

Late in the afternoon of June 13 the advance guard reached the James River, coming down to it past an impressive plantation once owned by the late President Tyler—the "Tyler too" of the rowdy campaign song. The river was broad and it glinted in the afternoon sun, and it was the first really pleasant-looking body of water anybody had seen since the campaign began. Yankee warships were anchored in the stream, white awnings spread against the heat, small boats coming ashore with rhythmical dip and swing of dripping oars.

An officer on Meade's staff found himself blinking and gaping at these Navy people as they came ashore. There seemed to be something wrong about them, and at last he realized what it was. They were all clean, their persons washed, their uniforms whole, unfaded, and unsullied. The officer discovered that he had got to the point where he was suspicious of anyone who was not dirty and in rags. He was used to soldiers, and where soldiers were concerned, "the more they serve, the less they look like soldiers and the more they resemble day-laborers who had bought second-hand military clothes." [25]

Only the leading echelons of the army reached the river that evening. They included a swarm of engineers who immediately went to work to lay a pontoon bridge over to the southern shore. The army had never built such a prodigious bridge before. It would be nearly half a mile long and it would require more than a hundred pontoons, and three schooners had to be anchored in the deep water out in midstream to support the central section of the bridge. The sappers got to work without delay, tugboats and barges bringing men and material to each shore, and along the bank where the advance guard was camped there was a great chopping and shoveling, because a grove of huge old cypress trees had to be cut down and it was necessary to build a causeway across a swamp to provide an approach to the bridge. Other details went to work to put a half-ruined wharf in proper shape, a little upstream from the place where the bridge was being built, and the transports were anchored just offshore to take men aboard as soon as the wharf was repaired. As many of the soldiers as could get down to the water went in swimming, whooping and splashing as they began soaking off the sweat and grime of weeks of fighting.

A mile or so from the water, Gibbon's division was camped on the plantation of Tyler-too. The enemy was many miles away, and the officers announced that the camp need not be fortified. Nevertheless, as soon as the men had stacked their muskets they began to dig a long trench all across the western edge of the plantation, and before they went to bed they had the place in shape to resist a regular assault. Meade's assistant adjutant general looked on their handiwork and concluded that the enlisted man was convinced that a rifle pit was "a good thing to have in a family where there are small children." [26]

4. Lie Down, You Damn Fools

Major General William Farrar Smith was a professional soldier who had nearly all of the qualities needed for success except a sense of the value of time and the ability to get along with his superior officers—to whom, as an admirer confessed, he was at times "a perfect Ishmaelite." His subordinates liked him immensely. He was kindly and courteous without condescension, he "looked after his men," in the army phrase, and his headquarters tents were a fabulous place to visit. Champagne was commonly served at dinner—it was so even at Cold Harbor, where Meade dropped in for lunch the day after the big assault and found things so pleasant he remained until dusk—and an overnight guest could expect to be awakened in the morning by a servant bearing a champagne cocktail. Yet with all of this, and the innumerable card games that were played, neither Smith nor his staff ever acquired the rake-hell reputation that clung about such a general as Joe Hooker.

Smith had been "Baldy" ever since his days as a West Point cadet, partly because of a thinned spot on his crown, but mostly, as a friend explained, because there were so many Smiths in the army that each one had to have an identifying nickname. Even men who did not like him—and, in the end, this included nearly all of the generals under whom he had served—admitted that he was brilliant. He ranked fourth in his class at the Academy on his graduation in 1845, he had gone into the engineers, and he had served for a number of years on the West Point faculty. On a tour of duty in Florida in the 1850s he had contracted malaria, from which he still suffered at times, and when the fever took him he was gloomy and morose. He had a sharp tongue and he never bothered to control it when he observed shortcomings in a superior officer, and this had done him much harm.[1]

In this war he had been up, and then down, and finally up again. He had organized and been first colonel of the 3rd Vermont Infantry, serving at the first battle of Bull Run and winning appointment as brigadier general and command of a division shortly thereafter. He fought well under McClellan on the peninsula, won promotion to major general and command of the IX Corps, which he led at Fredericksburg, and then he fell into trouble by giving vent to pointed public criticism of General Burnside.

Practically everybody was criticizing Burnside just then, but Burnside was backed by the powerful Committee on the Conduct of the War, which was suspicious of Smith anyway because he had been a close friend of McClellan. The upshot was that Smith lost both his corps command and his promotion, with the Senate refusing to confirm his nomination as major general, and for a time he dropped into obscurity. He showed up in Chattanooga in the fall of 1863 as chief engineer for the Army of the Cumberland, and in the dark days following Chickamauga he did a first-rate job of organizing and running the famous "cracker line" which saved the beaten army from starvation. (He had an extended row about this, later, with General Rosecrans, his commanding officer at the time, with both men claiming credit for the job.) When Grant moved in and put Thomas in Rosecrans's place he was highly impressed with Smith's capacities, and when Grant took command of all the armies he ordered Smith east and gave him an army corps under Ben Butler.

This brought Smith new troubles. It would have brought them to anybody, because serving under Butler was hard, but Smith was probably the last man in the army to adjust himself quietly to that officer's ruinous eccentricities. (To Grant, about this time, Smith burst out furiously, asking how he could retain in army command a man who "is as helpless as a child on the field of battle and as visionary as an opium eater in council.")[2] Since Butler was even more disputatious than Smith, and in addition possessed immense political influence, Smith's difficulties had been increasing by geometrical progression.

Probably no campaign in all the war was as badly mishandled as that of the Army of the James in the spring of 1864. While Grant was coming down through the Wilderness and Spotsylvania, Butler was taking his army up the James to menace Richmond from the south. He could have walked in and occupied Petersburg then almost without opposition, but apparently the idea did not appeal to him. Instead he wandered around the country, started for Petersburg and then turned back, lunged ineffectively toward Richmond, and wound up by letting a much smaller Confederate army lock him up in the formless peninsula of Bermuda Hundred— James River on the north and east, Appomattox on the south, and stout Rebel entrenchments running completely across the neck.[3]

When Smith was ordered to take his army corps away from there and help the Army of the Potomac at Cold Harbor, he went gladly, figuring that the fewer troops Butler commanded, the less harm was likely to result. But he found his reception in the clique-ridden Army of the Potomac lacking in warmth, and he was bitterly critical of the way Meade was running things, and when he brought his troops back to Bermuda Hundred he was not in a happy frame of mind.[4]

At Bermuda Hundred, however, new orders awaited him. Grant made a quick trip to see Butler, to outline the new campaign plans in person, and when Smith got his men off the transports he was told to take them over to the south side of the Appomattox and march on Petersburg without delay. Petersburg, he was informed, was held by a skeleton force and if he moved fast he could seize it, and the Army of the Potomac would follow to provide all necessary reinforcements. Smith's corps was badly thinned down—it had had heavy losses at Cold Harbor, there had been a great deal of straggling, and one division was to be left at Bermuda Hundred—and to bring him up to strength he was allotted a slim division of colored troops commanded by Brigadier General Edward W. Hinks.

These colored soldiers had been occupying City Point, a little steamboat landing on a low promontory on the south bank of the Appomattox at the point where that river flowed into the James. They had not yet been in any serious action, and most of the generals took it for granted that colored men would not make good soldiers, but Grant was in a hurry and there was no time to wait. So early on the morning of June 15 Smith's men crossed the Appomattox on a pontoon bridge a mile or two above City Point, picked up Hinks's soldiers, and set out for Petersburg. Altogether there were perhaps 10,000 men in the united column.

By an air line Petersburg was eight miles to the west. The ground was broken, with a series of north-and-south ridges coming down to the Appomattox, and the city might not be too easy to capture. If the Confederates could not spare many men for its defense, they had had plenty of time and abundant slave labor to fortify it, and a great semicircle of elaborate defenses ran all around it, starting in low ground by the Appomattox two miles east of town, cutting south in a great horseshoe curve, and coming up to the river again on the west. A few determined men could make these defenses very formidable, and after their experience at Cold Harbor Smith and his men were likely to be cautious when they saw Rebel trenches. Nevertheless, as the corps marched westward, raising an enormous cloud of dust and brushing Southern skirmishers out of the way, Smith was approaching one of the brightest opportunities an ambitious general could ask.

For the matter of that so was the Army of the Potomac, which was getting over to the south bank of the James as fast as it could, by pontoon bridge and by steamboat, in order to follow in his footsteps.

Never had the army been in a better strategic position than it was getting into on this fifteenth of June. Behind it were six weeks of the worst campaigning anybody had ever imagined, but all that had been endured might be justified by what lay just ahead. The army now was squarely in the rear of its opponent, the Army of Northern Virginia, which was still holding its trenches around Malvern Hill and Glendale, prepared to defend itself against an attack that was not going to take place. Grant had taken the army entirely out of Lee's reach, and in a few hours he would be able to strike where his enemy could not make an effective defense. Conclusive victory lay just ahead.

During the next few hours everything was going to be up to Baldy Smith and his 10,000. Smith took the men toward Petersburg, with his own divisions on the right and the colored troops on the left, and as the morning wore on the Rebel resistance grew stiffer, until at last Hinks had to move his men out into line of battle and storm a little hill where infantry and a couple of guns offered more than skirmish-line opposition. The colored boys went up the hill with a rush, driving away the defenders and capturing one of the guns, but the fight caused a delay and it was nearly noon when Smith's column came up against the main line of Confederate works.

These looked dangerous. The City Point Railroad ran half a mile or more south of the river, and between the railroad and the river the ground was low and the Rebel trench line slanted back toward the northwest, the ground in its front covered by guns mounted on bluffs on the far side of the river. Just south of the railroad the ground rose, and a long, uneven crest ran south for several miles, and this high ground was covered with fortifications that appeared to be stronger than anything that had been seen at Cold Harbor.

At intervals there were redoubts—square forts, solidly built, with embrasures for artillery. The redoubts were connected by ponderous raised breastworks, twenty feet thick at the base and six feet high. In front of the breastworks there was a ditch, fifteen feet wide by six or eight feet deep, and a few yards in front of the ditch there was an interminable slashing of felled trees anchored in place with branches all interlaced.

From end to end of the line the ground in front of the slashing was open for half a mile so that it could be swept by fire from the forest and trenches. Close to the slashing there were deep rifle pits for the skirmishers.[5]

All in all, it was no place to approach lightly. It seemed to Smith that the position was even stronger than the mountaintop line the Confederates had held at Chattanooga. That line, to be sure, had finally been stormed, but no one quite understood even yet how it had been done and one man who watched it wrote that the victory looked like "a visible interposition of God." Smith had to form his battle lines in deep woods and that took time, and it was two o'clock or later before he had everything ready.

Even when the lines were formed Smith was not disposed to be hasty. It was clear to him that if these Rebel trenches were held in strength, no attack could possibly succeed. Potentially, the place was a worse deathtrap than Cold Harbor, and Smith was not going to order an attack until he had studied things very carefully. He went out in front personally to do his looking, exposing himself to dangerous sniper fire, and he spent two full hours making his survey, going from end to end of the lines and studying the situation with the canny eye of a skilled engineer.[6]

Now these Confederate works were just as strong as they looked, but they had one glaring weakness: they contained hardly any soldiers.

Confederate commander here was the famous General Pierre Gustave Toutant Beauregard, a vain and theatrical personality, but at the same time a very good soldier. He was responsible for the defense of everything south of the James River, and after he had bottled Butler's army up at Bermuda Hundred he had to send some of his best troops across the river to help Lee, and on this day of June 15 he had no more than 7,000 soldiers in his command. Most of these were in the Bermuda Hundred lines, which was where most of the pressure had been so far, and in front of Petersburg there were barely 2,200 men, including home guards and cavalry. With several miles of trench to occupy, these were spread very thin, one infantryman to every four or five yards of trench. They could kill a certain number of Yankees but they could not possibly beat off a really determined attack, and no one knew it any better than Beauregard did. He had been calling for help, and a division of the troops that had been sent to Lee was on its way back to him, but it could not reach him until midnight or later and until then he was strictly on his own.[7]

As he studied the lines Smith began to discover that there was a scarcity of defenders, and he concluded that Rebel strength just now consisted mostly of artillery. He would not assault with massed troops, which could be ripped apart by the guns; instead he would use a succession of skirmish lines, against which the guns would not be effective. If the trenches were held as lightly as he was beginning to believe, the skirmish lines could carry them, and if he was wrong and there were lots of Rebels in the trenches, then no attack would have a chance anyway;[8] and by four o'clock, Smith finished his reconnoissance and ordered an attack.

Now came the first little hitch. Staff work had slipped, somewhere, and no one had warned the chief of artillery that a fight was imminent, so that officer had sent all of the artillery horses off to water. It seemed important to give the attacking troops plenty of artillery protection, and the guns could not be put into position until the horses got back. So there was a wait, and the afternoon died and evening came, and it was nearly sunset when everything was ready[9]—and north of the Appomattox, Confederate officers were driving lean columns down the roads, hurrying to get into the Petersburg lines before the war was lost beyond salvage.

Other troops were on the road, too—Union troops, two divisions of Hancock's II Corps, who had crossed the James during the night and now were struggling along to come up and give Smith's men a hand. Late in the afternoon, while he was waiting for the gunners to get their horses, Smith was told of their approach, and the news seems to have taken the edge off his eagerness. With strong reinforcements at hand, the delay in mounting the attack probably would not matter so much.

The artillery was moved forward at last and it began to smite the Confederate works, and around seven o'clock the Union lines rolled forward. The Confederates put up a good defense but their job was impossible. The Federal attackers simply swamped them, Hinks's colored troops going forward as stoutly as the rest, and by nine o'clock or a little earlier most of the formidable line was in Union hands, with sixteen guns and several hundred prisoners. The colored troops were exultant and they capered about their captured cannon with whoops of pride, and General Hinks was equally optimistic. Smith came riding over, and Hinks proposed that the entire command move boldly forward and march into Petersburg without further ado.

Night had come, but the moon was out and its clear thin light lay across the ridges and valleys and the empty roads to the little city. There were no more forts to storm, and the Confederates who had retreated were not even bothering to maintain a rear-guard fire. Hinks thought that the Federals could walk into Petersburg just about as they chose.

So did Beauregard. He wrote later that at that moment "Petersburg was clearly at the mercy of the Federal commander, who had all but captured it." But Smith did not think so. He told Hinks that Beauregard was going to be reinforced (which was true enough) and said that by the time the Federals could reach the town the defenders there would outnumber them (which was not true at all). He added that if they were not careful they would lose all that they had gained. It would be best to hold on where they were and wait for Hancock's men, and very likely something decisive could be done tomorrow. Smith sent Ben Butler a wire saying, "Unless I misapprehend the topography, I hold the key to Petersburg." Meanwhile, he ordered Hinks to make no advance.[10]

Hancock's men were just coming on the scene—two divisions, Birney's and Gibbon's, dusty and half-exhausted, but full of enthusiasm. They had had a very hard march, but they would have been on hand a great deal earlier except for a few little mistakes that had been committed here and there along the way. Altogether, these mistakes added up to nothing much except faulty staff work, and they would not be worth mentioning except that they helped to prolong the war by eight months.

The first mistake lay in the fact that somehow no one had told either Meade or Hancock that there was going to be a fight at Petersburg that day. Hancock's orders simply were to march to City Point, to wait long enough there to issue rations to his men, and then to march toward Petersburg and put his men in position at a spot where the City Point Railroad crossed something called Harrison's Creek. He was given a map showing all of the roads to Petersburg, and on this map his objective point was clearly marked. It was stated that the Federals already had field works there.

Hancock undertook to obey orders, but there were problems. The first was that there were no rations for him at City Point, and after waiting several hours he got impatient and had the column move on without them. The next trouble was that the map that had been given him turned out to be totally in error. Roads and streams did not run how or where the map said they did, and the troops were let in for a great deal of countermarching and backtracking. As the day wore on Hancock began to suspect that the spot he was going to did not exist; either the inhabitants of the region had never heard of any Harrison's Creek or they were refusing to share their knowledge with Yankees. (It turned out later that the designated place was well within the Rebel lines.) With all of this, the II Corps had a long day on the roads, and along toward 5:30 P.M a message arrived from U. S. Grant telling Hancock to hurry because Smith had carried the outer works of the Petersburg defense system and needed help at once. A few minutes later Hancock got a similar note from Smith.

Thus, for the first time, Hancock knew that he was supposed to be marching up to take part in a fight. If he had known this at dawn he could have had his men up beside Smith's by midafternoon, bad maps or no: instead, as he wrote in his report, "I spent the best hours of the day . . . in marching by an incorrect map in search of a designated position which, as described, was not in existence." As a result his men began to come up beside Smith's men after all of the fighting had stopped. Smith had made his decision, and when Hancock asked him, as the man on the spot, what was going to happen next, Smith simply suggested that Hancock have his men relieve Hinks's boys in the captured trenches. To-morrow would be time enough to renew the attack.[11]

The II Corps of the Army of the Potomac was a battle-wise outfit, and during the last six weeks it had been hammered so hard that most of the spring had gone out of it. Neverthe-less, it is recorded that for once in their lives the men in this corps made furious and profane objections when they were told that they would not immediately be rushed into battle.

During their march that day an electric sense of coming victory had gone through the ranks. The men had a fairly clear idea of what was going on, and they understood that at last a flank march had been fully successful. They had got ahead of their opponents, they were going to get to Peters-burg before Lee's army could get there, and they were strat-egists enough to know what that was going to mean.[12] So they tramped along perkily, while the sun went down and the twilight faded into ghostly moonlight, and up ahead they heard firing. They came up through the backwash of Smith's battle, at last, and they passed some of Hinks's colored sol-diers, gaily hauling brass cannon to the rear with long ropes, fifty men on a cannon, everybody shouting and laughing. The II Corps looked at this with interest and called out the obvi-ous question: Where did you get those guns? Proudly the col-ored soldiers replied that they had just captured them from the Rebels.

The deduction which Hancock's veterans drew from this was not complimentary to Hinks's division, but it sent II Corps morale sky-high. If these colored troops had captured guns in prepared earthworks, Hancock's men figured, that could only mean that Lee's veterans had not yet reached Petersburg. The Army of the Potomac was winning the race. Up and down the moving column the men shifted their blanket rolls, moved cartridge boxes around to where they could get at them more easily, and remarked to no one in particular: "Put us into it, Hancock, my boy, and we'll end this damned rebellion tonight!"

But instead of going into line of battle and making an advance, they filed into the captured works, watched Smith's troops retire, ate their supper and boiled their coffee, and put out sentinels for the night. Slowly the men came to understand that there would be no fight that night, and one of them wrote afterward: "The rage of the enlisted men was devilish. The most bloodcurdling blasphemy I ever listened to I heard that night, uttered by men who knew they were to be sacrificed on the morrow. The whole corps was furiously excited." [13]

So the II Corps went grumpily to sleep, and Smith's men went to sleep, and Beauregard's men stayed awake and worked hard. On a north-south ridge between the city and the works they had just lost, the Confederates were hard at it building new trenches and gun pits. During the night Hoke's division, which had been on loan north of the James, began to come in, and as the men were rushed out to the new defense line Beauregard took the last desperate step that was available: he ordered abandonment of the lines which held Butler's army immured at Bermuda Hundred, left a thin line of pickets there to watch the situation, and brought the men down to Petersburg. As a result of all of this, by morning he had 10,000 men or more in position to defend the town.[14] The odds against him were still long, but they were nothing like what they had been the day before, and it was just possible now that Beauregard could hold on until Lee's army could come down below the river and help.

Meade was busy, too. During the evening of June 15 he got word from Grant that Smith was fighting hard and that the rest of the army must come up as soon as possible, and so Burnside and his IX Corps crossed the river with orders to move up and take position on the left of Hancock's corps. The V Corps was to follow Burnside, artillery and trains and cavalry were to follow that, and Wright's VI Corps would hold the north bank of the James until everyone else was south of the river. Then the VI Corps would come up, the pontoon bridge would be removed, and everything would be south of the James with City Point as the new supply base.

Meade himself crossed the river on the morning of June 16, and as he rode up from City Point toward Petersburg, along toward noon, he met Grant, just returning from an inspection of the front. Grant was full of enthusiasm, and he told Meade: "Smith has taken a line of works stronger than anything we have seen this campaign. If it is a possible thing I want an assault made at six o'clock this evening." [15]

So ordered. Late in the day Hancock's and Burnside's troops were in line, the guns were in position in the captured works, and a great thunder of gunfire rolled out as the artillerists began to hammer the new Rebel trenches, which lay on the far side of a shallow valley. The sun was going down and the air was full of dust and smoke, and as Meade and his staff rode out to watch the fight there was a strange, coppery tinge in the atmosphere and on the landscape. Things looked posed and unreal, and one of Meade's party saw the gunners silhouetted against the unearthly light as they sponged out the guns and rammed the charges home and mused that they might have been lifted out of the old mezzotint engravings of Napoleon's battles which he used to see on the parlor wall of his parents' home. [16]

The Confederates had made good use of their time and the new line of works was strong. Hancock and Burnside sent their troops forward and there was bitter, inconclusive fighting. Gains were made, and the II Corps got in close around a commanding hill which anchored the left center of the Rebel line, but the Rebels lashed out with sharp counterattacks which made Meade think that Beauregard had a lot of troops in reserve, and in the end it was clear that the work could not be finished that day. The firing died out with a few spiteful rifle shots from the skirmish lines, and the hot guns on the ridge cooled as the sun went down, and Meade sent an officer back to City Point to give Grant a report.

This officer entered the general's tent and found Grant sitting on the edge of his cot, mostly undressed, just ready to go to sleep. He made his report, and Grant knew that Lee had only that afternoon begun to pull his troops out of the works north of the James to march for Petersburg; and he smiled a little and permitted himself a rare moment of self-congratulation, remarking: "I think it is pretty well, to get across a great river and come up here and attack Lee in the rear before he is ready for us." Then Grant went to bed and the staff officer returned to Meade, and everybody made ready for the next day.[17]

Next day ought to do it. Most of the army was up, by now —all of the II and V Corps, two divisions of Smith's corps and one of Wright's and three of Burnside's—in all, more than 80,000 fighting men. The men were very tired, for they had not yet had a chance to recover from six weeks' unbroken fighting and marching, and both Meade and Hancock noted that attacks now were not driven home as they used to be.[18] But morale was high, for the men sniffed victory in the air, and as June 17 dawned opportunity was bright.

Beauregard's trenches were strong, but the line was uneven. It ran south from the Appomattox for four miles, or thereabouts, and it had two principal strong points—the Hare house hill, around which Hancock's men had gained a foothold the night before, and a similar hill a mile or two south and a little east of there, crowned by the house of a man named Shand. This latter hill lay in front of Burnside, and it seemed likely that it could be flanked, and Meade considered that a hard joint attack by Hancock and Burnside ought to knock out both of these strong points and break the line wide open.

Farther south the prospects were even better. The Confederates months ago had built trenches completely encircling Petersburg, but they did not begin to have men enough to occupy all of them. Because the whole Yankee army was massed east of town, Beauregard had massed all of his troops there to meet the threat. On the south he was wide open. There was a country turnpike that dropped south from Petersburg, bearing the pleasing name of the Jerusalem Plank Road, and it and the country west of it held no Rebel troops at all, except for a thin cordon of cavalry pickets. Beauregard was painfully aware that he was defenseless in that quarter, and he wrote later that if Meade had put so much as one army corps over on the Jerusalem Road and told it to march due north, "I would have been compelled to evacuate Petersburg without much resistance." [19]

The army corps which might have made such a march was readily available—Warren's V Corps, which held the extreme left of Meade's line. It was the freshest outfit in the army, for it had not been involved in the hard fighting at Cold Harbor and had not, in fact, been heavily engaged since Spotsylvania. On June 16 Grant had wired Meade to get Warren over to the Jerusalem Road as fast as possible, and in a general way this was supposed to be Warren's objective on June 17. But Warren found Rebel skirmishers in his front and they were busy and seemed to be very bold and cocky, and Warren was cautious about pressing them too hard—and, in the end, nothing in particular was done and the empty country west of the Jerusalem Plank Road remained empty all day long.

On Warren's right there was hard fighting. Burnside dutifully moved up to attack the Shand house hill, where his men fought manfully but without intelligent direction. There was a ravine in front of the hill, and on the Yankee side the ground was full of gullies and patches of thick wood, which made it hard to form and move a line of battle. During the night Burnside's leading division, Potter's, struggled across this uneven ground. The going was hard, and the men had just made an all-night march after being under arms for thirty-six hours, and whenever a brigade or regiment was temporarily halted the men would drop where they were and go to sleep. When it was time to move on again they could be aroused only with much difficulty.

Line was formed close to the Confederate position. Orders were passed in a whisper, and the men were required to put their canteens in their haversacks so that they would not rattle. Just at dawn, with bayonets fixed, the division swept over the crest, plunged down into the ravine, and made for the Rebel position. [20]

The position was strong, but there were few Rebels in it,

and Potter's tired men seized the hill, dug some rifle pits, and looked around for the support that had been promised. On their right a division of the II Corps had been told to make a simultaneous attack, but orders had gone sour somewhere and the attack was not being made. (One trouble probably was that Hancock had finally been disabled by his old Gettysburg wound and had had to turn the corps over to the senior division commander, General Birney; in any case, liaison had broken down and the support was not there.)

In the rear things were no better. Another of Burnside's divisions, Ledlie's, had been supposed to follow on Potter's heels, but through some incredible breakdown in staff work nobody had told Ledlie about it and he and his men were sound asleep when the attack was launched. For the time being Potter's men could do nothing but dig in and wait.

Birney finally got his attack moving and it was successful, swamping the Confederate defenses on the Hare house hill, from which position the II Corps might have made a sweep toward the south, taking in flank what was left of the Confederate line. But control of the fight seems to have slipped out of Meade's hands, and no unit commander up front was concerned with anything except what lay immediately before him, and although the Confederate line had been broken in two places before noon nothing effective was done to exploit the openings.

Several hours passed. Burnside finally got a second division forward and it charged through Potter's troops and attacked the new line which Beauregard had patched up there. The men had to cross a railroad cut and climb a steep slope and there was a Confederate battery placed so that it could fire down the length of the railroad cut, and the new division was broken up and forced to retreat with nothing accomplished. Toward dusk, Burnside brought up Ledlie's division, and it went slamming down into the railroad cut and up the far side in the face of a furious fire. There were confused attacks and counterattacks all up and down the slope, and men used bayonets and clubbed muskets in desperate fights for gun pits. The 39th Massachusetts won an advanced position, losing three color-bearers, and at last was forced back, leaving its colors on the ground. Its colonel asked for volunteers to go out and get the flags. A corporal and a private responded and ran out to get them, and suddenly—and quite unexpectedly—the Confederates stopped firing, allowed the men to pick up the flags, and as they went back to the regiment the Rebels waved their hats and raised a cheer. Night came, and Ledlie's men got to the crest of the slope, seized the Confederate works there, and then had to stop because they had run out of ammunition.

So once more the Confederate line had been broken, and Beauregard wrote afterward that it then seemed to him that "the last hour of the Confederacy had arrived." But the Union command system just was not functioning this day, and the story at twilight was a repetition of the story at dawn: it had occurred to no one to have troops ready to follow up a success, and there had not even been any routine arrangements for getting ammunition up to the firing line, and the strategy which had enabled the army to fight for Petersburg with eight-to-one odds in its favor was totally wasted. The day ended and the fighting ended, and in the darkness Beauregard retired his entire line to a final position within easy gunshot of the town.[21]

There was still a chance. Lee was getting his Army of Northern Virginia down to Petersburg with driving speed—lean men in faded uniforms or no uniforms hurrying on through the night, desperately in earnest and handled by a soldier who knew precisely what he was doing and how to do it—but he had not got there yet and he would not be able to get there until several hours after daylight on June 18. A dim awareness of this fact seems to have been astir in the headquarters tents of the Army of the Potomac, and during the night Meade issued orders for an attack all along the line at the moment of dawn.[22]

When light came on June 18 it brought only more confusion. The Federals now were posted on a long ridge, with the Hare and Shand house hills in their possession, and Beauregard's last line was on an opposite ridge, and the different Federal commanders seem to have felt that they ought to explore this new position with some care before they attacked. Up near the river Baldy Smith's troops seized a Confederate skirmish line, took a number of prisoners, and then halted. Birney found himself unable to get his men moving until nearly noon, when he attacked with one division and was quickly repulsed. Burnside managed to edge some men forward and consolidated the position he had won the evening before on the far side of the railroad cut, but he waited for Warren to go into action on his left and this wait turned out to be rather long.

Warren began to move at dawn, as ordered, with all four of his divisions abreast, and he had the power to go sweeping through to the Jerusalem Road, wheel toward the north, and break things up once and for all. But he ran into skirmish fire, found the ground unfamiliar, and at six o'clock halted his men and told them to dig in while patrols examined the ground in their front.

In the rear Meade was in a foul temper, which kept growing worse, and he emitted a furious stream of orders in a completely futile attempt to bring about the united attack which had been designed. Hours passed, and the breakdown in the command system became complete, and by early afternoon Meade was wiring to his corps commanders: "I find it useless to appoint an hour to effect co-operation . . . what additional orders to attack you require I cannot imagine. . . . Finding it impossible to effect co-operation by appointing an hour for attack, I have sent an order to each corps commander to attack at all hazards and without reference to each other." [23]

Late in the afternoon, the attacks were finally made. It was too late, by now, for Lee's veterans were in the trenches at last and the eight-to-one odds had vanished forever; this was Cold Harbor all over again, with its cruel demonstration that trench lines properly manned could not be taken by storm. The chance had gone, and an attack now could result in nothing but destruction for the attackers.

The soldiers knew this even if their generals did not. In

mid-afternoon Birney massed his troops for a final attack. His principal column was formed in four lines, with veteran troops in the first two lines and oversized heavy artillery regiments, untried but full of enthusiasm, in the last two.

The men were lying down when the order to charge the Rebel works came in, and as the officers shouted and waved their swords the inexperienced artillerists sprang to their feet while the veterans ahead of them continued to lie prone. The veterans looked back, saw the rookies preparing to charge, and called out: "Lie down, you damn fools, you can't take them forts!"

One of the artillery regiments, 1st Massachusetts heavies, accepted this advice, lay down again, and made no charge. The other one, 1st Maine, valiantly stayed on its feet, ran forward through the rows of prostrate men, and made for the Confederate line. It was a hopeless try. The Confederate gun pits had been built low and the black muzzles of the guns that peered evilly out of the embrasures were no more than a foot or two above the ground, and when they fired the canister came in just off the grass so that nobody could escape. The whole slope was burned with fire, and in a few minutes more than 600 of the 900 men in the regiment had been shot down, the ground was covered with mangled bodies, and the survivors were running for the rear.[24]

In another part of the II Corps front, what remained of the veteran Excelsior Brigade of New York troops was moving up to the attack. The men passed through a line of artillery, and a gunner called out to ask if they were going to make a charge. A soldier answered him: "No, we are not going to charge. We are going to run toward the Confederate earthworks and then we are going to run back. We have had enough of assaulting earthworks."

The gunner who asked the question went to the rear shortly after this with a caisson to get more ammunition. He got his load and on his return he noticed that the road led over an open hill in such a way that he and his wagonload of explosives would be in clear view of a distant Confederate battery. While he was reflecting that he would undoubtedly draw

Confederate fire, he noticed that in a field on the reverse slope of the hill several hundred stragglers were lounging about little campfires, boiling coffee and enjoying themselves. He mused that these were the worthless bounty men and conscripts who had fled from the firing line, and whose mere presence in uniform weakened the entire corps, and he wished earnestly that something bad would happen to them: and just then the Rebel gunners caught sight of him, swung their guns in his direction, and let fly with a salvo.

The range was long and their aim was imperfect, and the shells missed the caisson and skimmed down into the very middle of the coffee boilers, where they exploded and sent campfires and coffee pots up in flying dust and sparks and smoke. On the ground were screaming men, fearfully wounded, and those who had not been hurt were running desperately for the woods; and the gunner reined in to enjoy the scene, and hugged his knees and rocked in wild laughter, and when he got back to his battery he told his mates it was "the most refreshing sight I had seen for weeks." [25]

The afternoon's attacks came to nothing at all. Warren and Burnside finally sent their men forward at three o'clock—the morning's opportunity gone with the morning's mists—and the Army of Northern Virginia was waiting for them in secure trenches, and the men were repulsed with heavy loss. The day ended, finally, and Meade wired Grant that nothing more could be done. He added piously that "our men are tired and the attacks have not been made with the vigor and force which characterized our fighting in the Wilderness; if they had been, I think we should have been more successful."

Grant replied that they would make no more assaults: "Now we will rest the men and use the spade for their protection until a new vein has been cut." [26]

So the men huddled in their trenches, and after dark they could hear the mocking sound of the belfry clocks in Petersburg striking the hours, and a man in a Connecticut regiment wrote that "this was the most intolerable position the regiment was ever required to hold." [27]

The men were used to occupying trenches under fire, and

in that respect the situation here was no worse than it had been at Cold Harbor or half a dozen other places. What made it truly intolerable was the realization, running from end to end of a tired, heartsick army, that the greatest chance of the war had been missed—and that, as a military critic expressed it years afterward, "the blame of the failure to take Petersburg must rest with our generals, not with our army." [28]

CHAPTER IV

White Iron on the Anvil

---

1. Changing the Guard

THE trenches ran south from the Appomattox for five miles, following the tops of the low ridges, and for all anyone could see the armies might stay there forever. There had been no rain for two weeks (nobody knew it, but another month would pass before there was as much as a light shower) and the dust was inches deep: a fine, powdery dust, like soiled flour, so light that every footstep sent up a cloud of it, and half a dozen men walking together along a trench or on open ground in the rear moved, invisible, in a choking mist of their own creation.

Sometimes the dust seemed to be the chief enemy. A Connecticut man wrote that taking a stroll was like walking in an ash heap, and he said that after a short time "one's mouth will be so full of dust that you do not want your teeth to touch each other." A gunner said that whenever a grasshopper hopped it raised so much dust that Rebel lookouts reported the Yankee army on the move, a New Yorker found the combination of 110-degree heat and 4-inch dust "is killing more men than the Johnnies," and a private from Michigan—remembering the cool pines and clear streams of his homeland—wrote despondently: "I think of the hottest days, in harvest time, away north in Michigan, and oh! how cool, compared with these." Every day men toppled over with sunstroke and were carried to the rear. Uniforms, faces, trees, shrubs, and grass were all a dull, ugly yellow gray. The air was heavy with the odor of unburied bodies, and the sun beat down day after day on men who cowered in deep slits in the earth.[1]

General Grant had said that they would use the spade, and they did. Each regiment in the line would dig a broad trench, and on the side facing the enemy there would be a solid wall of logs, with dirt banked up beyond it. Several yards in front of this there would be a ditch, six feet deep by ten feet wide, with the earth that came out of it added to the pile in front of the logs until the embankment was six or eight feet high and a dozen feet thick. Sandbags or logs would be arranged on top of the embankment, with slits or loopholes for men to stick their rifles through, and just behind the log wall there would be a fire step—a low ledge of packed earth, built so that a man who stood on it could put his musket through the loopholes. At intervals, leading to the rear, there would be covered ways, which were deep trenches zig-zagged to take advantage of the ground, built so that men could walk to the firing line from the rear without being exposed.

Out in front of the trenches, fifty or one hundred yards nearer to the enemy, there was an abatis. Much of the ground had been timbered, and the trees were felled with their bushy tops pointing toward the foe. The butts were embedded in shallow trenches to hold them in place, and the branches were sharpened and bound together so that it was almost impossible to get through them. In places there were several rows of these entanglements, with narrow lanes cut here and there so that pickets could go out to their stations. This abatis was supplemented very often by what were called *chevaux-de-frise:* heavy logs laid end to end and bound together with chains, bristling with six-foot stakes sharpened to a point and projecting in such a way that a man who tried to scramble over was certain to find his person or his clothing jagged and held fast.

On every hill or knoll there was a fort, a square enclosure of earth and logs with openings for the guns. These were arranged so that there was no place in front of the trenches that could not be reached by artillery fire. Farther to the rear there were pits like unroofed cellars where coehorn mortars were mounted. In these forts and pits, and adjoining all of the trenches, there were bombproofs—square holes in the earth roofed with logs and dirt, in which the men could hide when the enemy fired shells.[2]

That was the front. It was five miles long and the Rebel line was exactly like the Union line, and there was not the remotest chance that any part of either line could be taken by storm so long as a handful of defenders remained on duty and stayed awake. The dust and the sickening air and the killing sunlight lay on everything, and the sharpshooters and the gunners were always alert, and by day and by night there was intermittent heavy firing. A good many men were killed and wounded every day, to no particular end except to warn the survivors that they had better dig deeper and stronger trenches and hide in them every moment of their lives.[3]

On most of the line the trenches were not far apart, and in front of Burnside's corps there were hardly 150 yards between them, and the firing there was almost continuous. On each side sharpshooters with long-range rifles found vantage points a little behind the lines and kept their weapons trained on the firing slits in the opposing trenches, so that a man who looked out to see what he could see was quite likely to get a bullet in the face.

Toward the southern end of the line, however, where the V Corps was stationed, the works diverged. Here the Rebel trenches curved over toward the west and the Federal trenches continued in a southerly direction, and the rival lines were half a mile apart, and so there was much less shooting. Along here the pickets had made their usual arrangements with each other, and between the lines there was a little stream to which men from both armies came, in full light of day, to fill their canteens. When an officer came down the enemies would warn each other, because most officers had strong ideas about the need for keeping up a constant fire, and the general feeling was that officers were interlopers who ought to stay farther in the rear. One day the Union General Crawford came out to the picket line and stood up on a parapet and began examining the Rebel line through field glasses. A Reb scribbled something on a sheet of paper, wrapped the paper around a stone, and tossed it over into a Union rifle pit. The Federal soldier who picked it up found that the Southerner had written: "Tell the fellow with the spy glass to clear out or we shall have to shoot him."

When they were left to themselves the men in this particular sector faithfully observed the rules of their informal truce. There was a day when some recently conscripted Southerner was assigned to duty down here, and being full of the ideas his officers had drummed into him he leveled his musket and fired at the first Yankee he saw. The other Federals jumped into their holes and prepared to shoot back, but the Confederates called out: "Don't shoot—you'll see how we fix him." Thereafter, for the rest of the day, the ardent Southern recruit was seen pacing back and forth along the firing line ignominiously shouldering a fence rail, and the supposed enemies lounged on the grass, went for water, exchanged gossip, and kept a wary eye open for officers.[4]

But this was the exception. Along most of the line the two armies were playing for keeps, and it was considered certain death to expose oneself for more than a moment. Men cooked, ate, and slept in the earth, and when mortars were fired they ran for the bombproofs, although they soon discovered that most of these did not offer much protection against a direct hit by a shell of large caliber. On one part of the line certain Pennsylvania soldiers—time-expired members of the famous Bucktails, mostly, who had re-enlisted in another regiment when the Bucktails were paid off—found that it was highly amusing to fire ramrods at the enemy, because of the peculiar whirring noise and erratic flight of these iron arrows. Many men had been killed in this sector and there were discarded rifles all over the place, so the supply of surplus ramrods was large and some of the Pennsylvanians got so they could actually hit people with them. The fun was mostly in the noise, however, for the ramrods would go "whirling end over end, and every way, whipping out of the air a multitude of sharp screeches and cutting sounds." [5]

In some regiments men were under orders to fire a certain number of rounds per day, regardless. The more conscientious would try to find a good target before firing, but many of the men simply thrust their weapons over the parapet and fired at random.[6]

There did not seem to be any especial reason why this could not go on forever. Not even the major generals supposed any longer that Petersburg could be taken by assault, and it had become equally obvious that whatever else an army under Grant might do, it was not going to retreat. The strategy by which Grant had hoped to apply pressure elsewhere so as to compel Lee to retreat had fizzled out, so there was nothing for the Army of the Potomac to do but stay where it was, stand the hammering, and hope for the best.

Sheridan and his cavalry had got nowhere with the plan to team up with Hunter's forces at Charlottesville. Wade Hampton had gone in hot pursuit with Confederate cavalry, and he and Sheridan collided near Trevilian Station on the Virginia Central Railroad and had a desperate fight. Each general said afterward that he had beaten the other, but Sheridan had gone no farther west. He said this was because he had learned that Hunter was nowhere near Charlottesville and never would be, so that it was useless to go on. However that might have been, Sheridan rode north and east in a wide circle and got back into the Union lines.

Hunter had tried to go to Lynchburg instead of to Charlottesville, and he had bumped into a strong Confederate force led by the redoubtable Jubal Early. Hunter conceived that he did not have enough ammunition to carry him through a serious battle; conceived also, it may be, that Early and his men were pretty tough; conceived finally that he had best retreat, and did so, fleeing across the mountains into West Virginia, taking his command entirely out of the war for several weeks and nullifying this particular part of Grant's strategy as neatly as Lee himself could have wished. His departure left the Shenandoah Valley wide open, and Early promptly began to march down the valley toward the Potomac, taking a leaf from the Stonewall Jackson book of two years earlier.[7]

It was the railroads that made Petersburg important, and about the time the two armies settled down to unbroken trench warfare, Wilson was told to take his division of cavalry and ride far south to destroy the line that led to North Carolina. His men tore up much track, burned stations and freight cars, and wrecked bridges and culverts, but Sheridan's retreat from Trevilian had left Lee with a temporary surplus of cavalry and these rode hard and fast, overtaking Wilson, boxing him in, and coming close to destroying his entire command. He got back within the Union lines at last, minus his artillery and his wagons and a good many of his men, and his expedition looked like a flat failure. Actually, it had accomplished more than the Federal command quite realized. The break which it made in the vital Southern railway line was a bad one and it was not fully repaired for weeks, and while it lasted the Confederates were burdened with one of their worst supply problems of the war.[8]

There had been one other failure, and in some ways it was the worst of the lot. When Beauregard pulled his troops out of the Bermuda Hundred lines in order to save Petersburg, Butler's inactive army was released. For twenty-four hours the way was open for it to move forward, cut the railroad and highway from Petersburg to Richmond, and sever all communications between Beauregard and Lee. Butler's front-line commanders saw the chance and tried to do something about it, and Grant saw it and sent Wright and two divisions of the VI Corps over to help, but Butler flubbed the shot completely. He hesitated and considered and then launched a spate of orders which looked good on paper but which served only to confuse the generals who had to do the fighting, and before he could get himself rounded up Lee sent Pickett's division in, shoved the irresolute Federals back, and closed the gap for good.

Somewhere, in the tangled mesh of politics that lay between Washington and the fighting fronts, Butler possessed influence that even the commander of the armies could not break. Grant tried to have him removed, and failed. Then he worked out a scheme by which Butler would retain his command but would do all of his work down at Fortress Monroe, where there was administrative routine to be handled, leaving all military operations to Baldy Smith, his second-in-command. That could not be done, either. Butler held his job and he held it on his own terms, although Grant warned Halleck that relations between Butler and Smith were so bad that if Butler stayed Smith probably would have to go.

In the end, Smith did go; and in the end, when he went, it was Grant who sent him away. While he fought his losing fight to get rid of Butler, Grant seems to have done a good deal of thinking about Smith's performance on June 15, when he captured the Confederate forts and then sent his soldiers to bed instead of into Petersburg. In the end Grant concluded that Smith was a man he could do without, Butler or no Butler, and when he came to this conclusion he acted on it. Smith was quietly removed and sent up to New York—indignant, protesting bitterly, writing long afterward that the real trouble was that Butler had got Grant drunk and then had used his knowledge of the fact as blackmail to make Grant do as Butler wished.[9]

The tale can be taken or left alone, at anyone's choice. The chief trouble is that it is too simple, explaining too much with too little. There is of course no reason to suppose that Butler would have been above blackmailing Grant or anyone else if it would have served his purposes, but something much more intricate than a threat to let one small cat out of a bag was unquestionably involved in the fact that Butler could not be fired. His political power had been moving mountains long before he had any opportunity to lay Grant under threat of exposure.

Everything about Butler was fantastic, beginning with his personal appearance: lumpy oversized body, arms and legs that looked as if they had been attached as an afterthought, eyes that refused to mesh. As a Democratic politician, he had in 1860 been an ardent supporter of the extreme Southern viewpoint; two years later the Southerners were announcing that Ben Butler was the one Yankee who, if captured by Confederate forces, would be shot without trial. Abolitionists made a hero of him and considered him a great friend of the Negro, although at the beginning of the war he had said that he would not interfere with slavery in a slave state, and when the idea of enlisting Negroes as soldiers was first suggested to him in New Orleans he turned it down flatly. A private in the 25th Massachusetts wrote that "as a military governor he is a none-such . . . but as a commander of troops in the field he is not just such a man as I should pick out." [10]

Butler was the archetype of the fixer, the influence man, the person on whom nothing much is ever proved but who is always suspected of everything. Devout Confederates believed that in addition to committing an illegal hanging and insulting Southern womanhood he had in New Orleans personally stolen silver spoons with his own hands. A Northern general who served under him for a time in Virginia reported that Butler had become a dictator who "made laws and administered them, dealt out justice and inflicted punishment, levied fines and collected taxes," and he added that the air about him was thick with rumors and hints of corruption. A good part of Butler's territory in the Norfolk–Hampton Roads area was a queer no man's land in which contraband trade seemed to flourish, with cotton shipped into the Union lines in return for war goods which went to support Lee's army. Nobody was ever quite sure just who got the rake-off, but it seemed obvious that someone must be getting a good deal. A tremendous scandal was always on the edge of breaking, but the break never quite came. There was always something soiled about the man, but he remained uncanny and untouchable. [11]

There were times when it was all but impossible for a good man to work under him. He could send a subordinate an order phrased so as to constitute the most cruel of insults; then, when the officer protested, Butler would write a smooth letter insisting that no insult was intended and that he had the highest personal and professional regard for the man he had insulted. A brilliant lawyer, he knew how to handle words, and none of the professional soldiers who tangled with him could match phrases with him.

Just at the end of the period when his troops might have broken out of the Bermuda Hundred lines he sent to General Wright a curt order to attack the Rebel troops in his front at once. The situation at the front was not at all as Butler imagined it and Wright wired back that the proposed attack was impossible, suggested an alternative approach, and asked further instructions.

Immediately Butler replied: "At 7:10 this evening I sent an order to you and General Terry to do some fighting. At 10:30 I get no fighting, but an argument. My order went out by direction of the lieutenant general." When Wright, somewhat baffled, protested against what he termed an unmerited reproach, Butler blandly replied: "No reproach is given; a fact is stated," and added loftily that victory could not be won if orders were not obeyed.[12]

In his campaign to keep his job this summer Butler held one prodigious trump card which Grant could not see. This was a presidential election year, and just when Grant was trying to rid himself of this incompetent general the leaders of the Republican party, very much against their will, were in the act of renominating President Lincoln for a second term. It was no time to rock the boat, and Butler was just the man who could rock it to the point of capsizing it.

From the beginning, Lincoln's real problem had been political. He had a war to win and he had to find generals who could win it, but above everything else he had to control the war—not merely the fighting of it, but the currents which would finally determine what it meant and what would come of it all. So far, the war had brought nothing but death: death by wholesale, death in all its forms, death in hospitals, in blazing thickets, on ridges swept by exploding shell, in ravines where dust and battle smoke lay thick and blinding. Unless the whole thing was no better than fever and madness, all of this death must finally be swallowed up in a victory that would justify the cost. The spirit that would infuse this victory must have infinite breadth, because the country was

fighting no enemy: it was simply fighting itself. The death of
a South Carolinian, brained by a clubbed musket butt in a
fort in front of Petersburg, was fully as significant as the
death of a Pennsylvanian killed by a Minié ball in a swamp
at Cold Harbor. If what those men had bought, by dying, was
to be principally hatred and smash-'em-up, then both deaths
had been wasted and dust and ashes were the final truth.

There were strong men in the North who wanted revenge.
The old technique of plowing up the site of a conquered city
and sowing the ground with salt had fallen into disuse, since
the fall of Carthage, but they would do the best they could
with some modern variant. The Ben Wades and the Thad
Stevenses and the Zach Chandlers had great capacity for
hatred, and the South was not part of the country as they saw
it. Lincoln stood in their way, and because they could not
budge him they cried that he was soft and irresolute, and
they would put one of their own kind in his place if they
could. Standing with them were the men whose minds were
laudably high but deplorably narrow—the abolitionists, the
men who had taken scars in the long fight in the day when the
odds were all against them and who now were disposed to
judge a man by the iron which he was willing to put into the
matter of punishment for the slave-owners.

There was something to be said on their side. They could
remember Bully Brooks and his murderous assault on Sumner,
and the taunts and jibes of men like Texas's Wigfall, who
would have turned the Senate into a place where only an expert duelist could speak freely. If they were grim and implacable, it is at least possible to see how they got that way;
and in addition they were that part of the Union cause which
would never surrender or stop to haggle over costs. They provided a good part of the nerve and sinew which enabled the
North to bounce back from Fredericksburg defeats and Wilderness casualty lists, and neither Lincoln nor any other Republican was likely to win the election if they went actively
on the warpath.

What had kept them off the warpath so far was partly the
fact that Lincoln did seem to have most of the people with

him, and partly the old political truism: You can't beat somebody with nobody. To date, only nobodies had offered themselves against him, men like John Charles Frémont, who was
heading a rickety third-party slate. But Butler was a somebody. Soldiers might know him as a cipher, but with abolitionists and bitter-enders he was a mighty hero. He had
boundless ambition and a total lack of scruples, and he saw
himself as a presidential possibility. If the army suddenly
dropped him he would land in the arms of the political ex-
tremists. What that would mean, to the war and to the things
that would finally come out of the war, was nothing good
men could speculate about with easy hearts.

So the truth of the matter probably is that in the infinite,
complicated economy of the Civil War it was better to keep
Ben Butler a major general, even though soldiers were need-
lessly killed because of it, than it was to inject him back into
the political whirlpool. Washington saw it so, at any rate, and
Washington had to balance fearful intangibles when it made
its decision. And although there was not, fortunately, anyone
else quite like Butler, there were many other cases where
similar intangibles had to be balanced—cases where the Administration had to ask, in effect: Where will this man do the
least harm—as a general, or as a politician out of control?
Often enough the wrong guess was made, but that was the
kind of riddle the times were asking.

Halleck understood these matters, and when Grant first began suggesting that it would be easier to win the war with
Butler a civilian, Halleck tried to explain to him that political
considerations must at times override even the professional
judgment of the general in chief. A little earlier, Halleck had
frankly confessed in a letter to Sherman that "it seems little
better than murder to give important commands to such men
as Banks, Butler, McClernand, Sigel and Lew Wallace, and
yet it seems impossible to prevent it." [13] Halleck was right.
It was impossible to prevent it. The trouble was that the army
had to carry these costly misfits on its shoulders.

But the political generals were only part of the story, as far
as the army was concerned. As the army settled into its

trenches after four days of battle in front of Petersburg—four days which cost, roughly, as many killed and wounded as had been lost in all twelve days at Cold Harbor—some of its professionals were giving cause for worry.

Meade was on the verge of removing Warren, just when Grant was sending Smith into exile. Warren was increasingly given to broad interpretation and spontaneous revision of his orders, and Meade could hardly fail to note that the all-out attack which he had told Warren to make at dawn on the crucial eighteenth of June had not actually been delivered until 3:30 P.M. At one time Meade had definitely made up his mind to send Warren away, but the trouble was reconciled somehow and by July 1 Assistant Secretary of War Dana wired Stanton that "the difficulty between Meade and Warren has been settled without the extreme remedy which Meade proposed last week." [14]

Meade himself was showing the strain. His temper was always bad, but as June wore on into sultry July and frustration followed frustration he became as savage as a wounded grizzly, and Dana was presently telling Stanton: "I do not think he has a friend in the whole army. No man, no matter what his business or his service, approaches him without being insulted in one way or another, and his own staff officers do not dare speak to him unless first spoken to, for fear of either sneers or curses." Dana added that a change in command seemed probable.[15]

There was probably some exaggeration in this. Meade and Grant were never intimates, but in the main they got along well enough. Nevertheless, there was trouble. Meade had handled the Petersburg assaults about as ineptly as they could have been handled, and his angry complaint on the fourth day, that since he had found it impossible to co-ordinate attacks each commander should go ahead and do the best he could on his own hook, went far to merit the comment it got from General Wright—that the different attacks had been ordered "without brains and without generalship." [16] Grant seriously considered taking Meade out of the top spot and sending him up to the Shenandoah Valley, and he appears to have felt that if this happened Hancock was the man to take Meade's place.[17]

Yet that would hardly do, either. Hancock's wound still refused to heal. He returned to duty late in June, but a wound which remains open after nearly a year takes something out of a man, and Hancock's great days were over. Like Meade, he was getting irritable, and he was quarreling now with General Gibbon, who had been one of his best friends.[18] Worse yet was the fact that if Hancock was not himself his own immediate command, the famous II Army Corps, was in even worse shape.

The II Corps had been fought out and used up. It had been the most famous corps in the army. It had stormed Bloody Lane at Antietam, it had taken 4,000 casualties at Fredericksburg without flinching, it had beaten back Pickett's charge at Gettysburg, and it had broken the Bloody Angle at Spotsylvania. But now it was all shot to pieces, and instead of being the army's strongest fighting unit it was the weakest. Nothing but a long period of recruiting, drill, and discipline would bring it up to its old level.

Proof of this came in the latter part of June, shortly before Hancock returned to command, when the corps was sent out to the Jerusalem Plank Road in an effort to extend the army's left. Lee saw the move and sent A. P. Hill's veterans down to meet it, and these men caught the corps off balance, tapped at its flanks, crumpled it up, and sent it flying. The fight had not been a particularly hard one, and comparatively few men were killed or wounded, but the manner of the defeat was eloquent. No fewer than 1,700 men had been taken prisoner —more prisoners than the corps had lost at Antietam, Fredericksburg, and Chancellorsville put together—and whole regiments had surrendered without firing a shot. Among these were the remnants of regiments which had once been among the very best in the army. There was the 15th Massachusetts, for instance, which had had more than 300 casualties in the West Wood at Antietam but which, when forced to retreat from that doleful little grove, had proudly brought out not only its own flag but also the flag of a Confederate regiment with which it had come to grips. In this latest fight the 15th surrendered almost entire, flag and all, after no more than a token resistance. Also, the corps had lost four pieces of artillery, and its attempt to retake these guns had been very feeble.[19]

What had happened was clear enough. During the last two months almost all of the good men in the corps had been shot. The figures on Gibbon's division tell the story. This division crossed the Rapidan on May 5 with a total of 6,799 men in its three brigades. During May and June it had 7,970 casualties—more men, by a large margin, than the entire number under arms when the campaign began. It had received heavy reinforcements, to be sure, but its losses for the two months amounted to 72 per cent of its original strength plus all of the replacements. It saw forty regimental commanders killed or wounded, and, as Gibbon wrote, the losses showed plainly why it was that "troops which at the commencement of the campaign were equal to almost any undertaking, became toward the end of it unfit for almost any." [20]

Gibbon's division had had it worse than the other II Corps divisions, but only a little worse. Altogether, the corps had lost nearly 20,000 men in less than two months. More than a score of its brigadiers had been shot, and approximately a hundred regimental commanders. Naturally, the men who were lost were the best men—the officers who led the way, the enlisted men who ran ahead in a charge and were the last to leave when a position was given up. Numerically, most of the losses had been made good, but the new men were mostly substitutes and bounty jumpers, of whom a II Corps gunner said contemptuously that Lee's veterans could, if they chose, drown the lot by taking bean poles and pushing them into the James River.[21]

. . . There had been that dance for officers of the II Army Corps, in the raw-pine pavilion above the Rapidan on Washington's Birthday, and it had been a fine thing to see; and it had been a long good-by and a dreamy good night for the young men in bright uniforms and the women who had tied their lives to them. Most of the men who danced at that ball were dead, now; dead, or dragging themselves about home-town streets on crutches, or tapping their way along with a hickory cane to find the way instead of bright youthful eyes, or in hospitals where doctors with imperfect knowledge tried to patch them up enough to enable them to hope to get out of bed someday and sit in a chair by the window. There had been a romance to war once, or at least people said there was, and each one of these men had seen it, and they had touched the edge of it while the music played and the stacked flags swayed in the candlelight, and it all came down to this, with the drifting dust of the battlefields blowing from the imperfect mounds of hastily dug graves.

Famous old fighting units ceased to exist. At the end of June Gibbon's adjutant published orders consolidating what was left of the once mighty 15th, 19th, and 20th Massachusetts—there were about enough men left to make a slim battalion and thereafter they would serve as a unit, although separate regimental rolls would still be kept. The Philadelphia Brigade was broken up, the men in its five skeleton regiments being parceled out to regiments in other brigades. The survivors were angry, and jeered the next time they saw General Gibbon, and one man in the 106th Pennsylvania lamented that he and his comrades would no longer carry their prized regimental flag, which had been pierced (they had counted carefully) by thirty-nine bullets in its three years of service.[22]

The II Corps had been hit the hardest, but nobody had been on a picnic. General Lysander Cutler commanded what had been Wadsworth's division in the V Corps, and when he wrote his report for the campaign he explained why the report was going to be incomplete. Two regiments had been lost by expiration of their terms of service, he wrote, and one whole brigade had been transferred to another division. The regiments which still remained with the division had, when the campaign began, 3,742 enlisted men, and now they had 1,324, and the regiments which had been transferred had suffered in proportion. Furthermore: "The changes in the command have been so frequent, and the losing of nearly every original brigade, regimental and company commander render it impossible to make anything like an accurate report." [23]

In the 24th Michigan, which now had fewer than 100 men, there was one company with a total strength of two—one sergeant and one private—and on drill or parade a man remembered that "it afforded amusement to witness the evolutions of this little company." A man in the 12th New Hampshire said that his regiment had been under fire every day, and every night but one, over a period of seventy-two days, and a headquarters clerk in the V Corps wrote the age-old complaint of the soldier: "How often the words 'cruel war' are uttered, and how glibly people beyond the reach of its influence talk of the misery caused by it . . . but not one-thousandth part of the real misery is even guessed at by those who are not eyewitnesses of its horrors." [24]

Many men who had not been hit became unfit for service simply because they were worn out. Colonel Dawes of the 6th Wisconsin, appointed to a board to pass on officers' qualifications, recalled numerous cases of self-inflicted wounds. He remembered one captain whose fertile imagination led him to drink "a decoction of powdered slate pencils in vinegar" in order to unfit himself for further duty, and he reported sadly that "the excitement, exhaustion, hard work and loss of sleep broke down great numbers of men who had received no wounds in battle." Some men, he said, who had been noted for their bravery and leadership when the campaign began, became timorous, unstable, and all but useless toward the end of it. For a time the 150th Pennsylvania contained a unique detachment known as "Company Q," made up of line officers from other regiments who had been court-martialed and broken for cowardice but who were given the chance to serve as private soldiers and, if they could, redeem themselves. Company Q turned out to be a good fighting unit, and most of the men in it ultimately regained their commissions.[25]

Even the chaplains seemed to be showing the strain, and many of them quietly gravitated toward safe jobs far behind the lines. ("Undue susceptibility to cannon fever," a New England soldier complained, "ought to be regarded as a disqualification.") A surgeon in the 39th Illinois, on duty at a base hospital at Fortress Monroe, felt that the chaplains there were "pharisees who made it a business to pray aloud in public places . . . rotten to the core, not caring half as much for their souls' welfare or anybody else's as for the dollars they received." One chaplain ruined morale in his ward by coming in half a dozen times a day, sitting on the edge of some soldier's cot, and telling the man he looked bad and must prepare to die; a patient threw a plate at him one day and told him to go to the devil. The doctor added stoutly that he himself had "stood beside hundreds of soldiers when dying from disease or wounds, and he has never yet seen one manifest the least fear of death." [26]

In the 2nd Connecticut Heavy Artillery it was said that the chaplain got into a poker game one night and cleaned out an entire company, coming into regimental headquarters later to show a fat roll of bills and say, "There is my forenoon's work." An officer remembered seeing some dignified clergymen of the Christian Commission moving up toward the front, carpetbags in hand. They passed some soldiers, one of whom called out: "Hullo! Got any lemons to sell?" Gravely, one of the frock-coated contingent replied: "No, my friend, we belong to the army of the Lord." And from a blue-uniformed officer there came back: "Oh yes—stragglers! stragglers!" [27]

As usual, there were complaints that not all of the goods sent down for Christian and Sanitary Commission workers to distribute to the soldiers ever actually reached the men for whom they were intended. A soldier detailed as hospital orderly said that grafters and scroungers got most of these delicacies: "The articles to be distributed are first turned over to the surgeon in charge, he keeping out enough for himself and assistants, then the cooks take out enough for themselves and friends. The balance, should there be a balance, goes to the soldiers. I know the above to be true from personal observation." [28]

Underneath the grousing and the bills of complaint the army was trying to maintain a sense of the continuity of its own experiences and traditions. It had to do this, because actually this simply was not the army it used to be. Something like 100,000 combat men had come down across the Rapidan early in May (the flags were all flying and everything was bright and blowing and the dogwood blossoms lit the shadows in the woods) and 60,000 of them had been shot while many other thousands had been sent home as time-expired veterans, and so much the greater part of the men who had started out were not with the army any more. There were 86,000 men in the ranks at the end of June, and most of them were new men. What those who were gone had left behind them was the confusing raw material out of which a new morale would have to be made.

Always the army reflected the nation, and the nation itself was changing. Like the army, it contained many new people these days. The war had speeded everything up. The immigrant ships were coming faster, there were more factories and slums and farms and towns, and the magical hazy light that came down from the country's past was beginning to cast some unfamiliar shadows. The old unities were gone: unities of blood, of race, of language, of shared ideals and common memories and experiences, the very things which had always seemed essential beneath the word "American." In some mysterious way that nobody quite understood, the army not only mirrored the change but represented the effort to find a new synthesis.

What was going on in front of Petersburg was not the development of a stalemate, or the aimless groping of frozen men stumbling down to the last dead end of a cold trail. What was beginning meant more than what was ending, even though it might be many years before anyone knew just what the beginnings and the endings were. Now and then there was a hint, casually dropped, as the country changed the guard here south of the Appomattox River, and the choking dust hung in dead air under a hot copper sun. The men who followed a misty dream had died of it, but the dream still lived, even though it was taking another form.

There was in the 67th New York Infantry a young German named Sebastian Muller, who got off an immigrant ship in 1860 and walked the streets unable to find work because he could speak no English and because times in this land of promise were harder than he had supposed they would be. The war came and in 1861 a recruiting agent got him, and to his people back in the fatherland Muller wrote: "I am a volunteer soldier in the Army of the United States, to fight the rebels of South America for a sacred thing. All of America has to become free and united and the starry banner has to fly again over the new world. Then we also want to have the slaves freed, the trading of human beings must have an end and every slave should be set free and on his own in time. . . . Evil of all kinds, thievery, whoring, lying and deception have to be punished here."

Muller served in the 67th and on June 20, 1864, the regiment's time expired and it was sent back for muster-out. But he had enlisted a couple of months late, and he and a few others were held in service and were transferred to the 65th New York to serve out their time, and two days after the 67th went back home Muller was a picket in an advanced gun pit on the VI Corps front, and a Rebel sniper drew a bead on him and killed him. A German comrade wrote a letter of consolation to Muller's parents: "If a person is meant to die on land, he will not drown. If death on the battlefield is to be his lot, he will not die in the cradle. God's dispositions are wise and his ways are inscrutable." The chaplain added a note saying that Muller had died without pain and had been given "a decent Christian burial." [29] That was that.

In the 19th Massachusetts there was an Irish sergeant named Mike Scannell—the same who won his chevrons by carrying the flag at Cold Harbor—and in the II Corps debacle over by the Jerusalem Plank Road Mike and his flag were out in front and were taken by the Confederates, one of whom came at Mike with leveled bayonet, ordering: "You

damned Yankee, give me that flag!" Mike looked at the
Southerner and he looked at the bayonet, and he replied:

"Well, it is twenty years since I came to this country, and
you are the first man who ever called me a Yankee. You can
take the flag, for that compliment." [30]

Nothing much had happened. A German who could not
tell Virginia from South America had seen a sacred thing
in the war and had died for it, and an Irishman after twenty
years of rejection had been accepted, at the point of a bayonet but in the language of his time and place, as a full-
fledged American.

The synthesis was taking place.

2. I Know Star-Rise

The ravine was broad and it ran north and south, and
along the bottom of it there were a little brook and what
remained of the Norfolk and Petersburg Railroad. On the
western crest, which was the side toward the Rebels, there
was a line of Federal entrenchments, and the center of this
line was held by the 48th Pennsylvania Veteran Volunteer
Infantry.

The trench was high-water mark for the IX Army Corps
—the extreme limit of the advance, the place where tired
men who had fired all of their ammunition lay in the dark
to build little breastworks out of earth scooped up with bayonets, tin plates, and bare hands.

Since the fight the line had been made very strong. There
was a deep trench now, with a high parapet on the side toward the Rebels, and out in front there was a cunning tangle
of abatis. A quarter of a mile in the rear, on the eastern crest
of the ravine, there were gun pits, with artillery placed so
that it could knock down any hostile parties that might try
to storm the trench. The slope just behind the trench offered protection from Southern fire, and to make traffic to-

ward the rear even safer, there was a deep covered way, which left the trench almost at a right angle, crossed the ravine and ended behind the guns.

On the Confederate side things were much the same. The trench was deep and strong, and the point directly opposite the place where the 48th lived had been made into a fort, with brass cannon emplaced. Like the Federals, the Confederates had an abatis out in front, and covered ways leading to the rear, and batteries posted to beat back any attack. Five hundred yards behind the Confederate trench the ground rose to a long, rounded ridge, and just over this ridge was the Jerusalem Plank Road, which had once been an undefended avenue leading into Petersburg but which was undefended no longer.

As far as men could make them so, the opposing lines here were proof against assault. The soldiers who occupied them were always on the alert. They had to be, because the trenches here were closer together than at any point along the front. Everyone kept under cover, and any man who exposed himself for an instant was immediately shot at—and usually was hit, too, for the sharpshooters were keen and the range was short. There were mortars back among the gun pits, and they were active. And although the trenches were deep and the men took care of themselves, it was very expensive to hold this part of the line and divisional losses could run to 12 per cent in one month just from sniper and mortar fire.[1]

The 48th Pennsylvania came mostly from Schuylkill County, up in the anthracite region, and it fancied itself a crack regiment. When the IX Corps was sent West, in the spring of 1863, the 48th was briefly assigned to provost guard duty in Lexington, Kentucky, and the men proudly remembered that they had done the job so smoothly, and had kept themselves looking so trim and neat, with well-shined shoes, polished buttons, clean uniforms, and white gloves, that the citizens petitioned Burnside to keep them in that assignment. Burnside was willing, and so the 48th spent nearly six months in Lexington, living comfortably and missing a great deal of hard campaigning, including the latter part of the siege of Vicksburg. When the 48th was finally ordered away, the whole town turned out to say good-by, and a band paraded the boys down the street to the tune of "Auld Lang Syne," while the girls on the sidewalks waved handkerchiefs and cried sentimentally and the soldiers said that leaving Lexington was harder than leaving home.[2]

Early in 1864 the regiment had gone back to Schuylkill County to "veteranize." The mine fields were supposed to be full of strong Copperhead sentiment, with coal miners demonstrating against the draft so violently that troops had to be sent in to keep order, but the 48th had no trouble getting recruits to fill its ranks. It mustered rather more than 400 enlisted men for duty nowadays, and about a fourth of these men had been coal miners before they enlisted.[3]

Coming from mining country and having many miners, the 48th knew a thing or two about digging in the earth. One day its commander, passing along the trench, came on a soldier who was peering through the firing slit at the Rebel works. The man stepped down, turned to a comrade, and said: "We could blow that damned fort out of existence if we could run a mine shaft under it."

The commanding officer was Lieutenant Colonel Henry Pleasants, and that was talk he could understand because he was a mining engineer himself and before being a mining engineer he had done railroad construction work, and he had tunneled under obstructions before now. Born in the Argentine, the son of a Philadelphia businessman who married a Spanish woman and spent many years in South America, he was thirteen before he was brought to Philadelphia for a North American education. Trained as a civil engineer, he worked for the Pennsylvania Railroad in the early 1850s and he had had a hand in driving a 4,200-foot tunnel through the Alleghenies. A few years before the war he quit the railroad for coal mining and made his home in Schuylkill County. He was thirty-one now—slim, dapper, dark, and bearded—and as he passed along the trench he kept thinking about what the soldier had said. A little later he went down the ravine to a bombproof where the regimental officers lived, and he introduced the subject to them by saying bluntly: "That God-damned fort is the only thing between us and Petersburg, and I have an idea we can blow it up." [4]

Not long after this, Pleasants passed the suggestion along, more formally, to his division commander, Brigadier General Robert Potter, and Potter sent a staff officer around to see what this was all about. Pleasants took the man to a place in the trench where they could get a good view of the Rebel fort. While they were looking over the parapet, the staff man unfortunately was hit in the face by a Confederate bullet, but after he had been carried away Pleasants drew a rough sketch of the terrain and sent it to Potter, and a few days later Potter sent for him and took him back to corps headquarters to see Burnside.

It was a sweltering hot night, and the two officers found Burnside sitting in his tent, coat off, bald head glistening in the candlelight, a long cigar cocked up at the side of his mouth. Burnside put the young colonel at his ease at once, and listened intently while the plan was explained, mopping beads of sweat off his forehead with a big silk bandanna while they talked.

Modestly enough, Pleasants admitted getting his idea from a chance remark dropped by an enlisted man. He then went on to explain how they could begin a tunnel on a sheltered spot on the hillside, forty or fifty yards behind their trench, where the Rebels would not be able to see what they were doing. The shaft would slant uphill, which would take care of the drainage problem, and although it would probably have to be more than 500 feet long, Pleasants thought he could devise a means of ventilating it.

Burnside liked the idea and he said he would take it up with Meade. Meanwhile, he said, Pleasants should go ahead with it. So the next day Pleasants organized his coal miners into details, led them to a spot on the protected side of the ravine, and put them to work. Lacking picks, they began by using their bayonets, and in no time at all they were underground. [5]

Meade took very little stock in the project, but he felt that it was good to keep the troops busy. Also, his engineers had just reported that "the new era in field works has so changed their character as in fact to render them almost as strong as permanent ones," and every professional soldier knew that the only way to take permanent fortifications was through the long, ritualized processes of siege warfare.[6] This involved an almost endless dig-and-fill routine—an advance by regular approaches, in military jargon—the general object of which was to inch one's own lines forward far enough so that heavy guns could be mounted where they could flatten the enemy's works at short range. The trouble was that the conditions which would make siege warfare successful simply did not exist here. Petersburg was by no means surrounded, and the Federals did not begin to have the necessary preponderance of force.

So when Burnside came in with this new idea, Meade was prepared to be receptive. The same could not be said for his engineers, who pooh-poohed the whole proposal and said it was clap-trap and nonsense. They said loftily that there was nothing novel about mining the enemy's works—it was standard operating procedure, once the besieging party had brought its own trenches up to within a few yards of the objective point—but they declared that no army on earth had ever tried to do it at anything like the distance involved on Burnside's front. A mine shaft of that length, they went on, could not possibly be ventilated and the men who had to dig it would all be suffocated, if they were not first crushed under falling earth. Besides, the Rebels would find out about it and would interfere. The army's engineers, in short, would have none of it.

Meade himself felt much the same way, but Grant was anxious to get on with the war and he was pressing Meade to see if there was not some way to break the Rebel front. Meade had to confess that there did not seem to be any way, but he did tell Grant that Burnside had some men digging a mine "which General B. thinks when exploded will enable him by a formidable assault to carry the line of works." So with this cautious endorsement, and largely because there was nothing else in sight, the Schuylkill miners suddenly began to be very important people.[7]

Pleasants began by getting from each of his company commanders a list of all the men who were actually coal miners. He organized these men into shifts, with a non-com named Harry Reese as mine boss, precisely as if he were going to mine for coal, and he put them to work round the clock, seeing to it that each man got a dram of commissary whisky when he finished his stint. Picks and shovels were supplied, and although the picks were not the kind used in coal mines, there were plenty of blacksmiths in IX Corps artillery units and Pleasants persuaded them to remodel the implements. The work went faster than he had anticipated, and in a short time he needed timbers to shore up the ceiling and walls.

At this point he found that the army was letting him do this job rather than helping him do it. Meade had promised Burnside to send a company of engineers and any other aid that might be needed, but the company never showed up and when Pleasants asked for some timber nothing seemed to happen. So Pleasants sent a detail from his regiment down into the ravine behind the lines, tore down a railroad bridge, and used those timbers as long as they lasted. Then he discovered an abandoned sawmill four or five miles to the rear. He got Burnside to issue a pass and provide some horses and wagons, and he sent two companies back to operate the mill and cut the necessary lumber.

Pleasants also needed handbarrows to carry the dirt out of the tunnel and dispose of it in some place where Rebel lookouts would not see it. Army headquarters had promised sandbags, but the sandbags never arrived, so Pleasants collected cracker boxes, reinforced them with iron hoops taken from pork barrels, nailed stout handles on them, and detailed parties to lug these in and out of the shaft.

After a week progress came to a halt when the miners struck a belt of wet clay and the ceiling sagged, breaking the timbers and nearly closing the tunnel. Pleasants retimbered the shaft, shored up the ceiling with stouter props, and drove on. Next he struck a bed of marl which had a way of turning to rock soon after the air struck it. The soldiers amused themselves by carving tobacco pipes out of this in their spare time, but it was mean stuff to tunnel through and the colonel finally had to increase the tunnel's angle of climb so as to get into a softer earth stratum. He was making his tunnel five feet high, four feet wide at the bottom, and some two and one half feet wide at the top, and it was strongly timbered all the way—ceiling, both sides, and floor. Cutting and transporting all of this timber and getting it inside the mine, and taking all of the dirt out and concealing it in the ravine under fresh-cut bushes, kept calling for more and more hands, and before long practically the entire regiment was at work.[8]

When the shaft had gone a couple of hundred feet into the hillside, Pleasants felt that it was time to make some exact calculations about the spot where the powder magazine ought to go. (Obviously he would accomplish nothing if he dug past the Rebel fort or stopped short of it.) So he applied to the engineers for the instruments with which he could make the necessary triangulations. The engineers laughed this off, and a plea to Meade's headquarters was lost in the shuffle somewhere, and at last Burnside—who seems to have been the only important officer in the army who was disposed to be helpful—wired to a friend in Washington and had him send down a theodolite.

Pleasants had to take this into the front line to make his observations, and of course Rebel snipers were apt to shoot him while he was doing it. He got around this by having half a dozen soldiers put their caps on ramrods and raise them just above the parapet. While the sharpshooters peppered away at these, hitting them quite regularly and no doubt imagining that they were hitting human heads inside of them, Pleasants draped some burlap over his head and his instrument, got unobserved over the parapet level a few yards away, and made his observations.[9]

Farther and farther into the hillside went the tunnel. As the engineers had prophesied, ventilation was a problem, but

Pleasants solved it. Close beside the tunnel, at a point just behind the main Federal trench, he dug a vertical shaft whose lower end opened into a little recess in the tunnel wall and whose upper end discharged unobtrusively into a clump of bushes. Then he built a square tube of boards, reaching from the mouth of the tunnel all the way to its inner end, and he prepared a door by which the outer end of the tunnel could be sealed shut, leaving the open end of the wooden tube protruding out into the air. The rest was simple: close the door and build a fire in the little recess at the bottom of the vertical shaft. The smoke and heated air went up this chimney, the resultant draft pulled the bad air out of the tunnel, and fresh air from the outside was drawn in through the wooden tube.

On July 17, three weeks after the job had been begun, the inner end of the tunnel was squarely beneath the Confederate redoubt, twenty-odd feet underground and 510 feet from the entrance, and the miners could hear Confederate soldiers tramping about overhead. Pleasants then had his men dig a 75-foot shaft running across the end of the tunnel; a diagram of his work now would look like a capital T with a very long shank, with the crossbar of the T running along directly beneath the Confederate works.[10]

Pleasants then reported that the mine was ready for its charge of powder—at which point further operations were temporarily suspended because the Rebels had discovered that the Yankees were digging a mine and were sinking shafts of their own trying to find it.

Confederate luck right here was bad. Their engineers misjudged the direction the tunnel was taking, and their countermining shafts failed to intersect it. When Pleasants had his men stop working, the Rebels in underground listening posts could hear nothing, and in the end all of their protective measures failed. Meanwhile, the Southern privates who were going about their business directly above the dark sinister gallery began to treat the whole affair as another camp rumor, and now and then they would call across and ask the Yankees when the big show was going to begin.[11]

After a pause, with the digging and timbering all finished, Pleasants went to work to lay the powder charges. Burnside wanted to use eight tons of powder, but the army engineers had one good suggestion here—the use of explosives in quantity was a subject they really knew something about—and they pointed out that a smaller charge would actually be more effective. In the end, Burnside settled for four tons, and Pleasants had his men build eight open-topped wooden boxes in the lateral gallery for magazines. The powder was delivered behind the lines in 320 kegs, each containing 25 pounds, and there was day-and-night work carrying these into the mine and pouring the charges into the magazines.

All of the magazines were connected by wooden troughs half filled with powder, and these troughs met at the place where the gallery crossed the inner end of the main shaft. The engineers had promised Pleasants a supply of wire and a "galvanic battery" to touch off the charge, but this was another delivery that was never made, so Pleasants got a supply of ordinary fuses, spliced them together, introduced one end into the powder in the trough, and strung the rest of the fuse back along the tunnel for about one hundred feet. As a final step, earth was solidly tamped into place, filling the main shaft for thirty-eight feet from the place where it met the lateral gallery. All that remained now was to light the outer end of the fuse.[12]

Pleasants never doubted that the mine would blow a big hole in the Confederate line, but the only other officer of any consequence who really believed in it seems to have been Burnside himself, and according to his lights Burnside did his best to make a success of the attack that would follow the explosion.

His army corps contained four divisions. Three of these had been in action more or less continually since the army crossed the Rapidan, and they had had a solid month of trench duty in front of Petersburg. Each of these divisions contained about 3,000 men, all of whom by now were very battle-weary. The fourth division had never been in action to speak of, having spent practically all of its time guarding wagon trains and doing other back-area jobs, and its 4,300 men consequently were fresh. Obviously, a fresh division ought to be used to spearhead the attack, and so—about the time Pleasants was beginning to dig the lateral gallery— Burnside brought his division forward and told its commander, Brigadier General Ferrero, to give it special training for the assault; it was the outfit that was going to break the Rebel line and march into Petersburg and win the war. (Burnside himself was so confident the attack would succeed that he had all of his headquarters baggage packed so that he could move right into Petersburg on the heels of his victorious troops.)

Burnside's plan was perfectly logical. The three divisions which had been holding the trenches were worn out—during the last ten days of June and the month of July they lost more than a thousand men, altogether, just from sharpshooter and mortar fire—and the men had adjusted themselves to trench life so completely that they looked on soldiering as being largely a business of getting behind a protective bank of earth and avoiding enemy bullets. If unbloodied troops were available it was only common sense to use them, and in picking Ferrero's division Burnside was exercising perfectly sound judgment.[13]

The difficulty was that an imponderable entered into things here, deep as the ocean and unpredictable as a tornado at midnight. Ferrero's division was made up entirely of colored soldiers.

The use of colored troops was an experiment to which the Administration had been driven partly by the demands of the abolitionists and partly by sheer desperation, the supply of white manpower having slackened. The implications of this experiment were faced by few people, and there probably would be time enough to worry about them after the war had been won. At the moment the great riddle was whether it was possible to turn colored men into good soldiers.

Most of these ex-slaves were illiterate, used to servile obedience, and living (presumably) in deep awe of Southern white men. They were husky enough, and yet they somehow lacked physical sturdiness and endurance,[14] and they had been held at the bottom of the heap for so long that they seemed to be excessively long-suffering by nature. Somewhere, far back in dim tribal memories, there may have been traditions of war parties and fighting and desperate combat, but these had been overlaid by generations of slavery, and most colored folk saw themselves as pilgrims toiling up the endless slopes of heartbreak hill—pilgrims whose survival depended on the patient, uncomplaining acceptance of evil rather than on a bold struggle to overthrow evil.

That was the sticking point. The average Northern white man of that era might refuse to associate with the Negro and hold himself to be immeasurably the Negro's superior—the superiority, of course, grew out of the natural order of things, and need not actually be proved—but there was a war on and the country needed soldiers, and if Federal corpses were the price of victory, it hardly paid to be finicky about the original color of the corpses' skins. The real trouble lay in the assumption that while it was all right to let the Negro get shot it was foolish to expect him to do any serious fighting first.

A young officer who left his place in a white regiment to become colonel of a colored regiment was frankly told by a staff officer that "we do not want any nigger soldiers in the Army of the Potomac," and his general took him aside to say: "I am sorry to have you leave my command, and still more sorry that you are going to serve with Negroes. I think it is a disgrace to the army to make soldiers of them." The general added that he felt this way because he was sure that colored soldiers just would not fight.[15]

Most men felt the same way. In support of the belief it was pointed out that in many years of American bondage there had never been a really serious slave revolt. Even John Brown himself, carrying fire and sword below the Potomac, had been able to recruit no more than a dazed corporal's guard of colored followers. Surely this proved that even though slaves might not be happy with their lot they had no real combativeness in them?

There might be flaws in the argument. It quite overlooked the fact that for many years the fabulous underground railroad had been relieving the explosive pressures the slave system had been building up, and had been in fact a great deterrent to slave revolt, for it took out of slavery precisely the daring, energetic, intelligent slaves who might have planned and led an uprising if they had been unable to escape.[16] The argument also overlooked the fact that if American slaves rarely made any trouble the people who owned them were always mortally afraid that they would do so some day. The gloomy island of Haiti was not far enough away to let anyone forget that black men there had risen in one of the most bloody, desperate revolts in human history, winning their own freedom and practically annihilating the master race in the process. Oddly enough, the general belief that colored men would not fight ran parallel with a conviction that they would fight with primitive viciousness if they ever got a chance.

Yet whatever prejudice might say, the hard fact now was that colored men were being enlisted as soldiers in large numbers and that there were times when it was impossible to avoid using them in combat. The use of Hinks's division was an example. They had stormed rifle pits and captured guns, and although Hancock's veterans saw in that fact nothing more than evidence that the Confederacy had only second-rate troops in line, Baldy Smith—who was far from being prejudiced in their favor—said afterward that Negro soldiers under certain circumstances might be as good as any.[17]

No matter how it might use them, however, the army certainly had not assimilated them. It had not tried to and if it had tried it would have failed, and it did not matter much anyway for it was no longer possible for this army to be homogeneous. It had become a representative cross section of an extremely mixed population; and now, as a final step, it contained long columns of colored men whose memories, as one of their officers said, were "a vast bewildered chaos of Jewish history and biography," the residue of chanted spirituals and the preaching of untaught plantation clergymen,

men who in their innocence attributed every historic event to the doings of the great Moses.[18]

When Ferrero's dark battalions came up to the sheltered area just behind the front, they added a new dimension to army life and gave it a strange wild flavor. Always there had been groups of soldiers to sit around campfires in the evening, singing about their homesickness and the girls they wanted to get back to, about their comradeship, and, occasionally, about their patriotism, but when these black soldiers sang there was a haunting and a mystery in the air. For if the white soldier looked back with profound longing to something precious that had been left far behind, the colored soldier's homesickness seemed to be for a place where he had never been at all. He had nothing to look back to. Everything he could dream of lay ahead of him, and his dreams were apocalyptic, not to be expressed in ordinary words.

So when the colored troops met by the campfire to sing— and it was their favorite way to spend the evening—they sang made-up, spur-of-the-moment songs, which had never existed before either in words or in music, songs which grew out of the fire and the night and the dreams and hopes which hovered between fire and night forever.

All of the colored troops were officered by white men, and these white officers listened, fascinated, to the campfire singing, and when they wrote about it they tried to tell why it moved them so deeply. There would be a hundred men sprawled in a fire-lit circle, dark faces touched with fire; and one voice would go up, rich and soft and soaring:

> *I know moon-rise,*
> *I know star-rise—*

and half a dozen men would come in with a refrain:

> *—Lay dis body down.*

The singer would grope his way two lines nearer to the thought that was drawing him on:

> *I walk in de moonlight,*
> *I walk in de starlight——*

and now more voices would sound the refrain:

Lay dis body down.

Finally the song would be finished, and a white officer who listened said that the chanted refrain would sound like "a grand creation chorus":

> *I'll walk in de graveyard,*
> *I'll walk troo de graveyard*
>   *To lay dis body down.*
> *I go to de judgment in de evening of de day*
>   *When I lay dis body down.*
> *And my soul and your soul will meet in de day*
>   *When I lay dis body down.*[19]

They were men coming up out of Egypt, trailing the shreds of a long night from their shoulders, and sometimes they sang in the wild imagery of a despairing journey through parted waters to a land of promise:

> *My army cross over,*
> *My army cross over—*
> *O Pharaoh's army drownded—*
> *My army cross over.*
>
> *We'll cross de mighty river,*
> *We'll cross de River Jordan,*
> *We'll cross de danger water . . .*
>   *My army cross over.*[20]

Most of the men were straight from the plantation. On many matters their ignorance was absolute. Yet they were men without doubts, and always their faith reached out to the future. A man in the VI Corps, talking to one of them, learned that men who could not read one word of Scripture could cite Biblical authority for their belief that the North would win the war. There was a prophecy, they said, which foretold that while the South would prevail for a time, in the end it would be overthrown. The VI Corps soldier searched his own Bible and at last concluded that the reference was to words in the eleventh chapter of the Book of Daniel:

"And in those times there shall many stand up against the King of the South: also the robbers of thy people shall exalt themselves to escape the vision; but they shall fall. So the King of the North shall come, and cast up a mount, take the most fenced cities; and the arms of the South shall not withstand, neither his chosen people, neither shall there be any strength to withstand." [21]

A Rhode Island soldier who had served along the Carolina coast remembered how a group of fugitive slaves had come within the Union lines after a harrowing nine-day flight through swamps. One man explained his perseverance: "I seed de lamp of life ahead and de lamp of death behind," and another said that, on coming up to the Federal outposts, "When I seed dat flag, it lift me right up." Even before they left slavery, they had their own idea of what the war was about. A Pennsylvania soldier on that same Carolina expedition asked a slave if he knew why the Yankees had come, and the slave replied that of course he knew—"to kill Massa and set de darkeys free." A Wisconsin man who escaped from a prison pen in the Deep South took refuge in the hut of an aged slave who had never before seen a Union soldier, and he asked the old man if he would betray him. "No sah," replied the old man emphatically. "There's not a slave in South Carolina who would betray you." One officer discovered that before the war the Southern slaves had known about the Frémont campaign of 1856, and the campaign of 1860. Some of them told him that they had refused to work on March 4, 1861, expecting their freedom to date from that day.[22]

A Connecticut soldier who watched contrabands at work unloading ships at the Alexandria piers noticed that whenever there was a breathing spell some of the men would stretch out on the nearest pile of barrels or boxes, take out a spelling book, and laboriously study it. As a general thing, he said, they worked very hard: "All they want to encourage them is talk of freedom, and then the dirt will fly high and fast." They disliked to be called "contrabands," and when they were made soldiers they were intensely proud of their status as combat men. A white woman who visited her husband at army headquarters near Petersburg told about meeting a wounded Negro soldier who was trudging along the road toward the base hospital at City Point, loaded down with his musket, cartridge box, and haversack. Her husband told him to throw his load away, but the man begged to be allowed to carry it all the way to the hospital: "I don't want de fellows at de hospital to mistake me for a teamster." [23]

A Regular Army enlisted man watched some of Ferrero's men marching up toward Petersburg and noted that many of them had taken off their shoes and were carrying them on their bayonets, going along barefooted. In the evening he went to their camp and observed evening roll call: "There were so many Jacksons and Johnsons that the first sergeant numbered them as high as 'Johnson Number Five.' They appeared to be very proud of being soldiers and serving with white troops." [24]

From the beginning it was realized that the effectiveness of colored troops would depend largely on the way the regiments were officered, and what would now be called an officer-candidate school was set up in Philadelphia. Non-commissioned officers and privates in the Army of the Potomac could apply for admission to this school, and if recommended by their own officers and approved by an examining board they would get thirty days training and then would be commissioned to command colored soldiers. The rank and file seems to have been of two minds about this arrangement. Some felt that it was a good idea, that the standards were high and the training thorough—one man said he knew colonels in white regiments who could not get an examining board recommendation for a second lieutenancy—but others believed that the examinations and instructions "were not practical, but scholastic and theoretical," and that most of the men who were commissioned were not up to their jobs.[25]

Certain it was that these strange new regiments needed good leadership. They were reluctant to take orders from non-coms of their own color—it was common to hear the complaint, "I don't want him to play de white man over me"—and a company commander had to be careful to treat his sergeants with formal military courtesy, always addressing them by their titles and in general following precise Regular Army routine. The colored enlisted man who had a complaint or problem was quite likely to try to by-pass his company officers and go direct to his colonel, and one of the colonels meditated on the reason for this: "The Negroes have acquired such a constitutional distrust of white people that it is perhaps as much as they can do to trust more than one person at a time." He added that in training and disciplining the men it was vital "to make them feel as remote as possible from the plantation," and said that the habit of obedience was worthless unless the officer managed to instill a stout feeling of self-respect along with it. An officer of polished manners could do better with colored troops than with white volunteers, who preferred a certain roughness of manner in their officers.[26]

In camp, the colored men made excellent soldiers. They picked up the drill quickly, learning it more easily than white recruits did. The different companies in a regiment would vie with each other for excellence on the parade ground, and sometimes would get into furious fist fights while arguing as to which company was the best. During that Carolina expedition, where local contrabands were organized into a regiment, there was one day a parade of colored soldiers through the city of Beaufort, with the band of a Maine regiment leading the way, and it was a big experience. A colored sergeant said afterward: "When dat band wheel in before us and march on—my God! I quit dis world altogedder!" And a private related: "We didn't look to de right nor to de left. I didn't see nottin' in Beaufort. Every step was worth half a dollar."

Some of the ordinary problems of army discipline seemed to be non-existent. Desertion was utterly unknown, and there was very little drunkenness. The men especially enjoyed practice on the target range. When one made a good shot there would be a gleeful chorus of "Ki! Old man!" and if an unskilled recruit fired his piece into the dirt there would be "such infinite guffawing and delight, such rolling over and over on the grass, such dances of ecstasy" that the colonel would remember it and put it in his memoirs.[27]

There were a few little subsidiary problems connected with the use of colored troops. The colonel of the 36th U.S. Colored Infantry told how a detachment from his regiment in the spring of 1864 was sent across from Point Lookout to the Rappahannock River area to destroy certain Rebel installations. One group, commanded by colored non-coms and with no white officers present, had a fight with some Confederates and did very well, capturing certain prisoners; and the problem was that the men wanted to kill all of the prisoners forthwith, being restrained only by their sergeant. On the other side of the ledger there was the example of Fort Pillow, a Mississippi River post held by colored troops, which had been stormed in recent months by Bedford Forrest's command. After the surrender some of Forrest's tough troopers got out of hand and turned the occasion into something like a lynching bee. The colored troops with the Army of the Potomac could read no newspapers and got their information of far-off events Heaven knows how, but every one of them knew about Fort Pillow. General Hinks, with colored men in his command, urged that all of them be armed with repeating rifles in place of the regulation muzzle-loaders. His men, he said, "cannot afford to be beaten and will not be taken," and ought to have the best arms the country could provide. His request was ignored, but the making of it was significant.[28]

As a general thing the Negro soldiers seemed to hold very little personal animus against their former masters. A white officer discovered, rather to his surprise, that they had neither hatred nor affection for the men who used to own them. They never mentioned their masters except as natural enemies, yet it was the class they hated, not the individuals in the class. They saw slavery, said this man, as "a wrong which no special kindnesses could right." [29]

When Ferrero's troops were brought up the Confederates in the Petersburg line quickly learned about it, and they despised the whole IX Corps because of it. On Burnside's front the fighting became vicious. There were no picket-line truces and no lulls in the fighting. Off to the left, where Warren's men held the line, tolerant Southerners might call, "Down, Yank!" before opening fire, but there was no more of that in Burnside's sector. Sharpshooters kept their pieces trained on the firing slit and they were shooting to kill.[30]

The men in Ferrero's division, meanwhile, were immensely proud of their new assignment. As they sat about their campfires in the evening they made up a new song:

> We looks like men a-marching on;
> We looks like men o'war—

and they sang it on every possible occasion. Ferrero drilled them in the maneuvers that would be expected of them. After the mine was exploded, they were to charge straight ahead. White divisions would follow them, wheeling to right and left to protect their flanks, but they were to go straight on and seize the long ridge that overlooked Petersburg. That would come very close to ending the war, and for these colored men it would be a new beginning, and the soldiers were buoyant and worked hard on their behind-the-lines rehearsals.[31]

Yet there was a doom over the men, and an extra sense seemed to tell them that things were not going to be simple. A prodigious thing was happening, and it could not happen easily. Here were men who had been held on a level with the mule and the ox, animated property with no rights which anyone was bound to respect, and now they were becoming men, and the very word "American" was taking on a new meaning. The war had changed. The soldiers were different and the country was different, and only the dream that had possessed them would go on. It was a dream that nobody could ever quite put into words, but it was growing as men died for it, and now it appeared that colored men could share in it.

But the road out of Egypt was long, and black men who were coming up to the unparted deep-sea waters looked ahead and made up a little campfire song to tell how they felt about it:

> *For death is a simple ting,*
> *And he go from door to door,*
> *And he knock down some and he cripple up some*
> *And he leave some here to pray.*[32]

3. Like the Noise of Great Thunders

The ridge behind the Confederate trenches was not very high, and its slope was gentle and grassy, with dips and hollows here and there, and occasional clumps of trees. It lay naked under the July sun, and no one had ever climbed it (except for a few Confederate artillerists, who had parked some guns in the Jerusalem Plank Road), and it was like a mocking challenge to the Federal soldiers. If they could once reach the crest of that ridge, the war was over, for if they stood there they would be in rear of the entire Confederate line, and they would control Petersburg and everything that was in it, which meant that they could certainly capture Richmond and could probably destroy Lee's army. The crest was less than half a mile from the Union line, and between the crest and the Army of the Potomac there was nothing in particular except the Confederate trench which was about to be blown sky-high.

The Pennsylvania miners had brought the end of the war within whispering distance. Never before had there been a chance like this. A trench properly built and manned by a sufficiency of Southern riflemen and gunners could never be stormed, and by now everybody knew it; but if the trench and everyone in it could suddenly be obliterated the case would be very different, and if this business were handled right men could walk through and take the crest.

Grant finally saw it, and while he had certain doubts about this stunt of Burnside's, he was determined that it must at least be given a fair chance. He was commander of all the armies of the United States and he was not directly responsible for the tactics involved in an assault along half a mile of one front, but if strategy could insure success of this attack he proposed to use it, and so he laid a plan.

North of the James River, squarely in front of Richmond, there were miles of Confederate trenches held by a thin string of cavalry pickets. Potentially, this was the most sensitive part of Lee's entire line, and a Union attack there was certain to pull Confederate strength into the area just as fast as Lee could get it there. When Grant thought about ways to help Burnside's assault his mind naturally turned to those empty fortifications north of the river.

His plan was simple. He would send Hancock and the II Corps north of the James, accompanied by Sheridan and the cavalry. They would cross the Appomattox below Petersburg, march north back of Butler's lines, and cross the James by a new pontoon bridge at a place called Deep Bottom, and it would not hurt in the least if Lee saw them going. Presumably, Lee would take troops from the Petersburg lines to meet this threat. If Hancock and Sheridan could actually break the lines in front of Richmond, that of course would be all to the good. If they could not it would probably be because Lee had reduced strength in front of Petersburg in order to hold in front of Richmond. In that case Burnside's chance of success would be just so much better.[1]

So Grant planned and so it was ordered, and on the evening of July 26 the II Corps took the road north. The column got to the Appomattox bridge around midnight, and a newspaper correspondent on the north side of the river watched, fascinated, as the line of march wound past a huge bonfire which had been lit to show the way. The men came up out of the dark, passed through the pool of wavering light, and moved on into more darkness, marching steadily for the James River crossing, silent enough except when some brigade staff rode by with a jingling of scabbards and other equipment. Batteries rolled by now and then, firelight gleaming off the polished guns, and the reporter sat and watched for two hours, bemused by "that flow of men, like a river, passing, still passing, but never passed." [2]

Early on the morning of July 27 the corps crossed the James. Butler had laid two pontoon bridges at Deep Bottom somewhat earlier, and he had a detachment on the north bank to hold the bridgehead, and Sheridan took his cavalry over to strike the Charles City Road to Richmond, while the infantry fanned out along the banks of a little stream called Bailey's Creek. There was skirmishing all day long in the underbrush and forsaken fields by this brook, the Rebels apparently present in some strength with more coming up.

Back in front of Petersburg, Pleasants's men were carrying the kegs of powder down the long tunnel, each man stooping low under the ceiling and hugging the 25-pound keg against his belly. Over their heads the Confederates had stopped hunting for the rumored Yankee mine—partly, it seems, because Lee's engineers felt just the way Meade's felt: no soldiers could burrow 500 feet under a hill. A correspondent for the London *Times* who was visiting Confederate headquarters at the time helped to confirm this delusion. British army experience, he said, showed that 400 feet was the absolute limit for a tunnel of this kind. [3]

In any case, Grant's feint worked perfectly. Hancock's infantry and the dismounted cavalry gestured and skirmished and fought along a ridge back of Bailey's Creek and made threatening motions on the Charles City Road, and it looked as if a big attack was coming. One after another, Lee called veteran divisions out of the Petersburg lines, and by the morning of July 29 he had more than half of his army north of the James, leaving only 18,000 infantry to hold the five miles of line in front of Petersburg. More than a third of Hancock's people, meanwhile, had already gone back to Petersburg, and everybody else would go back as soon as the darkness came; [4] and Meade was sitting down with Burnside to draw up formal orders for the big attack, which was to begin at 3:30 o'clock the next morning, July 30.

By now, Meade was ready to support Burnside with everything he had. Burnside was to use his entire corps, and two army corps would be on hand to help him—Warren's corps, on the left, and Baldy Smith's old corps, now led by General E. O. C. Ord, on the right. A powerful mass of artillery had been quietly moved up into position during recent nights—eighty field pieces, eighteen huge 10-inch mortars, twenty-eight of the lighter coehorn mortars, and eighteen 4½-inch siege guns, all dug in where they could sweep the Confederate position.

Battle orders were precise. Burnside was to attack the moment the mine was sprung and he was to go straight for the crest of the ridge, pausing for no consideration whatever. The objective was a decisive break-through and final victory, and the only thing that counted was to get the troops up on the heights. They could get there only if they moved fast. Therefore they must be formed in columns of assault before the mine was exploded, and during the night Burnside's parapets and abatis must be leveled so that those columns could advance in line of battle. There must also be engineer parties at the heads of the columns, to remove Confederate obstructions and prepare a way for Yankee artillery to follow.

The plan was good, and it was about as Burnside had figured it. But Meade made one change in Burnside's original plan. He told Burnside that Ferrero's colored division must not be used as the first wave of the attack. The fight must be spearheaded by the white troops. If the colored troops were to be used at all they must go in later, as support.

Burnside objected, with heat, pointing out that Ferrero's was his biggest, freshest division and that it had been getting special training for weeks in the movements which would be involved in this assault. Meade refused to yield, and after a while Grant came in and Burnside appealed to him. Grant listened, and upheld Meade: the colored troops must not go in first. Profoundly disturbed, Burnside went back to his own headquarters to rearrange his plans and prepare new orders. The moment set for the explosion of the mine was now about twelve hours in the future.[5]

The Army of the Potomac was led to disaster many times, and there is a rather horrible fascination about tracing the steps by which, in each case, it reached that destination. Usually those steps seemed quite reasonable at the time, and they were generally taken with the best intentions in the world, and almost invariably they form a chain of events which might have been broken almost anywhere. So now.

It began with the decision not to put the colored division first. A little later Grant was to admit that this decision was a mistake, but it was made for what seemed excellent reasons. The battle that was coming up was a gamble at best. Nobody could be sure that the mine would actually have the effect Pleasants and Burnside believed it would have. If it did not, the troops that led in the assault would be butchered. If those troops happened to be colored men without combat experience it would immediately be argued that they had been sacrificed callously because no one cared what happened to them. (The argument would be made, incidentally, by some of the most vocal and determined arguers that ever lived, the abolitionists and the radical Republicans.) Neither Grant nor Meade felt that that was a proper risk to take.

But this decision started all the trouble, because its effect was to deflate Burnside completely. Until now, Burnside had done what a good corps commander ought to do. He had seen merit in an unorthodox plan proposed by a subordinate, he had fought to get the idea approved, and he had supported it when higher authority failed to support it. But from this moment on he was as poor a general as a grown man can be, and both the army and the Union cause as a whole would have been much better off if he had taken to his bed, pulled the covers over his handsome face, and let someone else take charge.

First of all he had to pick another division to lead the attack, and he called in the commanding officers of his three white divisions. These were General Potter, to whom Colonel Pleasants had first suggested the mine, a capable man with a good record; General Orlando B. Willcox, a veteran who had been commanding a division ever since Antietam; and Brigadier General James H. Ledlie, a civil engineer without military training or experience when the war began, who had come into the army as major in a New York heavy artillery regiment and who had only recently risen to division command.

Burnside seems to have been pretty numb when he talked with these three generals. He explained that plans had been changed and one of their divisions would have to lead the attack. He confessed that he could not for the life of him see any reason to prefer one division or one general over the other two. Therefore, said Burnside, why should they not simply draw lots to see which division should go in first? [6]

Down under the fabulous whiskers and the kindly dignity, Burnside was a gambler. In the Mexican War he had almost been cashiered because of his weakness for risking everything on the turn of a card. This time he was gambling far beyond his means, and chance played him false. The luck of the draw, when they finally got down to pulling for the short straw, decreed that Ledlie's division must take the lead.

Why Burnside did not immediately call for a new deal is past understanding. Of all of his divisions Ledlie's was the weakest, and of all of his generals Ledlie was the most unfit. The whole division had grown notoriously gun-shy during the past month, and one of its two brigades was made up largely of heavy artillery regiments and dismounted cavalry. Although the heavies had turned into first-rate soldiers for the rest of the army, they were not highly regarded in the IX Corps. A few weeks earlier Burnside himself had said of them: "They are worthless. They didn't enlist to fight and it is unreasonable to expect it of them. In the attack last night I couldn't find thirty of them." But chance had put Ledlie's division in the lead and Burnside let it ride; and chance further decreed that when Ledlie formed his men for the charge it was the weak brigade that was put in front.[7]

The real trouble, however, was in Ledlie himself.

The army contained a good many poor generals, but it

had very few who were ever accused of personal cowardice. Ledlie was one who was so accused. His subordinates knew him as a weakling. In the June 18 attack, while his men fought to carry a Rebel entrenchment, Ledlie had taken to the bottle, and at a climactic moment of the fight, he had been stretched out on the ground in a safe place, the world forgetting and by the world forgot. His soldiers knew it and his junior officers knew it, but the IX Corps somehow was the kind of corps in which a thing like that could escape the notice of the commanding general, so Burnside did not know it. Burnside combined the great virtue of being loyal to his underlings with the terrible weakness of being quite unable to tell a good operator from a bad one, and now he was entrusting the supreme assault of the army's career to a soldier who was taken with palsy whenever it came time to go out where enemy bullets were flying.[8]

For good or for ill, the day ended and there was a stir all along the line. The secret of the mine had not been too well kept, and there had been gossip about it for days, but most Federals had at last begun to treat it as the Confederates did —as a rumor which someone had probably dreamed up over a jug of commissary whisky—and few people had taken it very seriously. Still, as June 29 drew to a close, there were omens for all to see. Sick men in the field hospitals were sent back to City Point. There was a great riding to and fro of staff officers and couriers, and practically every unit in the corps was being moved from one place to another. Ferrero's colored troops were brought forward, after dark, and lined up in the bottom of the ravine. They were full of enthusiasm, because in all of the excitement no one had thought to tell them that assignments had been changed, and they still supposed that they were going to lead in the attack. Indeed, they were the only division in the corps which believed that it knew what was going to happen.[9]

During the night Hancock's men came back from the north side of the James, and Meade and Grant got up early and went to Burnside's headquarters, half a mile behind the front—a convenient place, connected with other commands by telegraph, which Meade had designated as temporary headquarters for the army.

Burnside, meanwhile, went forward to a fourteen-gun battery that had been built on a hill a few hundred yards back of the entrance to the mine. The night wore away, silent except for the shuffling of thousands of men moving to their places, and a little after three o'clock in the morning Pleasants sent a man into the mine and shaft to set fire to the fuse.

Back on the hills behind the line the artillerists were ready. They had previously trained their pieces on their targets, and the guns and mortars were all loaded, and from three o'clock on the gunners were standing by, lanyards in hand, ready to fire at the word of command.[10] In the trenches, Ledlie's men were standing up, not knowing what was coming except that they realized they were about to be pushed into a big fight. On the slope behind them, Potter's and Willcox's divisions were waiting, similarly tense and ignorant. Back of all of them were Ferrero's colored men, massed at the bottom of the ravine, expecting at any moment to get the word to go in and capture Petersburg. General Burnside stood in the battery, serene in his ineffable rectitude, conscious that his baggage was packed and that he could take up headquarters in the Rebel city on a moment's notice.

Half-past three came, with the high command fingering watches and staring off into the dark, and nothing happened. Another half hour went by, and half an hour more on top of that, and the silence was unbroken, except for the occasional discharge of some wakeful picket's musket. Grant got impatient, and at least he told Meade to have Burnside make his charge regardless: something had gone wrong with the mine, and there was no use waiting any longer.[11] In the east the sky was turning gray—and five eighths of Lee's army was north of the James River, with the full strength of the Army of the Potomac massed to smash through the fraction that was left.

Grant was impatient, and Meade was impatient, and probably even Burnside was getting a little restless; but the man who was really excited was Colonel Pleasants. About the time Grant was saying that the charge had better go ahead without the explosion, Pleasants called Sergeant Harry Reese, the mine boss, and told him to go into the tunnel and see what was the matter.

In went Reese, on as nerve-racking an assignment as the war could produce, groping forward all bent over along 400 feet of a dark tunnel, never sure that the solid earth ahead was not going to quake and heave and tumble to bury him forever. He got to the fuse, traced it, and found that the spark had died at a place where one fuse had been spliced to another. He started back to get a new fuse, found Lieutenant Jacob Douty coming in, at Pleasants's direction, with the material he needed, and he and Douty went back to the splice and made a new connection. Then he lit the spark again, and he and Lieutenant Douty came out of the tunnel as fast as they could travel [12]—and the sky grew lighter in the east, so that ridges and trees and hillocks became dark shadows outlined against the dying night, and the whole Army of the Potomac stood by gripping its muskets, waiting for nobody knew just what.

Four forty-five: and at last it happened.

To the men who were waiting in the front line it seemed to occur in slow motion: first a long, deep rumble, like summer thunder rolling along a faraway horizon, then a swaying and swelling of the ground up ahead, with the solid earth rising to form a rounded hill, everything seeming very gradual and leisurely. Then the rounded hill broke apart, and a prodigious spout of flame and black smoke went up toward the sky, and the air was full of enormous clods of earth as big as houses, of brass cannon and detached artillery wheels, of wrecked caissons and fluttering tents and weirdly tumbling human bodies; and there was a crash "like the noise of great thunders," followed by other, lesser explosions, and all of the landscape along the firing line had turned into dust and smoke and flying debris, choking and blinding men and threatening to engulf Burnside's whole army corps.

Different men saw it and felt it in different ways. A soldier in the 36th Massachusetts wrote that "we witnessed a

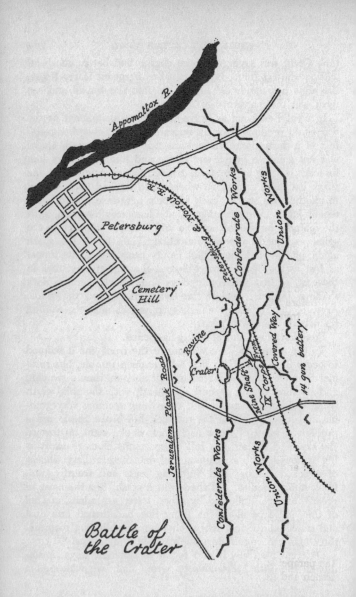

Battle of
the Crater

volcano and experienced an earthquake," yet an officer in Ferrero's division, standing not a third of a mile away from the explosion, recalled it as "a dull, heavy thud, not at all startling . . . a heavy, smothered sound, not nearly so distinct as a musket shot." A man in Pleasants's own 48th Pennsylvania remembered it as a "magnificent spectacle," and another soldier recalled that a bronze cannon was tossed nearly over to the Union line. To one man the whole thing looked like "a waterspout as seen at sea," another felt it as "a heavy shaking of the earth, with a rumbling, muffled sound," and to men in Hancock's corps, waiting behind the artillery, it seemed that the solid earth went up "like an enormous whirlwind." [13]

The gunners had been waiting a long time, and some of them had their eyes fixed on the Confederate redoubt, and they jerked their lanyards as soon as they saw the grounds begin to rise, so that the crash of their own guns rocked the air before the sound of the explosion reached them. There was a tremendous concussion from the artillery, with more guns being fired than the Union army had fired in the great artillery duel at Gettysburg. An overwhelming cloud of white smoke from the guns went tumbling down into the ravine and overflowed the farther crest to mix with the hanging black dust and smoke from the mine, so that all along the Yankee line the air was dark as midnight, lit by brief stabbing flames as the shell began to go off.[14]

The troops which had been waiting to make the charge saw a hillside fly up in their faces, and it looked as if the mass of earth was going to fall on them, so that many men turned and ran, and it was five or ten minutes before the officers could get them re-formed. Then the order for the charge was sounded and Ledlie's division started to make its attack— at which crucial moment the soldiers realized that nobody had prepared the way for them, so that the kind of charge which everybody had counted on was completely impossible.

In Meade's orders there had been a provision for leveling the parapet so that a line of battle could swing up out of the trench and go forward in fighting formation, but this assignment had dropped out of sight somewhere between "I ordered it done" and "Nobody told me to do it." Nothing whatever had been done. The leading brigade was standing in the bottom of an eight-foot ditch, and men who were loaded down with muskets and cartridge boxes and haversacks just could not scale the wall.

One officer, aware that time was a-wasting, had a squad improvise a ladder by jabbing bayonets into the log wall and holding the outer ends while their comrades climbed up and over. In another place, men tore down sandbags and piled them into a clumsy sort of stairway. Finally, with an additional ten minutes lost, a straggling line of men got up out of the trench and began to run forward by twos and threes —a thin trickle of wholly disorganized men, rather than the connected wave of a line of battle.[15]

Stumbling up the slope through dust and smoke, these men got to the place where the Confederate redoubt had been and found themselves peering down into a great smoking crater.

One hundred and seventy feet of the Confederate line had been blown up. In its place there was a huge chasm, 60 feet across and 30 feet deep. All around this crater, balanced on its rim and tumbled over the ground on every side, were big hunks of solid clay, broken timbers, dismounted guns, and lesser wreckage of every kind. Down at the bottom there was more of the same, including many human bodies. Some Southerners, still living, had been buried to their waists, some had only their heads above the earth. Others had been buried head downward, their legs protruding into the air. As the men of Ledlie's leading brigade came up they paused, stupefied by the sight; then they slid and scrambled down into the crater and began to uproot the buried Confederates. An officer got one squad together to dig out a couple of half-buried cannon.

Nothing could be seen very clearly, for smoke and dust still filled the air. To the rear the Federal guns kept up a furious bombardment, and there was no return fire. For 200 yards on each side of the crater the Confederate trenches were empty, the men who had inhabited them having taken to their heels when the mine blew up. Here and there a few stout souls began to fire their muskets into the haze about the crater, but half an hour would pass before their fire would have any appreciable effect.

Colonel Pleasants's little plan could not possibly have been more successful. Right in the middle of the impregnable Confederate chain of defenses it had created a gap of 500 yards wide, and all the IX Corps had to do was march through and take the ridge. It would need to move briskly, because the gap was not going to stay open very long, but at five o'clock on this morning of July 30 decisive victory was less than half an undefended mile away.

But the one thing which Burnside's corps could not do that morning was to move briskly.

While one of Ledlie's brigades was getting down into the crater and acting partly like a rescue squad, partly like a salvage party, and partly like a group of sight-seers, his other brigade came dribbling out of the Federal trenches to support it. Those engineer parties which were to have cleared the way for the attacking columns had not materialized, and so the only gap in the abatis and *chevaux-de-frise* was right in front of the crater, where the earth thrown out by the explosion had buried the entanglements. This second brigade thus came forward through a funnel which led it straight toward the crater, and since the men were not coming up in regular formation—getting over the parapet was still a matter of every man for himself—and since nobody in particular was shooting at them, the men trotted up to the rim to have a look. While stray officers were urging everyone to continue the advance, most of the men slid down to the bottom of the crater, and presently almost all of Ledlie's division was jammed in there, a confused and aimless mob wholly out of control.

Not a vestige of military organization remained. Officers could not find their men and men could not find their officers, and there was a good deal of rather aimless activity. Along the farther rim of the crater, some industrious souls were trying to prepare a defensive line. The officer who had been digging up the buried cannon was putting men to work to horse them up to the rim where they could be fired—a difficult job, since the final feet of the crater wall were practically vertical—and he had other details hunting about to find the Rebel gunners' magazine. Half-entombed Confederates were still being dug up, and a few files of dazed prisoners were being sent to the rear. A few officers were yelling themselves hoarse, trying to get the men to climb up out of the crater and go on with the attack, but hardly anyone was paying any attention to them.[16]

This, of course, was the kind of situation which generals in charge of infantry divisions had been created to unscramble. Now was the moment for the division commander to take charge, restore order, pull the men out of the pit, form a coherent line of battle, and make his attack. But General Ledlie, who commanded this division, was snugly tucked away in a bombproof 400 yards behind the line, plying himself with rum borrowed from a brigade surgeon. From first to last he never saw the explosion, the soldiers, the crater, or the charge. Now and then reports would come back to him, and he would dispatch a runner with the order that everyone must move forward to the crest of the ridge. Beyond that he did nothing and was capable of doing nothing.[17] And General Burnside, back in the fourteen-gun battery, serenely unaware that anything was wrong, was busily ordering fresh troops forward.

The fresh troops were Potter's and Willcox's divisions. Time would have been saved if these troops had been lined up in brigade front just behind the front-line trench, but it was held that troops moving forward to the front ought to go up through the covered way—after all, that was what the thing had been built for—and so two infantry divisions were sent up a winding ditch that was wide enough for no more than two or three men abreast, colliding with stragglers, walking wounded, couriers, and other persons, and in due time they got into the front-line trench and scrambled up sandbag stairways, bayonet ladders, and what-not and went forward through the gap toward the crater. Their officers steered them off to the right and left, so that the empty Confederate trenches adjoining the crater could be possessed, and very slowly and with much confusion a trickle of Federal troops began to come up into line on each side of Ledlie's disorganized division.[18]

Meanwhile, the Confederates were rapidly coming to. On the right and left, regiments were being formed so that they could fire on the flanks of the attacking column. Between the crater and the ridge there was a shallow ravine—luckily, from the Southern viewpoint, it was out of reach of the Federal cannon—and an alert Confederate general put troops in it, and the fire from these men was beginning to be very heavy. The golden half hour in which the ridge could have been taken effortlessly was gone forever, and any advance that was made now would be made only after a hard fight.

After Potter's and Willcox's men had moved out into the empty trenches they began to go forward. The going was very bad. The ground beyond the trenches was a labyrinth of bombproofs, rifle pits, covered ways, and support trenches, and in many places the advance was a hoptoad business of jumping into a hole in the ground, scrambling out on the other side, jumping into another hole, and then repeating the scramble. The rising tempo of Confederate musketry did not make this kind of progress any easier.

Worse yet, Rebel artillery was coming into action, with power. A quarter of a mile north of the crater there was a four-gun battery, and the Southern gunners who had decamped when the mine was blown up came back to these guns and trained them on the Yankees who were trying to advance from the captured trenches. Federal artillery pounded this battery mercilessly, but it was well protected by solid earthen traverses and, although the shell dug up the ground all about until it looked as if the whole area had been plowed, the guns remained in action, putting canister right down the flank of the Federal battle line. On the other side of the crater the story was somewhat the same, with a battery posted so as to enfilade the Federal line from the left.

This battery also drew a storm of fire, but there was one gun that could not be silenced and it kept firing canister at deadly close range.

Up on the ridge west of the crater the Rebels put sixteen guns in line. The Federal gunners swept the ridge with overwhelming fire, but the Jerusalem Plank Road was sunken and offered a natural gun pit, and although ten of the sixteen guns were wrecked, the six that remained could not be subdued. In addition, the Confederates had mortars tucked away in hollow ground beyond the crater, and these began to toss shell into the dense jam of Federal soldiers.[19]

Minute by minute the situation grew worse. Potter's men gained ground on the right of the crater, but they were under a killing fire and their battle line was slowly pressed back. Mixed elements from half a dozen different commands crawled forward a few dozen yards from the crater itself in a valiant attempt to reach and silence the guns on the ridge, but the Rebels had a good second line in operation now and and there were not enough men in this attack to break it. On the left of the crater Willcox's men could do nothing but cower in the captured trench and keep up an ineffective musketry fire.

Meade had been right: if the attack was to succeed at all it would succeed in the first rush. The first rush had failed, and the failure was both incredible and irretrievable. What could have been done easily at five o'clock had become a matter of great difficulty by six o'clock and by seven it had become virtually impossible. The fight now was just one more dreary repetition of the old attempt to capture entrenched positions. Most of the men in the attacking forces knew it perfectly well, and they hugged the ground. To all intents and purposes the battle was already lost.

But the high command did not know it. Both corps and army headquarters were helpless. Burnside's command post was a quarter of a mile behind the front and Meade's was half a mile behind that, and the fight was out of their hands. An officer might be sent forward to get news. He would spend five or ten minutes jostling forward along the covered

way, and take his look around, and then spend another
five or ten minutes getting back. By the time his report had
been assimilated and orders had been started forward the
situation would have changed completely—above all other
battles, this one was fluid and every minute counted—and
the new orders would be worse than useless.[20]

Burnside might well have been up at the crater himself—
Grant said later that if he had commanded a corps in a fight
like this, that was where he would have been[21]—but Burnside was a headquarters operator, and this was Fredericksburg all over again: reports coming in out of a blinding fog,
orders going forward into the fog, nothing that was ordered
having any relation to reality, the men who wrote the orders
never once seeing the place where the orders were to be
executed or the people who were to execute them; and all
Burnside could do was to tell all and sundry to attack and
keep on attacking. Meade might have gone forward, but he
had announced beforehand that he could be reached at IX
Corps headquarters and it seemed to him now that it would
only cause more confusion if he left that spot. So he com-
municated with Burnside by telegraph, and he told Warren
and Ord to get their own troops moving to help the attack;
and nothing that happened up around the tangle of crater
and captured trenches and broken earth was in the least as
the officers in the rear thought it was.

Warren went to talk to Burnside about where the V Corps
ought to go in, and Burnside suggested that he go forward
and take a look, and Warren did so, and when he got back
he and Burnside discussed the situation in some detail, after
which Warren went over to his own headquarters and ordered Ayres's division forward.

Ord tried to advance, but the way was jammed with IX
Corps troops and hardly more than a handful of his men
were able to move. At 7:20 Burnside sent a wire to Meade
saying that he was doing everything possible to push his
men forward to the crest but that it was very hard work, and
Meade lost his temper and sent an angry wire asking him
what on earth was going on and snapping: "I wish to know

the truth and desire an immediate answer." Then Burnside lost his temper and wired Meade that Meade had been "un-officer-like and ungentlemanly"; and up in front the Confederates stitched together a semicircle of fire around the attacking troops and the advance came to a hopeless standstill.[22]

At precisely which moment orders went down to the bottom of the ravine from corps headquarters telling Ferrero's division of colored troops to advance and seize the crest.

The colored boys had been under arms since dawn, and as far as they knew their original assignment was unchanged: charge straight across the place where the mine had exploded and take the high ground that overlooked Petersburg. Top authorities had said that they must not lead the charge lest they be sacrificed; now, with the battle lost beyond recall, they were being sent in for a job that was not even as good as a forlorn hope. They got into the covered way, struggled up to the front line, scrambled over the parapet and ran forward with a cheer. By now the Confederate defense was able to lay heavy fire on the ground between the Union trench and the crater, so that getting forward was costly. As the men advanced General Ferrero dropped off in the same bomb-proof that housed General Ledlie and borrowed a swig of his jug of rum, leaving his brigadiers to direct the fight.[23]

It was impossible to go through the crater, because it was full of white troops. The colonel of the leading regiment saw this difficulty and led the command off to the right. By this time most of Potter's men had been shoved out of the trenches they had seized, and the colored regiment found itself running along between the Rebel abatis and a trenchful of Southern infantry—so close to the trench that some of the men were bayoneted as they ran, and those who were shot bore powder burns from the flash of Rebel muskets. As soon as the tail of the regiment had cleared the crater the colonel gave the order: "By the left flank—march!" followed by "Charge!" and the men sprang into the trench, using bayonet and clubbed musket, taking prisoners and a stand of colors. A regimental officer had to intervene to keep the men from killing their prisoners.[24]

In the captured trench the colored troops re-formed for a further advance. It was not easy, because the trench was full of dead and wounded men of both armies, and from in front and from the right the Confederates were laying down a blistering fire. A colonel tried to organize a charge, but when he went over the parapet he could not get more than fifty men to follow him, and the hostile fire quickly knocked them back. Then, while officers were trying to figure out what to do next, a runner came up with a message from General Ferrero: "If you have not already done so, you will immediately proceed to take the crest in your front"—which may have sounded like a reasonable order to a man safely tucked away in a dugout far behind the front.[25]

Well, they tried. First the officers leaped up on the parapet, waving their swords and shouting, and most of these were shot before they took another step. Then a scattering of soldiers followed them—200 men, perhaps, from three regiments—and a thin little cheer went up, and the ragged line ran forward. They got almost to the hidden ravine where the Confederates were waiting, and the Rebels came out with a countercharge, and for a moment there was vicious combat rocking back and forth in the open. Then the charge broke, and the colored men came running back, most of their officers gone, regimental and company organizations wholly mixed up, furious Southern infantry on their heels. Such white troops as were on the ground were caught up in this retreat, and in another moment a disorganized mass of black and white soldiers in blue uniforms was running desperately for cover, diving into the trenches and rifle pits or streaming for the deep haven of the crater.

In the captured trenches there was a dreadful crush of men. An officer wrote afterward that people were packed so tightly that he literally could not raise his arms from his side. The Confederates had followed close, and they poked rifles over the edge of the trench and fired into the huddle at three-foot range. Some of them jumped down in with bayonets, and men began to surrender, and the soldiers remembered hearing the Confederates crying: "Take the white man—kill the nigger!" There was a blind flurry of bitter fighting in the maze of trenches and rifle pits and dugouts, and eventually the whole section of captured trench was lost and the Union survivors got into the crater and prepared to hang on as long as they could.[26]

It was all over now, except for the killing. Grant had recognized failure and had told Meade to get the men back and call the whole operation off, and Meade had passed the word on to Burnside, but Burnside still thought that the attack somehow could be reorganized and made successful, and no recall was sounded. Hundreds of Union soldiers were jammed into the crater, most of them down at the bottom where they could do no fighting whatever. Men up along the rim were standing on a slope so steep that after a man fired his rifle he had to turn around, dig in with his heels, and brace his shoulders against the dirt in order to reload.[27]

Confederate mortars had the range and they were dropping shell into the crater on a helpless target that they could not miss; men who got out alive remembered a horrible debris of severed limbs and heads flying through the air after each shell exploded. The sun was high in the sky now and it beat down with unrelenting heat, terribly magnified in this steaming pit, and thirst seemed to be a worse foe than Confederate infantry. A Rebel countercharge came to the very edge of the crater, and Negroes lined the rim and fired and drove the attackers back, and the noise and the heat and the exploding shell beat on men's brains and dazed them so that nothing was remembered very clearly afterward.

Here and there, officers were able to organize details to search among the dead and wounded for cartridges. Some men were ordered to run back to the Union line with a cluster of canteens to get water, and a few of them managed to make the round trip without being killed. More than 200 men dropped unconscious from sheer heat and exhaustion, and a captain in the 45th Pennsylvania wrote: "The loss of life was terrible. There was death below as well as above ground in the crater. It seemed impossible to maintain life from the intense heat of the sun." He noted that his regiment lost 67 of the 110 men who had gone in.[28]

Somehow, finally—long after noon—it ended. The men who could do so went back to the Union lines; the others stayed where they were and either died or went off to Confederate prison camps. Burnside continued to insist to Meade that the attack could still succeed, but Ord bluntly told Meade that it was nonsense, and defeat at last was accepted. Through it all, Colonel Pleasants had been standing on the parapet of the fourteen-gun battery where he could watch the proceedings, and he stormed and swore in unregimented fury, telling Burnside that he had "nothing but a damned set of cowards in his brigade commanders"; and one of the men in the 48th Pennsylvania recorded that "Pleasants was awful mad when he saw how things were going on." [29]

Mad Colonel Pleasants might well have been. Never before had the army met so completely ignominious a defeat. Grant summed it up by telling Halleck that it was "the saddest affair I have witnessed in the war," and he added: "Such an opportunity for carrying fortifications I have never seen and do not expect again to have." A man in the 36th Massachusetts wrote that this day had been "the saddest in the history of the IX Corps," and a boy in the 48th Pennsylvania wrote to his sister:

"I expected to write to you of one of the most glorious victories that was ever won by this army, but instead of a victory I have to write about the greatest shame and disgrace that ever happened to us. The people at home may look at it as nothing but a mere defeat, but I look at it as a disgrace to our corps." [30]

In the 115th New York, a sergeant blew his top from heat and fatigue, sprang up and cried, "We'll fight 'em till we die, won't we, boys?" and then dropped unconscious. And in Ferrero's division it was observed that the colored troops never again sang their song:

> *We looks like men a'marching on;*
> *We looks like men o' war.*[31]

As such things went, the great battle of the crater was not, perhaps, unduly expensive. When the butcher's bill was added up it recorded a loss of 3,798 men, more than a third of them in the colored division. Measured by the standards of the Wilderness and Spotsylvania, this was comparatively mild. Most of the casualties occurred after Grant and Meade had ordered the attack given up, when the men were trying to do nothing more than get back to their own trenches.

Yet the casualty lists did not tell the whole story, which indeed was a good deal more complex than most of the participants were able to understand.

Since May 4 everything that had happened had been part of one continuous battle, a battle three months long, with advance and retreat and triumph and disaster all taking place together, so that words like victory and defeat had lost their meaning. All that had gone before was no more than prelude. The nation itself had been heated to an unimaginable pitch by three years of war and now it had been put on the anvil and the hammer was remorselessly coming down, stroke after clanging stroke, beating a glowing metal into a different shape.

There would be change and the war was bringing it, even though it might be that the war could not bring victory. The war had taken on a new magnitude, and perhaps it was no longer the kind of struggle anybody could win. But it was moving inexorably toward its end, and when it ended many things would end with it, in the South and in the North as well. Some of these were things that ought to end because they shackled men to the past, and some of them were fit to be laid away in the shadowland of dreams that are remembered forever, but in any case they were being brought to an end. After that there could be a new beginning.

CHAPTER V

Away, You Rolling River

---

1. Special Train for Monocacy Junction

PRIVATE Spink belonged to the 147th Regiment of Ohio National Guard Infantry, and in a modest and wholly innocent way he symbolized what was wrong with the defenses of Washington.

The 147th was doing a 100-day tour of duty, and it had been sent to Washington to help occupy the defensive lines so that the troops regularly in garrison could go down to fight the Rebels around Petersburg. Presumably Private Spink was a good soldier. He had recently been made acting ordnance sergeant, and with six other privates of the 147th he had been detailed to take charge of a battery of fieldpieces at the eastern end of the Chain Bridge, the farthest upstream of three Potomac River bridges which connected the District of Columbia with Virginia. This bridge had been guarded against Rebel intrusion ever since the early days of the war, and it was a key spot in the capital's defenses, and Private Spink and his detail cleaned the guns daily and swept the wooden gun platforms, and periodically took the ammunition out of the magazine and exposed it briefly to the air so that it would not deteriorate. No one made any complaint about the way this duty was performed, but in July of 1864, when a Confederate army came north to menace the capital, it suddenly developed that cleaning the guns and airing the ammunition taxed the abilities of these seven guardsmen to their absolute limit.

Which is to say that not one of the seven knew anything at all about artillery. When the inspecting colonel from General Halleck's staff came out to look at the defenses he learned that neither Private Spink nor any of the men with him even knew how to load the guns, let alone fire them. This was quite natural, since they had been trained strictly as infantry, but the colonel wondered what they would do if the invading Confederates showed up across the river and tried to march over into the national capital. He asked the nearest officer—a Veteran Reserve Corps lieutenant, who with sixty-three men was responsible for this whole section of the defenses—and the lieutenant had a ready answer. In such case, he said, he would have his men remove the planks of the bridge flooring, and pile them up in a barricade at the Washington end. He would also close the gates which gave access to the bridge. He understood, further, that one of the western piers of the bridge had been mined so that it could be blown up, but when the inspector looked into it he found that this was not true.

It would have been unfair to blame any of this on the Reserve lieutenant or the acting ordnance sergeant, since neither man was in any way responsible. But the condition of things in their part of the line was fairly typical of the condition elsewhere. The next bridge downstream, for instance, was Aqueduct Bridge in Georgetown, and it was guarded by two dozen men under a Reserve captain. This man said that if attacked he would close the gates of the bridge at the Georgetown end. He believed there were heavy bars lying around somewhere, although he had never tried them to see whether they would fit the staples in the gate and stockade. The inspector took the trouble to find them and test them. They did fit. Comforted by that much, he went his way.

On the land front, the chief engineer of the Department of Washington reported with military horror that brush was growing all over the approaches to the line, in such quantities that attacking troops could easily get quite close to the parapet under cover. He urged strongly that details be assigned to cut this brush and provide the defense with a clear field of fire. At about the same time a War Department major general who had access to the White House told President Lincoln that the Rebels were really getting close and that "An enterprising general could take the city." He said that when he mentioned all of this to General Halleck he was told that the responsibility was Grant's and not Halleck's. This worried the major general, because Grant was quite busy down in front of Petersburg, and he told the President that Halleck seemed very apathetic. Mr. Lincoln nodded.

"That's his way," he said. "He is always apathetic." [1]

It was a bad time for apathy, because the approaching Confederates were under the command of Jubal Early, who was nothing if not enterprising. He had been moving down the Shenandoah Valley ever since General Hunter retreated from the vicinity of Lynchburg, and he had perhaps 15,000 men with him—veteran troops as good as any in the land, their number magnified by panic rumor to practically any figure which a frightened imagination cared to think of.

The Washington defenses were extremely strong if there were men to hold them. Much time and money had been spent on them, beginning 'way back in the McClellan era, and they had been laid out according to the best military standards of the day. From the banks of the Potomac northwest of Chain Bridge, all the way around the city to the Potomac shore opposite Alexandria, the lines ran in a ponderous unbroken horseshoe, with a fort on every hill, trenches connecting the forts, and heavy guns posted to cover all the ground out in front. Over on the Virginia side it was the same, with another semicircle of works running from above Chain Bridge down to the lower edge of Alexandria. No one could approach the city from any direction without running into powerful fortifications. Yet fortifications needed soldiers in order to be effective, and now the soldiers were lacking.

If Grant had risked something by taking the soldiers away, the risk had been carefully calculated. What had thrown the calculations out of gear was the eccentric notion of strategy held by General Hunter.

While the Army of the Potomac remained on the offensive, Lee could not bring his own army up across the border as he had done in 1862 and 1863. The only danger would come from lesser detachments advancing down the Shenandoah Valley, and as long as Hunter and his troops were in the valley that way was barred. As far as the security of Washington was concerned it did not matter much whether Hunter was advancing, retreating, or sitting down. If he and his men were in the Valley, that was enough.

But when Hunter found Early ready to fight him in front of Lynchburg, and decided to run for shelter, he concluded for some incomprehensible reason that he had better run off through the West Virginia mountains instead of back down the valley toward Winchester and Harper's Ferry. That took his entire army out of the way for more than a fortnight, and it left the valley wide open for any use the Confederates wanted to make of it. Of this opening General Early promptly took full advantage.

Hunter could never see what was wrong with his move. He wrote to Stanton and he wrote to Lincoln, protesting that he had done everything for the best and complaining that he was unfairly blamed. Six months later he was still at it, writing to Grant, reciting all of his troubles with the undisciplined troops and unskilled generals he had inherited from the blessed Sigel and complaining that no one ever told him he had anything to do with the defense of Washington. After the war he was obtuse enough to write to Robert E. Lee, asking if Lee did not agree that the retreat into the mountains had been strategically sound. Lee, who detested him, replied with dead-pan courtesy that he hardly felt competent to pass on Hunter's reasons for making that move, since he did not know what they were; but he said that the move itself had been a tremendous help to Lee personally and to the Southern Confederacy in general.[2]

An aging Regular with sagging cheeks, a stringy mustache, and a habit of writing ill-tempered letters, Hunter had had rather an odd career. In February of 1861 he had been one of four army officers assigned to guard Mr. Lincoln on the President-elect's trip from Springfield to Washington. Out of this experience Hunter got a dislocated shoulder, received when a crowd surged out of hand at Buffalo; but a little later, after Fort Sumter, he got a major general's commission, and when Frémont was removed from command in Missouri that fall it was Hunter who was put in his place. He did not last very long in that important job, and presently he was on the shelf in Kansas, with few troops and fewer responsibilities, and he complained about it so gracelessly that even Lincoln, who could put up with almost anything, told him it was hard to answer "so ugly a letter" in good temper.

Still later Hunter had been given command along the Carolina coast, where he had endeared himself to the radicals by proclaiming the emancipation of slaves some months before Mr. Lincoln was ready for such a policy. Naturally, he had been removed, and when the War Department this spring picked him to command in the Valley, Grant had approved on the simple theory that anybody would be better than Sigel.

His stay in the Valley had been brief enough and his exit had been disastrous, but in one way he had made his presence felt—by burning Virginia Military Institute and the home of Virginia's Governor Letcher. His troops took their cue from him and did a good deal of looting and house burning on their own hook, and when Early led his Confederates north of the Potomac the Southerners were not in a mood to be gentle with Northern civilians. One of Early's officers who surveyed the damage Hunter's troops had left behind them wrote that it was very hard to admit that vengeance belonged solely to the Lord.[3] So the Confederates levied heavy cash contributions on such towns as Frederick, Maryland, and when they seized horses and cattle and forage they were less urbane and polite about it than had been the case during the Gettysburg campaign. By the end of the first week in July they were destroying railroad bridges and other property in Maryland east of the South Mountain ridge, and the long-suffering Baltimore and Ohio Railroad was asking the Navy if it could send gunboats to protect railroad property in the upper reaches of Chesapeake Bay.

This call took Secretary Welles over to the War Department, where to his disgust he found that nobody knew anything about Early's army—"its numbers, where it is, or its destination." He wrote in his diary that an attack on Washington probably could not be resisted, and he predicted that such an attack would be made very soon. A couple of days later, on a Sunday, a Navy Department clerk hurried to Mr. Welles's office to tell him that Southern troopers had already crossed the district line and were prowling about in the outskirts of Georgetown. Welles had a low opinion of Halleck and Stanton anyway, and he wrote now that "on our part there is neglect, ignorance, folly, imbecility in the last degree." [4]

The War Department had not been quite as neglectful as Mr. Welles supposed. At the beginning of July Halleck had warned Grant that Early was becoming a menace, and Ricketts's division of the VI Corps had been sent up to Baltimore. There it joined a scratch contingent of miscellaneous troops pulled together by General Lew Wallace, the literary-minded soldier who eventually was to write *Ben Hur*, and Wallace took his command over toward Frederick, to fight the Rebels on the banks of the Monocacy. Early's veterans outnumbered him heavily and they pushed him aside without much delay, but the rest of the VI Corps was embarking on transports at City Point to come north and take a hand in the game, and ocean steamers were coming up the bay with veterans from Emory's XIX Corps, recently on duty in Louisiana. The situation would probably be all right if Early would just allow a few more days' grace.

Early was no time-waster, however. After routing Wallace's command he drove his men on mercilessly in mid-July heat, and by the morning of July 11 his weary advance guard was coming south through Silver Spring, its skirmishers creeping forward toward Fort Stevens, well inside the district line on the Seventh Street Road. Old Francis P. Blair's famous country home was occupied by Rebel officers, who took care not to damage the place unduly but did help themselves to the contents of Mr. Blair's excellent wine cellar. Not far away there was a house owned by Blair's son Montgomery, who was Postmaster General in Lincoln's cabinet, and this house the Rebels burned to the ground, leading Blair to remark bitterly that nothing better could be expected so long as "poltroons and cowards" had control of the United States War Department.[5]

To beat off Early's advance Halleck had very few troops, but he did have plenty of general officers. Among these was dignified Major General Alexander McD. McCook, temporarily without a command, and McCook was sent out to Fort Stevens and told to assume charge of the capital's defenses. He had very little to work with—a regiment of District of Columbia militia, some 4-F's from the Veteran Reserve Corps, a Maine battery, a few National Guard troops on 100-day duty, and a scattering of gunners in the different forts. He put these men in the trenches and had them begin shooting at Early's skirmishers. During the morning the military hospitals were combed out and a number of convalescents, representing nearly every regiment in the Army of the Potomac, was brought out the Seventh Street Road, together with some more Reserve Corps soldiers and odds and ends of dismounted cavalry. Meanwhile General Montgomery C. Meigs, the distinguished quartermaster general of the army, had donned his field uniform and was forming all of the clerks and detailed men of the Quartermaster Corps into a brigade and was marching them around to the arsenal to draw weapons. During the day he went trooping out to the scene of action with some 1,500 of these extemporized soldiers. At McCook's direction he occupied a mile or more of trench to the right of Fort Stevens.[6]

The forts and trenches were good, and this assemblage of soldiers might do well enough if nobody pushed very hard. General Early—closer to the Capitol dome than any other armed Confederate during all of the war—was peering south from the high ground a mile north of Fort Stevens, getting ready to push just as soon as he could figure out just what was ahead of him.

He was a salty and a picturesque character, this Jubal Early, and a very dangerous opponent to boot. A West Pointer who had given up the Army for the law some years previously, he had been prosecuting attorney of Rockingham County before the war, and he was stooped and grizzled and sardonic, not greatly loved by other ranking Confederate officers because of his habit of blunt, sarcastic speech; an exceedingly capable soldier, grim as old Stonewall himself, a driver who could be counted on to get the last ounce of advantage out of the baffling, almost incomprehensible opportunity which faced him on this eleventh of July.

When General Lee sent him north, neither he nor Early had much hope that Washington could actually be captured. The idea was principally to make trouble and to joggle Grant's elbow. In former years the Lincoln administration had shown itself abnormally sensitive to any threat to the capital, and there was a chance that this thrust might force Grant to raise the siege of Petersburg and come back to save Washington.

If this could not be done it was just possible that Early could slide clear around Washington on the northern side, strike down southeast, and capture the prison camp at Point Lookout on the shore of Chesapeake Bay, releasing some thousands of Confederate prisoners of war. Failing that, he could at least make a great nuisance of himself, collect supplies in Maryland, and in general disarrange Federal strategy. Early's problem this morning was to determine exactly how much of an opening was in front of him now, while inexpert tacticians were assembling third-rate troops in the lines adjoining Fort Stevens.

The balancing of risks and opportunities was delicate and perplexing, and if "Old Jube" swore and bit off another chew of tobacco—as he very probably did—it could hardly be wondered at. He knew that the trenches before him were too strong to be taken if any number of regular troops occupied them. He also knew that even if he broke the line and got all the way to downtown Washington he could not hope to stay there very long, since the country in his rear was all swarming with Federal troops—Wallace's men, and Sigel's, and Hunter's dispirited army coming back from West Virginia—and in time the Yankees would undoubtedly form these into a compact mass that would bar the way home. Early's own army was small and very tired, and a hard fight might cripple it so badly that it could never return to Virginia, and Lee was so pressed for manpower that he simply could not afford to lose these men. The forces that made for caution were strong.[7]

But the possibilities also were good. No hasty collection of convalescents, casuals, and government clerks could hope to bar the way for the lean veterans of the Army of Northern Virginia—the prospect of looting the rich depots of Washington was enough to make these men fight like desperadoes— and the results that would flow from even a temporary occupation of the Federal capital might well be incalculable. If, after all that had happened this spring, a wing of Lee's army could actually seize Washington, the whole course of the war might be different. Anyway, Early was a slugger who never listened to the voice of caution unless he had to, and at last he decided to make the assault. He put sharpshooters into farmhouses to pick off gunners in the Yankee forts, and he wheeled his artillery forward and pressed his skirmishers in closer, and he began to get ready for a big fight.

In the forts and the trenches there were pallid men from hospital and office—"a mild-mannered set," as one observer felt, who looked as if "they would never hurt anyone, not even in self-defense," obviously uncomfortable in their unweathered uniforms, uneasy at the prospect of passing the night in the open air. Downtown there were nervous civilians in the streets, wondering what was going to happen next, listening to the fluttering, pulsing sound of the distant cannon, contemplating flight but not certain where to fly to or how to get there.[8]

But down by the Seventh Street wharf fat-sided steamers were coming up the river, tarred heaving lines snaking ashore to be taken by waiting longshoremen, mates busy about the decks, whistles grunting hoarsely, ships' timbers creaking against the pilings. Then the gangplanks were slung to the wharf, and long lines of tanned men in ragged, dusty, sun-bleached uniforms were coming ashore, forming up on the dock with elbow nudgings and right-dress craning of necks. Up Seventh Street they came, a solid column of soldiers with the Greek cross on their caps and their banners, men who slouched along casually without bothering about alignment, seeming to be in no hurry at all but somehow covering the ground very rapidly.

They were hard-boiled and unemotional, and as they tramped along they looked cynically at the people on the sidewalks, and made mental note of the locations of saloons; and they marched behind tattered, faded, shot-torn banners, and the people on the sidewalk looked at them and set up a sudden cheer, and called out to one another in elated relief: "The Sixth Corps! That's the Sixth Corps!"

From time to time the column would halt for a breather, and every time it halted a certain number of the veterans would slip away and head for a barroom and a glass of something cold, and one of the men who made the march said that not even "the military genius of a Napoleon" could have taken them out that dusty street on a hot July day without loss. The men who did not fall out made caustic remarks about militia and quartermaster clerks and well-fed civilians, and in midafternoon they got up to Fort Stevens and took charge. The amateurs could relax now; the professionals were taking over.[9]

General Wright had galloped on ahead, and General Mc-Cook received him with feelings of great relief, and as the head of the corps came up the men of the Army of the Potomac filed right and left into the trenches. One of Wright's men wrote that they found "a rattled lot of defenders, brave enough but with no coherence or organization," and he mentioned seeing a surplus of brigadier generals and a vast number of home guards whose skins looked strangely white and untanned. Out beyond the trenches, he said, he and his mates could see Early's Southerners—"as fine a corps of infantry as ever marched to the tap of a drum"—but the VI Corps was here now and the door was locked, and at the last minute of the last hour the Washington lines were occupied by men who knew how to hold them.[10]

After that it was all over, except for the incidental drama and excitement.

General McCook asked Wright to hold his corps in reserve but to relieve the picket line, and so several hundred of the VI Corps went out beyond the trenches to exchange shots with Early's skirmishers. The fire seemed hot and heavy to the clerks and 100-day militia, but Wright's veterans considered it light and scattering and they went out with nonchalant competence. One of them remembered, with an amused chuckle, that the troops that were being relieved were "astounded at the temerity displayed by these war-worn veterans in going out beyond the breastworks, and benevolently volunteered most earnest words of caution."[11]

Early's skirmishers were 600 yards away, and they were being supported by shellfire, and the veterans moved out and sparred with them, and after a while darkness came and the opposing armies settled down for the night. General Meigs, unused to field work, went along his line of trenches, saw that his men had rations and blankets, and himself went a few hundred yards to the rear, tied his horse to a tree in an apple orchard, and spread his poncho on the ground for a bed—feeling, one gathers, innocently thrilled and pleased with himself. Secretary Welles, who had come out to see what was to be seen, rode back to the city in his carriage, looking at the campfires and knots of lounging soldiers and groups of stragglers and musing: "It was exciting and wild. Much of life, and much of sadness."[12]

Next morning Early tapped harder, just to make certain that the reinforced defenses were as solid as they looked. The VI Corps sent a whole brigade out to meet him, and in Fort Stevens and nearby Fort De Russey the long-range cannon came to life, plowing up the slopes where the Rebel skirmishers were in line and knocking down the houses where the sharpshooters were hiding. The noise echoed and rolled across the open country north of the city, a blanket of ragged white smoke slid down into the hollows, and a trickle of wounded men began to flow back to the rear. Then a carriage pulled up by the barracks that had been built just behind Fort Stevens, and a tall man in frock coat and stovepipe hat got out—an unmilitary figure among all of these soldiers, but moving nonetheless with the air of one used to exercising command—and here was Abraham Lincoln, out to see for himself a little of the death and destruction which he had been living with for three years and more.

General Wright was in the fort, and he greeted the President; and without stopping to think, never imagining that the invitation would be accepted, he asked if Mr. Lincoln would care to get up on the parapet with him and watch the battle. The President said he would like to very much, and while Wright wished earnestly that he could recall his thoughtless words the President clambered up on top of the parapet. He was tall and gaunt, towering over everybody, an obvious target, standing right where Southern sharpshooters were peppering the place with Minié bullets.

Wright begged him to get down, but Lincoln refused, the idea of personal danger seeming not to enter his head. A surgeon who had got up on the parapet was struck, just a few feet away from where Lincoln was standing, and other bullets flicked up the dirt near him, and Wright in desperation moved around to stand between the President and the enemy fire. His entreaties having no effect, Wright at last bluntly told the President that he, General Wright, was in charge of operations here at the fort and that it was his order that the President get down out of danger; and when Lincoln still failed to move, Wright threatened to get a squad of soldiers and remove him by force. This seemed to amuse the President, and while Wright gulped at his brashness in threatening to arrest the commander in chief, Lincoln got down obediently and sat with his back to the parapet.

He was safe enough now, unless some Rebel gunner happened to burst a shell overhead, and Wright felt better. He noticed, however, that Lincoln was forever spoiling the effect by jumping up and peering over the ramparts for another look, and Wright later wrote to a friend: "I could not help thinking that in leaving the parapet he did so rather in deference to my earnestly expressed wishes than from any consideration of personal safety." [13]

Meanwhile the fight was getting warmer. Wright's infantry went forward, taking losses, and Lincoln saw men killed and watched while wounded men were carried to the rear. But Early realized that the situation was hopeless, and after a while called in his skirmishers, and at dusk he ordered a retreat. He was in an acrid, festive humor, and as his troops fell into column for the march back to Virginia Early turned to an aide and remarked: "Major, we haven't taken Washington, but we've scared Abe Lincoln like hell!" The aide agreed that this was so, but he suggested that when the VI Corps line moved out to drive back Early's skirmishers there might have been a few Confederates who were equally scared. Early chuckled. "That's true," he said, "but it won't appear in history!" [14]

It had been a brisk scrap while it lasted, but one of Wright's veterans confessed that he supposed the Confederates had retired "more we think from the sight of the VI Corps flag than from the number assailing them." A man in the Vermont Brigade wrote that "the dignitaries in the fort returned to their homes, having witnessed as pretty and well-conducted a little fight as was seen during the whole war," and the War Department recorded that the whole business had cost the VI Corps some 200 in killed and wounded. General Meigs took his quartermaster details back to town, proudly writing that he had had command of a battle line two miles long containing 5,000 troops, and he presently got from Secretary Stanton a letter containing a brevet major general's commission and thanking him for his services. The Rebels drew off through Rockville, heading for the Potomac River fords, and some of General McCook's men advanced as far as the Sligo Creek post office, capturing a field hospital containing seventy-odd wounded Southerners plus a corporal's guard of surgeons and orderlies. Washington relaxed. The big scare was over.[15]

It was up to the VI Corps to pursue the enemy, and the pursuit was extremely vigorous. The Vermont Brigade remembered the first night's march out of Washington as one of the worst it ever made. The weather was hot and the roads were dusty, clogged with any number of stragglers and with obstructions which Early's men had thoughtfully left in their wake. By the time the veterans had seen the Confederates out of Maryland they were fully ready to call it quits and take a little rest.

The 2nd Connecticut Heavy Artillery came trailing back to Washington, and to its delight learned it was to get back its original assignment as heavy artillery—it had been front-line infantry beginning with Spotsylvania Court House, and it had had fearful casualties—and it snuggled down in a fort near Tenallytown, dispossessing an Ohio National Guard outfit "with its gawky officers" and luxuriating in new uniforms, new shoes, and regular rations. It was especially delighted to get, at last, crossed cannon to put on its caps, for these insignia belonged to heavy artillery and the men felt that this made the new incarnation official. They looked fondly at the comfortable living quarters in the fort and told one another that they were going to sleep for a week. However, the very next morning orders were changed and the regiment was put back in the VI Corps infantry column, crossed cannon and all, and it went off on a grinding hike to the Shenandoah Valley to keep Early from launching a new invasion, and it never saw the Tenallytown fort again.[16]

For the VI Corps the next two weeks were a nightmare. The men forded the Potomac and went up through Leesburg and Snickers' Gap to the banks of the Shenandoah, and down at City Point Grant concluded that the danger was over and sent orders for the corps to come back to Petersburg. So there was a hard forced march, and just as the troops reached Washington and prepared to board the transports Early sent his cavalry riding hard up into Pennsylvania, where the men burned the city of Chambersburg—another little dividend on Hunter's depredations in the upper Valley —so once again orders were changed and the corps marched back to Harper's Ferry as fast as it could go, crossing the Potomac there and starting up the Valley again.

There was much straggling on this march, due to heat and general exhaustion and, as a brigade surgeon confessed, to "bad whisky from Washington." The corps had no more than started up the valley than orders were changed once more and everybody had to hurry back into Maryland. In the first days of August the men made a bivouac along the Monocacy River not far from Frederick, wondering bleakly what the people in Washington were going to think of next.

Corps morale was down at low-water mark for the war. Originally the men had been delighted to leave Petersburg and come up to Washington, and their appearance as saviors of the capital, the only troops who had ever fought under the eye of Lincoln himself, made them think very highly of themselves. But the marching since then had been harder than anything they had had in all their experience—it was even worse than the man-killing marches they had made in the Gettysburg campaign, which they had always supposed were the worst possible—and when they got to the Monocacy the men were so dead-beat that most regiments made camp with no more than twenty men around the colors. The series of aimless marches and countermarches showed clearly that Washington did not know what it was doing, and one veteran admitted that by this time "the Sixth Corps was, in army parlance, 'about played out.'" Another man wrote that "the thinking soldiers about their campfires felt a discouragement the gloom of the Wilderness had failed to produce." [17]

Still, the campsites by the Monocacy were pleasant, and for a few days there was rest, and with the rest men's spirits rose again. One of the 2nd Connecticut heavies, adjusted at last to the fact that the comforts of the Washington forts would be forever unattainable, grew almost lyrical when he considered the present bivouac:

"The clear, sparkling river ran along the lower edge of it, and the surrounding woods abounded in saplings, poles and brush, for which soldiers can always find so many uses. Regular camp calls were instituted, company and battalion drills ordered, and things began to assume the appearance of a stay." An officer died while the corps was camped here and he was given a full-dress military funeral, whereat all the men wagged their heads. They had seen so many men of all ranks put under the sod without any ceremony at all that this seemed to be an infallible sign that they would stay here for a long time, resting, drilling a little, and regaining their strength.[18]

Emory's men in the XIX Corps felt the same way. They had spent all of the war in the humid heat of Louisiana, and when they made camp by the Shenandoah a few miles from Harper's Ferry they felt that they were in a new world. One soldier wrote glowingly of "the bracing air, the crystal waters, the rolling wheat fields and the beautiful blue mountains," sick men in the field hospitals returned to duty, straggling diminished, and the men looked about them at the open country and the excellent roads and felt that marching in this region might almost be a pleasure.[19]

While the soldiers caught their breath and hoped for the best, Grant had been living through what were probably his most trying moments of the war. He was at City Point, and some sort of curtain seemed to have come down between his headquarters there and the War Department in Washington. He had a good many things on his mind—the tragedy of the mine and the attempted break-through came right when all of this frenzied, useless countermarching was going on—and when he sent orders north to govern the use of the troops that were supposed to be rounding up Early's army the orders had to go through Washington, and on their way through things happened to them.

The pursuit of Early had been ineffective because too many men were in position to give orders to soldiers like

Wright and Emory. All lines of authority were crossed, and the War Department was buzzing and fretting and issuing innumerable orders, taking time along the way to modify, alter, or countermand the orders other people were issuing. Looking back long after the war, Grant wrote his verdict: "It seemed to be the policy of General Halleck and Secretary Stanton to keep any force sent there in pursuit of the invading army moving right and left so as to keep between the enemy and our capital; and generally speaking they pursued this policy until all knowledge of the whereabouts of the enemy was lost." [20]

The first step, obviously, was to put one competent soldier in charge of the whole operation with definite, overriding authority, and this step Grant took. He sent orders to pull Major General William B. Franklin out of retirement and give him command over everybody, and for a day or two he assumed that he had settled things. Then he got a fussy telegram from Halleck explaining that this just would not do. Franklin had been a McClellan man in the old days, and the grim Committee on the Conduct of the War considered that he was really responsible for Burnside's failure at Fredericksburg, and he was in very bad odor at the War Department—and Grant's order was nullified and Franklin was not appointed. It appeared that Halleck and Stanton were exercising a veto power over Grant's authority and substituting their own ideas of strategy for his.[21]

Now this was the old McClellan situation all over again, and in a sense it was the crisis of the war. This was a presidential election year and by every sign men could read the Northern people were tired and discouraged. Sherman had not taken Atlanta and Grant had not taken Richmond, casualty lists had been heavy beyond all previous experience, and now the Confederates had an army in the lower Shenandoah Valley, ravaging Northern towns and apparently quite as irrepressible as in the Stonewall Jackson days. Unless the general in chief could somehow regain control and put an end to the fumbling and meddling, the bottom might fall out of the whole war effort, with failure in the field leading to defeat at the polls, and with independence for the Confederacy coming along in due course.

In a very similar situation, McClellan wrote bitter letters to his wife, told his officers that Washington was villainously conspiring against him, and drifted on down to defeat. It remained to be seen what Grant would do.

On August 1—while he was still digesting the dismal story of the fiasco at the crater—Grant made his move. He ordered Phil Sheridan to go up to the Monocacy and take control of all the troops in that area, and he wired Halleck that he was instructing Sheridan to "put himself south of the enemy and follow him to the death." 22

The emphasis here, of course, was on the instruction to get *south* of the enemy. Whenever the Confederates invaded the North they were actually offering the Federals a priceless opportunity, and the real job of the Federal commander at such times was not to repel the invasion but to destroy the invading army. Lincoln had always seen it so, but he could never make his generals see it, and both Antietam and Gettysburg had been barren victories. Now there was a general with iron in him, who saw things as Lincoln did; and yet the old viewpoint still prevailed in the War Department, and the War Department had muscled in between general and President, on the one hand, and opportunity, on the other.

Grant's order was not at all the sort of thing Secretary Stanton was apt to approve. Under all his bluster, Stanton was timid, and the idea of following a pugnacious enemy to the death was just too much for him. Also, he felt that Sheridan was too young for an important independent command, and it appears that he did not like him very much personally, and what would happen to Grant's order regarding Sheridan was likely to be very similar to what had happened to his order regarding Franklin.

But just at this moment President Lincoln took a hand. He had been reading all of the correspondence, and now he sat down to send a telegram of his own to General Grant.

Grant's instructions to Sheridan, said the President, were just exactly right, and what Grant wanted done was precisely what the President wanted done. But Grant was invited to look over all of the dispatches he had received from Washington, and to consider everything he knew about the way the War Department did things, "and discover, if you can, that there is any idea in the head of anyone here of 'putting our army south of the enemy' or of 'following him to the death' in any direction."

Mr. Lincoln closed with the blunt warning:

"I repeat to you it will neither be done nor attempted, unless you watch it every day and hour and force it." [23]

The whole history of the Army of the Potomac passes in review in Mr. Lincoln's brief dispatch: the history of the army, and the most exasperating problem of the war itself. Over and over the war had been prolonged because of the timid, restrictive caution that could paralyze action—the habit of mind that was always too busy weighing risks to grasp opportunities. It developed now that that habit of mind had never been eradicated because when all was said and done it had its final roots in the War Department itself. The War Department could not act and the President could not make it act. The most he could do was support a general who was bold enough to ram action down the department's throat.

Now Lincoln was giving Grant the final tip-off, just as he had so often and so vainly tried, two years earlier, to give McClellan a similar tip-off. Tables of organization and lines of authority meant nothing in themselves. In the end everything depended on the general, and it was up to the general to act. McClellan had never been able to rise to this challenge. Grant was the last chance.

Two hours after he had received this wire from President Lincoln, Grant was on a fast steamer, coming up the Potomac. When the boat docked at Washington he stopped off neither at the White House nor at the War Department. Instead he went directly to the railroad station and took a special train to Monocacy Junction, and as soon as he got there he went to see General Hunter.

Technically, Hunter commanded the military department in which all of these troop movements were going on, and so technically he was responsible for everything that was being done. Grant had no intention of letting Hunter have control over the attempt to destroy Early's army but he was quite willing to let him down easy. Hunter could shelve himself in a Baltimore office if he wished, retaining nominal command of the department while Sheridan did the actual work, and Grant told Hunter this in so many words. But Hunter had had enough. He was getting on in years and he was not much of a soldier, and there was something mean in him which had led him to burn college buildings and homes when he should have been fighting Confederate armies, but during the last fortnight he had been more sinned against than sinning. He told Grant frankly that he had been pulled and tugged around so much by War Department orders that at this moment he simply did not know where Early and Early's troops were— and, in short, he would prefer to be relieved outright and let Sheridan carry the whole load.

Grant wasted no further time. "Very well, then," he said. Hunter was relieved, and without even waiting for Sheridan to arrive Grant ordered all of the Union troops in the vicinity to move at once to Halltown, a little village at the lower end of the Shenandoah Valley a few miles away from Harper's Ferry. No matter where Early was, a concentration of Federal soldiers in the Shenandoah was something the Confederacy could not endure. Early would come back quickly enough, once blue-uniformed troops displayed themselves in force around Halltown.[24]

Sheridan reached Monocacy Junction the next morning, after most of the troops had moved. Grant met him, outlined the job he wanted done, and took off for City Point, with very few people knowing that he had ever left the place, and Sheridan took a one-car special train for Harper's Ferry and rode from there to Halltown to take over his new command. There was a great deal of work to be done and it was going to take Sheridan a month or more to get acclimated and learn how to do what he had to do, but from now on the road led upward. This was the beginning of the end.

2. To Peel This Land

There may be lovelier country somewhere—in the Island Vale of Avalon, at a gamble—but when the sunlight lies upon it and the wind puts white clouds racing their shadows the Shenandoah Valley is as good as anything America can show. Many generations ago the Knights of the Golden Horseshoe climbed the Blue Ridge to look down on it in wonder, and ever since then it has been a legend and the fulfillment of a promise. There is music in its very name, and some quality in the region touched the imaginations of men who had never even seen it. The sailors on deep water sailing ships made one of their finest chanteys about it, and sent topsail yards creaking to the masthead in ports all over the world to the tune of "Shenandore":

> O Shenandore, I love to hear you—
> Away, you rolling river.

During the war it was known simply as the Valley: an open corridor slanting off to the southwest from the gap at Harper's Ferry, broad land lying between blue mountains with the bright mirror of a looped river going among golden fields and dark woodlands, pleasant towns linked along a broad undulating turnpike and rich farms rolling away to the rising hills.

Queerly enough, although it had been a vital factor in the war, in a way the war had hardly touched it. Stonewall Jackson had made it a theater of high strategy, and there had been hard fighting along the historic turnpike and near quaint villages like Front Royal and Port Republic, and most of the fence rails on farms near the main highway had long since vanished to build the campfires of soldiers in blue and gray. Yet even in the summer of 1864 the land bore few scars. East of the Blue Ridge and the Bull Run mountains the country along the Orange and Alexandria Railroad had been marched over and fought over and ravaged mercilessly, and it was a desolate waste picked clean of everything an army might want or a farmer could use. But the Valley had escaped most of this, and when Phil Sheridan got there it was much as it had always been—rich, sunny, peaceful, a land of good farms and big barns, yellow grain growing beside green pastures, lazy herds of sheep and cattle feeding on the slopes.

Originally, the Valley had drawn many settlers from Pennsylvania and the Cumberland Valley, and these were mostly Dunkers, with a sprinkling of Quakers, Mennonites, and Nazarenes: devout, frugal, and industrious folk who held firmly to a belief that war was sinful—a belief for which there may be a certain amount of backing, both in Scripture and in racial experience—and their religion forbade the faithful to take up arms. As non-resistants these people had been a problem to the Confederate government, since they would not volunteer and, because of the stubbornness with which they held to their faith, could not well be drafted. But before the war was very old they became an asset instead of a problem. The Confederate Congress in 1862 provided that they might be exempted from military service on payment of a $500 tax, and as a result the farms of the Valley had no shortage of manpower. And because the men were good farmers and the soil was fertile, the Valley became an incomparable granary and source of supply for Lee's soldiers. Rations might be short now and then, because of poor transportation and an incompetent commissariat, but as long as these sober pacifists continued to till their lands and raise their flocks and operate their gristmills, Lee's army could not be starved out of Richmond.[1]

An accident of geography made the Valley worth more to the South than to the North, strategically. Running from southwest to northeast, the Valley was the Confederacy's great covered way leading up to the Yankee fortress, the high parapet of the Blue Ridge offering concealment and protection. A Confederate army coming down the Valley was marching directly toward the Northern citadel, but a

Yankee army moving up the Valley was going nowhere in particular because it was constantly getting farther away from Richmond and Richmond's defenders. Nor did a Confederate force operating in the Valley have serious problems of supply. The Valley itself was the base, and it could be drawn on for abundant food and forage from Staunton all the way to Winchester and beyond.

Both Lee and Grant were thoroughly familiar with these facts. In the spring of 1862 Lee had used them, sending Stonewall Jackson down the Valley in such a way as to bring the North to stunning defeat. In the summer of 1864 he had used them again, and Early's foray had caused more trouble. From the moment he took command Grant had had to take these facts into consideration. Until he solved the problem of the Valley, the Army of the Potomac was never safe from an attack in its rear.

When the 1864 campaign began Grant tried to solve it, and the solution then would have been fairly simple. All that he needed was to establish a Federal army in the upper Valley —at Staunton, say, or Waynesboro, anywhere well upstream. That would close the gate and the Confederacy's granary and covered way would be useless. But nothing had worked out as he had planned. First Sigel went up the Valley, to be routed at Newmarket. Then Hunter took the same road, only to lose everything by wild misguided flight off into West Virginia. So now the problem was tougher, and the solution that would have worked in the spring was no good at all in midsummer.

Grant studied the matter, fixing his eyes on the fields and barns and roads of the Valley, and he had a deadly unemotional gaze which saw flame and a smoking sword for devout folk whose way led beside green pastures and still waters. The war could not be won until the Confederacy had been deprived of the use of this garden spot between the mountains. If the garden were made desert, so that neither the Southern Confederacy nor even the fowls of the air could use it, the problem would be well on the way toward being solved.

Grant put it in orders. In a message to Halleck, sent before Sheridan was named to the command, Grant was specific about what he wanted: an army of hungry soldiers to follow retreating Rebels up the Valley and "eat out Virginia clear and clean as far as they go, so that crows flying over it for the balance of the season will have to carry their provender with them." He spelled this out in instructions for the Union commander: "He should make all the Valley south of the Baltimore and Ohio railroad a desert as high up as possible. I do not mean that houses should be burned, but all provisions and stock should be removed, and the people notified to get out." [2]

Sheridan got the point. A soldier in Torbert's division of cavalry remembered the orders that came down from Sheridan's headquarters: ". . . you will seize all mules, horses and cattle that may be useful to our army. Loyal citizens can bring in their claims against the government for this necessary destruction. No houses will be burned; and officers in charge of this delicate but necessary duty must inform the people that the object is to make this Valley untenable for the raiding parties of the rebel army." [3]

It could be written out concisely, and the telegraph instruments would click it off, and adjutants could read it before the troops at evening parade, with deep shadows dropping down through the rich dusk; and a grim eternity of war and the hardening of many hearts had gone into it, romance of war and knightly chivalry dissolved forever in the terrible acid of enmity and hatred, settlement by the sword coming at last to mean all-out war, modern style, with a blow at the economic potential cutting across the farmer's yard and dooming innocent people to the loss of a lifetime's hard-bought gains.

There was a young fellow in the 2nd Ohio Cavalry who presided over some of this devastation: a lad who had seen values beyond life glimmering on the edge of the war when he enlisted, and who wrote in his diary about a talk he had with a farmer on the western fringe of the Valley whose farm lay in the road of military necessity:

"He owned a farm, sterile and poor, of 200 acres in among the hills. Moved there 34 years since when all was a wilderness. Had never owned a slave. Had cleaned up the farm, built a log house and made all the improvements with his own hands. It made him almost crazy to see all going to destruction in one night—all his fences, outbuildings, cattle, sheep and fowls. An only son at home, an invalid. Had always been true to the government. Only wished that God would now call him, that he might be with his many friends in the church yard—pointing to it near by—and the aspect of suffering and starvation be taken from it." [4]

The war had grown old, and it was following its own logic, the insane logic of war, which had been building up ever since Beauregard's cannon bit into the masonry of Fort Sumter. The only aim now was to hurt the enemy, in any way possible and with any weapon; to destroy not his will to resist but his ability to make that will effective. The will might remain and be damned to it: if the will and the bitterness could be made impotent, nothing else mattered.

There was much bitterness abroad by now—everywhere, perhaps, except in the army itself—and kindly, God-fearing people were demanding that their enemies be made to suffer. An example of this feeling can be seen in a letter which President Lincoln received just about this time from the good businessmen who made up the Chicago Board of Trade.

The president and the secretary of this organization wrote to Mr. Lincoln to recite the terrible evils which were befalling Union prisoners in the great Confederate prison camp at Andersonville, Georgia. In that overcrowded pen men lived in an open field without tents or huts, exposed to the hot sun and the driving rain, unclothed and badly fed, dying miserably of disease and malnutrition, all but totally uncared for, none of their sufferings minimized by wartime propaganda. So the Chicago civilians were soberly urging that the Federal government set aside an equal number of Confederate prisoners and subject them to the same treatment: that is, throw them together in such a way that most of them would die and the rest would lose their health and their minds, do it deliberately and with calculation, in order that there might be a fair extension of pain and death.

"We are aware," wrote the Chicagoans, "that this, our petition, savors of cruelty"—but it was no time to be squeamish. There was a war on and they felt obliged to "urge retaliatory measures as a matter of necessity"; and, in sum, here was a black flag fluttering on the hot wind, a rallying point for any ill will which had not yet been properly organized.[5]

Admittedly, Andersonville had a record which even today cannot easily be read without horror and sick disgust. So did most of the other prison camps in the Civil War, in the Confederacy and in the Union as well, and the terrible things which happened in them seem to have taken place not because anyone meant it so but simply because men were clumsy and the times were still rude.

Even when they were camped in perfect safety behind their own lines, getting the best their governments had to give, the soldiers of that day got miserable food and defective medical attention, so that simply being in the army killed many more men than were killed in battle. Only when an army commander was a first-rate military administrator, willing and able to devote a large part of his time to such matters, did the lot of the troops become anything better than just barely endurable. Inevitably, prisoners of war fared a great deal worse. A certain combination of incompetence and indifference can cause almost as much suffering as the most acute malevolence.

One does not need to read wartime propaganda to get a full indictment of the prison camps. Each side indicted itself, in terms no propagandist could make much more bitter.

A Confederate surgeon, completing an inspection of Andersonville, reported to his superiors at Richmond that more than 10,000 prisoners had died in seven months—nearly one third of the entire number confined there. More than 5,000 were seriously ill. Diarrhea, dysentery, scurvy, and hospital gangrene were the chief complaints, and there were from 90 to 130 deaths every day. He found 30,000 men jammed together on twenty-seven acres of land, "with little or no attention to hygiene, with festering masses of filth at the very doors of their rude dens and tents." A little stream flowed through the camp, and about it the surgeon found "a filthy quagmire" which was so infamous that a man who got a slight scratch on his skin, or even an insect bite, was quite likely to die of blood poisoning. A South Carolina woman, learning about similar conditions in the prison camp at Florence, wrote to the governor asking: "In the name of all that is holy, is there nothing that can be done to relieve such dreadful suffering? If such things are allowed to continue they will surely draw down some awful judgment upon our country." [6]

Thus in the South. In the North, an army surgeon inspected the camp for Rebel prisoners at Elmira, New York, and said that the 8,347 prisoners there exhibited 2,000 cases of scurvy. He asserted that at the current death rates "the entire command will be admitted to hospital in less than a year and 36 per cent die." Like Andersonville, the Elmira camp contained a stream, which had formed a dreadful scummy pond —"a festering mass of corruption, impregnating the entire atmosphere of the camp with the pestilential odors . . . the vaults give off their sickly odors, and the hospitals are crowded with victims for the grave." The camp surgeon had made repeated complaints but he could get no one in authority to pay any attention to them, and his requisitions for medicines had been entirely ignored.[7]

A little later, when the rival governments worked out a deal for the exchange of certain prisoners who were too ill to fight but not too sick to travel, a trainload of 1,200 such men was made up at Elmira and sent down to Baltimore to take a steamer for the South. Federal doctors who met this pathetic convoy at the dock wrote indignantly that many of the men were obviously unfit to travel. Five had died on the train and sixty more had to be hurried to hospital as soon as they reached Baltimore. There were no doctors, orderlies, or nurses on the steamer, and the whole setup indicated "criminal neglect and inhumanity on the part of the medical officers in making the

selection of men to be transferred." The commander at Elmira, meanwhile, was writing that he had hoped that getting
rid of his 1,200 worst cases would relieve overcrowding at
the camp hospital but that somehow it had not. Overcrowding was as bad as ever, and "if the rate of mortality for the
last two months should continue for a year you can easily
calculate the number of prisoners there would be left here
for exchange." [8]

There was a smoky moonlit madness on the land in this
fourth year of war. The country was striking blindly at
phantoms, putting scars on its own body. People can stand
only about so much, and they had been pushed beyond the
limit, so that what was monstrous could look as if it made
sense. Ordinarily decent, kindly citizens could seriously pro-
pose that some thousands of helpless prisoners be condemned
to slow death by hunger and disease, and the fact that the
authorities rejected this mad scheme did not help very much
because the reprisal was in fact already being inflicted.

That was what the climate of the war was like now. It
was a climate apt to produce hard deeds by hard men, and
some characters well fitted to operate in such a climate were
beginning to come forward; among them, Major General
Philip Sheridan, commanding the newly formed Army of the
Shenandoah.

When he first got it, it was hardly an army. It was simply
a collection of three infantry corps and three divisions of
cavalry, totaling perhaps 36,000 men, of whom 30,000 or
thereabouts could be classed as combat troops.[9] Its different
units stood for widely varying traditions, and both time and
leadership would be needed to turn them into an army.

At the bottom of the heap was the remnant of the army
that had been led by Hunter. Now denominated the VIII
Army Corps, it was led by George Crook, who was a very
good man, and it needed new equipment, a good rest, much
drill and discipline, and a thorough shot in the arm. An
observer saw Crook's men as "ragged, famished, discouraged,
sulky and half of them in ambulances." They had been over-
marched and underfed and they had been ruinously beaten

by the Rebels.[10] Someone would have to work on them before they would amount to much as fighting troops.

Much better were the two slim divisions of Emory's XIX Corps, just up from Louisiana. They were veterans of hard campaigning in the Deep South, and they had one asset, very uncommon among Union troops in the Virginia theater: they were used to victory rather than to defeat, and it never occurred to them to expect anything except more victories. It was only the army of Northern Virginia which bred an inferiority complex among Yankee troops, and that army the XIX Corps had never met.

Solid nucleus of Sheridan's new army was Wright's VI Corps. This was probably the best fighting corps the Army of the Potomac had, but at the moment it was a little worn and morose. It did not look the part of a crack corps. When it bivouacked, its regiments and brigades pitched their pup tents as the spirit of the individual dictated, instead of ranging them in formal rows with proper company and regimental streets. The men no longer kept their muskets brightly polished, preferring to steal clean ones from their neighbors. (An ordnance sergeant at this time confessed that as far as clean muskets were concerned, "we hain't had one in our brigade since Cold Harbor.") There were regimental officers who freely admitted that although they had not exactly lost confidence in General Grant they did have a good deal more confidence in General Lee, and even the famous Vermont Brigade was showing deficiencies in discipline, its historian confessing: "The regiments were organized somewhat on the town meeting plan, and the men were rather deferred to on occasion by the officers. . . . There was hardly the least rigidity, and camp life on the whole was of the easiest possible description." [11]

The VI Corps, in short, had had it, and how it would perform now might depend a good deal on Sheridan himself. The men were not very happy to see him. They did not know much about him except that he was supposed to be a hard and remorseless fighting man, and while they were willing to admire that quality from a distance they suspected that his assignment to command in the Valley meant that some very rough work lay ahead, and they had had about all of the rough work they wanted. When a general won a reputation as a fighter, these veterans understood perfectly well who it was that paid for that reputation.

They understood also, however, that the war was never going to be won by the aimless sort of maneuverings which had been going on during the last three weeks. Direct action might not be so bad if the man who was directing it knew what he was doing. As one man wrote, "We knew we were there for other purposes than a traveling procession, and the cause had been for a long time a failing one." [12]

So here was Sheridan, and they would see about him.

The first things they saw were the little things. When the army marched Sheridan was always up near the front, taking personal charge. If traffic jams or road blocks developed, the officer who galloped up to straighten matters out was Sheridan himself. Sometimes he stormed and swore, and sometimes, when others were excited, he was controlled and soft-spoken; either way, he struck sparks and got action. If infantry was ordered to march in the fields and woods so that wagons and guns could have the road, Sheridan got off the road too and went with the foot soldiers. Marches went more smoothly, and camp life ran as if someone was in charge again, and it began to dawn on the men that many of the pesky little annoyances of military existence were disappearing. Before long, VI Corps veterans were paying Sheridan one of the highest compliments they knew. Having him in command, they said, was almost as good as having Uncle John Sedgwick back.[13]

It was noticed, too, that army headquarters was managed without fuss and feathers. Headquarters in the Army of the Potomac had been elaborate and formal—many tents, much pomp and show, honor guards in fussy Zouave uniforms, a gaudy headquarters flag bearing a golden eagle in a silver wreath on a solferino background; the whole having caused U. S. Grant, the first time he saw it, to rein in his horse and inquire if Imperial Caesar lived anywhere near. Sheridan made do with two tents and two tent flies, and he had no honor guard. Instead he had a collection of two-gun scouts dressed in Confederate uniforms, who were probably the toughest daredevils in the army.

There were perhaps a hundred of them, the outgrowth of a small detail originally selected for special jobs from the 17th Pennsylvania Cavalry. They were a peculiar combination of intelligence operatives, communications experts, counterespionage men, and sluggers. They spent nearly as much time within the Rebel lines as in their own—they had "learned to talk the Southern language," as one of them put it, and they made themselves familiar with every regiment, brigade, and division in Early's army—and the biggest part of their job was to keep Sheridan at all times up to date on the enemy's strength, movements, and dispositions. If captured, of course, they could expect nothing better than to be hanged to the nearest tree, and they always ran a fair chance of being potted by Yankee outposts, since they did look like Rebels. They tended to be an informal and individualistic lot.[14]

In part, the existence of this group reflected one of Sheridan's pet ideas—that daring and quick reflexes were worth more than muscle. Standing by a campfire with his staff one evening, Sheridan remarked that the ideal cavalry regiment would consist of men between eighteen and twenty-two years of age, none weighing more than 130 pounds and not one of them married. Little, wiry men could stand the pounding better than the big husky ones, Sheridan felt, and a Pennsylvanian who heard him agreed. He had noticed that skinny little chaps from the coal breakers usually outlasted the brawny deer hunters and bear trappers who came down from the mountains. And only young bachelors were properly reckless.[15]

Even more, however, these scouts were the product of the kind of war that was developing in the Valley. Yankee soldiers here were not only up against Early's troops. They were also up against guerillas, some of them Colonel Mosby's, some of them answering to nobody but themselves, and guerilla warfare was putting an edge on the fighting that had been seen nowhere else in Virginia.

In modern terms, the Confederacy had organized a resistance movement in territory occupied by the hated Yankees; had organized it, and then had seen it get badly out of hand.

The Valley was full of men who were Confederate soldiers by fits and starts—loosely organized and loosely controlled, most of them, innocent civilians six days a week and hell-roaring raiders the seventh day. They owned horses, weapons, and sometimes uniforms, which they carefully hid when they were not actually using them. Called together at intervals by their leaders, they would swoop down on outposts and picket lines, knock off wagon trains or supply depots, burn culverts and bridges behind the Federal front, and waylay any couriers, scouts, or other detached persons they could find. They compelled Union commanders to make heavy detachments to guard supply lines and depots, thus reducing the number of soldiers available for service in battle. To a certain extent they unintentionally compensated for this by reducing straggling in the Federal ranks, for the Northern soldier was firmly convinced that guerillas took no prisoners and that to be caught by them was to get a slit throat.

So the guerillas gave the Federal commanders a continuing headache—and, in the long run, probably did the Confederacy much more harm than good.

The quality of these guerilla bands varied greatly. At the top was John S. Mosby's: courageous soldiers led by a minor genius, highly effective in partisan warfare. Most of the groups, however, were about one degree better than plain outlaws, living for loot and excitement, doing no actual fighting if they could help it, and offering a secure refuge to any number of Confederate deserters and draft evaders. The Confederate cavalry leader, General Thomas L. Rosser, called them "a nuisance and an evil to the service," declaring:

"Without discipline, order or organization, they roam broadcast over the country, a band of thieves, stealing, pillaging, plundering and doing every manner of mischief and crime. They are a terror to the citizens and an injury to the cause. They never fight; can't be made to fight. Their leaders are generally brave, but few of the men are good soldiers." [16]

Jeb Stuart, not long before his death, endorsed this sentiment, saying that Mosby's was the only ranger band he knew of that was halfway efficient and that even Mosby usually operated with only a fourth of his supposed strength, while Lee wrote to the Confederate Secretary of War strongly urging that all such groups be abolished, asserting: "I regard the whole system as an unmixed evil." [17]

The worst damage which this system did to the Confederacy, however, was that it put Yankee soldiers in a mood to be vengeful.

By this time the Union authorities had had a good deal of experience with guerillas and they were getting very grim about it. Much of this conditioning had been gained in states like Tennessee and Missouri, where neighbor was bitter against neighbor and barn burnings and the murderous settlement of old grudges went hand in hand with attempts to discomfit the Yankee invader, and most Federal generals considered guerillas as mere bushwhackers, candidates for the noose or the firing squad. An exception was generally (though by no means always) made in the case of Mosby's men, who were recognized as being more or less regular soldiers, but the attitude toward the rest was summed up by a Union general along the upper Potomac, who said: "I have instructed my command not to bring any of them to my headquarters except for interment." [18]

This attitude spread rapidly to the rank and file, particularly when the guerillas took to killing any Union stragglers they could catch. Overlooking the fact that lawless foraging and looting by stragglers and bummers could easily provoke angry reprisals, the soldiers simply argued that if a Southerner wanted to fight he ought to be in the Confederate Army. If he was not in the Army, but fought anyway, they considered that he was outside the law. Since the guerillas could not often be captured—they usually struck at night, vanished in the dark, and became innocent farmers before the pursuit got well organized—the tendency was to take it out on the nearest civilians, on the broad ground that if they let guerillas operate in their midst they would have to take the consequences.

Most Federal soldiers would have endorsed the words and acts of a Union officer in northern Alabama, where troop trains were fired on and railroad telegraph lines were cut by anti-Unionists in a little country town. This officer assembled the townsfolk and told them that henceforth "every time the telegraph wire was cut we would burn a house; every time a train was fired on we should hang a man; and we would continue to do this until every house was burned and every man hanged between Decatur and Bridgeport." He went on to put the army viewpoint into explicit words: "If they wanted to fight they should enter the army, meet us like honorable men, and not, assassin-like, fire at us from the woods and run." He concluded by warning that if the citizens let the bushwhackers continue to operate, "we should make them more uncomfortable than they would be in Hell." Having said all of this he burned the town, arrested three citizens as hostages for the good behavior of the rest, and went his way. He wrote that this action was spoken of "approvingly by the officers and enthusiastically by the men." [19]

Now it should be remembered that ordinarily the soldiers were the least bloodthirsty of all the participants in the war. Secretary Welles might write fondly of hangings, and the Chicago Board of Trade might ask that Confederate prisoners be allowed to die of hunger or disease, and it could be washed off as part of the inevitable idiocy of superpatriotism in time of war. But when the soldiers themselves began to feel an interest in creating a hell on earth for enemy civilians the moon was entering a new phase. The tragic part about it now was that this was happening in an army one of whose functions was to ravage and lay waste a populous farming area until even a crow could not support himself in it. The hand that was about to come down on the Shenandoah Valley was going to be heavy enough anyway. What the guerillas did was not going to make it come down any more lightly.

It was mid-August, and the Army of the Shenandoah had

marched more than a third of the way up the Valley. Lee sent reinforcements to Early, and the number of them was exaggerated by rumor, and Sheridan—still feeling his way with his new command, and behaving with unwonted caution—decided to move back to Halltown and wait for a better time and place to strike. The army paused, and then it moved slowly back in retreat, and as it moved innumerable squadrons of Federal cavalry spread out from mountain to mountain in a broad destroying wave and began methodically and with cold efficiency to take the Valley apart.

They were not gentle about it. The chaplain of the 1st Rhode Island Cavalry wrote grimly: "The time had fully come to peel this land and put an end to the long strife for its possession," and he had found the precise word for it.[20] The cavalry peeled the Shenandoah Valley as a man might peel an orange. The blue tide ebbed, leaving wreckage behind it, pillars of smoke rising by day and pillars of fire glowing by night to mark the place where they had been.

The general idea was simple. All barns were to be burned, and crops were to be destroyed. Farmers were to be left enough to see themselves through the winter, although the definition of "enough" was left to the lieutenants and captains commanding the detachments which had the matches, and there was no right of appeal. Anything that could benefit the Confederacy was to be destroyed, whether it was a corn-crib, a gristmill, a railroad bridge, or something that went on four legs. It was hoped that nobody would starve to death, and no violence was to be offered to any civilian's person, but the Valley was to feed no more Confederate armies thereafter.

The Rhode Island chaplain looked back on it, a dozen years later, and wrote:

"The 17th of August will be remembered as sending up to the skies the first great columns of smoke and flame from doomed secession barns, stacks, cribs and mills, and the driving into loyal lines of flocks and herds. The order was carefully yet faithfully obeyed. . . . The order led to the destruction of about 2,000 barns, 70 mills, and other property, valued in all at 25 millions of dollars." The chaplain went on to say that many guerilla bands had lived in this region and that it had finally been "purified" by fire: "As our boys expressed it, 'we burned out the hornets.' " [21]

A man in the 17th Pennsylvania Cavalry gave his picture of it:

"Previously the burning of supplies and outbuildings had been incidental to battles, but now the torch was applied deliberately and intentionally. Stacks of hay and straw and barns filled with crops harvested, mills, corn-cribs; in a word, all supplies of use to man or beast were promptly burned and all valuable cattle driven off. . . . The work of destruction seemed cruel and the distress it occasioned among the people of all ages and sexes was evident on every hand. The officers and soldiers who performed the details of this distressing work were met at every farm or home by old men, women and children in tears, begging and beseeching those in charge to save them from the appalling ruin. These scenes of burning and destruction, which were only the prelude to those which followed at a later day farther up the Valley, were attended with sorrow to families and added horrors to the usual brutalities of war, unknown to any other field operations in the so-called Confederacy." [22]

Not all of the people quite got the point of what was being done. Even General Hunter had felt obliged to point out to his men, a month earlier, that there were in the Valley many people of stout Unionist sympathy, who sheltered Federal wounded men and did their best to aid the Union army; such people, he pointed out, ought to be given a little protection, which unfortunately his own army did not seem able to provide. Now the Pennsylvania cavalryman said that "the few Union people, old men, women and children, could not be made to understand the utility or necessity of the measure, while the outspoken Confederates heaped upon us maledictions. . . . The common hatred of open foes seemed to deepen, and to blot out forever all hope of future goodwill between North and South." [23]

The soldiers did not exactly enjoy their job. The historian

of another regiment of Pennsylvania horse, the 6th, said that his regiment was lucky enough to avoid "the detail for this unpleasant duty," and said that he rode that day with the last element of the rear guard, marching in the wake of the men who had been swinging the torch. "The day had been an unpleasant one," he wrote, "the weather was hot and the roads very dusty, and the grief of the inhabitants, as they saw their harvests disappearing in flame and smoke, and their stock being driven off, was a sad sight. It was a phase of warfare we had not seen before, and although we admitted the necessity we could not but sympathize with the sufferers." [24]

A Michigan cavalryman remembered riding past a little home and seeing, in the gate of the fence by the road, an old woman, crying bitterly, blood flowing from a deep cut in one arm. He rode up to her and she told him that some soldier had struck her with his saber and then had taken her two cows. He wheeled and spurred after his regiment, found the officer in charge of the herd of confiscated cattle, recovered the two cows—or, at any rate, two cows which might have been the ones—and with the officer he tried in vain to find the man who had used the saber. Then he took the cows back to the woman, who thanked him in tearful surprise and told him that if he was ever captured by Mosby's men he should have them bring him to her home, and she would give testimony that would save him from being hanged.[25]

So the army made its way back down the Valley, leaving desolation behind it, and the war came slowly nearer its end in the black smoke that drifted over the Blue Ridge. The war had begun with waving unstained flags and dreams of a picture-book fight which would concern no one but soldiers, who would die picturesquely and without bloodshed amid dress-parade firing lines, and it had come down now to burning barns, weeping children, and old women who had been hit with sabers. In the only way that was left to it, the war was coming toward its close. Phil Sheridan passed the word, and his scouts laughed and went trotting off to spy on the Rebels and play a clever game with the threat of a greased noose; and the guerillas met in dark copses on the edge of the army and rode out with smoking revolvers to kill the cripples, and now and then one of them was caught.

It happened so with a group of Sheridan's scouts, who captured a Captain Stump, famous as a Rebel raider, a man they had long been seeking. He had been wounded, and when he was caught they took his weapons away and brought him to Major Young, who commanded the scouts, and Major Young had a certain respect for this daring guerilla, so he told him:

"I suppose you know we will kill you. But we will not serve you as you have served our men—cut your throat or hang you. We will give you a chance for your life. We will give you ten rods' start on your own horse, with your spurs on. If you get away, all right. . . . But remember, my men are dead shots."

Captain Stump was bloody and he had been hurt, but he was all man. He smiled, and nodded, and rode a few feet out in front of the rank of his captors—skinny young men, 130 pounds or less, unmarried, the pick of the Yankee cavalry. Major Young looked down the rank, and called out: *"Go!"*

A cavalryman wrote about it afterward:

"We allowed him about ten rods' start, then our pistols cracked and he fell forward, dead." [26]

3. On the Upgrade

From the Shenandoah Valley to Chicago it is perhaps 500 miles, as one of General Grant's unrationed crows might fly, and the binding threads of war spanned these miles and tied valley and city together in an invisible bond.

In the Valley, as August came to an end, the winds from the mountains carried away the last of the smudge from charred barns and hayricks, and whether or not anybody could see it those winds came from the hour just before sunrise and there was a promise in them. In Chicago, the hour looked like the spectral twilight of collapse and defeat, and the passenger trains were unloading a large assortment of people who were prepared to stake a good deal on the belief that the great Union of the States was dying.

With that belief Abraham Lincoln himself felt a certain agreement. On August 23 he had somewhat mysteriously asked members of his cabinet to sign a curiously folded paper, which he then tucked away in his desk. None of the men who signed knew what was in the paper. If they had known they would have gabbled and popped their eyes, for in Lincoln's handwriting it contained this statement:

"This morning, as for some days past, it seems exceedingly probable that this administration will not be re-elected. Then it will be my duty to so co-operate with the President-elect as to save the Union between the election and the inauguration; as he will have secured his election on such ground that he cannot possibly save it afterward."

A pessimistic appraisal, which since then has often been considered far too gloomy, hindsight having made clear many things not then apparent. But men in wartime have to operate without benefit of the backward glance, and in the summer of 1864 the war looked very much like a stalemate. Many men had died and there was much weariness, and as far as anyone could see the people had had about enough— of the Administration and of the Administration's war.

Lincoln was not the only pessimist. Horace Greeley, whose progress through the war years was a dizzy succession of swings from fatuous optimism to profoundest gloom, had recently written: "Mr. Lincoln is already beaten. He cannot be re-elected." His pink cherubic face fringed by delicate light hair which always seemed to be ruffled by a faint breeze from never-never land, Greeley spoke for many Republican stalwarts when he wistfully hoped that Lincoln might some-how be replaced on the party ticket by Grant, or Butler, or Sherman. In such case, mused Greeley, "we could make a fight yet." With other prominent Republicans, Greeley had been working on a scheme to hold a national convention of radical Republicans at the end of September, so as to concentrate support "on some candidate who commands the confidence of the country, even by a new nomination if necessary." [1]

What was worrying Lincoln, of course, was not so much the prospect of his own defeat as the conviction that this defeat would mean loss of the war. In this judgment he may or may not have been correct. It is perhaps worthy of notice that one man who was very well qualified to form an expert opinion on the matter agreed with him thoroughly. When a visitor from Washington told General Grant that there was talk of running him for the presidency, Grant hit the arms of his camp chair with clenched fists and growled: "They can't do it! They can't compel me to do it!" Then he went on to show how Lincoln's leadership looked from the special vantage point of the commanding general's tent at City Point: "I consider it as important to the cause that he should be elected as that the army should be successful in the field." [2]

Grant was the man who fought all-out, with few holds barred and with the annihilation of the opposing armies as the end to be sought. Yet Grant was quite able to see that although the war must be won on the battlefields it might very easily be lost back home—in Chicago, for example. The same thought had occurred to many others, including Jefferson Davis, and as a result a number of Confederate spies and military agents were converging on Chicago just now in the hope that they could stir up a great deal of trouble.

The immediate magnet was the national convention of the Democratic party, convening on August 29 to nominate a candidate to run against Lincoln. Broadly speaking, this convention was bringing together practically everybody who disliked the way the war was being run, with the single exception of the dissident Republicans who felt that Lincoln was not tough enough. Among the assembling Democrats were stout Unionists who opposed the forcible abolition of slavery and the reduction of states' rights; among them, also, were others who wanted only to have the war end—with a Union victory if possible, without it if necessary. And there were also men who saw the war consuming precious freedoms and creating tyranny, who blended extreme political partisanship with blind fury against the war party and who at least believed that they were ready to strike back without caring much what weapon they used.

So the waters in Chicago were very muddy, and to the Confederate government it seemed likely that they might offer good fishing.

For many months the Confederacy had been getting ready to exploit just this kind of situation. It had assembled a large number of operatives in Toronto under the general leadership of Colonel Jacob Thompson, who bore the vague title of Special Commissioner of the Confederate States Government in Canada and who possessed a letter from Jefferson Davis guardedly instructing him "to carry out the instructions you have received from me verbally in such manner as shall seem most likely to conduce to the furtherance of the interests of the Confederate States of America." Thompson's people were trying to do a little bit of everything. Early in the summer they had put out peace feelers, briefly hoodwinking none other than Horace Greeley himself, and although nothing much came of this venture the apparatus was hard at work on many other projects, most of them involving some form of sabotage in the Northern states.

Thompson had a wild, devil-may-care crowd at his command. One of the most effective was a slim, black-haired, almost effeminate-looking Kentuckian named Thomas H. Hines, formerly a captain in John Hunt Morgan's cavalry—the man, in fact, who had engineered Morgan's spectacular and still mysterious escape from the Ohio penitentiary a year earlier. Hines was very tough indeed, and he had been sent to Canada from Richmond immediately after the Dahlgren raid, his mission being to round up all escaped Confederate prisoners of war who could find their way north of the border and to carry out with them "any fair and appropriate enterprises of war against our enemies" that might occur to him.

The ideas these men had ranged all the way from stirring up draft riots in the Middle West to the burning of Northern cities, the capture of Northern prison camps, and the seizure of U.S.S. *Michigan*, the Navy's warship which patrolled the

Great Lakes. To a certain extent their program was frankly terroristic, and the papers which supposedly had been found on Colonel Dahlgren's body calling for the burning and sacking of Richmond were often mentioned as full justification for such a program.[3]

Colonel Thompson was an experienced politician well fitted for his shadowy role, and in Captain Hines he had as cool and capable a behind-the-lines operator as any fifth columnist could wish to have. Yet the results which these men obtained, from first to last, add up to nothing much more than a series of petty annoyances. Many of their operatives seem to have looked on the whole program as a glorified Tom Sawyer lark, with the sheer fun of conspiring and risking their necks offering a welcome outlet for restless spirits bored by the routine of ordinary army life. The whole operation was so effectively watched by Union spies that it had little chance to accomplish anything very sensational.

The really crippling thing, however, was that Thompson and Hines and everybody else made the same mistake which a number of good Republicans and Union generals were forever making: when they looked upon the vast body of supposedly militant Northern Copperheads, they took them seriously.

The Copperheads talked and at times acted as if they had both the means and the will to revolt against the Lincoln government, and they had grandiose plans for detaching from the Union various northwestern states and setting up a new confederacy actively friendly to the South. Their action arm was a mildly secret organization known as the Sons of Liberty, and their prophet was the famous Clement Laird Vallandigham, the former Ohio congressman whom Burnside in an excess of zeal had arrested in 1863 for seditious speechmaking and who had been rustled across the fighting lines and given to the Confederacy. Vallandigham had visited Richmond and had talked with government people there. Then he had flitted north to Canada, and in June of 1864 Captain Hines met him at Windsor, across the river from Detroit. Vallandigham talked largely about the size and power of the Sons of Liberty. They had 85,000 members in Illinois, he told Hines, 50,000 in Indiana, and 40,000 in Ohio, and with such an organization it seemed likely that a great deal could be done.[4]

Soon after this Vallandigham donned a false beard and smuggled himself across the river, going thence to Ohio, dropping the beard, and beginning to make speeches. (The Lincoln government carefully looked the other way, figuring that as long as it did not officially know that Vallandigham had returned it would not have to make a martyr out of him all over again by re-arresting him.) In his speeches, Vallandigham expressed a vague menace. He warned the Lincoln tyranny that "there is a vast multitude, a host whom they cannot number, bound together by the strongest and holiest ties, to defend, by whatever means the exigencies of the times shall demand, their natural and constitutional rights as freemen, at all hazards and to the last extremity." At the end of August he went to Chicago to take part in the Democratic convention.

Captain Hines and sixty of his boys were in Chicago, too, dressed in civilian clothes and carrying revolvers. They had money and they knew where there were more weapons, and they had had a series of annoying, protracted, but apparently fruitful conferences with Copperhead leaders looking toward direct action. The modest Federal garrison in Chicago had recently been increased, and there were Democrats who felt that this could only have been done for the purpose of suppressing their convention and thereby ending the last of America's civil rights. County chairmen of the Sons of Liberty, accordingly, had been notified to alert their members and stand by to strike a blow for freedom, and the leadership assured Hines that they were "sure of a general uprising which will result in a glorious success."

Hines, meanwhile, reflected that there were 5,000 perfectly good Confederate soldiers locked up at Camp Douglas, near Chicago, and 7,000 more in another prison camp at Rock Island. He appears to have hoped that the Copperheads would create enough trouble and confusion so that those prison camps could be seized and the prisoners released and armed. Then, with 12,000 good troops loose in northern Illinois, he could make trouble for the Yankees on a really impressive scale.[5]

Unfortunately, as the time for action came closer the leaders of the Sons of Liberty grew more and more nervous. Talking nobly about taking up arms for the constitutional rights of free men was all very well, as long as it was just talk. The trouble was that this quiet, blue-eyed Kentuckian was in deadly earnest and so were the men he had with him, and they proposed to turn this talk into action in which many Sons of Liberty would probably get shot, with the gallows looming large in the background for those whom the bullets missed. Copperhead leadership began to have second thoughts, and it hedged and temporized, grossly exaggerating the number of Federal troops present in Chicago and dwelling long on the probability of failure.

By convention time, the Confederates could see that the Sons of Liberty simply were not going to rise in any substantial number. Disgustedly, Hines made a final proposal: if as many as 500 armed Copperheads would come together he could at least capture one of the prison camps, and he would play it alone from then on in. There were more conferences, more shiverings and headshakings—and, at last, the Confederates had to slip back to Canada, with nothing accomplished. The Copperheads could deplore and conspire and denounce, but they would not fight and the real fighting men whom the Confederacy had sent to Chicago could do nothing with them. Men who thought themselves bold had had to confront men who really were bold, and the meeting gave them a permanent scare.[6]

This fiasco was the surface indication that a crisis had at last been met and passed. The North might be divided by bitter passions and half paralyzed by the numbness brought on by a long war, but the nightmare that had been dimly visible in the background for two years was at last fading out. Whatever happened, it was now certain that the war would not be lost because of revolt at home. The attempt to crush secession would not fail because of a second secession.

Vallandigham might roam Chicago, conferring with leaders and orating to street-corner crowds, forcing the Democratic convention to adopt a platform deploring the "failure" of the war and calling for "immediate efforts" to end all hostilities. In the end there was just going to be another presidential election, not an armed uprising. The Chicago gathering remained an ordinary political convention, and it made an ordinary political bet—that general war weariness and discontent over a military stalemate could be made to add up to a majority at the polls.

In making this bet the convention played it both ways. It adopted the Vallandigham peace plank, to pull in all of the people who were tired of war or who had not believed in war in the first place; then, for its presidential candidate, it nominated a soldier—George B. McClellan, the enduring hero of the enlisted man in the Army of the Potomac, a leader whom Democratic orthodoxy considered a military genius unfairly treated by petty politicians in Washington.

Immediately after this, the roof fell in.

To begin with, McClellan would not stay hitched. On reflection he found the platform altogether too much to swallow. Accepting the nomination, he quietly but firmly turned the peace pledge inside out, saying that he construed it as a mandate to carry the war through to victory and remarking that to do anything less than insist on the triumph of the Union cause would be to betray the heroic soldiers whom he had led in battle.

Worse yet, William Tecumseh Sherman captured Atlanta.

Sherman had moved against Joe Johnston's Confederate army the same day Grant crossed the Rapidan. From the distant North his campaign had looked no more like a success than the one in Virginia. If it had not brought so many casualties, it had seemed no more effective at ending Rebel resistance. Wise old Joe Johnston, sparring and side-stepping and shifting back, had a very clear understanding of the home-front politics behind the armies. His whole plan had been to keep Sherman from forcing a showdown until after the election, on the theory that victory postponed so long would look to the people up North like victory lost forever, and his strategy had been much more effective than his own government could realize. To President Davis, Johnston's course had seemed like sheer faintheartedness, and he had at last dismissed Johnston and put slugging John B. Hood in his place. Hood had gone in and slugged, and Sherman's army had more slugging power—so now, with the Democrats betting the election on the thesis that the war effort was a flat failure, decisive success had at last been won.

First Sherman, then Sheridan: and in the middle of September Grant quietly went up to the Valley and had a talk with Sheridan, the two men walking back and forth across a little field, Sheridan gesturing with nervous hands, Grant chewing a cigar and looking at the ground. A leathery Vermont sergeant leaned against a rail fence, watching them, and he looked moodily at Grant's stoop-shouldered figure.

"I hate to see that old cuss around," said the sergeant at last. "When that old cuss is around there's sure to be a big fight on hand." [7]

The sergeant was quite right. The old cuss had been growing impatient and he wanted action. Sheridan had a big advantage over Early in numbers, and Grant believed that he ought to be able to move to the Valley Pike somewhere below Winchester, get south of the Rebel army, and at last do what Grant had demanded two months earlier—follow it to the death. Early had his army in position behind Opequon Creek, covering Winchester, and Sheridan felt that it was going to be hard to get at him. Still, he had held this command for six weeks now, the shakedown period was about over, and it was time for action.

So Grant and Sheridan finished their talk and Grant went back to City Point, and at two o'clock on the morning of September 19 Wilson's cavalry trotted down to one of the fords of the Opequon, went spattering across the shallows, drove in the Rebel outposts, and rode on to feel the main Southern defensive line, horse artillery banging away hard, dismounted troopers laying down a sharp fire from repeating carbines.

The Opequon fords lay perhaps six miles east of Winchester and the VI Corps came over the water at dawn, the sun coming up behind their backs, dirty smoke piling up in the gray sky to the west. The veterans looked and listened, and one of them wrote that they "heard that sound which I believe strikes a chill through the bravest man that lives, and causes him to feel that his heart is sinking down, down till it seems to drop into his boots. I mean the dull rustling of air which is hardly more than a vibration, but which to the experienced listener betokens artillery firing at a distance. When one expects soon to join in the exercise, that signal is not inspiriting." [8]

According to Sheridan's battle orders the VI Corps was to come up on the heels of Wilson's cavalry, with Emory's and Crook's men close behind and the rest of the cavalry swinging in a half circle to come down on Winchester from the north. Speedy movement was essential. Early had scattered his forces, and most of his men were spread out somewhere between Winchester and Martinsburg. Perhaps a third of his infantry, supported by artillery and cavalry, was posted in the lines east of Winchester covering the road from the Opequon. If that infantry force could be smashed quickly, Early's troops north of town could be cut off and his army could be destroyed piecemeal. So the VI Corps pressed along and the offensive was under way at last.

Unfortunately, it was not under way very fast. Orders had gone awry somehow and there was an infernal traffic tie-up, and the army moved at a crawl. The road led up the length of a narrow valley, and in some way the whole baggage and supply train of the VI Corps, which was supposed to be side-tracked east of the creek, inserted itself into the line of march right behind the leading infantry divisions, with corps artillery behind it and all the rest of the army to follow. The infantry column thus was cut in half by miles of slow-moving wagons, ambulances, caissons, battery forges, and other lumbering vehicles, and the cumbersome procession could neither be parked by the roadside nor turned around and sent back, because road and valley were too narrow.

The foot soldiers left the road and tried to pass this tangle, but they found themselves scrambling along steep hillsides, through trees and underbrush, creeping up toward the fight at a rate not much better than a mile an hour. The slopes were clogged, as a man in the XIX Corps remembered, with "the hundreds of men who belong to an army but never fight—the cooks, the officers' servants, the hospital gangs, the quartermaster's people, the 'present sick' and the habitual skulkers"—not to mention various regiments of cavalry which had been told to wait by the road and let the infantry advance.[9]

The result was a bungled battle which nearly became a humiliating defeat. Early had plenty of time to pull his scattered divisions together, and when Sheridan finally attacked it was nearly noon, instead of 6 A.M. as he had planned. Even at noon he had only half of his infantry on hand, and a good deal less than half of his artillery, and his battle line had not gone far before it ran into trouble. The three divisions of the VI Corps were going in side by side, with one of Emory's divisions on their right, and somehow the two corps lost contact and let a gap develop, and the Rebels saw it and made a hard counterattack that stopped the VI Corps and sent Emory's men flying.

Emory's other division came up to check the rout, and Upton brought his brigade over to help plug the gap, and after a while the situation was stabilized. Nevertheless, by midafternoon the Federals were doing little more than hold their own, and they had had severe losses. Upton was knocked off his horse by a shell fragment and Sheridan told him to go to the rear and get into a hospital. Upton disobeyed—it was his theory that combat commanders ought to be up front with their troops—and after a doctor put a tourniquet on his wounded leg he got in a stretcher and made the stretcher-bearers take him along with the brigade through the rest of the battle.[10]

Meanwhile Sheridan was getting the mess straightened out

He was up and down the field in a fury, his dark face aglow, dripping perspiration, his eyes snapping, his black horse all flecked with foam. He had his staff officers take details and comb the woods for stragglers and shirkers, and these recruiting parties caught the spark and went through the underbrush with sabers swinging, herding their captives forward, making brand-new infantry companies out of them, and leading them into the fight with mighty saber thwackings for all laggards. A Connecticut officer who watched them chuckled that he had not seen so much spanking since he was a schoolboy.[11]

While the stragglers were being rounded up Sheridan demanded recapture of the ground which had been lost to the Rebel counterattack. This job fell chiefly to the 8th Vermont, a veteran regiment whose Colonel Stephen Thomas had once been a leading Democratic politician, stoutly opposed to all coercion of the South. Recently he had gone home on furlough and his former party associates had chided him for deserting the true faith. "Thomas, you've changed," they complained. "We haven't." A true Vermonter, Thomas replied: "Fools never do."

Now he was about to lead his regiment across a meadow and into a smoky grove of embattled Rebels, and the prospect was not inviting. Thomas sized it up, then rode out in front of his regiment, color-bearers beside him, and in his powerful spellbinder's voice he thundered:

"Boys, if you ever pray, the time to pray has come. Pray now, remember Ethan Allen and old Vermont, and we'll drive 'em to hell! Come on, old Vermont!" [12]

Then he wheeled about, his sword held high, and rode at a walk toward the Rebel firing line, without a backward glance. Old Vermont followed, cheering, and a regiment or two in the XIX Corps jumped up to join in the charge, and the Southern battle line began to draw back.

Sheridan went galloping over to the left of his own line, to where General Getty led a division of the VI Corps. Sheridan had at last got Crook's infantry out of the ravine and they were going into battle formation far over on the right, and beside them Sheridan's chief of cavalry, General Alfred Torbert, had two good mounted divisions ready to go, and Sheridan's army now formed a great crescent, five miles from tip to tip, far overlapping the Confederate left flank. It was Sheridan's idea that this crescent must now move forward, and when he came up to Getty—felt hat gripped in one hand, nobody riding with him but a lone orderly—he was all dust and sweat and fire, and he was shouting:

"General, I've put Torbert in on the right and told him to give 'em hell, and he's doing it! Crook too is on the right, and giving it to 'em. Press them, General—they'll run!" He swore a tremendous oath and repeated: "Press them, General —I know they'll run!" [13]

And now it was late afternoon, and behind the piled-up battle smoke the sky was streaked with crimson and pale green and yellow in a wild autumn sunset. The Federal battle line was rolling at last, and there was a tumult of artillery and musketry and cheering men—and suddenly it was like the old days, and there was a color and a shine and a drama to combat once more, and if battle was as terrible as ever it had at least begun to sparkle again.

Now and then as the line advanced a check would develop somewhere. Then one of Sheridan's staff would come up at a pounding gallop, to ride the length of the line pointing with his naked saber at the Rebel battle line, all gesture and compelling movement, saying never a word, and the line would lunge forward again. To the north could be seen Crook's battle line—a whole army corps tramping along in perfect order, skirmishers out in front, battle flags leaning forward, the ranks closing faultlessly as wounded men fell out, no one firing yet, every man yelling at the top of his voice.

Upton on his stretcher brought his brigade over to help Colonel Thomas and Old Vermont, and they took the Rebel position, chasing the Southern marksmen out of the wood and away from the hilltop they had been holding. The Vermonters drew up behind a stone wall to catch their breath, and suddenly a company officer gestured with his sword and cried: "Boys! Look at that!"

Beyond the lower ground in their front and to their right, two or three miles away, distinct in the clear sunset light, they saw what one man recalled as "a sight to be remembered a life-time"—two divisions of Yankee cavalry massed in solid columns, drawn sabers flashing in the sun like streaks of flame, thundering down at a full gallop to strike the flank and rear of the Confederate line. Southern artillery fired desperately to break the charge, but the charge could not be stopped. The outflanked Confederate line curled up, and the cavalry took guns and flags and prisoners, the squadrons riding wildly over broken fields after fugitive Confederates.

From their hilltop the Vermonters saw it, and they started forward again, and suddenly Sheridan was riding ahead of them, while Rebel bullets searched the dusk. The men saw him and cheered madly, and he swung his hat to them and called back: "Boys, this is just what I expected!" [14]

Most of the Union soldiers who were in that fight actually got a firsthand, close-up view of Sheridan before the day ended. This was a new thing for a Yankee army, since the commanding general was usually an off-stage presence rarely seen in battle. Sheridan seemed to appear from nowhere, attended by the solitary orderly who carried Sheridan's personal battle flag—a little swallow-tailed banner, half red and half white, bearing the two stars of a major general.

The experience of the 12th Connecticut was typical. The regiment was drawn up in a field, waiting for fresh ammunition, when an officer rode up to ask why they were standing there. While a regimental officer was explaining, a shell burst almost directly over the head of the mounted man. He was unhurt, and as the smoke blew away he called out to the men: "That's all right, boys—no matter—we can lick 'em!" And up and down the line men passed the word: "That's Sheridan!" and they cheered and laughed and waved their caps. Sheridan waved, told them to move forward as soon as they got their ammunition, and then went cantering off. [15]

The last Confederate resistance ended and darkness came

and the cavalry rode hard through Winchester, storming at
the Rebel rear guard. Early got his men and most of his
possessions away clean, and he was fully entitled to boast that
he had fought well against heavy odds, inflicting more loss
than he received and balking his foe's attempt to cut off his
retreat and destroy his army. It was also true that during the
first half of the day the Federal program had been handled
with an absolute minimum of skill.[16] Yet somehow these
facts were not in the least important.

What was important was that the war now was on the up-
grade. Sherman had taken Atlanta and sprightly old Admiral
Farragut had broken into Mobile Bay, and now the jaunty
Rebel army in the valley had been broken and sent streaming
off in defeat; and here was the point of rebound for the whole
war. The Chicago platform might bewail failure and call
for immediate peace, but now the war very clearly was not
a failure. Since spring the Confederacy's one hope had been
that the people of the North would get tired and quit. After
Winchester that hope no longer had any roots.

Sheridan followed up his victory. His army went along
the Valley Pike, and just south of Strasburg, where a roll
of high ground known as Fisher's Hill cuts across the Valley
from mountain to mountain, the Confederates made a stand.
Sheridan lined up his troops, telling them to keep up a heavy
fire whether or not they saw anything to shoot at, and while
he bluffed a frontal attack he swung Crook's corps far to the
west and brought it in on the Confederate flank. The blow
was struck at dusk on September 22, and the whole Rebel
line collapsed, losing twelve guns and a thousand prisoners.

Once again the Federal storming columns going up the
slope found Sheridan dashing across their front, orderly and
battle flag at his heels, Sheridan's black bullet head bare in
the breeze: and always he was waving the men on, calling
"Come on! Don't stop!" Once he came on a brigade which
was winded and had stopped to pant, and he reined up and
gestured toward the retreating Confederates, shouting: "Run,
boys, run! Don't wait to form! Don't let 'em stop!" Some

soldier piped up to tell him that for the moment they were just too bushed to run, to which Sheridan called back: "If you can't run, then holler!" And holler they did, while the general rode off to press the pursuit.

There was a note to all of this that these Union troops were not used to: a note of triumph assured, a driving flaming will to victory that would stop for no obstacles and accept no excuses. The men responded to it, and wherever Sheridan went now he was greeted by passionate cheers. A VI Corps veteran wrote that ever since McClellan's day it had been a point of pride with his outfit not to cheer any officers—but Sheridan was different, and "tumultuous hurrahs came unbidden from the bottom of every heart and conventional restraint was forgotten." [17]

While Early's main body had been trying to hold on at Fisher's Hill, the gray cavalry had been on the other side of the Massanutten Ridge, encamped at Front Royal. Sheridan sent in young General Wilson with his cavalry division to drive them out, and Wilson made his attack in the dense fog of an early morning, splashing through the Shenandoah fords and forming line of battle on the outskirts of the town.

No one could see thirty yards in the gray murk and Wilson was afraid his units would lose touch, so he passed the word that when his own buglers sounded the charge all of the other buglers in the division should pick the call up and repeat it. Since every battery, troop, regiment, and brigade in the division had its own buglers, this meant a lot of music; and the dripping quiet of early dawn was broken by the insistent notes of the charge, blown first by the men at division headquarters and immediately picked up all along the line, until 250 buglers were blaring away together, and the high imperious notes went echoing along the Blue Ridge until it sounded like the voice of ten thousand trumpets. Under it there was a great thunder of shod hooves on soft earth, and the Yankee cavalry went in on the gallop, sabers swinging, every man shouting with the jubilant confidence of an army that has begun to feel that it is invincible. Front Royal was taken and the gray troopers went back up the Valley, and Wilson's regiments assembled in the town and agreed that it was a great day in the morning.[18]

4. No More Doubt

Thurlow Weed, Republican boss of New York State, told Secretary Seward that "the conspiracy against Mr. Lincoln has collapsed," and those who had been looking for a hard-war man decided to climb on the band wagon. Salmon P. Chase, convinced at last that destiny would not tap his shoulder this year, began to make speeches urging Lincoln's re-election. Michigan's Senator Zach Chandler, bitter-end abolitionist, moved to make a little deal; after which John Charles Frémont, petulant darling of the Republican radicals' lunatic fringe, withdrew his third-party candidacy for the presidency. By Chandler's deal or by sheer coincidence, within forty-eight hours Lincoln accepted the resignation of Postmaster General Blair, whom all of the radicals hated—accepted it, in fact, before Blair had even submitted it.

As September came to an end Lincoln told his old friend Ward Lamon that although "Jordan has been a hard road to travel" he was beginning to think that he would wind up on the right side of the river. Dour old Gideon Welles wrote in his diary that "we are, I think, approaching the latter days of the rebellion." [1]

So a new feeling was abroad in the land; an exciting, growing conviction that a mighty tide was flowing at last. The armies had created this feeling, and the armies shared in it. Sheridan's troops were driving on up the Valley, surging all over the landscape as they moved, a double file of artillery and battle wagons on the roadway, half a dozen parallel columns of infantry tramping along on either side. The days were cool and sunny and the haunting mellow light of the war's last autumn lay on the land, and the men saw the panorama which they themselves were creating and rejoiced in it. The war had turned a corner, and for the first time these soldiers were learning what it felt like to be victors.

"Our march had been a grand triumphal pursuit of a routed enemy," wrote a man in the VI Corps. "Never had we marched with such light hearts; and although each day found us pursuing rapidly from dawn till dark, the men seemed to endure the fatigue with wonderful patience." [2]

Far out on either side of the marching columns were the cavalry flankers, guarding against surprise. In front moved the line of skirmishers, trotting lightly across fields which had long since lost their fences—"skirmishing only enough," the veteran felt, "to maintain a pleasant state of excitement."

Through Mount Jackson the army marched, to Harrisonburg, and beyond that to Mount Crawford, and the cavalry roved on ahead to Staunton and Waynesboro. As it moved, the army picked up a number of Confederate stragglers. These professed deep interest in the Northern election, and to a man they hoped that McClellan would win. A Connecticut soldier told about this in a letter home, adding: "I would state that the 'hero of the seven days retreat' is fast becoming unpopular in the army. Not that the soldiers dislike the man so much as the company he keeps." Another man expressed the same view: "There are a good many soldiers who would vote for McClellan but they cannot go Vallandigham for support." [3]

Sheridan now had the Valley in his possession, and he believed that Early was not capable of further offensive operations. To Grant it now seemed that Sheridan could break out of the Valley at its upper end, cutting across through Gordonsville and Charlottesville on the thrust Hunter had tried to make three months earlier and rejoining the Army of the Potomac around Petersburg. Sheridan objected. The move would take him far from his base of supplies, and the Rebel guerillas were being more pestiferous than ever. It would be better, he felt, to finish the job of ruining the Valley, take position much nearer to the Potomac, and then send Wright's corps back to Grant. Reluctantly, Grant deferred to his judgment, and on October 6 the army faced about and started back for the lower Valley.[4]

Morale was still high, but the brief atmosphere of holiday soldiering was gone. Guerilla warfare made men savage, and when the partisan rangers swept in for a fight neither side gave quarter. Cavalrymen said they would rather go into battle than patrol the Valley roads. One of Sheridan's aides was found in a field with his throat cut, and in hot fury Sheridan ordered every house, barn, and out-building within five miles burned to the ground. Farther down the Valley, Mosby's men struck at a supply train and its cavalry escort. Among the killed was a young Union officer who had been shot after he surrendered—or so, at any rate, the Federal troopers believed. Men from the 17th Pennsylvania Cavalry and the 2nd Regulars rode out for revenge, captured six of Mosby's riders, shot four of them, and hanged the remaining two. Under the dangling bodies they left a sign: "Such is the fate of Mosby's men." [5]

As the army withdrew Sheridan had the men get the matches out again, and the upper Valley got the treatment which the area below Strasburg had been given earlier. A cordon of cavalry brought up the rear, and behind it there was a blackened waste. A gunner said that "clean work was done," and a newspaper correspondent wrote: "The atmosphere, from horizon to horizon, has been black with the smoke of a hundred conflagrations, and at night a gleam brighter and more lurid than sunset has shot from every verge." Orders were to burn no dwellings, but if a burning barn happened to stand close to a house the house usually went up too, and the correspondent admitted that all of this incendiarism could not take place "without undue license" by stragglers and bummers; so "there have been frequent instances of rascality and pillage."

Nearly all barns and stables were destroyed, he recorded, most gardens and cornfields were ruined, and more than 5,000 head of livestock were driven off. Stout Union man though he was, this correspondent felt that the devastation "fearfully illustrates the horrible barbarity of war." Sheridan's orders were to leave each family enough to avert starvation, but marauding stragglers often carried away the last morsel. The newspaperman summed it up:

"The completeness of the devastation is awful. Hundreds of nearly starving people are going north. Our trains are crowded with them. They line the wayside. Hundreds more are coming; not half the inhabitants of the Valley can subsist on it in its present condition." [6]

A Confederate officer on Early's staff left bitter testimony: "I rode down the Valley with the advance after Sheridan's retreating cavalry beneath great columns of smoke which almost shut out the sun by day, and in the red glare of bonfires which, all across that Valley, poured out flames and sparks heavenward and crackled mockingly in the night air; and I saw mothers and maidens tearing their hair and shrieking to Heaven in their fright and despair, and little children, voiceless and tearless in their pitiable terror." [7]

Fully a year later, an English traveler wrote that the Shenandoah Valley looked like one vast moor. [8]

Heavy smoke, and blackened earth, and unending fires at night: and with the army as it moved there was an increasing stream of refugees, as if some strange emigrant train were off on an unimaginable journey. At many houses, as the cavalry approached, people were all packed and waiting. They could ride in army wagons, perhaps, and with the army there would be food, and if they were asked where they wanted to go they would reply: "Anywhere, to get out of this." Many of the Dunkers and Mennonites were setting out to join relatives in Pennsylvania, and there were scores and hundreds of contrabands who were departing for no one could imagine what goal. They had been told that the Yankees killed colored people, but with every barn for sixty miles going up in flames it seemed to them that they ought to leave.

These contrabands had many children, who looked in wide-eyed wonder at the odd things that were going on. The surgeon of the 77th New York reined in once by a rickety old cart drawn by an even more rickety horse. The cart seemed to be absolutely brimming over with small children, and the surgeon asked the bandannaed mammy who was driving: "Aunty, are these all your children?" She looked at him in mild surprise and protested: "They's only eighteen of 'em." [9]

Early pressed close behind the rear guard, and his cavalry struck whenever it found a chance. But things had changed since the early days of the war, when Confederate troopers could ride rings around the Yankees. The Rebel supply of horses was running out, and manpower was getting low, and the squadrons that came in on turnpike and field to harass the blue files no longer had the old advantage. A Confederate officer confessed glumly that Sheridan's cavalrymen nowadays "were more to be feared than their infantry—better soldiers all through." [10]

Sheridan grew irritated by the unending rear-guard actions, and at last he called in Torbert and told him to end the nuisance once and for all: "Whip or get whipped." On October 9 Torbert sent Custer and Merritt back for a head-on fight, and their seasoned divisions broke the Confederate mounted line to bits and chased the fragments up the Valley for twenty miles and more, capturing men and horses and eleven guns and inflicting, as one of the Southern riders confessed, "the greatest disaster that ever befell our cavalry during the whole war." [11] The Union army continued to retire at its leisure, smoke and flames still marking its passage, and by the middle of October Sheridan put it in position on a chain of low hills behind a little stream known as Cedar Creek, a little north of the town of Strasburg, twenty-odd miles south of Winchester.

For a few days the army rested in this camp. Early was not far away, but his army had been beaten twice in the past month and his cavalry had been thoroughly routed within the week, and the Yankees seem to have assumed that there was not much fight left in him—a risky assumption to make where Jubal Early was concerned, for he was as pugnacious a man as ever wore Rebel gray. And since there was a three-way disagreement between Grant, Sheridan, and the War Department as to what Sheridan ought to do next, Sheridan suspended the order transferring the VI Corps to Petersburg, put Wright in temporary command of the army, and went off to Washington for consultation. The situation of the rival armies seemed stable, and nothing much was apt to happen in his absence.[12]

Actually, the situation was highly unstable, principally because the destroying Yankee host had done its job so thoroughly. Early had perhaps 15,000 men with him, and the one thing these men could not do was stay where they were. The Valley had been so completely devastated that they could get no supplies of any kind from the surrounding country. Every mouthful of food for man and beast had to come up by wagon train, via Staunton and Waynesboro, and it was a hard pull for the worn-out Confederate transportation system. Early could either leave the Valley altogether, ceding the whole territory to the Yankees for the rest of the war —or he could attack.

To attack an army whose combat strength was twice his own would be, of course, to take fantastic risks. But the Confederate situation was desperate, and if fantastic risks were not taken the war was as good as lost. Early appears to have figured that Sheridan's force was not quite as solid as it looked anyway. The VI Corps was very good, but Confederate intelligence put a much lower estimate on the other two corps. Also, a good part of Sheridan's strength was in his cavalry, which did not ordinarily cut much of a figure in an infantry battle. Altogether, the odds could be worse.

In addition, there were two other encouraging factors. One was the obvious fact that nobody on the Federal side had any notion that the Confederates might take the offensive. The other was the position of the Union army.

Cedar Creek came down from the northwest to join the north fork of the Shenandoah River, and the chain of hills just behind the creek, on which the Federals were camped, ran from northwest to southeast. The VI Corps was on the Federal right, roughly a mile from where the Valley Pike crossed the creek and climbed through the higher ground. Next to it, north and west of the pike, was the XIX Corps. Southeast of the turnpike, anchoring the Union left, was

Crook's corps. It was in a good position to knock down any force which tried to come up along the main highway, but there was open ground nearly a mile wide between its own left and the point where creek and river met. Since the river just there lay in what looked like an impassable gorge, it seemed unlikely that the Confederates would be able to get across and make any trouble for this exposed flank.

Unlikely, except to soldiers who had to take fantastic risks anyway—the desperate, fifty-to-one sort of gamble that led Washington to take his army across the Delaware to attack the Hessian camp at Trenton. To Jubal Early the exposed Federal left looked like opportunity. He studied the ground carefully, and it seemed that an army corps could be led along that impassable gorge if the man who led it was thoroughly familiar with the layout and did not mind marching his entire command within 400 yards of the Yankee picket line.[13]

To lessen the risk, Early sent his cavalry and part of his infantry to the west, thrusting them forward as if he planned to attack the Yankee right flank. He put some more men in place where Wright's and Emory's men could see them, and he organized a third column to stand by for an advance directly along the turnpike. Then, with everything ready, he had General John B. Gordon take his army corps down into the gorge to get in behind the Federal left and open the attack. It meant an all-night hike, much of it in single file, and the men left canteens, cooking utensils, and everything except weapons and ammunition in camp so that no rattling or clanking of equipment would give them away.

So the army moved. Very early on the shivery, misty dawn of October 19, with fog hanging in the low places and the darkness lying thick in the graveyard hour between moonset and dawn, the Confederates rose up out of the gorge and came in yelling and shooting on the drowsy flank of Sheridan's army.

The day before, certain election commissioners from Connecticut had come into the Yankee lines to take the presidential vote of Connecticut soldiers, and they remained in camp overnight as special headquarters guests. They liked what they saw of army life, and to their hosts at supper they expressed regret that they could not see a fight before they went home. The officers who were entertaining them said they would like to accommodate them, but there just wasn't a chance: "it seemed very certain that Early would keep at a respectful distance." [14]

So here before reveille there was a popping and a racket off at the extreme left, and while nobody imagined it was anything except some little picket-line tussle there was a general stir in the Union camp, and the veterans began to cook breakfast on the theory that whether this was a false alarm or the real thing it would do no harm to eat and be ready. Then, suddenly, artillery began to pound, the infantry firing became sustained and intense, and a wild uproar came through the dark mist—and the election commissioners quickly found their clothes and ballot boxes and horses and took off for the North just as fast as they could go.[15]

Crook's corps was crumpled up in a twinkling, with Rebels coming in from the left and rear before the men even had time to grab their muskets. The corps had seven guns in line, and these were captured before they could fire a shot—to be spun about immediately by their captors and fired through the confusing mist into the middle of the Yankee camp. Crook commanded about 7,000 infantry that day, and in a matter of minutes those who had not been shot or captured were running for the rear, all 7,000 of them. For the next twenty-four hours, that corps did not exist as a usable military instrument.

Almost before the rest of the army realized that an attack was being made, Confederate Gordon had his infantry on the hill where Sheridan's headquarters had been—which meant that he was in rear of the entire army and that the men of Emory's and Wright's corps, who had as yet seen no Rebels, could do nothing on earth except retreat as speedily as possible. The surprise could not have been more complete.

General Wright came up from his own quarters, working to get troops over to the Valley Pike and check the rout. One of the men who went with him wrote that nothing was left of Crook's corps except "a disorganized, routed, demoralized, terrified mob of fugitives," and he sketched "the universal confusion and dismay" along the turnpike:

"Wagons and ambulances lumbering hither and thither in disorder; pack horses led by frightened bummers, or wandering at their own free will; crowds of officers and men, some shod and some barefoot, many of them coatless and hatless, with and without their rifles, but all rushing wildly to the rear; oaths and blows alike powerless to halt them; a cavalry regiment stretched across the field, unable to stem the torrent." [16]

Wright was in the middle of it, bareheaded, his beard all clotted with blood from a wound under the chin. He got the 2nd Connecticut heavies into line on a slope overlooking the highway, and as the men lay down to fire the sun came up and they found themselves looking directly into it, unable to see the Rebels, who were firing steadily: "We could see nothing but that enormous disk, rising out of the fog, while they could see every man in our line and could take good aim." The fog thinned, and more Confederates came in on the left and rear, and the regiment had to retreat, retreat turning quickly into a rout. General Emory brought over a brigade and sent it straight up the turnpike to break the Rebel charge and give time for a rally.

Federals and Confederates met head on and around the regimental battle flags there was furious fighting. A man in the 8th Vermont remembered that "men seemed more like demons than human beings as they struck fiercely at each other with clubbed muskets and bayonets," and at times it seemed that a dozen Confederates at once were reaching for each flagstaff. The colors tossed up and down in the dust and smoke. When they dropped the Southerners would cheer, and when they rose again the Northerners would cheer, and after a time the brigade got back out of the road and joined in the retreat. It still had all of its flags, but it had lost two thirds of its men.[17]

Step by step, the whole army retreated, and by the middle

of the morning it formed a shaky battle line four miles north of its original position. This line stretched away to the west of the pike, and there was a lull in the fighting, and the men scooped up little breastworks and got ready to meet another attack. Crook's corps was gone, and plenty of men had vanished from the other commands too, and all of these fugitives, together with the usual concourse of coffee boilers, wagoners, ambulance drivers, and the like were stretched out in steady flight all the way back to Winchester.

This flight was not a headlong rush, because even a frightened man cannot run so very far without pausing for breath. After the first panic wore off the men settled down to a walk, carrying on their flight, as one officer said, "in a manner as systematic as if they had been taught it." Now and then they would stop to make coffee and talk things over. Then they would go on again, sauntering along without haste but also without any intention of making a real halt anywhere. It was noticed, in this as in all similar cases, that it was almost impossible for any officer to rally and re-form such fugitives unless they recognized him as belonging to their own regiment or brigade. They would obey no strangers. They might fall into ranks obediently enough for a strange officer, but the ranks would evaporate as soon as he tried to lead them back into action.[18]

The triumphant Confederates meanwhile had seized all of the Union camps, and had 1,300 prisoners and 18 of Sheridan's cannon in their possession. Ahead of them, perhaps a mile and a half to the north, they could see the last Federal battle line; it was nearly two miles wide, and swarms of cavalry were forming up on either flank, and as Early looked at it he was jocund and full of confidence.

Exactly one month earlier his army had been running away from the Yankees, at Winchester. Now it was the Yankees who were in flight, and Early was in high spirits. A good many of his soldiers were leaving their commands to despoil the captured camps, with especial attention to the good food their foes had not been able to take with them, but this absenteeism did not worry him. He declared that the Yankee battle line visible west of the turnpike was no more than a rear guard. It would go away before long and the victory would be complete.

General Gordon was of a different notion.

"That is the VI Corps, general," he said. "It will not go unless we drive it from the field."

But Early would not listen to him. The Yankees had been beaten and most of them had run away: the rest would run away before long and that was all there was to it. Still, to play safe he put his staff to work to round up the camp looters and get them back into formation.[19] From his headquarters post on a hilltop he continued to look north with deep satisfaction. Banks and Sigel, Hunter and Sheridan—they were all alike, when they collided with a Rebel army in the Valley!

. . . On a rise of ground just north of Winchester, about fifteen miles from the battlefield, the 17th Pennsylvania cavalry had been in bivouac. They had come down from Martinsburg, guarding trains against guerillas, and they had been ordered to wait here for General Sheridan, who had reached Winchester the night before on his return trip from Washington.

The day of October 19 began as usual for these troopers, with "Boots and Saddles" sounding before sunrise. As the men fed their horses and got their own breakfasts they could hear the mutter of gunfire, far to the south. Nobody thought much about it, since the word was that Wright was going to make a reconnoissance in force that morning to find out just where the Rebel army was, and it was assumed that that was the cause of the firing. The men finished their meal and stood by, waiting for the general.

Sheridan rode out about nine o'clock, a few aides riding with him. It was a sunny morning, bare fields rolling away to the hills and mountains which blazed with autumn colors, a warm Indian summer haze thickening the air. Off to the south there was that continued sound of firing, perhaps a bit louder now than it had been earlier. Sheridan seemed to be puzzled. As he picked up his cavalry escort he halted, dismounted, and bent over with his ear to the ground, listening intently. When he got back on his horse his swarthy face was clouded.

Down the road went general, aides, and cavalry, horses moving at a walk. After a mile or so they came upon a wagon train all in a tangle, wagons turned every which way, nobody moving. Sheridan sent his Major Forsyth trotting on ahead to see what was wrong, and presently Forsyth came back at a mad gallop. The train had been bound for the front, he reported, and at this spot had met an officer heading for Winchester bearing news that the army had been routed and was coming back in full retreat—on hearing which the teamsters had begun to swing their wagons around without waiting for orders.

Sheridan told Major Spera, the cavalry commander, to give him fifty of his best mounted men and to spread the rest across the road as traffic police: untangle the wagon train, round up fugitives, and in general see that everybody who thought he was going to Winchester turned and headed back for the place where the fighting was going on. Then with his chosen fifty Sheridan set off down the road, the horses moving at a walk no longer.

First they met wagon trains, coming back to escape capture, and these were told to park in the fields and await orders. Then they met the outriders of defeat—sutlers, camp followers of high and low degree, artillerymen without their guns, headquarters trains, battery wagons, caissons, and little knots of stragglers and walking wounded. A little farther on, they saw groups of men in the fields, clustering about campfires, boiling coffee, and they met increasing numbers of men walking along the highway. And always the sound of the firing grew louder.

Here and there Sheridan would rein up and call: "Turn back, men! Turn back! Face the other way!" Once he told a group of stragglers: "Face the other way, boys—if I had been there this morning this wouldn't have happened! You'll have your own camps back before night!"

Most of the time, however, he did not come to a halt but

kept on at a gallop, swinging his hat in a great arc, now and then pointing toward the south, always calling: "Turn back, men! Turn back!"

The effect was electric. One group of coffee boilers, who had been stretched at ease around a fire, jumped up with a yell as he went past, kicked their coffeepots over, seized their muskets, and started back toward the battlefield. All along the way men sprang up and cheered. Those who were near the road turned and shouted, waving their arms in frantic signal, to attract the attention of men who were sauntering across fields a quarter of a mile away. They pointed to the speeding cavalcade in the road and at the top of their lungs they cried: "Sheridan! Sheridan!" [20]

The Valley Pike had been macadamized once, but in the war years it had seen many armies and no repairs, and its surface now was all pitted and broken, and a cloud of white dust rose as the mounted men galloped on, Sheridan in front, the rest trailing after him.

Sheridan was on his favorite horse, a tireless black named Rienzi, and it became a fable and a folk legend how Rienzi went a full twenty miles at a gallop without stopping. The legend outdid reality. There were a number of little halts, when Sheridan would pull up to ask for news, and at one halt he had Major Forsyth cut a little switch for him, with which he birched Rienzi into greater speed. Once he met a panicky man riding to the rear on a mule, and he asked the man how things were at the front. "Oh, everything is lost and gone," shouted the man, "but it will be all right when you get there"—after which the man got the mule to a gallop and kept on in the direction of Winchester. Once Sheridan stopped to look in on a field hospital, and talked to some of the wounded. Counting everything, Rienzi had a number of chances to catch his breath.

Yet the legendary picture is close enough to fact: black-headed man on a great black horse, riding at furious speed, his escort dim in the dust behind him, waving his arm and swinging his absurd flat little hat and shouting continually the order to turn around and get back into the fighting; a man followed for many miles by the cheers of men who spun on their heels and returned to the firing line because they believed that if he was going to be there everything would be all right again—and because the look of him, and his great ringing voice, and the way he moved and rode and gestured somehow made going back into battle with him seem light and gay and exciting, even to men who had been in many battles.

Major Forsyth wrote that every time a group of stragglers saw Sheridan the result was the same—"a wild cheer of recognition, an answering wave of the cap." In no case, he said, did the men fail to shoulder their arms and follow the general, and for miles behind him the turnpike was crowded with men pressing forward to the front which they had run away from a few hours earlier. And all along the highway, for mile on mile, and in the fields beside the road, there went up the great jubilant chant: "Sheridan! Sheridan!"

As they got closer to the front Sheridan became grimmer. Major Forsyth wrote: "As he galloped on his features gradually grew set, as though carved in stone, and the same dull red glint I had seen in his piercing black eyes when, on other occasions, the battle was going against us, was there now." [21]

They came at last to a ridge where there were batteries in action, dueling at long range; and up ahead, on the right of the road, they could see the ranks of the VI Corps, men standing in line waiting to be used. Sheridan came plowing up through the fainthearts and the skulkers, and his face was black as midnight, and now he was shouting: "Turn about, you damned cowardly curs, or I'll cut you down! I don't expect you to fight, but come and see men who like to!" And he swung his arm in a great inclusive gesture toward the VI Corps up ahead.[22]

These men had been waiting in line for an hour or more. As veterans, they knew that the army had been beaten in detail and not by head-on assault, and they were grumbling about it, making profane remarks about men who ran away —and then, far behind them, they heard cheering.

"We were astounded," wrote a man in the Vermont Brigade. "There we stood, driven four miles already, quietly waiting for what might be further and immediate disaster, and far in the rear we heard the stragglers and hospital bummers and the gunless artillerymen actually cheering as though a victory had been won. We could hardly believe our ears."

And then, while the men were still looking their questions at one another, out in front of the line came Sheridan himself, still riding at a swinging gallop—and the whole army corps blew up in the wildest cheer it had ever given in all of its career, and the roar went rocketing along the line as Sheridan rode on past brigade after brigade of the toughest veterans in the Army of the Potomac. The Vermont Brigade's historian wrote fondly:

"Such a scene as his presence produced and such emotions as it awoke cannot be realized once in a century. All outward manifestations were as enthusiastic as men are capable of exhibiting; cheers seemed to come from throats of brass, and caps were thrown to the tops of the scattering oaks; but beneath and yet superior to these noisy demonstrations there was in every heart a revulsion of feeling, and a pressure of emotion, beyond description. No more doubt or chance for doubt existed; we were safe, perfectly and unconditionally safe, and every man knew it."

All along the line went Sheridan, waving his hat, telling the troops: "Boys, we'll get the tightest twist on them they ever saw. We'll get all those camps back." To a colonel who rode up and said they were glad to see him, Sheridan replied: "Well, by God, I'm glad to be here!" And to another officer, still pessimistic from the morning's licking, who said that Early intended to drive them clear out of the Shenandoah Valley, Sheridan barked in fury: "What? Three corps of infantry and all of my cavalry; Jubal Early drive me out of the valley? I'll lick him like blazes before night! I'll give him the worst licking he ever had!" [23]

And that was the way of it, in the end. After Sheridan passed by the men in line retied their shoes, tucked pants legs inside their socks, tightened their belts, unfastened cartridge-box lids, slid ramrods down rifle barrels to make sure the weapons were loaded, and jerked their forage caps down lower on their foreheads. From the rear the returning stragglers came up in droves, wandering along the lines, finding their proper regiments and taking their places—to the tune of jibes from their comrades. Sheridan went to General Wright, who was lying on the ground, his throat and chin all swollen, blood on his coat. It was hard for him to talk, but he got up when Sheridan came, made his report, and prepared to go into action. Sheridan took plenty of time, waiting for his stragglers to come up, and it was nearly four in the afternoon when his battle line finally went forward.[24]

When it hit, it hit hard. Confederate ranks were thinned by the absence of men who persisted in foraging among what the Yankees had left, and if all of the absentees had been in line Sheridan still would have had more men than Early had. Anyway, this Federal army knew it was going to win, at last, and it rolled up to the Rebel lines with irresistible might.

One of Emory's men reported that the Confederates were retreating presently "in precisely the same kind of disorder we had exhibited that morning," and he wrote that they pursued eagerly because "the sight of so many rebel heels made it an easy thing to be brave." On a ridge, by and by, the Confederates made a stand, and with their heels no longer visible the joys of pursuit were not quite so overpowering; but Sheridan had a great mass of cavalry swinging in on the flank like a scythe, and it sheared in behind the Rebel infantry and the whole line gave way, and a disordered rout went southward as dusk came down.

Cheering madly, the Federal infantry pressed on, determined not to stop until they had at least got past their old camping grounds. At times it seemed as if the front were all flags, since the color sergeants were not loaded down with weapons and accouterments and so could run faster than the others. The infantry pressed on so hard that George Custer once turned to his mounted men, pointing, and cried: "Are you going to let infantry get ahead of you?"[25]

It was the cavalry that made the victory complete. It cannoned into the Confederate wagon and artillery train, smashed a bridge near the town of Strasburg, and went bucketing up and down and back and forth through the whole confused retreat. All of the Federal guns and wagons that had been lost that morning were retaken, together with twenty-five Confederate guns and any number of wagons, and Early's army was ruined.

At times the cavalry was going too fast to take prisoners. Rebels who surrendered would be told, "You stay here!" while the captors rode off to get more—after which most of the prisoners would disappear in the dark and try to rejoin their comrades. A South Carolina officer who got away recalled that he had surrendered five times during the retreat. The 5th New York boasted that one of its troopers, a tough Montenegrin named Heiduc, had personally sabered the two teamsters of a Confederate baggage wagon and had himself brought the vehicle back to camp.

Sheridan's word was good. The troops occupied their old camps that night, and at least some of them found that hardly any of their things had been taken; possibly fewer Rebels left the ranks for plunder than Early afterward alleged. A field in front of Sheridan's headquarters was filled with captured matériel—guns and ambulances and baggage wagons and stacks of muskets—and Sheridan's hell-for-leather scouts equipped themselves with a score of captured Confederate flags and paraded wildly across the firelight with them. General Emory watched Sheridan ride proudly by and he mused: "That young man has made a great name for himself today." [26]

A few days after the battle a Connecticut soldier looked over the long files of prisoners and wrote to his family that the Rebs were "smart healthy-looking men," clad in neat gray uniforms and slouch hats. "They are very quick, walk like horses," he added, and he found most of them quite cheerful, laughing and joking all of the time. And all of them, he said, "from officers down to privates, said they were tired of the war and that peace was worth more than the C.S.A." [27]

CHAPTER VI

Endless Road Ahead

---

1. Except by the Sword

A LUMINOUS mist of Indian summer lay on the desolate plains around Petersburg, and on the horizon the surviving woodlands were as remote and unreal as the memory of peace, magical with rich color, cool green of pines blending into the deep russet brown of oaks and the flaming red of maples and dogwood. Near the trees were thousands of tents and canvas-roofed huts, and across the fields and hills where there were neither tents nor trees were mile upon mile of trenches, scarring the earth with grotesque irregular patterns, the ground between them bristling with tangles of abatis and sinister sharpened stakes of *chevaux-de-frise*. Autumn sunlight sparkled on rifle barrels and bayonets, in the trenches and the skirmishers' rifle pits and the big square forts, and gleamed from the bright metal of the guns; and at night all the front glowed with flashing fires as the armies sniped and bombarded each other, and the great mortar shells climbed the sky in high slow parabolas, fuses burning red in the black sky.

The rival lines of forts and trenches ran for more than thirty-five miles. They began north of the James, at gloomy White Oak Swamp, and from the swamp they curved and twisted for eight miles to the north bank of the James. Along the river itself there was a four-mile stretch where Confederate artillery, mounted on the bluffs along the southern shore, barred the way against the Yankee monitors and gunboats. Then the trenches began again, running for five miles across the Bermuda Hundred neck to the Appomattox River, and here again, for four miles along the river bank, there was artillery. Then, below the river, due east from Petersburg and so close to the city that Yankee gunners could throw shells into warehouses and churches and dwellings if they chose, there were trenches once more.

These followed the battle lines that had been fixed in June, and they led south for four or five miles to the Jerusalem Plank Road—never very far apart, the men who occupied them always under fire, the hideous red wound of the mine crater lying just back of the Rebel parapets. Below the Plank Road the lines swung southwest, and here, early in the summer, they had ended, the Confederate system anchored by a work named Fort Mahone, the Yankee line tied to an opposing work named Fort Sedgwick. By day and by night, month after month, these forts dueled with each other, and the soldiers of the two armies had named the Federal work "Fort Hell" and the Confederate work "Fort Damnation." [1]

Always the lines had been creeping off toward the southwest. Since the day the mine was exploded the Federals had made no more frontal assaults. Grant resumed the old habit of edging constantly around by his left, looking always for a chance to strike in past the Rebel flank. There had been a series of moves of this kind during late summer and autumn, with Federal troops trying to get west from Fort Hell. None of these moves came to very much, and some had ended in humiliating defeat. The II Corps, for instance, was roundly whipped at a place called Reams's Station, men running in panic from a Rebel counterattack which the old II Corps would have beaten off with ease, Hancock riding among the routed troops waving his hat and crying: "Come on! We can beat them yet! Don't leave me, for God's sake!" [2]

Yet after each of these moves, somehow, the Union position was a little better and the Confederate position was a little worse. Lee was forever being compelled to stretch his line farther and farther, which meant that it was steadily growing thinner. While Confederate manpower was declining, he was being given more and more ground to hold. Month after month the Union army reached out, slowly but inexorably drawing closer to the railroad lines behind the Confederate right and rear which Lee must keep unbroken if his army and Richmond were to live.

Behind Grant's army was visible the enormous power of the North. City Point, which had been the sleepiest of riverside hamlets, had become one of the world's great seaports. Wharves lined the waterfront for more than a mile, with more docks extending up the Appomattox. An average day would see 40 steamboats, 75 sailing vessels, and 100 barges tied up or anchored along the waterfront. An army hospital that covered 200 acres and could accommodate 10,000 patients crowned a bluff above the river. There were vast warehouses for quartermaster, commissary, and ordnance departments; bakeries, blacksmith shops, wagon-repair shops, barracks for soldiers, quarters for civilian workers. Two steam engines had been set up to pump a water supply for this strange military city, and half a dozen sprinkling carts had been imported to lay the dust in its streets. The quartermaster general boasted that the facilities here were so extensive that he could easily supply an army of 500,000 men if he had to, and he had four passenger steamers providing daily service between City Point and Washington. (Very bad service, too, according to a newspaper correspondent, who found the boats dirty, crowded, and odorous and the food hardly fit to eat.)[3]

To connect this seaport with the army, the government had built a twenty-one-mile railroad, complete with freight yards, coal docks, roundhouse, repair shops, and all the rest. Nucleus of this was a prewar line which connected Petersburg with City Point, but of that seven-mile stub nothing much remained except the right of way; it had been a five-foot-gauge affair, and the military road was built to the standard four feet eight and one half inches. Branches had been built to run up and down behind the front, so that all of the military area below the Appomattox could be serviced by rail.

This railroad was enormously useful, since it meant that the fighting line could be kept supplied even in the worst weather, and it made the speedy reinforcement of any part of the line comparatively simple. The railroad amused the soldiers immensely. Even while it was contemporary, it managed to look quaint. It had been built in a great hurry and there had been almost no grading of the right of way, the tracks simply being laid on unprepared ground. As a result the railroad snaked up and down over hills and hollows, and it was said that watching a train go by was like watching a fly walk down a corrugated washboard. When a well-loaded train was at the top of a grade the engineer would open the throttle and go thundering down into the valley, hoping that the added momentum would get him up the opposite slope. If it did not he would back up and make a fresh start. If he carried troops, the men often would be ordered to get out and push.

The line had been built by railroad men. Army engineers had said that the road could never be operated—the grades would be too steep and cargo-carrying capacity would be too small. The railroad men knew better and went ahead with their program, and by fall the line was operating eighteen trains a day, with from fifteen to two dozen cars in each train, and was doing a fair passenger business besides.[4]

An Episcopal bishop from Atlanta, who had come north on a pass from General Sherman and who stopped off to visit Grant on his trip back south, was greatly impressed by the abundance of military supplies at City Point—"not merely profusion, but extravagance; wagons, tents, artillery, ad libitum. Soldiers provided with everything." He thought of the Confederate armies' lean rations and then looked in amazement at the comforts available to the Yankees. Bakeries were turning out thousands of loaves of fresh bread, sutlers' shops were everywhere, soldiers were forever buying extras to supplement their regular diet, and to him this reflected the wealth of the North.

The bishop believed that the consciousness of wealth and power had a direct effect on the mental attitude of the Northern soldiers and the Northern people. Everyone he talked to seemed obsessed with the greatness and destiny of the Federal Union. He found "a universal horror of rebellion," which made people feel that Rebels were almost "outside the pale of humanity," so that it was no sin to commit almost any sort of outrage on Southern people or property. It seemed to the good bishop that this was not merely a purse-proud complacency; it was something that looked far past the present, beyond the war to a future greatness for the whole country that would go beyond all present comprehension. He wrote: "Their idol is less the Union of the past than the sublime Union of the future, destined soon to overshadow all the nations." [5]

There was power in this sentiment, and as the fall progressed it seemed to overshadow everything else. It even dominated the one great emotional drive which had been bred into the very bones of the Army of the Potomac—the love which the army still felt for General McClellan. As election day approached there was much talk of McClellan among the veterans. A Quaker nurse at the City Point hospital wrote in September that "if it is left to the soldiers, his election is sure," and it was clear that the old affection for the handsome little general still ran strong. [6]

"Soldiers' eyes would brighten when they talked of him," one veteran recalled. "Their hard, lean, browned faces would soften and light up with affection when they spoke of him" —and yet, he continued, it was affection only. There was not, in the showdown, anything in it that would carry the election. Talking things over, the veterans agreed that they had been a better, stronger army in 1862, when McClellan commanded, than they were now in 1864, under Grant. Yet they also agreed that if Grant had commanded in 1862 the war would have been won in that year, while if McClellan had commanded in 1864 "he would have ended the war in the Wilderness—by establishing the Confederacy."

A man in the 20th Maine wrote that McClellan still was

"almost worshiped" by the soldiers, but that very few would vote for him. By and large, they interpreted his candidacy much as the Confederates did: to vote against Lincoln would be to consent to dissolution of the Union. An officer in what was left of the Iron Brigade, musing about the election, put his thoughts on paper: "On one side is war, and stubborn, patient effort to restore the old Union and national honor; on the other side is inglorious peace and shame, the old truckling subserviency to Southern domination, and a base alacrity in embracing some vague, deceptive political subterfuge instead of honorable and clearly defined principles." [7]

And so, when election day came, the veterans voted by resounding majorities against McClellan, voted for Lincoln and for war to the bitter end—and, voting so, swung shut forever a door into their own past.

For McClellan had always been the great symbol. He was the trumpets these soldiers had heard and the flags they had carried and the faraway, echoing cheers they had raised: the leader of an unreal army which had come marching out of the horn gates with golden light on its banners, an impossible sunrise staining the sky above its path, and now it had gone into the land of remembered dreams. Everything that these men had, one supposes, they would have given to be again the army McClellan had commanded and to have him again for a leader, and yet they did not try to vote the past back into existence because they were fond young men no longer. They had come of age and they gave history something new to look at, not seen before in all the record of wars and men of war—the sight, that is, of veteran soldiers who had long outlived enthusiasm and heroics walking quietly up to ballot boxes and voting for more war to be fought by themselves instead of voting for an end to it and no more fighting.

No one did any fancy talking about it, and it is probable that very little fancy thinking was done. It is even possible to doubt that many of the veterans were consciously voting for freedom and Union. At bottom, what counted most may have been nothing more than a simple refusal to admit they could be beaten. An officer wrote that "they were unwilling that their long fight should be set down as a failure, even though thus far it seemed so," and that probably says it. The men were not quitters, and when it came time to vote they said so according to their understanding of the case. But it is not hard to agree with the New England soldier who, looking back after the war, remarked that the Army of the Potomac was never pluckier than when it voted by a big majority for Lincoln's re-election and the continuation of the war.[8]

Not long after the soldiers had cast their ballots the army was ordered to load all of its cannon, train them on suitable Rebel targets, and fire 100 rounds from each gun—a colossal salute in honor of Sheridan's victory at Cedar Creek. There had been many salutes of that kind this fall—salutes for Sheridan's army, and for Sherman's, and for victories by the Navy —and it seems to have occurred to no one that although this army was constantly firing salutes to celebrate somebody else's triumph, no one was ever firing salutes for the Army of the Potomac.

Its role was inglorious, as men then figured glory. It won no victories and earned no applause; its job was just to hang on and fight and make final victory possible. By election day the army had been in intimate contact with its foes for six unbroken months. During all of that time there had been two or three days when contact was maintained by cavalry alone. All the rest of the time, in sunlight and in darkness, infantry and artillery had been in action somewhere along the front. During August, September, and October—months when the front was relatively inactive—the army's siege artillery alone threw nearly six tons of shell every day into the Rebel lines.[9]

The Confederates gave as much as they received. A Pennsylvania soldier whose outfit was moved into Fort Sedgwick that fall wrote that "we are now in fort hell and it seems pretty much like it. On Tuesday of last week the Rebs threw 132 mortar shells into our camp . . . last Friday they threw 129 . . . every few days we have to practice on dodging shells to save our top knots." Artillerists on both sides had a way of firing any kind of scrap iron when there was work at close quarters, and a soldier who was wounded by such a salvo in a fight near Drury's Bluff explained: "the damned rebels fired a whole blacksmith shop over here, but nothing happened to hit me but the anvil." [10]

In such ways as they could the soldiers tried to make things easier for themselves. During daylight, the picket lines did little or no firing. When dusk came the men would call across to each other, "Get into your holes!" and the shooting would begin. In some parts of the line the rival marksmen agreed to fire high, and if someone accidentally put a bullet close to his enemies there would be an angry protest.

Even the IX Corps began to find trench life a little easier. Its colored division was transferred over to the Army of the James, and when the Confederates learned about it they dropped their old habit of shooting to kill every time a member of this luckless corps raised his head. When the corps was moved down to the left of the line, where there was a considerable distance between the trenches, one man wrote that "it was a great relief to be able to stand upright without the certainty of being shot," and another said: "It doesn't seem like war here. We can walk clear over to their picket line and trade coffee, tea, etc., for articles of theirs."

When the Irish Brigade found itself stationed opposite Mahone's Confederate division, which contained many Irish soldiers, it had a fine time and its historian reported: "The soldiers on both sides mingled freely, exchanged newspapers, coffee, tobacco and sometimes whisky." He added that this did not mean that the Rebels were losing any of their combativeness, for "when it came to actual fighting, they fought like bull-dogs." [11]

The comment was characteristic. The queer, upside-down comradeship which six months of battle-front intimacy had begun to create between the armies did not mean that anybody had ceased to fight hard. Being sensible men, the soldiers tacitly agreed to defang the day-to-day picket-line firing, which would not affect the outcome of the war very much if it went on for a century, but battles were going to be as grim and deadly as ever. A Michigan soldier in the II Corps remembered how his brigade got flanked and cut to pieces during a brisk little fight beyond the extreme left, late in October, and he commented drily: "Of course it would not be gallant to say that anybody run, but if there was any tall walking done during the war, we did it crossing that field." [12]

In December, Warren's corps and some cavalry were sent on a long raid aimed at Southern railroad lines and supply bases near the Meherrin River. The Weldon Railroad, which came up to Petersburg from the south, had long since been cut, but the Confederates were bringing up supplies on it to a point some twenty miles from Petersburg and then hauling them the rest of the way by wagon, and Grant wanted this traffic broken up.

It began like an enjoyable diversion. Once out of the trenches, the soldiers were in country which, at least by contrast with what they had been looking at, seemed untouched by war. It was nice to be in such country, even though a sleety December drizzle had set in, and one man felt that "the lowing of the cow and the tinkling of sheep bells suggested that quieter days than those that came to us still dawned upon the world." As a more tangible boon, there was good foraging, and the men ate many chickens and turkeys.[13] The Atlanta bishop had understood the matter: the Union soldier saw no wrong in taking chickens and turkeys owned by men who were in rebellion.

The big idea of this raid was to destroy so much of the railroad that it would no longer be practical for Lee's commissariat to run a wagon line to the end of the track, and once the infantry got into position the work of destruction began, soldiers working for miles up and down the right of way. The work went on far into the night, and a rookie in the 198th Pennsylvania saw it as strange and exciting: "As far as the eye could reach were seen innumerable glowing fires, and thousands of busy blue coats tearing up the rails and piling up the ties. It was a wild, animated scene, and the fatigue of the long day's march was forgotten." [14]

It was not all pure fun. Rebel cavalry hung around the fringes of the force, and irregular troops came into action as well, giving the V Corps a taste of guerilla warfare. Stragglers were waylaid and killed, and as the troops finished their work and began to move back to Petersburg they found stripped, mutilated bodies of their comrades lying in field and road. Just how many cases of this kind there actually were is not clear, nor can it be told now how many Union soldiers, if any, looked upon mutilated corpses and how many merely heard about them; but the news went through the army fast, and it raised murderous fury, and the command became a destroying host as it moved back northward. A man in the 9th Massachusetts battery saw many buildings on fire, and heard that every building in sight from the line of march was destroyed. "One thing is certain," he said. "The burning was approved by the commanders, and there was cause for it; probably murders were the cause of it. We believed it at the time." [15]

To a man in the Iron Brigade, this raid was "the most vindictive that the army ever engaged in." He said the men had been infuriated by the work of the guerillas, but he admitted that "the destruction of the houses of peaceable women and children, though venomous in their Union hatred, cannot be justified," and he added proudly that "the Iron Brigade had no share in the vandalism." [16]

The year drew to an end: 1864, the year of the Wilderness and the Bloody Angle, of Cold Harbor and the Crater; the year that killed John Sedgwick and saw Abraham Lincoln under fire; the terrible year when war became total; the year of U. S. Grant. In the Shenandoah Valley snow drifted over black ruins, and what was left of Early's army huddled in a winter camp near Waynesboro, and Sheridan sent the VI Corps back to Petersburg. The people of the North put on a big campaign to give the soldiers a good Christmas dinner, and boxes and barrels of turkeys, doughnuts, mince pies, and cakes came down to City Point. The men in the huge hospital got an especially lavish turkey dinner, and a nurse reflected afterward that "there is not a class of persons in the world more cheerful than a ward full of wounded who are doing well." New Year's Day came in clear and cold, and below

Fort Hell details went out to cut firewood from a stand of timber between the lines. They found Rebel details out on the same mission, and the woodsmen declared a truce, had a chat, and then pitched in together and cut wood until dusk, at which time they made a fair division of the firewood and went back to their respective lines.[17]

There was a severe winter that year, and life in the trenches was even less comfortable than usual. Army headquarters frowned upon idleness, and there were drills and work details for everybody, with brigade dress parades every afternoon for all except those actually on the firing line. Orders came through to comb out the non-combat details and get men back into combat roles, and a clerk in V Corps headquarters estimated that this would add fully 6,000 men to the army's combat strength. Discipline became sharper. Bounty-jumpers, draftees, and substitutes were going to be made soldiers in spite of themselves, and a special court was set up at City Point to give speedy trials to deserters. It hanged seven men in one day.

The army began to get back some of its old-timers. Some were men who had been wounded, earlier, recovered now and returning to their old regiments for duty. Others were men who had been mustered out when their enlistments expired, who had joined up again and were coming down to the front. Some of the new, high-number regiments were almost entirely made up of such veterans. These regiments would be as good as any the army ever had.[18]

Two generals the army had lost—two who had done much, for better or for worse, to shape its fate. One was Winfield Scott Hancock, still plagued by his Gettysburg wound, gone north now with some vague mission to recruit a new corps of time-expired veterans and bring it to the upper Shenandoah Valley; a mission that somehow never came to much, and Hancock was out of the war. He had not been himself for months, had never really been the same since Gettysburg, but he had been one of the men who gave spirit and color to the army and he had been in the middle of its most desperate fights. The army would not be the same, without

Hancock. In his place at the head of the II Corps went Andrew A. Humphreys, Meade's chief of staff, a hard fighter and the sternest of disciplinarians.

The other loss was sheer gain. Ben Butler had gone home, and although technically he had never belonged to the Army of the Potomac, it had had to pay for a number of his mistakes. In December, Army and Navy had mounted a big expedition to take Fort Fisher in North Carolina, the last seaport open to the Confederacy, and since the operation fell in his department Butler had elected himself commander of it. He had planned to destroy the fort by exploding a ship filled with powder as close to the ramparts as possible; did explode it, at dead of night, damaging the fort not at all, making in fact so little impression that the defenders vaguely supposed a Yankee boiler had burst. Butler then got troops ashore, grew discouraged, ordered them aboard ship again, and sailed away reporting that the fort could not be taken.

That was his last act. The admiral on this expedition was tough David Porter, who had been on intimate terms with Grant ever since the Vicksburg campaign, and Porter told Grant the fort could be had any time they sent a competent general to take it. The presidential election was over and the war was on the downhill slope, and it was suddenly realized that Butler no longer need be handled with tongs. So Grant relieved him of his command and sent him back to Massachusetts, and Lincoln sustained Grant, and the one man who ever bluffed those two citizens had lost all of his terrors.

Another expedition went out, Fort Fisher was captured, and the Confederacy was sealed away from the outside world. Sherman was beginning to come north from Savannah, and for the Army of the Potomac it was a winter of rising confidence. "There was hope in the air," wrote a veteran in the VI Corps. "All were beginning to feel that the next campaign would be the last." [19] Much of this was due to the realization that the men in the opposing trenches, the indomitable veterans of Lee's magnificent army, were themselves beginning to lose hope.

The Confederacy was visibly failing—in manpower, in rations, in equipment. A Union man in Fort Hell, peering through the wintry air, saw a stooped and ragged Confederate detail marching out to relieve the picket line and wrote that "I could not help comparing them with so many women with cloaks, shawls, double-bustles and hoops, as they had thrown over their shoulders blankets and tents which flapped in the wind." An officer of the day on the VI Corps front recorded that forty deserters had come into his lines in forty-eight hours, and he said that this was about average; "if we stay here, the Johnnies will all come over before the 4th of July." To another Union officer, the "starved and wan appearance" of the deserters proved that "the Confederacy was on its last legs." [20]

In the lines facing Richmond, Union pickets one night heard a great hallooing and cursing from a swamp out in front, and they crept out and rescued an indignant Rebel conscript who had got stuck in the mud while trying to desert. They took him to their campfire and found that he was fat and sixty, a man who ordinarily wore a wig, spectacles, and false teeth, but who had lost all three while floundering in the swamp. They dried him off and gave him coffee; he drank, looked about the circle, and then began to curse the Confederacy:

"He cursed it individually, from Jeff. Davis and his cabinet down through its Congress and public men to the lowest pothouse politician who advocated its cause; he cursed its army, from General Lee down to an army mule; he cursed that army in its downsittings and uprisings, in all its movements, marches, battles and sieges; he cursed all its paraphernalia, its artillery and its muskets, its banners, bugles and drums; he cursed the institution of slavery, which had brought about the war, and he invoked the direst calamity, woe and disaster upon the Southern cause and all that it represented; while the earnestness, force and sincerity with which it was delivered made it one of the most effective speeches I ever heard, and this together with his comical appearance and the circumstance of his capture made the men roar with laughter."

The Union man who told about all of this added, perhaps unnecessarily, that "the best element in the Southern army" did not desert.[21]

A New England private said that each evening the men in his company would speculate about the number of deserters who would come in that night: "The boys talk about the Johnnies as at home we talk about suckers and eels. The boys will look around in the evening and guess that there will be a good run of Johnnies." Heavy firing on the picket lines was always taken to mean that the enemy was trying to keep deserters from getting away. Many deserters were willing to enlist in the Union army, and before 1864 ended it was ordered that all such should be sent West to fight the Indians—it would go very hard with them if the army from which they had deserted should recapture them. When these men talked about the Southern cause, it was said, they would remark that it was a rich man's war and a poor man's fight.[22]

Yet there was always one striking point to remember. Confederate soldiers might be deserting in increasing numbers, but up to the moment of desertion they fought just as hard as ever. A VI Corps officer admitted that "the Army of Northern Virginia was still a most formidable foe," and when he studied the battle front he found that "their forts, with five lines of abatis in front, looked as if they could defy any attack." As the winter wore away the tension actually increased. Men felt that Lee would find some way to strike a blow before desertions crippled him, and it was agreed that when the blow fell it would come with savage force.[23]

At the end of January there was an odd, revealing incident. Over the Rebel parapet near the old mine crater came a white flag, with a bugler to blow a parley, and a message came over for General Grant. As it happened, Grant was away just then, and there was a twenty-four-hour delay before the message reached him. During the delay, by the mysterious army grapevine, word went up and down the rival lines: the Confederacy was sending a peace commission to meet Lincoln and Seward to see whether they could not agree on terms to end the war.

The peace commissioners were men of note. One was John A. Campbell, former justice of the United States Supreme Court, now the Confederacy's Assistant Secretary of War. Another was Senator R. M. T. Hunter, former Confederate Secretary of State. The third was the Vice-President of the Confederacy, wizened Alexander Stephens, who had been in Congress with Lincoln and who, in 1848, made a speech which caused Lincoln to write to his law partner, Herndon, that "a little, slim, pale-faced consumptive man" had just made the best speech he had ever heard, a speech which moved him to tears. He and Stephens had been drawn to each other, somehow. Members of the Whig party, they had worked together in 1848 to help nominate Zachary Taylor.

Jefferson Davis once had used words of poetry to refer to Stephens as "the little pale star from Georgia." He would not use such tender language about him now, for he and Stephens had drifted far apart. Davis considered Stephens a defeatist, and Stephens considered Davis a despot, and said so in public; and now, against his will, Stephens was head of a mission sent to confer with Lincoln "for the purpose of securing peace to the two countries."

By the time Grant got the message, consulted Washington, and made arrangements to get the commissioners through the lines, it was the afternoon of January 31. Both armies knew what was up, and when the carriages came out the Jerusalem Plank Road from Petersburg, bearing the three dignitaries and any number of anxious private citizens, the parapets of Union and Confederate trenches were jammed with soldiers as far as the eye could see.

There was an expectant hush. The commissioners' carriage turned and made for an opening in the Confederate lines— and suddenly all of the soldiers who could see it, blue and gray alike, swung their hats and raised a tremendous cheer. A gunner who looked on remembered: "Cheer upon cheer was given, extending for some distance to the right and left of the lines, each side trying to cheer the loudest. 'Peace on the brain' appeared now to have spread like a contagion. Officers of all grades, from lieutenants to major generals, were to be seen flying in all directions to catch a glimpse of the gentlemen who were apparently to bring peace so unexpectedly."

Slowly the carriage came through, jolting over the uneven ground. The cheering died down. Having yelled, the men seemed to be holding their breath in nervous anticipation. The Federal soldiers now saw something which they had never seen before, or dreamed of seeing—a large number of ladies, dressed in their frilly best, standing on the Confederate parapet.

The carriage stopped and the commissioners got out, tiny Stephens weighed down and made almost helpless with an enormous overcoat. The Confederates began to cheer again, and the three civilians walked across no man's land to the place where Grant had ambulances waiting for them. As they reached these a couple of soldiers helped Stephens climb in, and the Northern troops cheered. The ambulances drove away, and as they passed from sight a Confederate picket sprang out, turned to face his comrades, and proposed three cheers for the Yankee army. These were given, after which a Union man led his side in three cheers for the Confederates. When this shouting died down somebody proposed three cheers for the ladies of Petersburg and both sides joined in, and the ladies fluttered their handkerchiefs prettily.[24] Then the winter day ended, and the ladies went back to town, and the men climbed down from the parapets, and there was a quiet buzz of talk all up and down the lines. No soldier on either side seems to have asked what sort of peace terms were apt to come out of the conference. On this one afternoon, nobody was thinking of victory or defeat. It was enough to think that perhaps the war could end with no more killing.

For anti-climax, the conference came to nothing. One side insisted on an independent Confederacy and the other side insisted on a restored Union, and the conferees presently were reduced to nothing much more than an interchange of expressions of personal good will. It developed that Stephens's nephew, a Confederate officer, had for twenty months been a prisoner of war on Johnson's Island, in Sandusky Bay. Lincoln made a note of it, and a few days later that surprised young officer found himself called out of prison and sent down to Washington, where he was taken to the White House for a chat with President Lincoln; after which he was sent through the lines to Richmond. The Confederates returned the favor, picking at random a Union officer of the same rank, and so the 13th New Hampshire presently welcomed the return of its Lieutenant Murray, who was delighted and surprised by the whole business.

So the conference ended, and in the North the radicals reacted to it with bitter suspicion, shouting their fear that Lincoln was trying to revive "the old policy of tenderness toward the rebels." Congressman George W. Julian of Indiana, to whom, long ago, Burnside had confided that the real trouble with the Union soldiers was that they did not hate their enemies sufficiently, took the floor to warn that the sole purpose of the war now was subjugation, crying: "Both the people and our armies, under this new dispensation, have been learning how to hate Rebels as Christian patriots ought to have done from the beginning."

Lincoln meanwhile called a cabinet meeting and coolly proposed that the Federal government offer to the Southern states four hundred million dollars in six per cent government bonds, as compensation for the property values which would be destroyed by emancipation, on condition that the Southern states return to the Union within two months. The Cabinet was stunned and slightly indignant. In vain Lincoln pointed out that if the war lasted only another hundred days it would cost all of the money he was now proposing to spend. No one would agree that this was the way to get peace and reunion, and at last Lincoln put away the draft of his proposal, saying: "You are all opposed to me."

In Richmond, Davis addressed a patriotic rally, inviting all Southerners to "unite our hands and hearts" in the fond belief that before midsummer it would be the Yankees who would be crossing the lines to ask for terms. Stephens conceded that Davis made a brilliant speech, although he considered it "not much short of dementation," and when Davis asked what he proposed to do next the little Vice-President was blunt: "Go home and stay there." [25]

No peace, then, except by the sword, and the eerie light that had so briefly touched the winter sky faded out. It had been building up to this for four years, and here it was, visible and final: the war would end only when one side or the other had been pounded into helplessness, for men had passed beyond the point where they could negotiate or compromise. It was up to the soldiers, after all.

The soldiers were hopeful, but sober, for the war had worked on them. In the Petersburg trenches and camps, no one was ever heard to sing "Tenting Tonight," once the favorite campfire song: "That song is especially dedicated to the brave and stalwart homestayers." There was little horseplay, little joviality, few campfire jokes and pleasant yarns—not, as one man wrote, because men had grown discouraged, but simply because the wide range of a regiment's personal characteristic now "is narrowed to almost the definiteness of one special class: the steady and sober men." Yet there was little complaining, and very little self-pity: "The army laughs far more than it weeps." [26]

A Massachusetts gunner sat down and figured that in another 200 days his battery would reach the end of its enlistment and could go home, and he tried to write down what the rest of his term of service would amount to:

". . . only 200 more days of service, of which 33 are guard duty and the same of regular fatigue; three times mustered for pay—marching, fighting, perhaps; 2,000 hard tack, 75 pounds of pork, 125 pounds of beef to eat, 72 gallons of coffee to drink, part of it every day, and it will be done." [27]

2. Great Light in the Sky

Fort Stedman was a square box of a place, with solid walls enclosing a space for the guns. Inside the enclosure were sodded mounds over the dugouts in which the soldiers slept and kept their stores. In front and on each side were the spiky entanglements of the abatis, and to right and left were the trenches which tied Fort Stedman into the main line of Federal works facing Petersburg.

The fort had stood here for nine months, and there was nothing in particular to distinguish it from several dozen other forts in the Federal lines except that it was in bad repair. It was less than 200 yards from the Confederate works, and that was easy range even for average marksmen, and so when the fort's walls settled that winter the authorities did not order them rebuilt because the men who worked on them would probably be shot. Behind the fort there was higher ground from which one could look into the fort, and there was no abatis in the rear, and all in all Stedman was one of the weakest spots in the whole Federal line. That did not matter much, however, for it seemed very improbable that the Rebels would ever make an attack. The New York heavy artillery regiment which held this part of the line kept pickets out in front—they were almost within handshaking distance of the Rebel pickets, the lines here were so close—but as long as these men stayed awake and the works behind them were adequately manned the weakness of Fort Stedman seemed nothing to worry about.[1]

This was sensible enough, as good sense goes in wartime. But the old balances were falling, and suddenly now the war was going to go with a rush and a roar toward the final smashup, all of the tensions built up in nine months of strained equilibrium letting go in one comprehensive explosion. Fort Stedman had been built across the path of Fate,

375

and its imperfect walls enclosed the spot from which a man who looked sharply might see the beginning of the end.

It was four in the morning of March 25, 1865, black and still as polar midnight, with never a sound from the picket lines. Half a mile north of Stedman was another Union strong point, Fort McGilvery, and a sergeant in this fort peered off to the south, listened intently, and then went to rouse his commanding officer: "Captain, there is some disturbance on our left in the direction of Fort Stedman, but I can't make out what it is." The captain went to have a look, and the men could see a few pin-pricks of flame, and then they could hear scattered musket fire. Then they saw one of Stedman's cannon fired—not in front, toward the Rebel army, but off toward the rear.[2]

Several hundred yards south of Fort Stedman a Catholic chaplain had been saying predawn mass for sixty-odd communicants in Union Fort Haskell. He heard rifle firing, and the boom of cannon, and he got through the service as soon as he decently could, after which the worshipers took their weapons and ran to the parapets. And then there was a rising swell of firing, and the sound of men shouting, and there was a flashing of heavy guns in the Confederate lines —and Rebel infantry was past Fort Stedman, running out to seize Union trenches and batteries to right and left, and an assaulting column was swinging around to attack Fort Haskell while other troops were forming for a drive straight through to the Union rear.[3]

This part of the line belonged to the IX Corps. Burnside had gone home long since, the attack on the crater having been his final contribution, and the corps was in command of his former chief of staff, a pleasant-faced, competent general named John G. Parke. Parke was asleep at corps headquarters, well to the rear, when the fighting began. When he was roused and learned that he had a fight on his hands he also was told that Meade was temporarily absent and that, by seniority, he himself was in command of the Army of the Potomac. He notified the other commands that the Rebels were attacking, and got troops moving toward the danger area. Also, he brought up his own third division which had been in reserve and sent it in to mend the break.

This division was made up of six new Pennsylvania regiments, which had enlisted just before Christmas and were still under training. They seem to have contained good men —not all of the recruits were worthless bounty-jumpers and substitutes—and they were commanded by a first-rate soldier, General John Hartranft, who as a colonel had led the successful attack on Burnside's bridge at Antietam Creek in one of the battles of the long ago. Hartranft took his men forward, and Federal artillery began to open a heavy bombardment as soon as dawn brought enough light to make targets visible.

The 200th Pennsylvania charged in against the Confederate advance, wrecking itself but blunting the spearhead of the Southern charge and forcing it to a halt. The garrison of Fort Haskell beat off the column that was attacking there, and in Fort McGilvery men hoisted cannon over the embankments by hand so that they could fire on the high ground behind Stedman. Hartranft got a solid battle line strung out across the open country to the rear—and before long it was clear that the crisis was over. The Confederates had punched a clean hole in the Union line but they could not widen the hole enough to mount a new attack that would break the secondary defenses, and by eight o'clock Lee sounded the recall.[4]

Many of the Confederates never returned to their own lines. Yankee artillery was laying a heavy fire on the ground they had charged across and to retreat was as dangerous as to advance, and when Parke finally sent the Pennsylvanians smashing forward to recover Fort Stedman and the lost trenches and batteries hundreds of Confederates surrendered. In the end the attack cost Lee's army 4,000 men—twice the total of Union casualties—and the lines were as they had been before.

Meade got back from City Point just as the fighting died down, and he reasoned that Lee must have weakened his forces elsewhere to make this attack. He ordered the II

Corps and the VI Corps, accordingly, to attack the entrenched Rebel picket lines in their front. They did so, seizing the lines, taking hundreds of prisoners, and gaining excellent positions from which to assault the main Southern defenses if that should ever seem advisable.[5]

The grimy Federals who cleared the recaptured trenches, sent wounded men and prisoners to the rear, and put the burial squads to work had had a bigger day than they could realize. They had beaten off the last great offensive thrust of the Army of Northern Virginia.

That army had struck at its Yankee antagonists many times—at Gaines's Mill and at Bull Run, at Chancellorsville and at Gettysburg, and on many other fields, and always it struck with terrible power, tough soldiers running forward under the shrill yip-yip of the Rebel yell, red battle flags sparkling above flashing muskets, cold fury of battle lighting the eyes of the gray warrior who directed the blows. It would never happen again. It was a new war now, and the end was coming.

In the afternoon there were visitors on the battlefield—Abraham Lincoln and U. S. Grant, coming up by rattletrap military train from City Point, Meade and his staff officers going to meet them. Lincoln walked over the field, saw wounded men not yet removed to hospital, and dead men for whom graves were not yet ready. Grant had seen this many times and on many dreadful fields and Lincoln had never seen it at all except for a little at Fort Stevens; and these two men who were so very different were much alike in that neither one was ever able to forget the human cost of glorious victories, or his own responsibility for that cost. An army surgeon told how Lincoln once visited a hospital in Washington and afterward stopped to chat with the doctors. One of these was telling about a difficult operation just performed, in which a wounded soldier's arm had been removed at the shoulder joint, and he went into much technical detail, the other doctors listening intently. At last, as he finished, and the others were asking this and that about the operation, Lincoln burst out with the one question that interested him, the one question which no doctor had thought to ask: "But how about the soldier?" [6] Neither Lincoln nor Grant, who remorselessly held the country up to month after month of wholesale killing, ever got far away from that question.

Back to City Point went Lincoln and Grant, to talk by headquarters campfires, their shadows falling longer and darker over the dwindling borders of a fading Confederacy. Presently there came to join them another man who also cast a long and portentous shadow, a lean and wiry man with unruly red hair and a short stubble of a close-cropped beard, dancing lights in the alert eyes that peered out of a hard face—William Tecumseh Sherman, who had made his name terrible to the South, here now for a last conference before returning to the tough, devil-may-care army which he had left in the pine hills of North Carolina.

In a sense, Sherman was responsible for the attack on Fort Stedman. What remained of the Southern Confederacy was the ground that lay between his army and Grant's, and its doom was absolutely certain if he continued his relentless advance until the two armies made contact. If Lee could break away, get south fast, pick up the inadequate army with which Joe Johnston was opposing Sherman, beat Sherman by a quick, hard blow, and then turn to deal with Grant—if all of that could be done, then the Confederacy might survive. The blow at Fort Stedman had been an attempt to knock the Army of the Potomac back on its heels and cripple it just long enough to give Lee the start he would need on a move to the south.

The odds against the success of any such program were fantastically long, and both Lee and Grant knew it. But they also knew one other fact—that the people of the North were weary of the war with a deep, numb, instinctive weariness, so that one more major disappointment might be too much for them. Whether or not he could beat Sherman, Lee might at least prolong the war for six months if he could get away from Grant, and if he could do that there was a fair chance that the North would give up the struggle.

So Grant figured it, at any rate. [7] Lee may have reasoned

in the same way, or he may have followed nothing more subtle than the born fighter's refusal to quit as long as he can stay on his feet and lift his fists waist high. In any case he was going to play out the string, and if the Northern generals did not watch him very carefully the triumph which was so near might drift off into nothingness like battle smoke blown down the wind. So Lincoln, Grant, and Sherman were taking counsel, in the armies' nerve center at City Point.

Yet they had not met just to discuss means of insuring victory. They had held the war firmly in their hands for nearly a year now; a few more weeks of vigilance and driving energy and it would all be over. They were thinking not so much about the ending of the war as about the new beginning that must lie beyond that. They were almost incredibly different, these three—Sherman quick, nervous, and volatile, Grant stolid and unemotional and relentless, Lincoln ranging far beyond them with brooding insights, his profound melancholy touched by mystic inexplicable flashes of light—but each held the faith that the whole country, North and South together, must ultimately find in reunion and freedom the values that would justify four terrible years of war.

The discovery of those values would by no means be automatic. Much hatred and bitterness existed, and there could easily develop a program of revenge and reprisal that would make real reunion forever impossible. There was talk of hangings and of proscription lists and of conquered provinces. There were powerful leaders in the North who meant to see these threats carried out in all their literal grimness, and it was not in the least certain that they could be kept from having their way. So the principal order of business for the President and the two generals was not so much to checkmate the Confederacy as to checkmate the men who would try to make peace with malice and rancor and a length of noosed rope.

When the Southern armies surrendered the two generals would be the ones to say what the terms of surrender must be, and they would take their cue from Lincoln. If the terms expressed simple human decency and friendship, it might be that a peace of reconciliation could get just enough of a lead so that the haters could never quite catch up with it. On all of this Lincoln and Grant and Sherman agreed.

It was a curious business, in a way. The Confederacy had no more effective foes than these men. Lincoln had led the North into war, had held it firmly to its task, and had refused to hear any talk of peace that was not based on the extinction of the Confederate Government. Grant seemed to be the very incarnation of the remorseless killer, and Sherman was destruction's own self, his trail across the South a band of ruin sixty miles wide. Yet it was these three who were most determined that vindictiveness and hatred must not control the future. They would fight without mercy as long as there must be fighting, but when the fighting stopped they would try to turn old enemies into friends.

They spoke for the soldiers. The Northern and Southern armies had less bitterness now than they had had when the war began. On every picket line the cry "Down Yank!" and "Down Reb!" always preceded an outburst of firing. A veteran in the V Corps spoke for the rank and file when he said that the opposing troops in front of Fort Hell "decided that we would respect one another, as the lines at this point were very close and to keep up constant firing would make it very uncomfortable for one or the other." [8] These were the men who climbed on the ramparts to give three cheers for peace, and then gave three cheers for each other, and then returned to their fighting, and they did not need to be told that it would be well to make peace mean comradeship. All they needed was to see somebody try it.

So Lincoln and Grant and Sherman had their talk and agreed that it must be tried, and at one point there was a faint, ironic echo from the days of McClellan, forever critical of Washington. This came when Lincoln abruptly asked Sherman:

"Sherman, do you know why I took a shine to Grant and you?"

Sherman confessed that he did not know, and he added

that he had received from the President kindness beyond his due.

"Well," said Lincoln, "you never found fault with me." [9]

Back to North Carolina and his restless, destructive army went Sherman, and as he went out Sheridan's cavalry came in, Phil Sheridan at its head, and the Army of the Potomac was ready to begin its last campaign.

Sheridan and his cavalry had wintered near Winchester, and as February ended they moved up the Valley to Staunton, two divisions of veteran mounted troops, 9,400 officers and men. The weather was vile, rain on the mountains and slush on the roads, every little stream over its banks, mud on everything, the burnt-out region looking more Godforsaken than ever. At Staunton, Sheridan learned that Early and a pitiful remnant of an army were entrenched on a knoll near Waynesboro, by the western entrance to Rockfish Gap, and he rode over there to get them. His men came into Waynesboro through a two-day rain, men and horses all dripping and plastered with mud, and Sheridan sent Custer's division up to obliterate the last Confederate force in the Shenandoah Valley.

Custer dismounted most of his men and attacked Early's flanks with carbines sputtering, and then he took the 8th New York and 1st Connecticut and drove them straight in on the middle of the line, charging in a galloping column of fours, bugles sounding in the raw March air. Straight over the breastworks went the mounted squadrons, and the flankers broke in the ends of Early's line, and all resistance collapsed, while the mounted men rode hard through the town of Waynesboro, sabering fugitives on the streets. Early and some of his officers and the merest handful of men hid out in friendly houses and escaped. When the fighting ended Sheridan counted 1,600 prisoners, 11 guns, 200 loaded wagons, and nearly a score of battle flags. [10]

Prisoners, guns, and wagons he sent back down the Valley, with a mounted brigade for escort. The battle flags he took with him, and as he rode into the Petersburg lines his band of scouts came cantering at his heels proudly bearing

these trophies[11]—and if the North wanted a soldier who
knew how to wear a conqueror's pride, perhaps Sheridan was
the man for it. The Valley was dead, and Lee's army was
half immobilized because the forage for cavalry and artillery
horses that used to come from there was no longer available.
Grant pulled the cavalry around to the extreme left of the
long Union line and made ready to destroy the Army of
Northern Virginia.

As always, that army was dangerous. Month after month it
had been perfecting its defenses—raising parapets, digging
deep ditches, mounting new guns and mortars, building
double and triple lines of abatis, tying everything together
with a crisscross of support and approach trenches—and
when these lines were properly manned it was quite impossible to carry them by assault. But Lee had come to the end
of his resources, and his lines were stretched to the very
limit. His right flank rested along the marshy banks of a little
stream called Hatcher's Run, eight or nine miles southwest
of Petersburg in an air line, substantially farther by road.
Grant's plan now was to send a strong force prowling around
that flank. The chance was good that this would either induce
Lee to pull his army out in the open for a finish fight—which
Grant had vainly been trying to bring about for ten months—
or compel him to stretch his thin line until it snapped.

There remained to the Confederates in Petersburg one
vital railway line—the Southside Railroad, which ran west
from Petersburg to Lynchburg, crossing the Richmond and
Danville line at the junction town of Burkeville, fifty miles
west of Petersburg. The Petersburg end of this line ran only
a few miles in rear of Lee's outposts at Hatcher's Run, and
a blow past the flank which broke the Southside Railroad
would break Lee's principal supply line and force him to
retreat.

Obviously, therefore, Grant's best move was to extend his
left flank once more—a repetition of the move that had been
made so many times since the army crossed the Rapidan.
In preparation, Grant was shifting men about even before
Sherman got to City Point.

In the Bermuda Hundred lines and directly before Richmond was the Army of the James, now under General Ord. This army was composed of two infantry corps, one containing three divisions of white troops and the other, three divisions of colored troops. Unnoticed by the Confederates Ord quietly took two white divisions and one colored division out of the trenches one evening and led them down to Petersburg on a grueling thirty-six-mile hike.

To occupy the lines facing Petersburg, Grant detailed Ord's three divisions plus the IX Corps and the VI Corps. For a movable force to menace Lee's flank he thus had two full army corps—Humphreys and the II Corps and Warren and the V Corps. He also had three superb divisions of cavalry under Sheridan, and from the moment he began to plan this move he seems to have concluded that the operation as a whole would be pretty largely under Sheridan's command.

He would start by sending Sheridan and the cavalry to the little hamlet of Dinwiddie Court House, half a dozen miles south and slightly west of the Hatcher's Run area. While Sheridan made this move Humphreys and Warren were to take their men up through the flat, wooded country closer to Hatcher's Run. They were not supposed to attack Confederate trenches there, but their presence might induce Lee to make a new extension of his line. At the very least it would cover Sheridan—who, from Dinwiddie Court House, could march northwest ten or twelve miles and strike the Southside Railroad. After that Sheridan might go on and break the Richmond and Danville road as well, and in the end he might even go down cross country and join Sherman. Plans were fluid. The chief idea was to shake things loose and end the long deadlock.[12]

It was March 29, at last, three o'clock of a clammy damp morning, with low clouds blotting out the stars, and behind the Union lines the grim columns began to move. Many times since they reached Petersburg different parts of the army had marched toward the left, and each time the result had been, if not an actual rebuff, nothing more exciting than a mere extension of the Union lines. But now men seemed to feel that the last act was beginning. Lincoln had been at City Point (was still there, as a matter of fact, to wait for news) and Sherman had been there, and Sheridan had come down from the Valley, and spring was in the air—and, altogether, perhaps this was it. A general in the V Corps wrote that men felt it so, and he said that as they took to the road it was almost as if, overhead, they saw "a great light filling the sky." [13]

Yet there were skeptics. A private in the 11th Pennsylvania wrote that "there was nothing borne on the wings of the wind" to hint that this move was going to be any different than all the earlier ones had been. "Four years of war," he said, "while it made the men brave and valorous, had entirely cured them of imagining that each campaign would be the last." Many times in the past high hopes had been disappointed. This morning as they moved out of winter quarters a soldier raised the butt of his musket to knock down the stick-and-clay chimney of one of the shacks. A contraband serving as company cook begged him not to destroy it: "We'll be back ag'in in a week, and I'll want to use it." [14]

The infantry reached their designated position, and had a sharp little fight with Confederate infantry which came down to see what the Yankees were up to. Farther west and south, Sheridan pushed Rebel skirmishers out of the way and put his men in bivouac near Dinwiddie, making his headquarters in a big frame tavern opposite the courthouse building. As evening came down it brought rain, the rain continued all night long, and there was no letup with the dawn. All of the country around Hatcher's Run and Dinwiddie Court House was low, covered with second-growth timber and seamed by many little brooks and creeks, and by noon of March 30 the whole area was a swamp. Sheridan put Custer's entire division to work corduroying the roads in rear of his position, the roads having become all but totally impassable for wagons and guns. A trooper remembered spending an atrocious night "with rations all soaked and blankets all wet, and spongy beds under leaking shelters." [15]

The rain refused to stop. Grant moved headquarters from City Point out to a waterlogged field near Gravelly Run, toward the left end of the line, and he remembered that the ground was so soggy that a horse or mule, standing quite motionless, would suddenly begin to sink out of sight and would have to be pulled out by a squad of soldiers. Men asked each other when the gunboats were going to come up and suggested that what the army needed now was Noah rather than Grant. The top echelons in the Army of the Potomac, remembering an occasion near Fredericksburg when the army had got hopelessly stuck in the mud, urged Grant to call everything off, get everybody back to camp, and start again a week or two later when the ground was drier. Grant himself seems to have wavered, for a time. First he told Sheridan to forget about the railroads and smash straight for Lee's flank and rear; then he sent another message suggesting that all forward movement be suspended until the weather improved.[16]

When he got this last letter Sheridan rode over to Grant's headquarters. The rain was still coming down and the mud was so deep that even Sheridan's horse could manage nothing better than a walk, sinking to his knees at every step, but Sheridan was all for action. To Grant's staff he expounded on the iniquity of delay—now was the time to move, Rebel cavalry could be knocked out of the way any time the commanding general pleased, and if Lee sent infantry out he was writing his own doom. Sheridan tramped back and forth in the mud and rain, striking his hands together. An officer asked how he would get forage for his 13,000 horses if the roads remained impassable.

"Forage?" echoed Sheridan. "I'll get all the forage I want. I'll haul it out if I have to set every man in the command to corduroying roads, and corduroy every mile of them from the railroad to Dinwiddie. I tell you I'm ready to strike out tomorrow and go to smashing things."

Staff suggested that Grant liked to hear that sort of talk, partly because it was so different from anything he ever got from top generals in the Army of the Potomac, and urged

Sheridan to go speak his piece to the lieutenant general. Sheridan demurred: Grant hadn't asked him to come over, he was just sounding off to relieve his mind. A staff officer, however, slipped into Grant's tent and suggested that it would be good for him to talk to his cavalry commander, and in another moment Sheridan was repeating his little speech to Grant, strongly backed by impetuous Chief of Staff John Rawlins, with his pale cheeks and feverish burning eyes.

Grant made up his mind: the move would go on, bad roads or no bad roads, and it would not stop until there had been a final showdown. Long afterward he confessed that he believed the country to be so desperately tired of the war that unless the move to the left was a complete victory it would be interpreted as a disastrous failure.[17]

On March 31, therefore, with rain still falling and the country looking like the bottom of a millpond, the advance was resumed. Sheridan still had Custer's division at work behind Dinwiddie, fixing the bottomless road so that forage and provisions could be brought in, and he was holding most of a second division at Dinwiddie; and he sent the rest of the men marching north, and at a lonely country crossroads known as Five Forks they ran into the Rebels in strength.

Five Forks was nowhere at all, but it was important because it was where the road from Dinwiddie Court House to the Southside Railroad crossed the east-and-west road that led to Lee's right flank and rear. Lee's army could not stay in Petersburg if the Yankees held this crossroads, and so Lee had scraped his last reserves to make a fight for the place. Dug in behind temporary breastworks were five brigades of infantry under the legendary George Pickett. With the infantry was practically all of Lee's cavalry.

Up against this powerful force came one division of Yankee cavalry led by General Thomas C. Devin, a former New York militia colonel who had become enough of a soldier to suit the most exacting of Regulars. He had been a favorite of tough John Buford in the old Gettysburg days, and nowadays he was dubbed "Sheridan's hard hitter"—which, considering the general reputation of Sheridan's cavalry, was a fairly substantial compliment. This day he had his hands full. When his patrols reported Rebel infantry at Five Forks he dismounted his division and got ready to fight on foot. Pickett immediately obliged him, rolling forward a heavier battle line than Devin's men could handle, and before long the blue cavalry was in full retreat.

The Federals fought hard, withdrawing as slowly as they could manage and maintaining a steady fire, but they were heavily outnumbered and Confederate cavalry kept curling in around both flanks, and presently Devin had to warn Sheridan that he was badly overmatched and that they might have trouble holding Dinwiddie itself. He kept his fighting line dismounted because the men could put up a more stubborn resistance that way, and as they fought the area immediately behind the firing line was a howling madhouse.

All of the division's horses were here, four thousand and odd of them, one trooper to every four horses. The country was densely wooded, with few roads and many rail fences, and the air was full of smoke and bullets and shouting men, and the conditions under which one mounted man could easily lead three riderless horses did not exist. The horses became panicky and fractious, and they kept running on the wrong side of trees, or colliding with each other, creating fearful tangles of kicking, plunging animals and snarled reins and cursing soldiers—and, said one of the men afterward, the whole business was enough to make anybody understand why an exceptionally profane man was always said to swear like a trooper.[18]

While Devin's men gave ground Sheridan got the rest of his men strung out in line in front of Dinwiddie Court House, and at dusk the Confederates came storming up to drive the whole lot of Yankee cavalry back where it belonged. When Devin's men came in Sheridan put them into line with the rest, and he rolled forward all the guns he could lay his hands on. Then he rounded up all of the regimental bands and put them up on the firing line and ordered them to play the gayest tunes they knew—play them loud and keep on playing them, and never mind if a bullet goes through a trombone, or even a trombonist, now and then.

The late afternoon sun broke through the clouds, and all of these bands were playing, and there was a clatter of musketry and a booming of cannon and a floating loom of battle smoke. Sheridan got his little battle flag with the two stars on it and rode out in front of his lines, going from one end to the other at a full gallop, waving his hat and telling every last soldier—by his presence, by his gestures, and by the hard look in his black eyes—that nobody was going to make them retreat another step.

They held the line. At dusk Sheridan tried a counterattack, ordering Custer to make a mounted charge on a line of Rebel infantry. A man who saw him giving Custer his orders remembered Sheridan's emphasis: "You understand? I want you to *give* it to them!" Custer nodded, and he drove his squadrons forward—to a muddy anticlimax. The field across which the men tried to charge was so soupy with wet clay and rain water that the horses immediately bogged down, the charge came to nothing, and at last it was dark, with the Federals holding the town and the Confederates facing them just out of musket range.[19]

It looked like trouble, for these venturesome Confederates had more men than Sheridan had and they were well behind the left end of the main Union line. But Sheridan saw it as opportunity; it was Pickett's force and not his that was in trouble, the Rebels were isolated and they could be cut off, and if the business were handled right none of them should ever get back to Lee's army. Off through the night to Grant went Sheridan's couriers with the message: "Let me have the old VI Corps once more and I can really smash things."

The VI Corps Sheridan could not have, because it was too far off and with the roads as they were it would take two days to get it to him. Warren and the V Corps were available, however, no more than half a dozen miles away, and late that evening Warren was ordered to get his men over to Dinwiddie at top speed. Sheridan was told that they would show up at dawn, and they would be coming in from the northeast, behind Pickett's flank. Warren had much more infantry than Pickett had, and Sheridan had much more cavalry. Between the two of them they might be able to destroy his entire force.[20] Lee was so pinched for manpower that a loss of such dimensions would practically bankrupt him.

So Sheridan put his men into bivouac and waited impatiently for the morning. It was a restless night, since every square foot of open space behind the line was jammed with led horses and their grouchy caretakers, and it was an all-night job to get all of these straightened out so that the squadrons could be mounted next day if necessary. Trains of pack mules came up, bringing forage and rations, and the ambulances had got through—that work on the roads had been effective—and lanterns twinkled in the damp groves as stretcher parties went through, gathering up the wounded men.[21]

It was the last day of March 1865, and the Army of the Potomac had just nine more days of campaigning ahead of it.

3. The Soldiers Saw Daylight

Major General Gouverneur Kemble Warren and his V Army Corps had been having a bad day. The corps had been in position, wet and uncomfortable, a little west of Hatcher's Run, presumably a trifle south of the extreme right flank of Lee's main line, and during the morning—while Devin's troopers were meeting Rebel infantry in front of Five Forks and were beginning their difficult withdrawal to Dinwiddie Court House—Warren sent one division forward to make a reconnoissance and find out just where the Rebels might be.

By ill chance this division began to advance just when Lee ordered a force of his own to move forward and pick a fight with the Yankees in order to protect the move which Pickett was making a few miles farther west. This force caught the

Federal infantry division off guard and piled into it with savage vigor, and the Federals were driven back in disorder. In their retreat they ran through the bivouac of the second of Warren's three infantry divisions, and these troops were all gathered around smoky campfires trying to dry their clothing and their blankets, no one having alerted them to the fact that there might be action. So this second division was routed, too, and Warren had to send in his third division and call for help from the II Corps, over on his right, in order to restore the situation.

By evening he had won back the ground that had been lost, but his men had had a hard all-day fight, with painful losses; and now, just as they were collecting their wounded and trying to get snug for the night, there came these orders to make a forced march over to join Sheridan.[1]

It was a foul night to move troops. It was so dark, as one soldier said, that it was literally impossible to see a hand before one's face. The rain had stopped, but the roads were deep with mud, every little creek had overflowed, and there was a completely unfordable stream flowing straight across the principal highway that the troops had to use. Warren's engineers tore down a house and used the timbers to build a bridge, but construction work at midnight with everybody exhausted was slow work.

Warren had received conflicting orders about the routes he was to take, so that there was a good deal of wearing counter-marching for some units, and there was much confusion about maps and place names. Also, at the time he got his marching orders Warren's skirmish line was in contact with the enemy, and he felt that he should use much caution in getting his men away. Some regiments started on time, but most of them did not, nothing that could conceivably go wrong went right, and by five in the morning—the hour at which it had been hoped that the whole corps would be taking position at Dinwiddie Court House—two of his divisions were just beginning to move.[2]

Sheridan was furious. He met the head of the infantry column in a gray dawn as the men came splashing up to the rendezvous, and he demanded of the brigadier commanding: "Where's Warren?" The brigadier explained that Warren was back with the rear of the column, and Sheridan growled: "That's where I expected to find him. What's he doing there?" The officer tried to explain that Warren was trying to make sure that his men could break contact with the Confederates without drawing an attack, but Sheridan was not appeased. Later, when Warren arrived, the two generals were seen tramping up and down by the roadside, Sheridan dark and tense, stamping angrily in the mud, Warren pale and tight-lipped, apparently trying to control himself.[3]

Wherever the fault lay, the early-morning attack that had been planned could not be made. It was noon before the V Corps was assembled, and by that time the Confederates were gone. During the night Pickett had got wind of the Yankee move, and around daybreak he took his entire force back to the breastworks at Five Forks.

These works ran for a mile or more along the edge of the White Oak Road, and they faced toward the south. At their eastern end, for flank protection, the line made nearly a right-angle turn and ran north for a few hundred yards. With his men in and behind these works, and cavalry patrolling both flanks, Pickett seems to have taken it for granted that he was safe from assault for the rest of the day. With a few other ranking officers he retired to a campfire some distance in the rear to enjoy the pleasures of a shad bake.

As far as Sheridan was concerned, however, Pickett was in as much danger as he had been in before. There was still a wide gap between his force and the rest of Lee's army, with only the thinnest chain of cavalry vedettes to maintain contact, and in that gap Sheridan could see a dazzling opportunity. He had his cavalry maintaining pressure along Pickett's front, and he had a whole mounted division waiting in reserve, ready to go slashing in around the Confederate right at the proper time. If, while the cavalry held the Southerners' attention, he could drive 16,000 good infantrymen into the open gap and bring their entire weight to bear on Pickett's left flank, just where the Rebel breastworks angled back toward the north, the war would be a good deal nearer its close by nightfall.

The 16,000 good infantrymen were at hand, and a comparatively short walk would put them into position. They were dog-tired. They had fought all of the day before, and they had spent practically all of the night and morning on the march, and while Sheridan and Warren discussed battle plans they were catching forty winks in some fields near a little country church. When Warren at last came over to move them up to the jump-off line they were sluggish, and getting them formed was slow work, and it seemed to Sheridan —watching the afternoon sun get lower in the sky, and reflecting that the whole situation might be very different by tomorrow morning—that Warren was not doing much to make things go faster.[4] But the men would fight well when the time came, because they considered themselves a crack outfit and they had a great tradition.

The V Corps was one of the famous units of the whole Federal Army. Fitz-John Porter had commanded it, and it had been McClellan's favorite corps, and in general orders he had held it up as a model for the other corps to emulate, which caused jealousies that had not entirely worn away even yet. (It caused War Department suspicions, too, and promotion for higher officers in this corps was harder to get, it was said, than in the rest of the Army of the Potomac.) The corps had been built around a famous division of Regulars, and in the beginning all of its ranking officers had been Regulars, mostly of the stiff, old-army, knock-'em-dead variety. Its discipline tended to be severe, there was strict observance of military formalities, and the Regular Army flavor endured, even though many of the old officers and all of the Regular battalions had disappeared.[5]

This was the corps which Sheridan now was preparing to use as his striking force. When Grant first sent the corps out to operate on Lee's flank, he did two curious things. He detached it from Meade's command and put it entirely under Sheridan, promising to do the same with the II Corps if Sheridan needed it—which was a bit odd, considering that

Sheridan was simply the cavalry commander, while Meade commanded the Army of the Potomac—and he specifically authorized Sheridan to relieve Warren of his command, if it seemed necessary, and to put someone else in his place.[6]

Grant's subsequent explanation of these acts was brief and vague, but what he was actually trying to do was to find a solution for the old, baffling command problem that had beset the Army of the Potomac from its earliest days.

Time and again the Army of the Potomac had missed a victory because someone did not move quite fast enough, or failed to put all of his weight into a blow, or came into action other than precisely as he was expected to do. This had happened before Grant became general in chief and it had happened since then, and the fact that Warren had been involved in a few such incidents was not especially important. What Grant was really shooting at was the sluggishness and caution that were forever cropping out, at some critical moment, somewhere in the army's chain of command. With the decisive moment of the war coming up Grant was going to have no more of that. Instinctively, he was turning to Sheridan, Sheridan the driver—giving him as much of the army as he needed and in effect telling him to take it and be tough with it.

Sheridan was the man for it. As Warren's brigades struggled into position Sheridan was everywhere, needling the laggards, pricking the general officers on, sending his staff galloping from end to end of the line. He rounded up the cavalry bands, which had made music on the firing line the evening before, and he put them on horseback with orders to go into action along with the fighting men when the advance sounded. It was four o'clock by now, and there would not be a great deal more daylight, and at last the infantry began to move. Sheridan spurred away to send the cavalry forward too. There was the peal of many bugles and then a great crash of musketry, and thousands of men broke into a cheer, and the battle was on.

A skirmisher trotting forward a few hundred yards ahead of the V Corps turned once to look back, and he saw what neither he nor any of his mates had seen in a dreary year of wilderness fighting and trench warfare, and he remembered it as the most stirring thing he had ever looked upon in all of his life. There they were, coming up behind him as if all the power of a nation had been put into one disciplined mass —the fighting men of the V Corps, walking forward in battle lines that were a mile wide and many ranks deep, sunlight glinting on thousands of bright muskets, flags snapping in the breeze, brigade fronts taut with parade-ground Regular Army precision, everybody keeping step, tramping forward into battle to the sound of gunfire and distant music. To see this, wrote the skirmisher, was to see and to know "the grandeur and the sublimity of war." [7]

It was grand and inspiring—and, unfortunately, there was a hitch in it.

Warren was sending his men in with two divisions abreast and a third division following in support, and by some mischance he was hitting the White Oak Road far to the east of the place where he was supposed to hit it. Instead of coming in on the knuckle of Pickett's line, he was coming in on nothing at all. His men were marching resolutely toward the north and the battle was going on somewhere to the west, out of their sight and reach.

The left division in the first line was commanded by General Ayres, a hard-bitten survivor of the original old-army set of officers, and the left of his division brushed against the left flank of Pickett's force and came under a sharp fire. Ayres spun the whole division around, brigade by brigade, making almost a 90-degree turn to the left—hot enough work it was, too, with Rebel infantry and cavalry firing steadily and the ground all broken—and as he turned the rest of the corps lost contact with him. The division that had been advancing beside him was led by General Crawford, who fell a good deal short of being one of the most skillful soldiers in the army, and Crawford kept marching to the north, getting farther away from the battle every minute. Most of the third division followed Crawford, Ayres's men were for the moment so entangled in their maneuver that they could not do much fighting—and, in sum, instead of crunching in on the Rebel flank with overpowering force, the V Corps was hardly doing more than giving it a brisk nudge.[8]

A confusing long-range fire, heavy enough to hurt, kept coming in from the left, and smoke fog was drifting through woods and fields. Warren had gone riding frantically on to try to find Crawford and set him straight, and entire brigades had lost touch with their corps and division commanders. One of these, presently, got into action, led by one of the most remarkable soldiers in the army, the hawk-nosed theologian turned general, Joshua Chamberlain of Maine.

Before the war Chamberlain had done nothing more militant than teach courses in natural and revealed religion, and later on in romance languages, at Bowdoin College. In 1862 he had been given a two-year leave of absence to study in Europe. Instead of going to Europe he had joined the army, and in a short time he showed up at Gettysburg as colonel of the 20th Maine Infantry, winning the Congressional Medal of Honor for his defense of Little Round Top. Since then he had been several times wounded—he had an arm in a sling today, as a matter of fact, from a wound received twenty-four hours earlier in the fight near Hatcher's Run—and he had twice won brevet promotions for bravery under fire. It was occurring to him now that since bullets were coming from the left there must be Confederates over that way, so he took his brigade over to do something about it.

Beyond a gully, Chamberlain could at last see a Confederate line of battle. He got his brigade into line, took it down into the little ravine, came out on the far side, and headed for the enemy. The fire was hot, now—and here, in the thickest of it, came Sheridan, riding up at top speed as always, his mounted color-bearer riding behind him. Sheridan pulled up facing Chamberlain, his dark face glowing.

"By God, that's what I want to see! General officers at the front!" cried Sheridan. He asked where Warren and the rest of the corps might be, and Chamberlain gestured toward the north, trying to explain what had happened. Sheridan interrupted, saying that Chamberlain was to take command of everybody he saw in the immediate vicinity and press the attack—and then Sheridan rode off fast, looking for Warren and the missing infantry.[9]

All along the breastworks on the White Oak Road dismounted Yankee cavalrymen were attacking—looking, as a man who watched them said, with their tightly fitting uniforms, natty jackets, and short carbines, as if they had been especially designed for crawling through knotholes. Many of the carbines were repeaters, and at close range the troopers had terrific fire power, and a deafening racket went up from the narrow aisle in the woods. Around the angle Ayres's division and Chamberlain's brigade and fragments of other commands were still in some confusion, but they were beginning to get it straightened out now, and they were hitting the Confederates from flank and rear. Far to the north, the troops that had gone off at a tangent were at last being wheeled around so that they could cut across the Confederates' rear.[10]

Sheridan was all over the field. When a skirmish line met a severe fire, wavered, and seemed ready to fall back, up came Sheridan at a gallop, shouting to the men: "Come on—go at 'em—move on with a clean jump or you'll not catch one of 'em! They're all getting ready to run now, and if you don't get on to them in five minutes they'll every one get away from you!" An infantryman at his side was struck in the throat and fell, blood flowing as if his jugular vein had been cut. "You're not hurt a bit!" cried Sheridan. "Pick up your gun, man, and move right on!" The soldier looked up at him, then obediently took his musket, got to his feet, and staggered forward—to drop dead after half a dozen steps. Chamberlain came up to Sheridan once and begged him not to expose himself on the front line, promising that the rest of them would press the attack. Sheridan tossed his head with a grin which, Chamberlain felt, "seemed to say that he didn't care much for himself, or perhaps for me," and promised to go to the rear—and then dashed off to a sector where the fire was even hotter.

Finally the line was formed as Sheridan wanted it. In a boggy woodland, heavy smoke clouding the last of the sun-

light, Sheridan looked down the shifting mass of soldiers,
turned in the saddle, and called: "Where's my battle flag?"
Up came his color-bearer. Sheridan took the flag from him,
raised it high over his head, and went trotting along the
front. The line surged forward and got up to the Rebel
works, Sheridan put his horse over the breastworks, and the
infantry went over in a riot of yelling jubilant men—and the
Rebel flank was broken once and for all, and the men of the
V Corps fought their way down the length of Pickett's battle
line taking prisoners by the score and the hundred.[11]

By this time Warren had Crawford's errant division far
around to the Rebel rear, rounding up fugitives and cutting
off the line of retreat, and Warren sent his chief of staff over
to tell Sheridan about it. This officer found Sheridan on the
battlefield and trotted up proudly. But the great fury of battle
was on Sheridan. Warren's corps had been late getting to
Dinwiddie and it had been late getting into position at Five
Forks, and when it attacked two thirds of it had gone astray
and Warren had gone with it; Sheridan did not in the least
care whether the reasons for all of this were good or bad, and
he did not want to receive any more reports from General
Warren.

"By God, sir, tell General Warren he wasn't in that fight!"
he shouted. The chief of staff was dumfounded. Warren had
been doing his best, no one in the Army of the Potomac ever
spoke that way about a distinguished corps commander—but
Sheridan was clearly implacable, his face black, his eyes
flashing. The officer managed to say at last that he disliked to
deliver such a message verbally—might he take it down in
writing?

"Take it down, sir!" barked Sheridan. "Tell him by God he
was not at the front!"

Warren's man rode away, stunned. The next to come up
was General Griffin, ranking division commander in the V
Corps—Regular Army to his fingertips, rough and tough and
gifted with a certain magnetism—a man, in fact, cut somewhat after the Sheridan pattern. Bluntly, Sheridan hailed him
and told him that he was now in command of the V Corps.

Then he sent a courier to find Warren and deliver a written message relieving him of his command and ordering him to report to General Grant at headquarters.[12]

Pickett's force was wholly wrecked, by now, with the front broken in and victorious Yankees charging in from the flank and rear to make ruin complete. Yet Sheridan still was not satisfied. The enemy must be annihilated, all escape must be cut off, that railroad line must be broken, no one must relax or pause for breath as long as there was anything still to be accomplished. . . . He was in a little clearing in the forest, directly behind what had been the main Confederate line, and through the clearing went the road that led from Five Forks to the Southside Railroad, the railroad Lee had to protect if his army was to live; and just then there came up to Sheridan some now unidentified officer of rank, to report triumphantly that his command was in the Rebel rear and had captured five guns.

Sheridan gave him a savage greeting:

"I don't care a damn for their guns, or you either, sir! What I want is that Southside Railway!"

The sun was just disappearing over the treetops, and the clearing was dim with a smoky twilight. Many soldiers were in and about the road through the clearing, their weapons in their hands, conscious of victory and half expecting to be told that they had done a great thing and were very fine fellows. Sheridan turned to face them, and he suddenly stood up in his stirrups, waving his hat, his face as black as his horse, and in a great voice he roared:

"I want you men to understand we have a record to make before that sun goes down that will make Hell tremble!"

He waved toward the north, toward the position of the railroad, and he cried: "I want you there!"

He turned and rode to the north. Meeting Griffin and Ayres and Chamberlain, he called to them: "Get together all the men you can, and drive on while you can see your hand before you!"

While the officers formed the men into ordered ranks and prepared to move on, a pale, slight man rode up to Sheridan and spoke to him quietly: General Warren, the written order clutched in his hand, asking Sheridan if he would not reconsider the order that wrecked a soldier's career.

"Reconsider, hell!" boomed Sheridan. "I don't reconsider my decisions! Obey the order!" Silently, Warren rode off in the dusk, and Sheridan went on trying to organize a force to break through to the railroad.[13]

Actually, no more could be done that night. No more needed to be done. To all practical purposes, Pickett's force had been wiped out. Thousands of prisoners were on their way back to the provost marshal's stockades, and there were so many captured muskets that Sheridan's prisoners were using armloads of them to corduroy the roads. Some of the Rebel cavalry elements which had got away were swinging about to rejoin Lee's army, but the infantry that had escaped was beaten and disorganized, drifting off to the north and west, effectively out of the war. Sheridan could have the railroad whenever he wanted to march his men over to it, and he might just as well do it tomorrow as tonight because the force which might have stopped him had been blown to bits. There was no need to put exhausted troops on the road before morning, and in the end even Sheridan came to see it. Cavalry and infantry went into bivouac where they were.

Around General Griffin's campfire the new commander of the V Corps talked things over with division and brigade commanders. These men were deeply attached to Warren. They felt that his troubles today had mostly been caused by General Crawford, and it seemed very hard that Warren should be broken for mistakes and delays which had not, after all, affected the outcome of the battle. This was the first time in the history of the Army of the Potomac that a ranking commander had been summarily fired because his men had been put into action tardily and inexpertly. Sheridan had been cruel and unjust—and if that cruel and unjust insistence on driving, aggressive promptness had been the rule in this army from the beginning, the war probably would have been won two years earlier. . . .

As the generals talked, a stocky figure stepped into the light of the campfire—Sheridan himself.

He was in a different mood, now, the battle fury quite gone, and he spoke very gently: If he had been harsh and demanding with any of them that day he was sorry, and he hoped they would forgive him, for he had not meant to hurt anyone. But—"you know how it is; we had to carry this place, and I was fretted all day until it was done." So there was this apology for hot words spoken in the heat of action, and there was the general's thanks for hard work well done; and then Sheridan went away, and the generals gaped into the dark after him. General Chamberlain, who was one of the circle, reflected that "as a rule, our corps and army commanders were men of brains rather than magnetism"; but Sheridan, now—well, "we could see how this voice and vision, this swing and color, this vivid impression on the senses, carried the pulse and will of men."[14]

Several miles to the east, one of Grant's staff officers who had been with Sheridan this day finished a tiring ride over crowded, watery roads, and pulled up his horse by the open fire at Grant's headquarters. His fellow officers there crowded around him before he had dismounted, eager for news, and he shouted it to them in breathless sentences—complete victory, Rebels utterly routed, the way to Lee's railroad and Lee's rear wide open, roads all clogged with prisoners—and they shouted, tossed hats and caps in the air, slapped one another on the back, capering in wild enthusiasm; all but Grant himself, who stood in their midst impassive, cigar in his teeth, and as soon as he could make himself heard in the din asked the staff officer the question that seemed to be his private gauge for measuring a victory: How many prisoners? The officer said that the best estimate was about five thousand, and for a moment Grant looked pleased, almost enthusiastic. Then he went over to the telegraphers' tent, coming out a moment later to remark: "I have ordered an immediate assault all along the lines."[15]

Great things might have been done on the flank, but the Army of Northern Virginia still lay directly in front, and from the moment he crossed the Rapidan River Grant's basic idea had always been, not to make that army retreat, but to break it. Now the time had come when it could be broken. Yet "immediate" did not actually mean "right away." Orders had to go from Grant through Meade and Ord to corps and division commanders. Artillerists had to frame and distribute orders to batteries and gun pits. Orders for the infantry had to filter down from army to corps to division to brigade and regiment; and it was likely to be dawn, or close to it, before the assault could really be made.

On the right, where the lines were close together and where the Confederate defenses were most tightly knit, Parke would send his IX Corps straight in from their trenches. Farther around, west of Fort Hell, the big push would be made by the VI Corps, with Ord holding his men ready to follow the moment there was a sign of success. In this part of the front the lines were a mile or more apart, and in the counterblow after Fort Stedman the Federals had taken the Confederate picket lines; so in here there was a little room to maneuver, and around midnight the men of the VI Corps filed out of their trenches to go into position.

General Wright had gone out ahead of them to pick the target. There was comparatively high ground here, and along part of the front there was no water in front of the Confederate works. There were five lines of abatis to be crossed, very stout and formidable, but the pickets had reported a singular fact: there was a pathway through these entanglements, used by enemy details which came out to get firewood or go on picket duty, and at night the Rebels kept a bonfire alight toward the rear in line with this pathway. If the Federals who formed on the higher ground would simply guide their advance on this bonfire, then, they would get through the abatis and up to the trenches.

Wright formed his corps wedge-shaped, with the third brigade of the second division as the thin end of the wedge— 1,600 men in six veteran regiments, the rest of the corps in echelon to right and left. With the advance there would be a detail of gunners with rammers and primers, ready to turn captured guns on the defenders. It was understood that the advance would begin as soon as a signal gun was fired from Federal Fort Fisher, in the rear.

The night was bewilderingly dark, and there was a mist that made the gloom even thicker. The VI Corps these days was known as the army's high-morale outfit—the men had shared in the great Shenandoah Valley victories, and they were cocky about it—but they were glum and silent as they left their trenches and took their places. The high command might know that when Lee detached troops to operate under Pickett at Five Forks he left his main line so badly under-manned that it could at last be broken, but the infantry knew nothing of this. All that the veterans understood was that these terrible fortifications which they had learned to consider unconquerable were at last to be attacked, and they took it for granted that the hour of doom had arrived.[16]

When company commanders read off the orders, soldiers here and there were heard to mutter: "Well, good-by, boys—this means death." As always, the men got ready for the fight in their different ways. Some scribbled hasty letters home, others threw away decks of playing cards, still others examined cartridge boxes and canteens to make sure that they were filled, a few put pipe and tobacco within easy reach. And tonight a good many did what they never did except when they figured they were about to be slaughtered. They wrote their names and addresses on slips of paper and pinned these to their uniforms, so that their bodies could be identified after the battle.[17]

Huddled close to the ground in the creepy no man's land between the armies, utter darkness and graveyard silence all around, the men waited nervously for the signal gun that would send them on their way. But once again there had been a mix-up in the arrangements. What finally came, jarring and stunning them and seeming to pin them down by sheer weight of violence, was not the report of one cannon but the crash of a tremendous bombardment, with every gun and mortar in the Federal lines opening fire.

There were miles upon miles of gun positions, all the way

from the Appomattox to the works near Hatcher's Run, and from every weapon in this crescent there came the most intense and sustained volume of fire the gun crews could manage. Never before, not even at Gettysburg, had the army fired so much artillery so fast and so long. The whole sky pulsed and shuddered with great sheets of light. Jagged flames lit the horizon as the Confederate guns replied. In the blackness overhead the battle smoke piled up in monstrous thunderheads, fitfully visible in the flash of exploding shell.

A gunner wrote proudly of "a constant stream of living fire" pouring from the flaming gun pits, and a front-line infantryman said that the very ground shook and trembled with the concussion. Miles away to the west, men in the V Corps said the sky was lighted up as if by aurora borealis. How long it all lasted, nobody ever knew. After a time men realized that the Confederate batteries had stopped firing, and then the crash of the Union guns seemed definitely lighter —and now, as the bombardment slowly tapered off, staff officers from corps headquarters were going to brigade and regimental commanders asking why the men were not moving: the signal gun had been fired, somewhere in the midst of all of this uproar, and the attack should have been made ten minutes ago.[18]

Officers prodded men to their feet, and the smoky sky began to turn gray, although it was still too dark to see anything a hundred yards away, and presently the whole great wedge of infantry was moving. And then the guns stopped altogether, and there was silence on the battlefield, and in this silence an officer realized that there was a mysterious, pervasive noise that seemed to be the sound of a deep, distant rustling, "like a strong breeze blowing through the swaying boughs and dense foliage of some great forest." He realized at last that this was the noise made by 14,000 soldiers tramping forward over soft damp ground.[19]

Rebel pickets came to life and began to shoot, and then rolling volleys of musketry lit the main line of Confederate works, and the guns opened heavily. The VI Corps raised a cheer and began to run forward. The leading brigade lost sight of the path through the abatis, but the whole corps was running now, details with axes were smashing at the entanglements, sheer weight of numbers was breaking a dozen openings—and the tide flowed on, past the abatis and into the ditch, with the black loom of the fortifications rising just ahead.

Far to the rear, on the parapet of a Union fort, an army surgeon had been watching, and in the predawn gloom he could see a twinkling, flashing line of fire half a mile wide—the rim of the Confederate works, lit by musketry. As he watched he saw a black gap in the center of this sparkling line, and then there was another gap a little to one side, and then a third one, and as he watched these gaps widened and ran together, and suddenly the whole chain of lights was out and he knew that the line had been captured.

It was not done easily, for if the defenders were few they died hard, and there was hand-to-hand fighting along the works. Storming parties got over in squads, stabbing and clubbing muskets. There was no cheering—everyone was too much out of breath for that—but the men coming up in the support brigades realized that the trenches had been taken when they saw Confederate cannon reversed, firing toward the Confederate rear. In some cases Union infantry refused to wait for the parties of artillerists who had been sent over to work the captured guns, and tried to operate them themselves. The 11th Vermont claimed to have fired twelve rounds from one battery, overcoming the want of primers simply by discharging muskets into the vents of the loaded pieces.[20]

Dawn came at last, and the whole line of works was black with Union soldiers. Beyond the line lay the Confederate camps, with eager parties of VI Corps hot-shots pushing on through them, every man for himself—some of them running on to reach the unguarded rear areas, some looking through tents and huts for loot, some just going, kept moving by the excitement of victory. Far to the right, the IX Corps had stormed the whole first line of deadly trenches but met stubborn resistance on the second line, and the sound of artillery and musketry rolled across the pine flats. On the left, the entire line of defense had dissolved. Ord's troops, and the II Corps, were breaking through on the west, cutting the defenders' organizations into fragments and driving these broken units before them. By twos and threes and by disorganized squads, the Federals broke clear through past the railroad to the edge of the Appomattox. In a chance encounter by a bit of wood, some of these killed the famous General A. P. Hill.

In the Confederate camps the VI Corps made merry. One man remembered seeing a burly buck private outfitting himself in the tinseled gray dress-uniform coat which some Confederate officer would never need again, and another soldier was wrapping a Confederate flag about his shoulders as if it were a toga. The whole corps was up, now, overflowing the trenches, scampering around among bombproofs and huts and tents, staring out over ground which no armed Yankee had previously seen. Up into their midst came a group of mounted men, Grant and Meade and Wright trotting over to reorganize the storming columns and make the break-through complete.[21]

"Then and there," wrote a Connecticut soldier exultantly, "then and there the long-tried and ever faithful soldiers of the Republic *saw daylight!*" And the whole corps looked up and down the Petersburg lines—broken forever, now—and took in what had been done, and caught its breath, and sent up a wild shout which, the Connecticut man said, it was worth dying just to listen to.[22]

4. The Enormous Silence

The end of the war was like the beginning, with the army marching down the open road under the spring sky, seeing a far light on the horizon. Many lights had died in the windy dark but far down the road there was always a gleam, and it was as if a legend had been created to express some obscure truth that could not otherwise be stated. Everything had changed, the war and the men and the land they fought for, but the road ahead had not changed. It went on through the trees and past the little towns and over the hills, and there was no getting to the end of it. The goal was a going-toward rather than an arriving, and from the top of the next rise there was always a new vista. The march toward it led through wonder and terror and deep shadows, and the sunlight touched the flags at the head of the column.

For a long time the Army of the Potomac had wanted to enter Richmond, and it almost seemed as if that was the object of everything that it did, but when Richmond fell at last the army did not get within twenty-five miles of it—not until long afterward, when everything was over and the men were going home to be civilians again. Most of the army did not even get into Petersburg, which had been within sight but out of reach for so long. Instead the troops moved off on roads that led to the west, pounding along in hot pursuit of Lee's army—no victory was final as long as that ragged army still lived and moved.

Only the IX Corps entered Petersburg, and it did so chiefly because the town lay right across its path. It moved in on the morning of April 3 a few hours after the last Confederate soldiers had moved out. The corps came in proudly, flags uncased and bands playing, but the town was all scarred by months of shellfire, the cheers and the music echoed through deserted streets, and there seems to have been a desolate, empty quality to it all that made the jubilation sound forced and hollow. Officers and newspapermen who had breakfast in Petersburg hotels found the fare poor, as was natural in a starved beleaguered city, and noticed that the hotel proprietors would not accept Confederate money.

In the dwelling houses the blinds were all drawn, and here and there an expressionless face could be seen peering out through parted curtains. Men remarked that there was not a woman to be seen; only a few old men, and an occasional cripple, and of course an awed concourse of colored folk. One officer saw Grant standing in a doorway, gesturing with his cigar as he dictated orders to his staff, utterly matter-of-fact, displaying rather less emotion and pride than the ordinary brigadier would show at a routine review of troops, and looking "as if the work before him was a mere matter of business in which he felt no particular enthusiasm or care." [1]

In refusing to allow the army to relax and celebrate Grant was simply following common sense. From his viewpoint he had not actually won anything yet. From the moment when he headed down to the Rapidan fords, eleven months and many thousands of lives ago, he had had just one idea in mind: to destroy Lee's army. Now Richmond had fallen, and so had Petersburg, but Lee's army still lived and if it was to be destroyed it must first be caught. It would never be caught by pursuers who let days or hours go to waste; not that army, led by that general. So the Army of the Potomac would keep moving, and if there was to be a celebration it could come later.

Beaten and reeling in flight, the Rebel army was still dangerous. Proof that its men still wanted to fight came this morning at the prisoner-of-war stockade. Nearly 5,000 of the men captured at Five Forks were herded together there, and the Federal provost marshal had them paraded and made a little speech to them, pointing out that their cause was doomed and inviting everyone to step up, take the oath of allegiance, and then go home and fight no more. Out of the 5,000 present, fewer than 100 moved out to take the oath—and they were bitterly derided by all the rest, who profanely denounced them as cowards and traitors. [2]

So although the grim Petersburg trenches were empty and harmless, and troops from the Army of the James were in Richmond putting out the fires that threatened to destroy the whole city—the Confederate rear guard had fired arsenals and storehouses, and the flames had got out of hand—nothing had really been settled. The Army of the Potomac had not yet brought its adversary to bay, and it would have to march long and fast to do it.

There were certain advantages. Leaving Petersburg, Lee

had gone north of the Appomattox River. Somewhere above that river he was picking up the troops that had come down from Richmond and was collecting the fragments that had been sent flying when Sheridan took Five Forks and the VI Corps broke the Petersburg line. With everybody assembled, he would try to join Joe Johnston in North Carolina, and to do that he would have to go west and south. The Army of the Potomac was nearly as far west as he was, and it was a good deal farther south. Properly handled it ought to be able to head him off because it had a shorter distance to travel.

The railroads were important. There were two lines that mattered: the familiar Southside Railroad, and the Richmond and Danville, which latter went slanting down into Joe Johnston's territory and bisected the Southside line halfway between Petersburg and Lynchburg. Lee's quickest route would put him on the Richmond and Danville at Amelia Court House, sixteen miles northeast of the point where the two railroads intersected.

If the Federals moved west by the shortest route, they should strike the Richmond and Danville road at or near the junction before Lee's people could get down there via Amelia Court House. If that happened, it would be impossible for Lee to meet Johnston. He would have only two alternatives: to stand and make a finish fight of it, a fight that could end in but one way, or to keep on going west in the hope that he could reach Lynchburg, where he might get supplies and win some sort of breathing space in the wooded folds of the mountains.

So the task was not to overtake his army but to get ahead of it. Every march was to be a forced march. Sheridan and his cavalry were leading the way. Meade and three infantry corps were following close behind, and Ord and three divisions from the Army of the James were moving on parallel roads just a little farther south. The men carried extra rations, for there would be no waiting for supply trains, and a thirty-mile hike—ordinarily a perfect prodigy of a march—would be considered no more than a fair day's work. Officers in the V

Corps called out to the men: "Your legs must do it, boys!" [3]

Spring had come, and the world was turning green and white and gold with new leaves and blossoms. The cramping misery of the trenches had been left behind, and men's spirits were so high that even dogtrotting along in the wake of the cavalry did not seem a bad assignment. The rank and file was not entirely clear about just what had happened, but it was clear that the Johnnies were on the run at last. Grant summed it up in a telegram to Sherman: "This army has now won a most decisive victory and followed the enemy. That is all that it ever wanted to make it as good an army as ever fought a battle." [4]

They might be victorious, but the men were still cagey. Midway of the first day out, excited staff officers rode down the columns shouting the news—Richmond taken, the Union flag flying over the Confederate capital! The veterans perked up, and then they remembered that they had been had before. When an especially hard march was to be made, staff officers often circulated false announcements of good tidings just to keep everybody stepping along briskly. So the men jeered at each bearer of good news, calling out: "Put him in a canteen! Give him a hardtack! Tell it to the recruits!" But pretty soon the bands began to play, and the colonels formally announced the news to their own regiments, and up and down the line of march the men began to realize that for once the good news was true.

"Stack your muskets and go home!" yelled one of Ord's men, when General Gibbon announced the fall of Richmond. As the army bivouacked that night, one veteran told another: "I feel better tonight than I did after that fight at Gettysburg." [5]

Far out in front, fantastic outriders of victory, went Sheridan's scouts. Sometimes they rode dressed as Confederate officers or couriers, and sometimes they wore faded jeans and rode decrepit horses or mules with makeshift bridles and saddles, pretending to be displaced farmers or roving horse doctors. Either way, they visited Rebel picket posts, rode blithely through cavalry cordons, ambled alongside Lee's wagon trains, paused to chat in Confederate camps. Most of them got back alive, and they kept Sheridan informed about where the enemy's people were and where they were going to be next.

As they did all of this, riding under no man's control, they appear to have found unheard-of opportunities for loot. They visited farms and plantations and collected much food for themselves, they got new horses when they felt that they needed them, and (as other cavalrymen reported enviously) they were not always above helping themselves to more substantial valuables, taking cash and jewelry from planters' homes and leaving their victims quite at a loss to say just who robbed them.[6] They were a wild, lawless crew, carrying their own lives and other people's property in their naked hands, and they feared nothing in particular except the black scowl of Phil Sheridan.

They swarmed all around the head of the cavalry column, exploring the whole network of country roads and learning where every lane and cowpath led. Behind them came hard columns of questing cavalry, slashing through to nip at the flanks of Lee's moving army, driving Confederate troopers off the roads, harassing the plodding columns with quick thrusts and then pulling away fast to strike again a mile or two farther on. Back of these, in turn, came Sheridan and the main body of cavalry; and two days out of Five Forks Sheridan led his men into a country town called Jetersville, which place was important then for two reasons—it was on the Richmond and Danville Railroad and Lee and his army had not yet reached it.

Sheridan sent one division west and north to see what was to be seen and to cause as much trouble as possible for the Confederacy. The rest he led northeast, and after a few miles his men ran into Rebel cavalry patrols and drove them back. Then Sheridan called a halt and had his men build breastworks, and a little later General Griffin came up with the V Corps and threw his men into line of battle beside them, and the rest of the infantry was not far away. Meade himself was coming up, in an ambulance. He had taken ill, from indigestion and general nerve strain, after the fall of Petersburg, but he was coming along with the army regardless.[7] So here was the Army of the Potomac getting ready to fight its old antagonist, and for the first time in its history its battle line was facing toward the northeast. It had won the race and if Lee was to go any farther south he would have to fight.

Lee's army was at Amelia Court House, half a dozen miles short of the spot where Meade's infantry was going into line. It could not stay there because it had used up all of its rations and there was nothing in Amelia Court House for it to eat, and after surveying the Yankee line carefully Lee concluded that his army was not strong enough to fight its way through. Since the army could not retreat—there were Yankees in both Richmond and Petersburg now—only one move remained on the board: to go west, cross country, and strike the western part of the Southside Railroad. Provisions could be brought up from Lynchburg by this line, and if the army moved fast and had luck there was an outside chance that it could still slip around the Federal flank and get south. Failing that, it might at least reach Lynchburg and try to survive there for a time. There was nothing else it could even try to do.

Sheridan did not believe it should be given any leeway. His whole instinct was to attack before anybody got six hours older, and he seems to have feared that Meade would be content to wait for Lee to start the fight. At any rate, Sheridan wanted the boss; so one of his scouts, dressed like a Confederate colonel, took a note which Sheridan scribbled on tissue paper, folded the tissue paper in tin foil, concealed that in a wad of leaf tobacco, and shoved the tobacco in his mouth—after which he went trotting off cross country to find U. S. Grant.

Grant was with Ord that day, a dozen miles away, and the scout reached him toward evening, narrowly missing getting shot by Ord's pickets as he came cantering in. So Grant got Sheridan's message, which described the situation, suggested that Lee's army might be captured, and urged Grant to come and take charge in person. With his staff and a small mounted escort Grant immediately set out, guided by the gray-uniformed scout, following rambling country roads in the dark—with his staff wondering uneasily just what would happen to the war if the little party should blunder into the Confederate lines by mistake. It was late at night when Grant reached Sheridan's tent, and nothing could be done with the troops until morning.[8]

If Sheridan feared that Meade would sit down and wait for the fight to be brought to him, he was mistaken. Meade wanted to fight and he started the infantry toward Amelia Court House at dawn, but Lee was no longer there. He had put his tired, half-starved troops on the road for a night march, trying the last chance that was left to him, striking due west for the town of Farmville, on the Southside Railroad. When the flight was discovered Meade ordered pursuit, but Grant modified the order: let part of the infantry follow in Lee's rear, pressing him and making him stand and fight whenever it could, but let the rest follow the cavalry and get west as fast as possible, keeping always south of the Confederates. The idea still was to win a race, and if they could plant infantry across Lee's path just once more it would all be over.

So the foot race was on again and away they went, infantry and cavalry and the lumbering guns. It was April 6, and the Petersburg break-through was four days behind them, and some of the infantry units were doing thirty-five miles a day and more. In some ways it was like any other hard march—woods and swamps and wispy fields, muddy roads churned into quagmire by thousands of horses, a hard pull on the long hills and everybody too winded to say much. Yet now it was all different, because for all anyone knew the thing they had been marching toward for four years might lie just the other side of the next hill.

On every side there were multiplying signs of Confederate defeat, littering roads and fields like driftwood dropped by an ebbing tide: broken wagons and ambulances, guns with broken wheels, discarded muskets and blanket rolls, stragglers bedded down in fence corners or stumbling listlessly through the woods—and, every so often, "dropped in the very middle of the road from utter exhaustion, old horses literally skin and bones, and so weak as scarcely to be able to lift their heads when some soldier would touch them with his foot to see if they really had life." Every regiment had its congenital pessimists, as one soldier confessed, men who fought well but who always darkly prophesied ultimate Rebel victory; but now, this man said, "the utter collapse of the rebellion was so near that no one could fail to see it, and the croakers were compelled to cheer in spite of themselves." [9]

Humphreys was driving the II Corps in on Lee's rear guard, and the day was a long succession of savage little fights wherever the Confederates could find a defensive vantage point. On other roads the other corps struggled to gain ground, and up ahead and along the way there was the cavalry—always the cavalry, with Sheridan sending galloping columns in to skirmish, wheel, and dash away again, forcing weary Southerners to halt, form line of battle, and then go on with their march. He had three divisions doing this, probing always for a weak spot, slowing down the enemy's march, relentless and seemingly tireless. In mid-afternoon he found, at last, the opening he was looking for.

Custer spied a Confederate wagon train winding through hill country, the bleak woods glistening from the spring rains, and he whistled his squadrons in on the dead run with sabers swinging. Confederate infantry fell into line to repel the attack, but up ahead a gap developed in the moving column and Custer's men went pouring through it, stopping the wagon train, cutting the traces and driving the teams away, sabering drivers, breaking wagon wheels with axes, and setting fire to the wreckage. More and more cavalry went into the gap, and Sheridan sent couriers back to bring up the infantry: here is a whole section of Lee's army cut off, come on up quick and we can bag the lot! [10]

Nearest infantry was the VI Corps, which had marched all night and all day without food and was just filing into some fields to make coffee and eat bacon and hardtack when Sheridan's messengers came up. Down the lines went staff officers

and colonels to tell the men the news: Sheridan is just ahead
and he wants help, and we can all eat later perhaps. The
men fell into ranks cheering and they stepped off eagerly, and
before long they formed a battle line on a slope looking down
to a little creek, on the far side of which there was a Confederate battle line. Sheridan rode up, and the VI Corps
veterans who had followed him in the Valley pointed and
told each other: "There's Phil! There's Phil!" and yelled their
heads off. One of their officers mused: "The sight of that
man on the field was more gratifying than rations, more inspiring than reinforcements." [11]

On the horizon was the burning Confederate wagon train.
Straight in front was a fair piece of the Rebel army, brought
to bay at last, the men dangerous as so many wounded
panthers; and off to the left were four brigades of Yankee
cavalry, moving forward at a walk as if passing in review,
heading for the Confederate flank. For a minute or two everything seemed to hang in suspense, as if the army had gone to
great pains to pose a dramatic picture. Then the wild high
notes of the bugles sounded from end to end of the line, and
everybody went forward on the run, cavalry and infantry
alike, and there was a great shouting and the smoke from
thousands of muskets banked up over the valley. Then the
cavalry had broken through, and the infantry was tussling
in the shallows, and suddenly there was no more Rebel
battle line, nothing but groups of men throwing down
their arms, cavalry ranging far and wide to round up fugitives,
thousands of Confederates surrounded and surrendering—
among them, picturesque one-legged General Dick Ewell,
who had been Stonewall Jackson's lieutenant when the world
was young. Far in the distance, Lee on a hilltop watched it
all and told an officer beside him: "That half of our army has
been destroyed." [12]

There was exaggeration in the remark, but not a great deal.
What remained of two Confederate army corps had gone to
pieces, with thousands of men taken prisoner, only a few es-
caping through the woods. The rear guard hung on until
dark and then the Confederates followed their last fading

chance to the north side of the Appomattox River, burning the bridges behind them. If they could keep the Federals south of that still unfordable river and go on with desperate forced marches it might yet be possible . . . just barely possible . . . to get away and join Johnston, or reach the mountains, or find somewhere a chance to rest and refit and make the war go on a little longer.

Along the creek where they had won their triumph the Federals cheered and danced. Someone found barrels of Confederate paper money in a headquarters wagon not yet burned, and the men went scampering about with handfuls of it, tossing it in the air, using it to kindle fires, offering great bundles of it to the gloomy prisoners. All of the ground was covered with the debris of the broken army, and as the VI Corps moved away the men found the road for two miles so littered with discarded muskets that it was hard to move to move without stepping on them. A major of the 65th New York was mortally wounded when someone's horse trod on one of these muskets and caused it to go off and shoot him.[13]

If the VI Corps found a few hours to relax, Humphreys kept the II Corps moving, and it got to one of the river crossings just as a Rebel rear guard was firing the last bridge. Barlow had the advance, and he sent his men down to the bridge a-running, fighting Confederate skirmishers and beating out the flames at the same time. In the end they saved the bridge and drove off the Confederate guards, and the whole army corps went pouring over to the north side of the river and pushed on to harry the rear of the Army of Northern Virginia and make any breathing spell impossible.

Two Confederate armies Grant had captured entire, in this war, and now the third and greatest of them was stricken, limping pathetically in its effort to get away from him. The increasing signs that the army was ready for destruction simply made Grant drive his own troops all the harder. Sheridan's cavalry ranged west, untiring, and Griffin's and Ord's troops followed as if the mounted men were pulling them on. North of the Appomattox, the II Corps continued to press the Confederate rear. Since this corps was miles away from the rest of the Union army, there was danger that Lee might turn suddenly and destroy it, and so Grant ordered the VI Corps to cross the river and march with Humphreys's men.

It was April 7 now, and Grant was in the little town of Farmville by the Appomattox. Evening had come, and the troops in Farmville had lighted bonfires all along the main street, and Grant was sitting on the veranda of the homely country hotel there when the head of the VI Corps came marching through on its way to the north side of the river. As they marched between the fires the men saw the unassuming little general on the porch, and they suddenly realized that this man was at last leading them to the victory they had dreamed of so long. They broke ranks briefly, seized brands from the bonfires and made torches, and then paraded past Grant, waving the burning torches and yelling hysterically. Brigade bands materialized, and the VI Corps marched by to music. Men who had no torches waved their caps, and the corps went on out of the firelight into the darkness, crossing the Appomattox. After they had passed, Grant went inside the hotel and wrote a formal note to be delivered to Robert E. Lee under a flag of truce, inviting Lee to surrender.[14]

Of this note the soldiers knew nothing. They knew only that in all its existence the Army of the Potomac had never been driven as hard as it was being driven now. Wagon trains were left far behind, whole brigades and divisions marched without food, and every rod of the way the army dribbled stragglers. These stragglers found the foraging in this part of Virginia very good, since marching armies had not previously been here, but the land's plenty was of little help to the men who remained in the ranks. The army was moving too fast to bother with foraging details.

A soldier in the 20th Maine said that "we never endured such marching before," and another man in the V Corps remembered making a forty-two-mile march that went clear through from one sunrise to another. Whenever the column stopped for a five-minute rest, he said, men would drop in their tracks and go instantly to sleep, and when the column moved on many of the men who stumbled to their feet, shouldered their muskets, and went lurching down the road would still be sound asleep. The very utmost men could do was demanded of them now, and the only reality was the road itself.[15]

It was a bad road to march on, like all the roads of war— deeply rutted, fouled by the march of the cavalry up ahead, by turns heavy with mud or deep with the dust that would make marching a gray choking agony. Yet this was the road the army had been marching toward from the very beginning, and many thousands of men had died in order that this road might at last be marched on; for this was the road to the end of the war, and on over the horizon to the unimaginable be- ginnings and endings that would lie beyond that. Also, and more intimately, it was the beginning of the long road home.

It was April 8, by now, and tomorrow would be Palm Sunday, and the land was rich and warm with spring. Below the Appomattox, that day, the road wound interminably through deep woods, so that dusk came down early. Ord's di- visions were on the road, and all of the V Corps, together with much artillery, and the artillery was supposed to have the road while the infantry filed along on each side. But the road was very narrow, so that there was much crowding and confusion, and the men were very tired and quarrelsome, and some time after dark a tremendous fight broke out be- tween infantry and artillery. Infantry complained that the gunners were driving their six-horse teams recklessly, forcing men off the road and causing injuries. Gunners declared that infantrymen were hitting artillery horses over the head with musket butts. Everybody was hungry, irritable, and half out of his mind with fatigue, and the yelling and cursing and hitting and general uproar went up from the dark lane for an hour or more.

When it was finally settled it was after midnight, and the troops were led off the road to make a supperless bivouac. They got very little rest—one regiment at the tail of the col- umn complained that it was roused just fifteen minutes after it turned in—because couriers came riding in from Phil Sher- idan, who was a few miles farther on, near a little place called Appomattox Court House. He had his cavalry squarely in front of the Rebel army, and he was writing that if the infantry could be there first thing in the morning they could probably wind the whole business up.[16]

Sheridan's scouts had come to him earlier in the day with word that several freight trains with food had pulled in at Appomattox Station, a mile or so from the courthouse town, and that Lee's wagons would presently be alongside, loading up. Sheridan sent Custer off at a gallop, and Custer's division took the Confederates by surprise, seizing the trains just as they were ready to unload. There were former railroad men among the Yankee troopers, and these flung themselves from the saddle and raced for the locomotives, climbing into the cabs with much clumping of heavy boots and clanking of sabers. They threw out the Southern train crews, blew whistles and rang bells, and bumped the trains back and forth in aimless celebration until someone finally had them run the cars up the track a few miles so that they would be out of reach of any Confederate counterthrust.

Custer took the main body of his troops on past the station, seized a big wagon park and artillery train, and chased fugitives eastward along a road that led uphill through deep woods. He came out into the open just at dark, and saw a rude breastwork cutting across the highway with gray-clad infantry behind it. Beyond, many campfires put a soft red glow on the sky. They were the campfires of Lee's army—and Custer's cavalry was due west of them.[17]

Sheridan came up soon after, with the rest of the cavalry. He sent hurry-up messages for the infantry, put half of his men in line, dismounted, facing the Rebel breastworks, and ordered the rest into bivouac near the railroad a mile to the south.

The road his cavalry was on was the main road to Lynchburg, which lay twenty miles to the west. Of all the world's roads, this was the only one that mattered now to the Army of Northern Virginia. If, when morning came, that army could knock the Yankees out of the way and march west on this road it might still hope to live for a while—a day or two, a fortnight, a few months. If it could not do that, it would cease to exist within twenty-four hours. Cavalry alone could not bar the way very long, but if the blue infantry came up in time then it would be taps and dipped flags and good-by forever for Lee's army.

Federal infantry was on the road in the dark hours before dawn, with very little sleep and no breakfast at all. The men were told that if they hurried this was the day they could finish everything, and this inspired them. Yet they were no set of legendary heroes who never got tired or hungry or thought about personal discomfort. They were very human, given to griping when their stomachs were empty, and what really pulled them along this morning seems to have been the promise that at Appomattox Station rations would be issued. Most of the men who made the march that morning, one veteran admitted, did so because they figured it was the quickest way to get breakfast. Even so the straggling was abnormally heavy, and there were regiments in the column which had no more than seventy-five men with the colors.[18]

It was Palm Sunday, with a blue cloudless sky, and the warm air had the smell of spring. The men came tramping up to the fields by the railroad station with the early morning sun over their right shoulders, and they filed off to right and left, stacked arms, and began collecting wood for the fires with which they would cook the anticipated rations. The divisions from the Army of the James were in front, Ord and John Gibbon in the lead, and the V Corps was coming up close behind. Gibbon and Ord rode to a little house near the railroad where Sheridan had his headquarters, and Sheridan came out to greet them and explain the situation.

The Lynchburg Road lay about a mile north of cavalry headquarters. It ran along a low ridge, partly concealed by timber, with a boggy little brook running along a shallow valley on the near side, and a couple of miles to the east it dipped down to a little hollow and ran through the village of Appomattox Court House. In and around and beyond this village, with its advance guard holding the breastworks half a mile west of it, was what remained of the Army of Northern Virginia. Off to the east, out of sight beyond hills and forests but not more than six or eight miles away, was Meade with the II Corps and the VI Corps, coming west on the Lynchburg Road to pound the Confederate rear. In effect, the Federals occupied three sides of a square—cavalry on the west, infantry on the south, Meade and the rest of the army on the east. The Rebel army was inside the square, and although the north side was open that did not matter because the Confederates could find neither food nor escape in that direction. Their only possible move was to fight their way west along the Lynchburg Road.

So Sheridan explained it, warning the generals that he expected the Rebels to attack at any moment and that they had better get ready to bring their troops up in support.[19]

While he was talking the sound of musket fire came down from the ridge. It was sporadic, at first, as the skirmishers pecked away at each other, but it soon grew much heavier and there was the heavy booming of field artillery. The big push was on, and Sheridan sprang into the saddle, ordering the rest of his cavalry up into line and telling the officers to bring their infantry up as fast as they could. Then he was off, and the generals galloped back to put their men in motion.

The hopeful little breakfast fires died unnoticed, nothing ever cooked on them, and the infantry took their muskets, got into column, and went hurrying north to get astride of the Lynchburg Road. The crossroad they were on led through heavy timber and the men could see nothing, but the noise of the firing grew louder and louder as they marched. Then, for the last time in their lives, beyond the trees they heard the high, spine-tingling wail of the Rebel yell, a last great shout of defiance flung against the morning sky by a doomed army marching into the final sunset.

The Federals got across the Lynchburg Road, swung into line of battle facing east, and marched toward the firing and the shouting. As they marched, dismounted cavalry came drifting back, and the troopers waved their caps and cheered when they saw the infantry, and called out: "Give it to 'em —we've got 'em in a tight place!"[20]

In a clearing there was Sheridan, talking with Griffin and other officers of the V Corps; Sheridan, talking rapidly, pounding a palm with his fist; and the battle line marched on and came under the fire of Rebel artillery. One brigade went across somebody's farm, just here, and as the firing grew heavier a shell blew the end out of the farmer's chicken house, and the air was abruptly full of demoralized chickens, squawking indignantly, fluttering off in frantic disorganized flight. And here was the last battle of the war, and the men were marching up to the moment of apotheosis and glory—but they were men who had not eaten for twenty-four hours and more, and they knew Virginia poultry from of old, and what had begun as an attack on a Rebel line turned into a hilarious chase after fugitive chickens. The battle smoke rolled down over the crest, and shells were exploding and the farm buildings were ablaze, and Federal officers were waving swords and barking orders in scandalized indignation. But the soldiers whooped and laughed and scrambled after their prey, and as the main battle line swept on most of this brigade was either continuing to hunt chickens or was building little fires and preparing to cook the ones that had been caught.[21]

The Confederates had scattered the cavalry, and most of the troopers fled south, across the shallow valley that ran parallel with the Lynchburg Road. As the last of them left the field the way seemed to be open, and the Confederates who had driven them away raised a final shout of triumph —and then over the hill came the first lines of blue infantry, rifles tilted forward, and here was the end of everything: the Yankees had won the race and the way was closed forever and there was no going on any farther.

The blue lines grew longer and longer, and rank upon rank came into view, as if there was no end to them. A Federal officer remembered afterward that when he looked across at the Rebel lines it almost seemed as if there were more battle flags than soldiers. So small were the Southern regiments that the flags were all clustered together, and he got the strange feeling that the ground where the Army of

Northern Virginia had been brought to bay had somehow blossomed out with a great row of poppies and roses.[22]

So the two armies faced each other at long range, and the firing slackened and almost ceased.

Many times in the past these armies had paused to look at each other across empty fields, taking a final size-up before getting into the grapple. Now they were taking their last look, the Stars and Bars were about to go down forever and leave nothing behind but the stars and the memories, and it might have been a time for deep solemn thoughts. But the men who looked across the battlefield at each other were very tired and very hungry, and they did not have much room in their heads for anything except the thought of that weariness and that hunger, and the simple hope that they might live through the next half hour. One Union soldier wrote that he and his comrades reflected bitterly that they would not be here, waiting for the shooting to begin, if they had not innocently believed that tale about getting breakfast at Appomattox Station; and, he said, "we were angry with ourselves to think that for the hope of drawing rations we had been foolish enough to keep up and, by doing so, get in such a scrape." They did not mind the desultory artillery fire very much, he said, but "we dreaded the moment when the infantry should open on us." [23]

Off toward the south Sheridan had all of his cavalry in line again, mounted now with pennons and guidons fluttering. The Federal infantry was advancing from the west and Sheridan was where he could hit the flank of the Rebels who were drawn up to oppose that infantry, and he spurred over to get some foot soldiers to stiffen his own attack. General Griffin told Chamberlain to take his brigade and use it as Sheridan might direct. Men who saw Sheridan pointing out to Chamberlain the place where his brigade should attack remembered his final passionate injunction: "Now smash 'em, I tell you, smash 'em!"

Chamberlain got his men where Sheridan wanted them, and all of Ord's and Griffin's men were in line now, coming up on higher ground where they could see the whole field.

They could see the Confederate line drawing back from in front of them, crowned with its red battle flags, and all along the open country to the right they could see the whole cavalry corps of the Army of the Potomac trotting over to take position beyond Chamberlain's brigade. The sunlight gleamed brightly off the metal and the flags, and once again, for a last haunting moment, the way men make war looked grand and caught at the throat, as if some strange value beyond values were incomprehensively mixed up in it all.[24]

Then Sheridan's bugles sounded, the clear notes slanting all across the field, and all of his brigades wheeled and swung into line, every saber raised high, every rider tense; and in another minute infantry and cavalry would drive in on the slim Confederate lines and crumble them and destroy them in a last savage burst of firing and cutting and clubbing.

Out from the Rebel lines came a lone rider, a young officer in a gray uniform, galloping madly, a staff in his hand with a white flag fluttering from the end of it. He rode up to Chamberlain's lines and someone there took him off to see Sheridan, and the firing stopped, and the watching Federals saw the Southerners wheeling their guns back and stacking their muskets as if they expected to fight no more.

All up and down the lines the men blinked at one another, unable to realize that the hour they had waited for so long was actually at hand. There was a truce, they could see that, and presently the word was passed that Grant and Lee were going to meet in the little village that lay now between the two lines, and no one could doubt that Lee was going to surrender. It was Palm Sunday, and they would all live to see Easter, and with the guns quieted it might be easier to comprehend the mystery and the promise of that day. Yet the fact of peace and no more killing and an open road home seems to have been too big to grasp, right at the moment, and in the enormous silence that lay upon the field men remembered that they had marched far and were very tired, and they wondered when the wagon trains would come up with rations.

One of Ord's soldiers wrote that the army should have

gone wild with joy, then and there; and yet, he said, somehow they did not. Later there would be frenzied cheering and crying and rejoicing, but now . . . now, for some reason, the men sat on the ground and looked across at the Confederate army and found themselves feeling as they had never dreamed that the moment of victory would make them feel.

". . . I remember how we sat there and pitied and sympathized with these courageous Southern men who had fought for four long and dreary years all so stubbornly, so bravely and so well, and now, whipped, beaten, completely used up, were fully at our mercy—it was pitiful, sad, hard, and seemed to us altogether too bad." A Pennsylvanian in the V Corps dodged past the skirmish line and strolled into the lines of the nearest Confederate regiment, and half a century after the war he recalled it with a glow: ". . . as soon as I got among these boys I felt and was treated as well as if I had been among our own boys, and a person would of thought we were of the same Army and had been Fighting under the Same Flag." [25]

Down by the roadside near Appomattox Court House, Sheridan and Ord and other officers sat and waited while a brown-bearded little man in mud-spattered uniform rode up. They all saluted him, and there was a quiet interchange of greetings, and then General Grant tilted his head toward the village and asked: "Is General Lee up there?"

Sheridan replied that he was, and Grant said: "Very well. Let's go up." [26]

The little cavalcade went trotting along the road to the village, and all around them the two armies waited in silence. As the generals neared the end of their ride, a Yankee band in a field near the town struck up "Auld Lang Syne."

ACKNOWLEDGMENTS

It would be harder to write this kind of book, and the final result would be poorer, if one did not get so much help from so many kindly people. In listing the sources from which material was drawn the writer must express his abiding gratitude for a great deal of generous assistance.

Of particular value has been the opportunity to study various collections of unpublished letters written by Federal soldiers. These letters not only provide useful source material; they leave one feeling that he somehow had personal friends in the Union army—and, now and then, give him the odd illusion that he actually served in that army himself.

The following manuscript collections were made available:

Letters of Edwin Wentworth, of the 37th Massachusetts Infantry, loaned by Miss Edith Adams, of Auburn, Maine. These letters provide a singularly appealing glimpse at the experiences and emotions of a typical New England soldier, and one feels a sense of personal loss upon discovering that the last letter in the collection is a note to next of kin announcing Private Wentworth's death at the Bloody Angle.

Letters of Lewis Bissell, of the 2nd Connecticut Heavy Artillery, loaned by Mr. Carl H. Bissell, of Syracuse, New York. Extremely valuable as an unrevised, day-to-day account of the experiences of a VI Corps veteran, these letters also provide a useful check on the formal regimental history of this Connecticut regiment, whose author is frequently mentioned in Private Bissell's letters.

Letters of Henry Clay Heisler, of the 48th Pennsylvania Veteran Volunteers, loaned by Mr. Donald M. Hobart, of Philadelphia. Written by a soldier in the regiment which dug the famous Petersburg mine, these letters shed a revealing light on that operation and on the reaction of Burnside's soldiers to Burnside's last battle. (Interestingly enough, this regiment apparently blamed the fiasco on Burnside's subordinates rather than on Burnside himself.)

Letters of Sebastian Muller, of the 67th New York Infantry: in the manuscript collection of the Library of Congress. Quaint and stilted in their formal, old-world phraseology, these letters show how the war looked to an immigrant who supposed he had enlisted to fight "the rebels of South America."

Manuscript diary of Corporal S. O. Bryant, of the 20th Michigan Infantry, loaned by Mr. Donald C. Allen, of Washington. In this diary another of Burnside's soldiers expresses himself about the war, and in a complaint about Spotsylvania foreshadows the disaster at the crater.

Letter of Sergeant George S. Hampton, of the 91st Pennsylvania Veteran Volunteers, loaned by Mr. J. Frank Nicholson, of Manassas, Virginia. Written some years after the war, this letter contains a priceless glimpse of men of the two armies at the moment of the cease-fire at Appomattox Court House.

The writer's especial thanks are due to Mr. Ralph Happel, historian, the Fredericksburg and Spotsylvania County National Military Park, for the loan of his excellent manuscript studies of the Wilderness-Spotsylvania battles, and for guidance in study of the terrain.

Dr. James Rabun, of the Department of History, Emory University, kindly forwarded a reprint of his article, "Alexander Stephens and Jefferson Davis," in the *American Historical Review*.

Major General U. S. Grant, III, was most helpful in recalling anecdotes and family recollections about his distinguished grandfather.

Colonel Charles G. Stevenson, state judge advocate, New York National Guard, provided interesting material on the history of the famous "14th Brooklyn" Regiment, and traced that regiment's lineal descent to the 955th Field Artillery Battalion recently active in Korea.

Finally, a substantial debt of gratitude for many acts of helpfulness is owed to various librarians—specifically, to Dr.

David Mearns and Dr. Percy Powell of the Manuscript Division, Library of Congress; to Colonel Willard Webb of the Stack and Reader Division and to Mr. Legare Obear of the Loan Division in that library; to Mr. Paul Howard, librarian of the Department of the Interior, and to Miss Georgia Cowan of the History Division of the Public Library of the District of Columbia.

BIBLIOGRAPHY

CHIEF reliance of course has been placed on the invaluable *War of the Rebellion: A Compilation of the Official Records of the Union and Confederate Armies,* published by the War Department in 1902. Unless otherwise noted, volumes cited in the footnotes are from Series I of this compilation. Reference has also been made to Appleton's *Cyclopedia of American Biography,* edited by James Grant Wilson and John Fiske and published in 1888, and to the more modern *Dictionary of American Biography,* edited by Dumas Malone and published in 1943. In addition, the following works were consulted:

GENERAL HISTORICAL WORKS

"Alexander Stephens and Jefferson Davis," by James Z. Rabun. *American Historical Review,* Vol. LVIII, No. 2.

Battles and Leaders of the Civil War, edited by Robert Underwood Johnson and Clarence Clough Buel. 4 vols. New York, 1884–87.

Campaigns of the Army of the Potomac, by William Swinton. New York, 1882.

Civil War Atlas to accompany Steele's American Campaigns: prepared by the Department of Civil and Military Engineering, U.S. Military Academy.

Confederate Operations in Canada and New York, by John W. Headley. New York and Washington, 1906.

The Crisis of the Confederacy, by Cecil Battine. London and New York, 1905.

Divided We Fought: a Pictorial History of the War, 1861–1865, edited by David Donald. New York, 1952.

Experiment in Rebellion, by Clifford Dowdey. New York, 1950.

Foreigners in the Union Army and Navy, by Ella Lonn. Baton Rouge, La., 1951.

The Generalship of Ulysses S. Grant, by Colonel J. F. C. Fuller. New York, 1929.

A History of Negro Troops in the War of the Rebellion, by George W. Williams. New York, 1888.

History of the Shenandoah Valley, by William Couper. 2 vols. New York, 1952.

History of the United States from the Compromise of 1850, by James Ford Rhodes. 9 vols. New York, 1899.

Lee, Grant and Sherman, by Lieutenant Colonel Alfred H. Burne. New York, 1939.

Lincoln and the War Governors, by William B. Hesseltine. New York, 1948.

Lincoln's War Cabinet, by Burton J. Hendrick. Boston, 1946.

The Long Arm of Lee, by Jennings C. Wise. 2 vols. Lynchburg, Va., 1915.

The Military Genius of Abraham Lincoln, by Brigadier General Colin R. Ballard. London, 1926.

Mr. Lincoln's Army, by Bruce Catton. New York, 1951.

The Northern Railroads in the Civil War, 1861–1865, by Thomas Weber. New York, 1952.

Numbers and Losses in the Civil War, by Thomas L. Livermore. Boston and New York, 1900.

Papers of the Kansas Commandery, Military Order of the Loyal Legion of the United States. 1894.

Papers of the Military Historical Society of Massachusetts, edited by Theodore Dwight. 10 vols. Boston, 1906.

Photographic History of the Civil War, edited by Francis Trevelyan Miller. 10 vols. New York, 1911.

President Lincoln as War Statesman, by Captain Arthur L. Conger: Separate No. 172 from the Proceedings of the State Historical Society of Wisconsin for 1916.

The Rebellion Record: a Diary of American Events, edited by Frank Moore. 12 vols. New York, 1868.

Regimental Losses in the American Civil War, by Lieutenant Colonel William F. Fox, U.S.V. Albany, 1889.

Report of the Committee to Recruit the Ninth Army Corps, prepared by the Secretary. New York, 1866.

The Shenandoah Valley and Virginia, 1861 to 1865: a War Study, by Sanford C. Kellogg. New York and Washington, 1903.

The Shenandoah Valley in 1864, by George E. Pond. New York, 1885.

Statesmen and Soldiers of the Civil War, by Major General Sir Frederick Maurice. Boston, 1926.

The Virginia Campaign of 1864 and 1865, by Major General Andrew A. Humphreys. New York, 1883.

War Papers Read before the Commandery of the State of Wisconsin, Military Order of the Loyal Legion of the United States. Milwaukee, 1891.

AUTOBIOGRAPHIES, BIOGRAPHICAL STUDIES, MEMOIRS, ETC.

Abraham Lincoln, by Benjamin Thomas. New York, 1952.

Abraham Lincoln: the Prairie Years, by Carl Sandburg. 2 vols. New York, 1926.

Abraham Lincoln: the War Years, by Carl Sandburg. 4 vols. New York, 1939.

Army Life in a Black Regiment, by Thomas Wentworth Higginson. Boston and New York, 1900.

Campaigning with Grant, by General Horace Porter. New York, 1907.

Captain Sam Grant, by Lloyd Lewis. Boston, 1952.

Charles Francis Adams: an Autobiography. Boston and New York, 1916.

Correspondence of John Sedgwick, Major General. 2 vols. Privately printed, De Vinne Press, 1902.

Days and Events: 1860–1866, by Colonel Thomas L. Livermore. Boston, 1920.

A Diary from Dixie, by Mary Boykin Chesnut, edited by Ben Ames Williams. Boston, 1949.

The Diary of Gideon Welles, with an introduction by John T. Morse, Jr. 3 vols. Boston and New York, 1911.

Fifty Years in Camp and Field: Diary of Major General Ethan Allen Hitchcock, edited by W. A. Croffut. New York, 1909.

Following the Greek Cross; or, Memories of the Sixth Army Corps, by Brevet Brigadier General Thomas W. Hyde. Boston, 1894.

From Chattanooga to Petersburg under Generals Grant and Butler, by Major General William F. Smith. Boston and New York, 1893.

General Hancock, by Francis A. Walker. New York, 1894.

Gideon Welles: Lincoln's Navy Department, by Richard S. West, Jr. Indianapolis, 1943.

Gouverneur Kemble Warren: the Life and Letters of an American Soldier, by Emerson Gifford Taylor. Boston and New York, 1932.

"Grant Before Appomattox: Notes of a Confederate Bishop," by the Right Rev. Henry C. Lay. *The Atlantic Monthly,* March, 1932.

Jeb Stuart, by John W. Thomason, Jr. New York, 1930.

Jefferson Davis: the Unreal and the Real, by Robert McElroy. 2 vols. New York, 1937.

Kilpatrick and Our Cavalry, by James Moore. New York, 1865.

Lee's Lieutenants, by Douglas Southall Freeman. 3 vols. New York, 1942–44.

Letters of a War Correspondent, by Charles A. Page. Boston, 1899.

The Life and Letters of Emory Upton, by Peter S. Michie; introduction by James H. Wilson. New York, 1885.

The Life and Letters of George Gordon Meade, by George Meade, Captain and Aide-de-Camp. 2 vols. New York, 1913.

The Life of John A. Rawlins, by Major General James Harrison Wilson. New York, 1916.

The Life of Ulysses S. Grant, by Charles A. Dana and Major General James Harrison Wilson. Springfield, Mass., 1868.

Major General Ambrose E. Burnside and the Ninth Army Corps, by Augustus Woodbury. Providence, 1867.

Memoir of Ulric Dahlgren, by Rear Admiral John A. D. Dahlgren. Philadelphia, 1872.

Military Memoirs of a Confederate, by E. Porter Alexander. New York, 1907.

Pemberton, Defender of Vicksburg, by John C. Pemberton. Chapel Hill, 1944.

Personal Memoirs of U. S. Grant. 2 vols. New York, 1885.

Personal Recollections of the Civil War, by Brigadier General John Gibbon. New York, 1928.

R. E. Lee, by Douglas Southall Freeman. 4 vols. New York, 1934.

Ranger Mosby, by Virgil Carrington Jones. Chapel Hill, 1944.

The Rebel Raider: a Life of John Hunt Morgan, by Howard Swiggett. New York, 1937.

A Rebel War Clerk's Diary, by J. B. Jones, edited by Howard Swiggett. 2 vols. New York, 1935.

Recollections of the Civil War, by Charles A. Dana. New York, 1898.

Recollections of War Times, by Albert Gallatin Riddle. New York, 1895.

Reminiscences of Winfield Scott Hancock, by His Wife. New York, 1887.

The Rise of U. S. Grant, by A. L. Conger. New York, 1931.

Robert E. Lee: the Soldier, by Major General Sir Frederick Maurice. Boston and New York, 1925.

Sheridan: a Military Narrative, by Joseph Hergesheimer. Boston and New York, 1931.

Sherman: Fighting Prophet, by Lloyd Lewis. New York, 1932.

South After Gettysburg: Letters of Cornelia Hancock, from the Army of the Potomac, 1863–1865, edited by Henrietta Stratton Jaquette. Philadelphia, 1937.

Ulysses S. Grant, by William Conant Church. New York, 1897.

Under the Old Flag, by Major General James Harrison Wilson. 2 vols. New York, 1912.

A War Diary of Events in the War of the Great Rebellion, by Brigadier General George H. Gordon. Boston, 1882.

A Woman's War Record, 1861–1865, by Septima M. Collis. New York, 1889.

REGIMENTAL HISTORIES, SOLDIERS' REMINISCENCES, ETC.

Annals of the 6th Pennsylvania Cavalry, by the Reverend S. L. Gracey. Philadelphia, 1868.

Army Letters, 1861–1865, by Oliver Willcox Norton. Chicago, 1903.

Army Life: a Private's Reminiscences of the Civil War, by the Rev. Theodore Gerrish. Portland, Me., 1882.

Berdan's United States Sharpshooters in the Army of the Potomac, by Captain C. A. Stevens. St. Paul, 1892.

A Brief History of the 100th Regiment, by Samuel P. Bates. Newcastle, Pa., 1884.

Campaigns of the 146th Regiment New York State Volunteers, compiled by Mary Genevie Green Brainard. New York, 1915.

Camp-Fire Chats of the Civil War, by Washington Davis. Chicago, 1884.

Civil War Echoes: Character Sketches and State Secrets, by Hamilton Gay Howard. Washington, 1907.

Deeds of Daring: or, History of the 8th New York Volunteer Cavalry, by Henry Norton. Norwich, N.Y., 1889.

The Diary of a Line Officer, by Captain Augustus C. Brown. New York, 1906.

The Diary of a Young Officer, by Josiah M. Favill. Chicago, 1909.

Diary of Battery A, First Regiment Rhode Island Light Artillery, by Theodore Reichardt. Providence, 1865.

Down in Dixie: Life in a Cavalry Regiment in the War Days, by Stanton P. Allen. Boston, 1888.

The Fifth Army Corps, by Lieutenant Colonel William H. Powell. New York, 1896.

First Connecticut Heavy Artillery: Historical Sketch, by E. B. Bennett. Hartford, 1904.

The 48th in the War, by Oliver Christian Bosbyshell. Philadelphia, 1895.

Four Years Campaigning in the Army of the Potomac, by D. G. Crotty. Grand Rapids, 1874.

Four Years in the Army of the Potomac: a Soldier's Recollections, by Major Evan Rowland Jones. London, 1881.

The Fourteenth Regiment Rhode Island Heavy Artillery in the War to Preserve the Union, by William H. Chenery. Providence, 1898.

Henry Wilson's Regiment: History of the 22nd Massachusetts Infantry, by John L. Parker and Robert G. Carter. Boston, 1887.

History of Durrell's Battery in the Civil War, by Lieutenant Charles A. Cuffel. Philadelphia, 1904.

History of the Corn Exchange Regiment, by the Survivors' Association. Philadelphia, 1888.

History of the 8th Cavalry Regiment, Illinois Volunteers, by Abner Hard, M.D. Aurora, Ill., 1868.

History of the 8th Regiment Vermont Volunteers, by George N. Carpenter. Boston, 1886.

History of the 87th Regiment Pennsylvania Volunteers, by George R. Prowell. York, Pa., 1903.

History of the 5th Regiment Maine Volunteers, by the Rev. George W. Bicknell. Portland, Me., 1871.

History of the 50th Regiment Pennsylvania Veteran Volunteers, by Lewis Crater. Reading, Pa., 1884.

History of the 51st Regiment of Pennsylvania Volunteers, by Thomas H. Parker. Philadelphia, 1869.

History of the First Connecticut Artillery, by John C. Taylor. Hartford, 1893.

History of the First Regiment of Heavy Artillery, Massachusetts Volunteers, by Alfred Seelye Roe and Charles Nutt. Worcester and Boston, 1917.

History of the 19th Army Corps, by Richard B. Irwin. New York, 1892.

History of the Ninth Massachusetts Battery, by Levi W. Baker. South Framingham, Mass., 1888.

History of the 9th Regiment Connecticut Volunteer Infantry, by Thomas Hamilton Murray. New Haven, 1903.

History of the 150th Regiment Pennsylvania Volunteers, by Lieutenant Colonel Thomas Chamberlin. Philadelphia, 1895.

History of the 198th Pennsylvania Volunteers, by Major E. M. Woodward. Trenton, N.J., 1884.

History of the 106th Regiment Pennsylvania Volunteers, by Joseph R. C. Ward. Philadelphia, 1883.

History of the Philadelphia Brigade, by Charles H. Banes. Philadelphia, 1876.

History of the Sauk County Riflemen, by Philip Cheek and Mair Pointon. Privately printed, 1909.

History of the Second Army Corps, by Francis A. Walker. New York, 1886.

History of the 2nd Connecticut Volunteer Heavy Artillery, by Theodore F. Vaill. Winsted, Conn., 1868.

History of the 17th Regiment Pennsylvania Volunteer Cavalry, by H. P. Moyer. Lebanon, Pa., 1911.

History of the 7th Connecticut Volunteer Infantry, compiled by Stephen Walkley. Southington, Conn., 1905.

The History of the 10th Massachusetts Battery of Light Artillery in the War of the Rebellion, by John D. Billings. Boston, 1881.

History of the 3rd Pennsylvania Cavalry, compiled by the Regimental History Association. Philadelphia, 1905.

History of the 3rd Regiment of Wisconsin Veteran Volunteer Infantry, by Edwin E. Bryant. Madison, 1891.

The History of the 39th Regiment Illinois Volunteer Veteran Infantry, by Charles M. Clark., M.D. Chicago, 1880.

History of the 36th Regiment Massachusetts Volunteers, by Henry Sweetser Burrage. Boston, 1884.

History of the 12th Massachusetts Volunteers, by Lieutenant Colonel Benjamin F. Cook. Boston, 1882.

History of the 12th Regiment New Hampshire Volunteers, by Captain A. W. Bartlett. Concord, N.H., 1897.

History of the 24th Michigan of the Iron Brigade, by O. B. Curtis. Detroit, 1891.

History of the 29th Regiment of Massachusetts Volunteer Infantry, by William O. Osborne. Boston, 1877.

I Rode with Stonewall, by Henry Kyd Douglas. Chapel Hill, 1940.

In the Defenses of Washington: or, the Sunshine in a Soldier's Life, by Stephen F. Blanding. Providence, 1889.

The Irish Brigade and Its Campaigns, by Captain D. P. Conyngham. Boston, 1869.

The Iron-Hearted Regiment; being an Account of the Battles, Marches and Gallant Deeds Performed by the 115th Regiment New York Volunteers, by James H. Clark. Albany, 1865.

Journal History of the 29th Ohio Veteran Volunteers, by J. Hamp Se Cheverell. Cleveland, 1883.

The Last Hours of Sheridan's Cavalry, by H. E. Tremain. New York, 1904.

A Little Fifer's War Diary, by C. W. Bardeen. Syracuse, N.Y., 1910.

Meade's Headquarters, 1863–1865: Letters of Col. Theodore Lyman from the Wilderness to Appomattox, selected and edited by George R. Agassiz. Boston, 1922.

Memoirs of a Volunteer, by John Beatty, edited by Harvey S. Ford. New York, 1946.

Memoirs of Chaplain Life, by the Very Rev. William Corby, C.S.C. Notre Dame, Ind., 1894.

Military History of the Third Division, Ninth Corps, Army of the Potomac, compiled and edited by Milton A. Embick. Harrisburg, Pa., 1910.

Music on the March, by Frank Rauscher. Philadelphia, 1892.

Musket and Sword, by Edwin C. Bennett. Boston, 1900.

My Diary of Rambles with the 25th Massachusetts Volunteer Infantry, by D. L. Day. Milford, Mass., 1883.

My Life in the Army, by Robert Tilney. Philadelphia, 1912.

The Passing of the Armies, by Joshua Lawrence Chamberlain, Brevet Major General, U.S. Volunteers. New York, 1915.

Personal and Historical Sketches and Facial History of and by Members of the 7th Regiment Michigan Volunteer Cavalry, compiled by William O. Lee. Detroit, 1907.

Personal Narratives, Second Series, the Rhode Island Soldiers and Sailors Historical Society. Providence, 1880–81.

Personal Recollections of Distinguished Generals, by William F. G. Shanks. New York, 1866.

Personal Recollections of the War of 1861, by Charles A. Fuller. Sherburne, N.Y., 1914.

Recollections of a Private Soldier in the Army of the Potomac, by Frank Wilkeson. New York, 1887.

Record of Service of Company K, 150th Ohio Volunteer Infantry, by James C. Cannon. Cleveland, 1903.

Red-Tape and Pigeon-Hole Generals: as Seen from the Ranks during a Campaign in the Army of the Potomac, by a Citizen-Soldier. New York, 1864.

Red, White and Blue Badge: Pennsylvania Veteran Volunteers, by Penrose G. Mark. Harrisburg, 1911.

Reminiscences and Record of the 6th New York Veteran Volunteer Cavalry, by Alonzo Foster. Privately printed: 1892.

Reminiscences of the 19th Massachusetts Regiment, by Captain John G. B. Adams. Boston, 1899.

Reminiscences of the War of the Rebellion, by Colonel Elbridge J. Copp. Nashua, N.H., 1911.

Reminiscences of the War of the Rebellion, 1861–1865, by Major Jacob Roemer. Flushing, N.Y., 1897.

The Road to Richmond: the Civil War Memoirs of Major Abner R. Small, of the 16th Maine Volunteers, edited by Harold Adams Small. Berkeley, Cal., 1939.

Sabres and Spurs: the First Regiment Rhode Island Cavalry in the Civil War, by the Rev. Frederic Denison. Central Falls, R.I., 1876.

Service with the Sixth Wisconsin Volunteers, by Rufus R. Dawes. Marietta, Ohio, 1890.

Shot and Shell: the Third Rhode Island Heavy Artillery Regiment in the Rebellion, by the Rev. Frederic Denison. Providence, 1879.

A Soldier's Diary: the Story of a Volunteer, by David Lane. 1905.

The Story of the 15th Regiment Massachusetts Volunteer Infantry, by Andrew E. Ford. Clinton, Mass., 1898.

The Story of the First Massachusetts Light Battery, by A. J. Bennett. Boston, 1886.

The Story of the 48th, by Joseph Gould. Philadelphia, 1908.

The Story of the Regiment, by William H. Locke. Philadelphia, 1868.

The Sunset of the Confederacy, by Morris Schaff. Boston, 1912.

Ten Years in the Ranks, U.S. Army, by Augustus Meyers. New York, 1914.

Thirteenth Regiment of New Hampshire Volunteer Infantry in the War of the Rebellion: a Diary, by S. Millett Thompson. Boston and New York, 1888.

Three Years in the Army: the Story of the 13th Massachusetts Volunteers, by Charles E. Davis, Jr. Boston, 1893.

Three Years in the Sixth Corps, by George T. Stevens. New York, 1870.

Thrilling Days in Army Life, by General George A. Forsyth. New York, 1900.

The Tragedy of the Crater, by Henry Pleasants, Jr. Boston, 1938.

The Vermont Brigade in the Shenandoah Valley, by Aldace F. Walker. Burlington, Vt., 1869.

A Volunteer's Adventures, by John W. DeForest, edited by James H. Croushare. New Haven, 1946.

War Diary of Luman Harris Tenney. Cleveland, 1914.

War Years with Jeb Stuart, by Lieutenant Colonel W. W. Blackford. New York, 1945.

NOTES

Chapter One: Glory Is Out of Date

A BOY NAMED MARTIN

1. The atmosphere of army dances during the winter of 1864 is well described in *A Woman's War Record, 1861–1865,* by Septima M. Collis, pp. 34–36. The II Corps ball is depicted in *History of the 106th Regiment Pennsylvania Volunteers,* by Joseph R. C. Ward, p. 193, and in *The Diary of a Young Officer,* by Josiah M. Favill, pp. 277–80, and the corps' battle casualties are listed in Francis Walker's *History of the Second Army Corps,* p. 397. There are references to the ball and to the entertainment of the women guests, in *South After Gettysburg: Letters of Cornelia Hancock from the Army of the Potomac,* edited by Henrietta Stratton Jaquette, p. 53, and in *The Life and Letters of George Gordon Meade,* by Captain George Meade, Vol. II, p. 167.

2. *Meade's Headquarters, 1863–1865: Letters of Col. Theodore Lyman from the Wilderness to Appomattox,* selected and edited by George R. Agassiz, p. 73.

3. *Under the Old Flag,* by James Harrison Wilson, Vol. I, pp. 369–73; *Meade's Headquarters,* p. 75.

4. *Civil War Echoes: Character Sketches and State Secrets,* by Hamilton Gay Howard, p. 214.

5. *Official Records,* Vol. XXXIII, pp. 170–72; *Kilpatrick and Our Cavalry,* by James Moore, p. 143.

6. Correspondence regarding the Butler fiasco, culminating in a tart interchange between Sedgwick and Halleck during the post-mortem phase, is in the *Official Records,* Vol. XXXIII, pp. 338, 502, 506–7, 512, 514–15, 519, 530, 532, 552 ff. The business is summarized in William Swinton's *Campaigns of the Army of the Potomac,* pp. 398–99.

7. *Memoir of Ulric Dahlgren,* by Rear Admiral John A. D.

Dahlgren, pp. 1–66, 92–116; *The Rebel Raider: a Life of John Hunt Morgan,* by Howard Swiggett, p. 208.

8. *Memoir of Ulric Dahlgren,* pp. 159–62, 169, 185 ff., 204–11.

9. *History of the 17th Regiment Pennsylvania Volunteer Cavalry,* by H. P. Moyer, p. 233; *Official Records,* Vol. XXXIII, pp. 170, 172–74.

10. Kilpatrick's report, *Official Records,* Vol. XXXIII, p. 183; *History of the 17th Regiment Pennsylvania Volunteer Cavalry,* p. 234.

11. *History of the 17th Regiment Pennsylvania Volunteer Cavalry,* p. 235.

12. *Personal and Historical Sketches and Facial History of and by Members of the 7th Regiment Michigan Volunteer Cavalry,* compiled by William O. Lee, pp. 28, 198; report of Captain Joseph Gloskoski, 29th New York Infantry, a signal officer attached to Kilpatrick's column, *Official Records,* Vol. XXXIII, p. 189; *History of the 17th Regiment Pennsylvania Volunteer Cavalry,* pp. 235–36.

13. *Personal and Historical Sketches . . . 7th Regiment Michigan Volunteer Cavalry,* p. 29; *Official Records,* Vol. XXXIII, pp. 184–85, 192.

14. *History of the 17th Regiment Pennsylvania Volunteer Cavalry,* pp. 242–44; *Personal and Historical Sketches . . . 7th Regiment Michigan Volunteer Cavalry,* pp. 30–31; *Official Records,* Vol. XXXIII, p. 193.

15. *The Rebel Raider,* p. 208.

16. *Campaigns of the Army of the Potomac,* p. 400; *Memoir of Ulric Dahlgren,* p. 214; *Official Records,* Vol. XXXIII, p. 195.

17. The best account of this period of the expedition is perhaps that of Captain John F. B. Mitchell, 2nd New York Cavalry, in the *Official Records,* Vol. XXXIII, pp. 195–96.

18. *Memoir of Ulric Dahlgren,* pp. 219–22; report of Lieutenant James Pollard, 9th Virginia Cavalry, *Official Records,* Vol. XXXIII, p. 208; *The Rebellion Record,* edited by Frank Moore, Vol. VIII, Part 2, p. 589.

19. There is a thoughtful analysis of the treatment ac-

corded Dahlgren's body and effects in Swiggett's excellent *The Rebel Raider*, pp. 208–11. The photographic copies of the Dahlgren papers, forwarded by Lee to Meade, are now in the National Archives in *Union Battle Reports*, Series 729 of the Records of the Adjutant General's Office, Record Group 94. They are faded and are very nearly illegible, but it is fairly easy to see that the signature is misspelled—"Dahlgren" for "Dahlgren"—which would hardly be the case if it were genuine. The affair is discussed indignantly in *Memoir of Ulric Dahlgren*, pp. 225–35. The Bragg-Seddon-Lee correspondence is in the *Official Records*, Vol. XXXIII, pp. 217–18, 222–23.

20. *The Rebellion Record*, Vol. VIII, Part 2, pp. 572, 574, 581, 591–92; *Official Records*, Vol. XXXIII, pp. 178, 180.

21. *History of the 17th Regiment Pennsylvania Volunteer Cavalry*, p. 257.

TURKEY AT A SHOOTING MATCH

1. *Army Life in a Black Regiment*, by Thomas Wentworth Higginson, p. 310.

2. *Reminiscences and Record of the 6th New York Veteran Volunteer Cavalry*, by Alonzo Foster, pp. 102–04.

3. An interesting account of the adventures of Custer's men, and of the behavior of the contrabands who followed them, appears in *Annals of the 6th Pennsylvania Cavalry*, by the Rev. S. L. Gracey, pp. 228–29.

4. *History of the 17th Regiment Pennsylvania Volunteer Cavalry*, pp. 245–46.

5. *Ibid.*, pp. 247, 251–52. The reference to the chalk line in the row of black faces is borrowed from this account.

6. *Journal History of the 29th Ohio Veteran Volunteers*, by J. Hamp Se Cheverell, p. 21.

7. *The Road to Richmond*, by Major Abner R. Small, p. 193. For an interesting depiction of a typical Army of the Potomac veteran early in 1864, see *Three Years in the Army: the Story of the 13th Massachusetts Volunteers*, by Charles E. Davis, Jr., p. 262.

8. An excellent analysis of the way the draft and bounty laws worked occurs in *Lincoln and the War Governors,* by William B. Hesseltine, pp. 290 *ff.* This writer points out that the draft actually brought in few new men; its chief effect was to compel the state governors to raise troops. See also the report of James B. Fry, provost marshal general, *Official Records,* Series III, Vol. V, pp. 599 *ff.*

9. *History of the 12th Regiment New Hampshire Volunteers,* by Captain A. W. Bartlett, pp. 152–53.

10. *Official Records,* Series III, Vol. V, p. 831; *Three Years in the Army,* pp. 131, 264. The report of Thomas A. McParlin, medical director of the Army of the Potomac (*Official Records,* Vol. XXXVI, Part 1, pp. 213 *ff.*), gives a horrifying account of the defective human material which came to camp in the winter of 1863–64.

11. *Three Years in the Army,* p. 270.

12. *History of the 12th Regiment New Hampshire Volunteers,* p. 155.

13. *History of the 2nd Connecticut Volunteer Heavy Artillery,* by Theodore F. Vaill, p. 45.

14. *Three Years in the Army,* p. 302. The gambling and fighting are described by Stephen F. Blanding in *In the Defenses of Washington; or, the Sunshine in a Soldier's Life,* pp. 8–10.

15. *The History of the 39th Regiment Illinois Volunteer Veteran Infantry,* by Charles M. Clark, M.D., pp. 240–42.

16. There is a detailed and rather dreadful account of life on this island camp in *Henry Wilson's Regiment: History of the 22nd Massachusetts Infantry,* by John L. Parker and Robert G. Carter, pp. 359–60, 362–70.

17. *A Little Fifer's War Diary,* by C. W. Bardeen, pp. 261–62; *History of Durrell's Battery in the Civil War,* by Lieutenant Charles A. Cuffel, p. 167; *History of the 12th Regiment New Hampshire Volunteers,* pp. 156–57.

18. The reader who wants an extended account of one of these sea voyages is referred to Frank Wilkeson's *Recollections of a Private Soldier in the Army of the Potomac,* pp. 14–19—one of the most graphic and least romanticized of all

the Civil War reminiscences, with a tone of bitter disillusionment which sounds almost as if it had come out of World War II.

19. *Ibid.*, pp. 1–14, 20. For the way the bounty men vanished on the way to camp, see *The Story of the 15th Regiment Massachusetts Volunteer Infantry*, by Andrew E. Ford, p. 290.

20. *Four Years Campaigning in the Army of the Potomac*, by D. G. Crotty, p. 141.

21. *Musket and Sword*, by Edwin C. Bennett, p. 200; *The Irish Brigade and Its Campaigns*, by Captain D. P. Conyngham, pp. 425–38. The writer of *History of Durrell's Battery in the Civil War* remarks (p. 168) that the 79th New York was the only IX Corps regiment which failed to re-enlist that winter. All regiments which re-enlisted were re-enforced by drafts of new recruits. See also the pamphlet, *Report of Committee to Recruit the Ninth Army Corps*, printed in New York in 1866.

22. *Official Records*, Series III, Vol. V, pp. 600, 669. In the summer of 1864 U. S. Grant wrote to Secretary of State Seward that not one in eight of the high-bounty men ever performed good service at the front. (*Official Records*, Series II, Vol. VII, p. 614.)

23. *History of the 7th Connecticut Volunteer Infantry*, compiled by Stephen Walkley, p. 150.

24. *Recollections of a Private Soldier*, pp. 32–34.

25. *Four Years Campaigning in the Army of the Potomac*, pp. 117–18; *My Diary of Rambles with the 25th Massachusetts Volunteer Infantry*, by D. L. Day, p. 110; *Three Years in the Army*, pp. 302–3.

26. *History of the 5th Regiment Maine Volunteers*, by the Rev. George W. Bicknell, p. 296. The manuscript letters of Edwin Wentworth of the 37th Massachusetts, made available through the kindness of Miss Edith Adams of Auburn, Maine, show how the high-bounty system could affect a veteran's decision. Early in the winter, Private Wentworth was writing to his wife that he would not re-enlist: "There are plenty of men at home, better able to bear arms than I am, and I am willing they should take their chance on the battlefield and

have their share of glory and honor." Later, however, he reflected that with the bounty he could buy a home and some
land—"it will enable me to provide you a good home and a
chance to live comfortably." In the end, Private Wentworth
re-enlisted, and was killed at Spotsylvania Court House.

27. *A Brief History of the 100th Regiment*, by Samuel P.
Bates, p. 21; *Service with the 6th Wisconsin Volunteers*, by
Rufus R. Dawes, p. 235; *Official Records*, Vol. XXXIII, p.
776.

28. *Reminiscences of the 19th Massachusetts Regiment*,
by Captain John G. B. Adams, pp. 79, 89.

FROM A MOUNTAIN TOP

1. *Music on the March, 1862–65*, by Frank Rauscher, pp.
122, 141, 145, 151; *History of the 3rd Pennsylvania Cavalry*,
compiled by the Regimental History Association, pp. 409–11.

2. *Campaigning with Grant*, by General Horace Porter,
pp. 15, 22, 28.

3. *Ibid.*, p. 30.

4. For various glimpses of Grant, see *Captain Sam Grant*,
by Lloyd Lewis, pp. 99–100; *Campaigning with Grant*, pp.
45, 56; *Army Life: a Private's Reminiscences of the Civil
War*, by the Rev. Theodore Gerrish, p. 324; *A War Diary of
Events in the War of the Great Rebellion*, by Brigadier General George H. Gordon, p. 351; *Three Years in the Army*,
p. 315; *Following the Greek Cross; or, Memories of the Sixth
Army Corps*, by Brigadier General Thomas W. Hyde, p. 181.

5. *Meade's Headquarters*, p. 81; *Correspondence of John
Sedgwick, Major General*, Vol. II, pp. 177–78.

6. For soldiers' comments on Grant, see *Down in Dixie:
Life in a Cavalry Regiment in the War Days*, by Stanton P.
Allen, pp. 187–88; *Four Years in the Army of the Potomac: a
Soldier's Recollections*, by Major Evan Rowland Jones, pp.
128–29; *The Road to Richmond*, p. 130.

7. *Campaigning with Grant*, pp. 46–47; an incident described to General Porter after the war by Longstreet himself.

8. Congressional doubts in regard to Grant's drinking, and

the reliance placed on Rawlins, are touched on by General James H. Wilson, who was fairly intimate with both Grant and Rawlins, in *Under the Old Flag*, Vol. I, pp. 345–46. Dana's comment is cited in *Abraham Lincoln: the War Years*, by Carl Sandburg, Vol. II, p. 542. The whole question of the extent to which alcohol was a problem to Grant is carefully examined in Lewis's fine book, *Captain Sam Grant*. (His conclusion: that it wasn't nearly as big a problem as some people have assumed.)

9. References to heavy drinking among Army of the Potomac officers abound in regimental histories and personal memoirs. Specifically, see *Days and Events: 1860–1866*, by Colonel Thomas L. Livermore, p. 297; *South After Gettysburg*, p. 55; *Camp-Fire Chats of the Civil War*, by Washington Davis, pp. 284–85.

10. *The Life of Ulysses S. Grant*, by Charles A. Dana and Major General James Harrison Wilson, p. 185; *The Generalship of Ulysses S. Grant*, by Colonel J. F. C. Fuller, p. 210; *The Life and Letters of George Gordon Meade*, Vol. II, p. 201; *The Life of John A. Rawlins*, by Major General J. H. Wilson, pp. 426–27.

11. *Memoirs of a Volunteer*, by John Beatty, edited by Harvey S. Ford, p. 210; *History of Durrell's Battery in the Civil War*, p. 150.

12. *Recollections of a Private Soldier*, pp. 36–37.

13. *Down in Dixie*, pp. 180–82.

14. *Letters of a War Correspondent*, by Charles A. Page, p. 110; *Musket and Sword*, p. 198.

15. There is a good pen picture of Sheridan in Gerrish's *Army Life*, p. 249, and Sheridan's crack about the bob-tailed brigadiers is to be found in *Personal Memoirs of John H. Brinton*, p. 267. For the cavalryman's complaint about hard work, see *Deeds of Daring: or, History of the 8th New York Volunteer Cavalry*, by Henry Norton, pp. 106–7. Other details are in the *Official Records*, Vol. XXXIII, p. 711, and *Under the Old Flag*, Vol. 1, pp. 331, 374–75.

16. *History of the 10th Massachusetts Battery of Light Artillery in the War of the Rebellion*, by John D. Billings,

pp. 37-38. (Incidentally, this book contains a good account of the assignments and duties of members of a Civil War gun crew, pp. 18-19.) See also *Recollections of a Private Soldier*, p. 22.

17. *Official Records*, Vol. XXXIII, p. 907.

18. *Memoirs of Chaplain Life*, by the Very Rev. William Corby, p. 357; *Reminiscences of the 19th Massachusetts Regiment*, pp. 84, 86.

19. *Three Years in the Army*, p. 316; *Service with the 6th Wisconsin Volunteers*, pp. 241-42.

20. *Reminiscences of the War of the Rebellion*, by Major Jacob Roemer, p. 30; *The Diary of a Line Officer*, by Captain Augustus C. Brown, p. 11; *History of the First Regiment of Heavy Artillery, Massachusetts Volunteers*, by Alfred S. Roe and Charles Nutt, pp. 124-36; *History of the 12th Massachusetts Volunteers*, by Lieutenant Colonel Benjamin W. Cook, p. 126; manuscript letters of Carl Bissell, of the 2nd Connecticut Heavy Artillery.

21. *History of the 2nd Connecticut Volunteer Heavy Artillery*, p. 81; *Official Records*, Vol. XXXVI, Part 3, p. 110.

22. *The Road to Richmond*, p. 195.

23. *Official Records*, Vol. XXXIII, pp. 638-39, 688, 717; *History of the Second Army Corps*, p. 400. Soldiers of the Army of the Potomac usually identified themselves first with their regiment and next with their army corps. Brigades and divisions generally (with a few striking exceptions) claimed less of their loyalty.

24. *Correspondence of John Sedgwick, Major General*, Vol. II, pp. 168, 175; *Personal Recollections of the Civil War*, by Brigadier General John Gibbon, pp. 209-10. One of the most fascinating might-have-beens of the Civil War is this move which almost put Sedgwick in charge of operations in the Valley. If he had been there instead of Sigel, the story in 1864 would have been very different. Meade planned to give John Gibbon command of the VI Corps.

25. Brigadier General Hazard Stevens, in *Papers of the Military Historical Society of Massachusetts*, Vol. IV, pp. 178-79 (referred to hereafter as *M.H.S.M. Papers*).

26. Francis A. Walker, in *M.H.S.M. Papers*, Vol. X, pp. 51, 53, 56-57.

27. For Warren, see *Gouverneur Kemble Warren: the Life and Letters of an American Soldier*, by Emerson Gifford Taylor, pp. 5 ff.; *The Road to Richmond*, p. 126; *Days and Events*, p. 304; *Three Years in the Army*, p. 349.

28. *South After Gettysburg*, p. 73; *History of the 87th Regiment Pennsylvania Volunteers*, by George R. Prowell, p. 117.

29. *Three Years in the Army*, p. 309; *History of the 8th Cavalry Regiment, Illinois Volunteers*, by Abner Hard, pp. 292-93; *A Little Fifer's War Diary*, p. 168.

30. *Down in Dixie*, pp. 165-66.

31. *The Road to Richmond*, pp. 129-30.

Chapter Two: Roads Leading South

WHERE THE DOGWOOD BLOSSOMED

1. *Following the Greek Cross*, p. 182; *Recollections of a Private Soldier*, pp. 42-43; *Meade's Headquarters*, p. 180; *Army Life: a Private's Reminiscences*, pp. 156-57; *The Road to Richmond*, p. 130.

2. *Down in Dixie*, p. 206.

3. Discussions of the courses open to Grant at the beginning of the 1864 campaign in Virginia are practically without number. A good brief summary of the alternatives can be found in *The Virginia Campaigns of '64 and '65*, by Major General Andrew A. Humphreys, pp. 9-12. (This book is authoritative, comprehensive, and unfortunately rather dull; it is cited hereafter as Humphreys.) For an extended study, see *The Generalship of Ulysses S. Grant*, pp. 209 ff. Grant discusses the matter in some detail in the *Official Records*, Vol. XXXVI, Part 1, pp. 12-18. I am greatly indebted to Ralph Happel, historian, Fredericksburg and Spotsylvania County National Military Park, for the loan of his manuscript account of the Battle of the Wilderness, which contains an excellent analysis of the strategy of the Wilderness campaign

and its relation to the grand strategy of the final year of the war.

4. *Down in Dixie*, p. 210.

5. *Campaigning with Grant*, pp. 42-43.

6. *Recollections of a Private Soldier*, pp. 43-46; *M.H.S.M. Papers*, Vol. IV, p. 185; *The Road to Richmond*, p. 131. Note the comment by Brigadier General Rufus Ingalls, chief quartermaster: "Our troops are undoubtedly loaded down on marches too heavily even for the road, not to speak of battle. . . . Our men are generally overloaded, fed and clad, which detracts from their marching capacity and induces straggling." (*Official Records*, Vol. XL, Part 1, p. 39.)

7. *Campaigns of the 146th Regiment New York State Volunteers*, compiled by Mary Genevie Green Brainard, p. 176; *Down in Dixie*, p. 176.

8. *Recollections of a Private Soldier*, pp. 49-51; *The Story of the Regiment*, by William Henry Locke, p. 323.

9. *Campaigns of the 146th Regiment New York State Volunteers*, p. 179.

10. *Army Life: a Private's Reminiscences*, pp. 217, 345-46.

11. *Campaigns of the Army of the Potomac*, pp. 420-22; *M.H.S.M. Papers*, Vol. IV, p. 188; *Following the Greek Cross*, p. 183.

12. *Campaigning with Grant*, pp. 50, 64-65.

13. *Army Life: a Private's Reminiscences*, p. 161.

14. *The Fifth Army Corps*, by Lieutenant Colonel William H. Powell, pp. 608, 610.

15. Colonel Theodore Lyman, in *M.H.S.M. Papers*, Vol. IV, pp. 167-68; also in *Meade's Headquarters*, pp. 90-91.

16. Report of Emory Upton, *Official Records*, Vol. XXXVI, Part 1, p. 665.

17. *History of the Corn Exchange Regiment*, by the Survivors' Association, p. 400; *Four Years in the Army of the Potomac*, p. 129; *Three Years in the Sixth Corps*, by George T. Stevens, pp. 309-10; *Army Life: a Private's Reminiscences*, p. 170.

18. *Campaigns of the Army of the Potomac*, p. 422; *Three Years in the Army*, pp. 329-30; *Official Records*, Vol.

XXXVI, Part 1, p. 614; *Campaigning with Grant*, p. 72.

19. There is a good account of Wadsworth's and Crawford's advance in the *M.H.S.M. Papers*, Vol. IV, pp. 127-32. For a glimpse of Crawford, see *The Road to Richmond*, p. 149.

20. *Campaigns of the 146th Regiment New York State Volunteers*, p. 195; *Official Records*, Vol. XXXVI, Part 1, pp. 601, 610-11, 614.

21. *M.H.S.M. Papers*, Vol. IV, pp. 189-94; General Getty's report, *Official Records*, Vol. XXXVI, Part 1, pp. 676-77.

22. *M.H.S.M. Papers*, Vol. IV, pp. 192-93.

23. *Official Records*, Vol. XXXVI, Part 1, pp. 696-98; *Recollections of a Private Soldier*, pp. 66-67.

24. *A Little Fifer's War Diary*, pp. 110-11, 302; *M.H.S.M. Papers*, Vol. IV, pp. 142, 193-94. For a good discussion of Federal difficulties in adjusting to woods fighting, see *The Crisis of the Confederacy*, by Cecil Battine, p. 382.

25. *The Road to Richmond*, p. 133.

SHADOW IN THE NIGHT

1. *Reminiscences of the 19th Massachusetts Regiment*, pp. 87-88; *Official Records*, Vol. XXXVI, Part 1, pp. 218-19; *History of the Corn Exchange Regiment*, p. 403; *M.H.S.M. Papers*, Vol. IV, pp. 101-2; *The Road to Richmond*, p. 133.

2. *Recollections of a Private Soldier*, pp. 52-54.

3. *Meade's Headquarters*, pp. 93-94; *Official Records*, Vol. XXXVI, Part 1, pp. 320-21, 667.

4. The classic account of this, of course, is Douglas Southall Freeman's, in *R. E. Lee*, Vol. III, pp. 286-88.

5. *Four Years in the Army of the Potomac*, p. 130; *Official Records*, Vol. XXXVI, Part 1, p. 403; *The Diary of a Line Officer*, p. 35; Humphreys, p. 56.

6. *Recollections of a Private Soldier*, p. 201.

7. *Ibid.*, pp. 57, 206; *Army Life: a Private's Reminiscences*, p. 170; *A Little Fifer's War Diary*, p. 86.

8. *M.H.S.M. Papers*, Vol. IV, p. 196; *History of the Second Army Corps*, pp. 428-29.

9. *Official Records*, Vol. XXXVI, Part 1, p. 438; *M.H.S.M. Papers*, Vol. IV, p. 151.

10. *History of the Second Army Corps*, pp. 417, 422.

11. Brigadier General Alexander Webb in *Official Records*, Vol. XXXVI, Part 1, pp. 437 *ff.*; also in *Battles and Leaders of the Civil War*, Vol. IV, pp. 159 *ff.*

12. "Battle of the Wilderness and Death of General Wadsworth," by Captain Robert Monteith, in the *War Papers Read before the State of Wisconsin Commandery, Military Order of the Loyal Legion of the United States*, Vol. I, p. 414; *Official Records*, Vol. XXXVI, Part 1, pp. 477, 934.

13. *History of the Philadelphia Brigade*, by Charles H. Banes, p. 231; *Meade's Headquarters*, p. 95; *Official Records*, Vol. XXXVI, Part 1, p. 488.

14. *M.H.S.M. Papers*, Vol. IV, pp. 154-55, 200; *Official Records*, Vol. XXXVI, Part 1, p. 624; *History of the 150th Regiment, Pennsylvania Volunteers*, by Lieutenant Colonel Thomas Chamberlin, pp. 187-88.

15. Hancock discusses all of this in some detail in his report, *Official Records*, Vol. XXXVI, Part 1, pp. 320-23, 325. After the war a sharp argument over the misunderstanding developed between Hancock and Gibbon; Gibbon tells about it in his *Personal Recollections*, pp. 387 *ff.*

16. *History of the 106th Regiment Pennsylvania Volunteers*, pp. 201-2; *Official Records*, Vol. XXXVI, Part 1, p. 514; *Recollections of a Private Soldier*, p. 73. For a very vivid account of this phase of the battle, see *The Crisis of the Confederacy*, p. 385.

17. Grant's *Personal Memoirs*, Vol. II, p. 201.

18. *Campaigning with Grant*, p. 59.

19. *Ibid.*, p. 52. For glimpses of Grant's earlier relations with Hays, see *Captain Sam Grant*, pp. 128, 172.

20. *Meade's Headquarters*, p. 98; *History of the 5th Regiment Maine Volunteers*, p. 305; *Following the Greek Cross*, pp. 186-87; *History of the 3rd Pennsylvania Cavalry*, p. 419.

21. *Letters of a War Correspondent*, p. 57; Colonel Theodore Lyman, in *M.H.S.M. Papers*, Vol. IV, p. 105n.; *Campaigning with Grant*, pp. 69-70.

22. *Four Years in the Army of the Potomac*, p. 131; *Following the Greek Cross*, p. 188.

23. The extent to which Grant was shaken, and the way in which he concealed his alarm, are set forth by his firm admirer, General Wilson, in *Under the Old Flag*, Vol. 1, pp. 390-91.

24. *Campaigning with Grant*, p. 74.

25. *History of the Philadelphia Brigade*, p. 235; *Reminiscences of the 19th Massachusetts Regiment*, p. 88; *Annals of the 6th Pennsylvania Cavalry*, p. 237.

26. *The Road to Richmond*, p. 134; *Campaigning with Grant*, p. 79; *History of the 3rd Pennsylvania Cavalry*, p. 421.

27. *Recollections of a Private Soldier*, p. 79. Major General U. S. Grant, III, grandson of the Civil War general, says that as a young lieutenant just out of West Point he served under an elderly officer who had been an enlisted man in the Army of the Potomac. This officer one day remarked that the most thrilling moment of the whole war, to him, came when his column turned south at the Chancellorsville crossroads and the men realized that they were advancing instead of retreating. As Historian Ralph Happel says, in his manuscript study previously referred to, Grant's decision to continue south after the Wilderness was "one of the most important decisions in American history."

28. *Following the Greek Cross*, p. 189.

ALL THEIR YESTERDAYS

1. *Following the Greek Cross*, pp. 189-90.

2. *History of the 3rd Pennsylvania Cavalry*, pp. 421-22. In General Warren's journal entry for May 7 (*Official Records*, Vol. XXXVI, Part 1, p. 540) there is reference to a delay caused by Meade's cavalry escort. Major Small refers to it in *The Road to Richmond*, p. 135, and General Webb mentions it in *Battles and Leaders*, Vol. IV, p. 164. It should be added, of course, that various other factors delayed the move to Spotsylvania Court House, the most important probably

being the job done by the Confederate cavalry under Fitz-hugh Lee.

3. *History of the 12th Massachusetts Volunteers,* p. 129.

4. There is an excellent description of the approach, assault, and repulse of Robinson's division, by Brigadier General Charles L. Pierson, in the *M.H.S.M. Papers,* Vol. IV, pp. 214-16, supplemented by Colonel Theodore Lyman, pp. 238-39. See also the *Official Records,* Vol. XXXVI, Part 1, pp. 594, 597, 619; *The Story of the Regiment,* p. 333; *Military Memoirs of a Confederate,* by E. P. Alexander, pp. 510-12.

5. *Campaigning with Grant,* p. 84; *Meade's Headquarters,* pp. 105-6,*n.*

6. *Down in Dixie,* p. 316; "Sheridan's Richmond Raid," in *Battles and Leaders,* Vol. IV, p. 189.

7. *Down in Dixie,* pp. 276-77.

8. The handling of the Wilderness wounded is treated in detail in the report of Surgeon Thomas A. McParlin, Medical Director of the Army of the Potomac, in the *Official Records,* Vol. XXXVI, Part 1, p. 220. See also *Down in Dixie,* p. 276; *Red-Tape and Pigeon-Hole Generals,* by a Citizen-Soldier, p. 242; *Army Life: a Private's Reminiscences,* p. 171.

9. Surgeon Edward B. Dalton, chief medical officer of Depot Field Hospital, in *Official Records,* Vol. XXXVI, Part 1, p. 270; also Surgeon McParlin's report, in that volume, p. 234; *South After Gettysburg,* pp. 85-86, 88; *Three Years in the Sixth Corps,* p. 343.

10. *Three Years in the Sixth Corps,* pp. 344-45.

11. Report of Surgeon McParlin, *Official Records,* Vol. XXXVI, Part 1, pp. 227 *ff.*

12. *Ibid.,* pp. 235, 271-74.

13. *History of the First Regiment of Heavy Artillery, Massachusetts Volunteers,* p. 151.

14. *South After Gettysburg,* pp. 88, 90.

15. *Army Life: a Private's Reminiscences,* p. 177; *Recollections of a Private Soldier,* p. 88; *History of the Corn Exchange Regiment,* p. 410.

16. *Following the Greek Cross,* pp. 191-93; *Campaigning with Grant,* pp. 89-90; *Correspondence of John Sedgwick,*

Major General, Vol. II, p. 210; *Battles and Leaders*, Vol. IV, p. 175.

17. *Abraham Lincoln: the War Years*, Vol. III, p. 47.

18. *Campaigning with Grant*, p. 83.

SURPASSING ALL FORMER EXPERIENCES

1. *The Life and Letters of Emory Upton*, by Peter S. Mitchie, pp. 1-9, 12-37, 51-68.

2. *Ibid.*, pp. 96-98. Upton's formal report on this assault is unusually detailed and graphic. It is in the *Official Records*, Vol. XXXVI, Part 1, pp. 665-68.

3. *Military Memoirs of a Confederate*, p. 517; *Official Records*, Vol. XXXVI, Part 1, pp. 667-68.

4. *History of the Philadelphia Brigade*, pp. 242-43.

5. *Ibid.*, p. 244; *M.H.S.M. Papers*, Vol. IV, p. 436.

6. Upton's report, *op. cit.*, p. 668.

7. *War Diary of Luman Harris Tenney, 1861-1865*, p. 115; *Meade's Headquarters*, p. 110.

8. *Official Records*, Vol. XXXVI, Part 1, p. 230; *Battles and Leaders*, Vol. IV, p. 170.

9. *The Long Arm of Lee*, by Jennings C. Wise, Vol. II, pp. 787-88.

10. Hancock's report, *Official Records*, Vol. XXXVI, Part 1, p. 334.

11. *Ibid.*, p. 335. General Barlow described the movement of his division in the *M.H.S.M. Papers*, Vol. IV, pp. 245-270. His article has been drawn on liberally in the preparation of this chapter.

12. *Personal Recollections of the War of 1861*, by Charles A. Fuller, pp. 9-10; *The Irish Brigade and Its Campaigns*, by Captain D. P. Conyngham, p. 474; *Mr. Lincoln's Army*, by Bruce Catton, pp. 209-10.

13. Barlow's account, *M.H.S.M. Papers*, Vol. IV, p. 247. See also, in the same volume, the article by Lieutenant Colonel William R. Driver, p. 277.

14. *Official Records*, Vol. XXXVI, Part 1, pp. 409–10.

15. *History of the 106th Regiment Pennsylvania Volun-*

teers, p. 206; *Official Records*, Vol. XXXVI, Part 1, pp. 335, 470; *History of the Second Army Corps*, p. 470.

16. *History of the Philadelphia Brigade*, p. 246; Barlow, in *M.H.S.M. Papers*, Vol. IV, pp. 251–52; *The Long Arm of Lee*, Vol. II, pp. 789–90; *Military Memoirs of a Confederate*, pp. 519–20.

17. *Lee's Lieutenants*, by Douglas Southall Freeman, Vol. III, pp. 404–6; *Service with the 6th Wisconsin Volunteers*, p. 268; *Official Records*, Vol. XXXVI, Part 1, pp. 373–74; *M.H.S.M. Papers*, Vol. IV, pp. 281–82.

18. *Military Memoirs of a Confederate*, p. 522; *Reminiscences of the 19th Massachusetts Regiment*, p. 91; *History of the Philadelphia Brigade*, p. 247.

19. *Military Memoirs of a Confederate*, p. 522; Barlow's story, in *M.H.S.M. Papers*, Vol. IV, pp. 254–55; *History of the Philadelphia Brigade*, p. 248; *History of the Second Army Corps*, p. 473.

20. Brigadier General Lewis A. Grant, in *M.H.S.M. Papers*, Vol. IV, p. 269. This fighting is graphically described by G. Norton Galloway in *Battles and Leaders*, Vol. IV, pp. 170–74. See also *Following the Greek Cross*, p. 202. Incidentally, it may be well to emphasize that the famous "bloody angle" was here, and not at the tip of the salient where Barlow's men first broke the line.

21. *Battles and Leaders*, Vol. IV, pp. 171–72; *Official Records*, Vol. XXXVI, Part 1, pp. 537, 539; *History of the 150th Regiment Pennsylvania Volunteers*, pp. 196–97.

22. *History of the 24th Michigan of the Iron Brigade*, by O. B. Curtis, p. 243; *History of the Second Army Corps*, p. 475.

23. *Reminiscences of the 19th Massachusetts Regiment*, p. 91; *History of the 106th Regiment Pennsylvania Volunteers*, p. 207; *Service with the 6th Wisconsin Volunteers*, p. 266; *Following the Greek Cross*, pp. 200–1.

24. *Following the Greek Cross*, p. 200; report of Brigadier General Lewis Grant, *Official Records*, Vol. XXXVI, Part 1, p. 704; *Reminiscences of the 19th Massachusetts Regiment*,

p. 92; *History of the 24th Michigan in the Iron Brigade*, p. 244.

25. *The Road to Richmond*, p. 141; *Campaigns of the 146th Regiment New York State Volunteers*, pp. 205–6.

26. *Recollections of a Private Soldier*, pp. 83–86; *M.H.S.M. Papers*, Vol. IV, pp. 297–98; *Letters of a War Correspondent*, p. 72; *History of the First Regiment of Heavy Artillery, Massachusetts Volunteers*, pp. 152–58. It might be noted that veteran troops called up to stand in support of the heavies in this fight put in a profitable afternoon looting the knapsacks which the green troops had piled in a row before going into action.

27. *My Life in the Army*, by Robert Tilney, p. 53.

Chapter Three: One More River to Cross

THE CRIPPLES WHO COULD NOT RUN

1. Grant's report of the final year's operations, *Official Records*, Vol. XXXVI, Part 1, pp. 20–21; *Campaigning with Grant*, pp. 124–25.

2. *Recollections of a Private Soldier*, pp. 91–93.

3. *Recollections of the Civil War*, by Charles A. Dana, p. 199.

4. *Four Years in the Army of the Potomac*, p. 190.

5. *Four Years Campaigning in the Army of the Potomac*, pp. 132, 134.

6. For these incidents involving punishment for cowardice, see *The Story of the 48th*, by Joseph Gould, pp. 177–78; *Reminiscences of the War of the Rebellion*, p. 200; *Reminiscences of the 19th Massachusetts Regiment*, p. 94; *Berdan's United States Sharpshooters in the Army of the Potomac*, by Captain C. A. Stevens, p. 355.

7. *Musket and Sword*, p. 169; *A Little Fifer's War Diary*, p. 119.

8. *History of the Philadelphia Brigade*, p. 247.

9. *The History of the 10th Massachusetts Battery*, p. 181.

10. The point is emphasized in Humphreys, p. 118.

11. *Army Life: a Private's Reminiscences*, pp. 187–90.

12. *Down in Dixie*, p. 86.

13. *History of the Corn Exchange Regiment*, p. 426; *History of the 51st Regiment of Pennsylvania Volunteers*, by Thomas H. Parker, p. 555; *Letters of a War Correspondent*, p. 81; *Official Records*, Vol. XXXVI, Part 1, p. 405; *The Story of the First Massachusetts Light Battery*, by A. J. Bennett, pp. 153–54; *The Road to Richmond*, p. 200.

14. *Musket and Sword*, p. 238.

15. *Three Years in the Army: the Story of the 13th Massachusetts Volunteers*, p. 132.

16. *History of the Philadelphia Brigade*, pp. 255–56.

17. *Meade's Headquarters*, pp. 99–100; Gibbon's *Personal Recollections*, p. 229.

18. *History of the Sauk County Riflemen*, by Philip Cheek and Mair Pointon, p. 110.

19. The organization of the Veterans Reserve Corps, and the amazing adventures of the regiment as described in the text, are fully recovered in the report made at the end of the war by Captain J. W. De Forest, acting assistant adjutant general, to Brigadier General James B. Fry, provost marshal general. It is found in the *Official Records*, Series 3, Vol. V, pp. 543–55.

20. *Four Years Campaigning in the Army of the Potomac*, p. 140; *History of the 12th Massachusetts Volunteers*, p. 142; *History of the 24th Michigan*, p. 241.

21. *M.H.S.M. Papers*, Vol. VI, p. 389.

JUDGMENT TRUMP OF THE ALMIGHTY

1. The enlisted men of the Army of the Potomac referred to this constant shift to the left as "the jug-handle movement." (*History of the Corn Exchange Regiment*, p. 432.)

2. *Three Years in the Army; the Story of the 13th Massachusetts Volunteers*, pp. 356, 364; Major William P. Shreve in *M.H.S.M. Papers*, Vol. IV, p. 316; *Service with the 6th Wisconsin Volunteers*, p. 279; manuscript letters of Lewis Bissell; *History of the 51st Regiment of Pennsylvania Volun-*

teers, p. 548. Note the sentiment expressed in *History of the 50th Regiment Pennsylvania Veteran Volunteers,* by Lewis Crater, p. 62: "Notwithstanding the regiment had lost fully 330 men killed, wounded and captured during the month, the very best feeling was exhibited, from the fact that all felt that some progress was being made and that the end of the rebellion was prospectively drawing near."

3. *In the Ranks from the Wilderness to Appomattox Courthouse,* by the Rev. R. E. McBride, p. 62.

4. *M.H.S.M. Papers,* Vol. V, p. 3; *Following the Greek Cross,* p. 214.

5. *M.H.S.M. Papers,* Vol. IV, pp. 326–28.

6. *Following the Greek Cross,* p. 208; *Three Years in the Sixth Corps,* p. 350; *History of the 2nd Connecticut Volunteer Heavy Artillery,* pp. 54–55.

7. Grant to Halleck, dispatch of May 22, *Official Records,* Vol. XXXVI, Part 1, p. 7; Grant to W. F. Smith, *Official Records,* Vol. XXXVI, Part 3, p. 371; Smith to Rawlins, *ibid.,* p. 410.

8. *History of the 2nd Connecticut Volunteer Heavy Artillery,* p. 58.

9. *Ibid.,* pp. 60–62, 65–66; *Three Years in the Sixth Corps,* pp. 352–53; *Official Records,* Vol. XXXVI, Part 1, pp. 662, 671.

10. A brief summary of the reasons for attacking at Cold Harbor is given in Humphreys, p. 181. See also *Lee, Grant and Sherman,* by Lieutenant Colonel Alfred H. Burne, p. 50. For a detailed account of the battle, strongly critical of Grant, see "Cold Harbor," by Major General Martin T. McMahon, in *Battles and Leaders,* Vol. IV, pp. 213 *ff.*

11. An extensive discussion of the way the rifle-trench combination had revolutionized tactics by 1864 can be found in Fuller's *The Generalship of U. S. Grant,* pp. 51–52, 57–58, 61.

12. *Official Records,* Vol. XXVII, Part 1, pp. 761, 775, 778, 831–32; Humphreys, pp. 75–76.

13. *History of the 36th Regiment Massachusetts Volun-*

teers, by Henry Sweetser Burrage, p. 189; *M.H.S.M. Papers,* Vol. V, p. 9.

14. *Meade's Headquarters,* p. 138.

15. *History of the Second Army Corps,* p. 506.

16. *Meade's Headquarters,* p. 139.

17. *Official Records,* Vol. XXXVI, Part 3, pp. 482, 489, 491–92, 505, 506; Humphreys, pp. 176–78, 182; *History of the Philadelphia Brigade,* p. 269; *Recollections of a Private Soldier,* pp. 127–28; *History of the 106th Regiment Pennsylvania Volunteers,* p. 219.

18. The point is stressed by Captain Charles H. Porter in *M.H.S.M. Papers,* Vol. IV, p. 339.

19. *Letters of a War Correspondent,* p. 96.

20. *Battles and Leaders,* Vol. IV, p. 217.

21. *Recollections of a Private Soldier,* p. 129; *History of the 10th Massachusetts Battery,* p. 200.

22. *Reminiscences of the 19th Massachusetts Regiment,* pp. 98–99.

23. Hancock's report on Cold Harbor is in the *Official Records,* Vol. XXXVI, Part 1, pp. 344–46. See also Gibbon's report, in that volume, p. 433, and Barlow's, p. 369. Humphreys' account, accurate but somewhat prosy, is in his book, pp. 182–85. There are graphic glimpses of the II Corps assault in *History of the Philadelphia Brigade,* pp. 270–72, and *History of the 106th Regiment Pennsylvania Volunteers,* pp. 220–21. See also *Following the Greek Cross,* p. 211, and *Meade's Headquarters,* p. 144.

24. *Army Life: a Private's Reminiscences,* p. 194. The very weight of Confederate fire seems actually to have kept the VI Corps from suffering as many casualties as Hancock's men had, by pinning the assault waves down from the very beginning. Reading the reports of division and brigade commanders in this corps leads one to believe that June 1 was a worse day for the VI Corps than June 3. Emory Upton's report, for instance, disposes of the June 3 assault with the simple statement that "another assault was ordered, but being deemed impracticable along our front was not made." For the VI Corps reports, see the *Official Records,* Vol. XXXVI,

Part 1, pp. 662, 671, 674, 680, 689–90, 708, 720, 727, 735, 739, 744, 750, 753. Most of these reports contain little indication that June 3 was especially different from any other day at Cold Harbor.

25. *History of the 12th Regiment New Hampshire Volunteers*, pp. 202–8. The account of Cold Harbor in this regimental history is one of the best contemporary battle descriptions in Civil War literature.

26. Offhand, it would seem both difficult and unnecessary to exaggerate the horrors of Cold Harbor, but for some reason—chiefly, perhaps, the desire to paint Grant as a callous and uninspired butcher—no other Civil War battle gets as warped a presentation as this one. It is usually described as a battle in which the entire Federal army attacked "all along the line," losing 13,000 men thereby. Actually, the 13,000 casualties are the total for nearly two weeks in the Cold Harbor lines, and the June 3 assault involved only part of the army. The V Corps did not attack at all on that day and the IX Corps did little more than drive in the Confederate skirmish lines. The VI Corps, as mentioned above, fared worse on June 1 than on June 3, and the real weight of the June 3 attack was borne by two of Hancock's divisions and one—Martindale's—of Smith's. In those three divisions, of course, the loss was genuinely frightful.

27. *Campaigning with Grant*, p. 109; manuscript letters of Lewis Bissell.

SECONDHAND CLOTHES

1. *Official Records*, Vol. XXXVI, Part 3, pp. 672, 870.
2. For trench life at Cold Harbor immediately after the June 3 attacks, see *History of the 106th Regiment Pennsylvania Volunteers*, pp. 223–24; *Army Life: a Private's Reminiscences*, p. 195; *History of the 12th Regiment New Hampshire Volunteers*, p. 214; *In the Ranks from the Wilderness to Appomattox Courthouse*, p. 54; *Three Years in the Sixth Corps*, pp. 357–58.

3. *Recollections of a Private Soldier*, p. 120; *History of Durrell's Battery in the Civil War*, pp. 190, 229.

4. *Official Records*, Vol. XXXVI, Part 1, p. 365.

5. *Official Records*, Vol. XXXVI, Part 3, p. 647.

6. There is a good discussion of this point by Major William P. Shreve in *M.H.S.M. Papers*, Vol. IV, p. 316.

7. *Diary of Battery A, First Regiment Rhode Island Light Artillery*, by Theodore Reichardt, p. 139.

8. *History of the 12th Regiment New Hampshire Volunteers*, p. 214; *History of the 106th Regiment Pennsylvania Volunteers*, p. 224; *History of the Corn Exchange Regiment*, p. 469.

9. *Service with the 6th Wisconsin Volunteers*, pp. 277, 284–85; *Meade's Headquarters*, p. 147.

10. *Campaigning with Grant*, pp. 107–8.

11. *Following the Greek Cross*, p. 211.

12. *The Life and Letters of Emory Upton*, pp. 108–9. In view of the violent criticism that has descended on Grant because of Cold Harbor, it might be noted that Upton is specifically blaming the army's troubles there, not on Grant, but on the various generals of the Army of the Potomac.

13. *Under the Old Flag*, Vol. I, p. 400.

14. *Four Years Campaigning in the Army of the Potomac*, p. 151.

15. *The Iron-Hearted Regiment*, by James H. Clark, p. 131.

16. A Connecticut soldier in the VI Corps, at about this time, declares himself in respect to civilians: "I suppose that all those miserable hounds who stay at home, that have no more courage than a chicken, who do all they can to encourage others to enlist but stay at home themselves, are marrying all of the smartest girls up there and leave the soldier boys without any or of the poorest quality." (Manuscript letters of Lewis Bissell.)

17. *History of the 12th Regiment New Hampshire Volunteers*, p. 208; *Letters of a War Correspondent*, p. 99.

18. *M.H.S.M. Papers*, Vol. V, p. 15; *Reminiscences of the 19th Massachusetts Regiment*, p. 100; *History of the Corn*

Exchange Regiment, p. 469; *The Diary of a Line Officer*, p. 68.

19. *The Diary of Gideon Welles*, Vol. II, pp. 43–44.

20. *Under the Old Flag*, Vol. I, p. 445.

21. Humphreys, p. 194.

22. For diametrically opposite verdicts on Grant's strategy up to this point the reader is referred to two studies in Vol. IV of the *M.H.S.M. Papers*—"Grant's Campaign in Virginia in 1864," by John C. Ropes, which is highly critical, and "Grant's Campaign Against Lee," by Colonel Thomas L. Livermore, which is very laudatory.

23. Grant's plans and the reasons assigned for them are set forth in his dispatch to Halleck dated June 5, *Official Records*, Vol. XXXVI, Part 1, pp. 11–12.

24. *History of the 2nd Connecticut Volunteer Heavy Artillery*, p. 69; *History of the Philadelphia Brigade*, pp. 277–78.

25. *Meade's Headquarters*, p. 163.

26. Colonel Theodore Lyman in *M.H.S.M. Papers*, Vol. V, p. 21.

LIE DOWN, YOU DAMN FOOLS

1. *Following the Greek Cross*, p. 117; *Meade's Headquarters*, p. 148; *Days and Events*, p. 372; *Under the Old Flag*, Vol. I, p. 271. There is a good sketch of Smith's career in the *Dictionary of American Biography*.

2. *Official Records*, Vol. XL, Part 2, p. 595.

3. Butler's moves are briefly summarized in Grant's report, *Official Records*, Vol. XXXVI, Part 1, pp. 20–21. There is a good picture of the way this fumbled campaign looked to the men in the ranks in *History of the 12th Regiment New Hampshire Volunteers*, pp. 171–85.

4. *From Chattanooga to Petersburg Under Generals Grant and Butler*, by Major General William Farrar Smith, p. 36.

5. This description is taken from Colonel Livermore's *Days and Events*, p. 369.

6. *M.H.S.M. Papers*, Vol. V, p. 89.

7. "Four Days of Battle at Petersburg," by General Beauregard, in *Battles and Leaders*, Vol. IV, p. 540.

8. *M.H.S.M. Papers*, Vol. V, p. 56.

9. *Ibid.*, p. 90.

10. *Ibid.*, p. 68; *Battles and Leaders*, Vol. IV, p. 541; *Official Records*, Vol. XL, Part 2, p. 83.

11. Hancock's report, *Official Records*, Vol. XL, Part 1, pp. 303–5; Grant's report, *Official Records*, Vol. XXXVI, Part 1, p. 25; *M.H.S.M. Papers*, Vol. V, pp. 64–72, 93–96; *Days and Events*, pp. 361–62; *History of the Second Army Corps*, pp. 527–32.

12. *Recollections of a Private Soldier*, p. 157: "We were in high spirits. . . . We knew that we had out-marched Lee's veterans and that our reward was at hand."

13. *Ibid.*, pp. 158, 160, 162.

14. *Battles and Leaders*, Vol. IV, p. 541.

15. *M.H.S.M. Papers*, Vol. V, pp. 28–29; *Official Records*, Vol. XL, Part 2, p. 86.

16. Colonel Theodore Lyman in *M.H.S.M. Papers*, Vol. V, p. 30.

17. *Ibid.*, p. 31. See also *History of the Second Army Corps*, pp. 532–36. For a detailed and judicious critique of the operations of mid-June, see "The Failure to Take Petersburg on June 16–18, 1864," by John C. Ropes, in *M.H.S.M. Papers*, Vol. V.

18. *Official Records*, Vol. XL, Part 2, pp. 91, 117.

19. Letter of General Beauregard to General C. M. Wilcox, printed in *M.H.S.M. Papers*, Vol. V, p. 121.

20. Ropes, *op. cit.*, pp. 167–68; Humphreys, pp. 217–18.

21. Ropes, *op. cit.*, pp. 169–72; *History of the 51st Regiment of Pennsylvania Volunteers*, pp. 564–70; *History of the 29th Regiment of Massachusetts Volunteer Infantry*, by William H. Osborne, pp. 304–5; *Battles and Leaders*, Vol. IV, p. 543; *History of the Second Army Corps*, p. 539; Humphreys, p. 219; manuscript letters of Henry Clay Heisler.

22. *Official Records*, Vol. XL, Part 2, p. 120.

23. *Ibid.*, pp. 167, 179, 205; *Battles and Leaders*, Vol. IV, p. 544.

24. *History of the First Regiment of Heavy Artillery, Massachusetts Volunteers*, pp. 173–75; *History of the Second Army Corps*, pp. 541–42.

25. *Recollections of a Private Soldier*, pp. 166-67, 180–81.

26. *Official Records*, Vol. XL, Part 2, pp. 156–57.

27. *History of the 2nd Connecticut Volunteer Heavy Artillery*, p. 74.

28. Ropes, *op. cit.*, p. 184.

Chapter Four: White Iron on the Anvil

CHANGING THE GUARD

1. Manuscript letters of Lewis Bissell; *History of the 10th Massachusetts Battery*, pp. 228–29; *The Diary of a Line Officer*, p. 91; *A Soldier's Diary: the Story of a Volunteer*, by David Lane, p. 177; manuscript letters of Henry Clay Heisler; *M.H.S.M. Papers*, Vol. V, p. 29.

2. *A Soldier's Diary: the Story of a Volunteer*, p. 225; *Musket and Sword*, p. 291; *Campaigns of the 146th Regiment New York State Volunteers*, p. 230; *Army Life: a Private's Reminiscences*, pp. 203–4.

3. *Days and Events*, p. 377; *Ten Years in the U. S. Army*, by Augustus Meyers, p. 323.

4. *Meade's Headquarters*, pp. 181–82.

5. *The Story of the 48th*, p. 281; *In the Ranks from the Wilderness to Appomattox Courthouse*, pp. 93–94; *Thirteenth Regiment of New Hampshire Volunteer Infantry in the War of the Rebellion: a Diary*, by S. Millett Thompson, p. 529.

6. *In the Ranks from the Wilderness to Appomattox Courthouse*, p. 97; manuscript letters of Lewis Bissell.

7. Humphreys, pp. 230–35, 243; *Battles and Leaders*, Vol. IV, pp. 233–39.

8. *Under the Old Flag*, Vol. I, pp. 457–82.

9. *From Chattanooga to Petersburg under Generals Grant and Butler*, pp. 5, 52–53, 174–78; *Official Records*, Vol. XL, Part 2, pp. 558–59.

10. *My Diary of Rambles with the 25th Massachusetts Volunteer Infantry,* p. 109. Theodore Lyman described Butler as "the strangest sight on a horse you ever saw . . . with his head set immediately on a stout, shapeless body, his very squinting eyes, and a set of legs and arms that look as if made for somebody else and hastily glued to him by mistake." (*Meade's Headquarters,* p. 192.) For an understanding of what Colonel Lyman had in mind the reader is urged to study the photograph of Butler in *Divided We Fought,* edited by David Donald, p. 95.

11. *A War Diary of Events in the War of the Great Rebellion,* by Brigadier General George H. Gordon, pp. 359, 365.

12. *Official Records,* Vol. XL, Part 2, pp. 131–32, 188.

13. *Official Records,* Vol. XXXIV, Part 3, pp. 332–33. For an illuminating exchange of letters between Grant and Halleck on the general subject of politics and military appointments, with especial reference to General Banks, see that same volume, pp. 252–53, 293, 316, 332, 409–10.

14. *Official Records,* Vol. XL, Part 1, p. 28.

15. *Ibid.,* p. 35.

16. *Recollections of the Civil War,* p. 227.

17. Grant to President Lincoln, *Official Records,* Vol. XXXVII, Part 2, p. 433. It should be pointed out that in suggesting Meade as commander in the Valley Grant warmly endorsed him: "With General Meade in command of such a division I would have every confidence that all the troops within the military division would be used to the very best advantage from a personal examination of the ground."

18. Gibbon's *Personal Recollections,* pp. 243–44, 248–51.

19. *History of the Second Army Corps,* pp. 544–47; *Official Records,* Vol. XL, Part 2, pp. 304, 330, 468. The corps' historian calls this "perhaps the most humiliating episode in the experience of the Second Corps."

20. Gibbon's *Personal Recollections,* pp. 227–28; *Official Records,* Vol. XL, Part 1, p. 368.

21. *History of the Second Army Corps,* p. 556; *Recollections of a Private Soldier,* p. 194.

22. *Official Records*, Vol. XL, Part 2, pp. 444–45; *History of the 106th Regiment Pennsylvania Volunteers*, p. 232.

23. *Official Records*, Vol. XL, Part 1, p. 474.

24. *History of the 24th Michigan*, p. 275; *History of the 12th Regiment New Hampshire Volunteers*, p. 229; *My Life in the Army*, p. 95.

25. *Service with the 6th Wisconsin Volunteers*, pp. 299–300; *History of the 150th Regiment Pennsylvania Volunteers*, pp. 197–98.

26. *Musket and Sword*, p. 183; *History of the 39th Regiment Illinois Volunteer Veteran Infantry*, p. 208.

27. Manuscript letters of Lewis Bissell; *Meade's Headquarters*, p. 232.

28. *A Soldier's Diary: the Story of a Volunteer*, p. 150.

29. Manuscript letters of Sebastian Muller, Library of Congress.

30. *Reminiscences of the 19th Massachusetts Regiment*, p. 105.

I KNOW STAR-RISE

1. Burnside's testimony at the Court of Inquiry on the Petersburg Mine, *Official Records*, Vol. XL, Part 1, p. 60; the three white divisions in the IX Corps lost 1,150 men between June 20 and July 20, and on the latter date mustered 9,023 enlisted men for duty. See also *Major General Ambrose E. Burnside and the Ninth Army Corps*, by Augustus Woodbury, pp. 420–21.

2. Manuscript letters of Henry Clay Heisler.

3. *The Story of the 48th*, p. 160; *The Tragedy of the Crater*, by Henry Pleasants, Jr., p. 35.

4. *The Tragedy of the Crater*, p. 32; *The 48th in the War*, by Oliver Christian Bosbyshell, pp. 163–65.

5. *The Tragedy of the Crater*, pp. 34–37.

6. Report of Major Nathaniel Michler, Corps of Engineers, *Official Records*, Vol. XL, Part 1, p. 291.

7. *The Tragedy of the Crater*, p. 41; *Battles and Leaders*,

Vol. IV, p. 545; *Official Records*, Vol. XL, Part 1, p. 45; Part 2, p. 619.

8. Manuscript letters of Henry Clay Heisler; *The 48th in the War*, pp. 167–68; *Official Records*, Vol. XL, Part 1, pp. 556–58; Part 2, pp. 396–97, 417; *The Tragedy of the Crater*, p. 38.

9. *The Tragedy of the Crater*, pp. 44–45; Colonel Pleasants' report, *Official Records*, Vol. XL, Part 1, p. 558.

10. *Official Records*, Vol. XL, Part 1, pp. 557–58. Cross sections, diagrams, and general plans of the mine shaft, magazines, and ventilating shaft can be found in that volume, pp. 559–63, and in *Battles and Leaders*, Vol. IV, p. 548.

11. *History of the 36th Regiment Massachusetts Volunteers*, p. 228; *Grant's Personal Memoirs*, Vol. II, p. 314; *The Long Arm of Lee*, Vol. II, p. 846.

12. *Official Records*, Vol. XL, Part 1, p. 557.

13. *Major General Ambrose E. Burnside and the Ninth Army Corps*, p. 430; *Meade's Headquarters*, p. 201.

14. *Official Records*, Series III, Vol. V, p. 669.

15. *Papers of the Kansas Commandery, Military Order of the Loyal Legion of the United States*, p. 11.

16. This point is made in *A History of Negro Troops in the War of the Rebellion*, by George W. Williams, p. 170.

17. *Ibid.*, pp. 235–36.

18. *Army Life in a Black Regiment*, p. 36—one of the most fascinating books, incidentally, in Civil War literature.

19. *Ibid.*, p. 74; *The Negro in the Late War*, by Captain George E. Sutherland; *War Papers, Wisconsin Commandery, Military Order of the Loyal Legion of the United States*, Vol. I, p. 183.

20. *Army Life in a Black Regiment*, p. 274.

21. *Three Years in the Sixth Corps*, pp. 275–76.

22. *Shot and Shell: the 3rd Rhode Island Heavy Artillery Regiment in the Rebellion*, by the Rev. Frederic Denison, pp. 214, 229; manuscript letters of Henry Clay Heisler; *Service with the 6th Wisconsin Volunteers*, p. 296; *Army Life in a Black Regiment*, p. 31.

23. Manuscript letters of Lewis Bissell; *A Woman's War Record*, p. 56.

24. *Ten Years in the U. S. Army*, p. 327.

25. *Memoirs of a Volunteer*, p. 231; *Musket and Sword*, p. 315; *Official Records*, Vol. XXXIII, p. 898.

26. *Army Life in a Black Regiment*, pp. 39, 71–72, 350.

27. *Ibid.*, pp. 14–15, 80; *The Fourteenth Regiment Rhode Island Heavy Artillery in the War to Preserve the Union*, by William H. Chenery, p. 18.

28. *Official Records*, Vol. XXXIII, p. 1020; Vol. XXXVII, Part 1, pp. 71–72; *A History of Negro Troops in the War of the Rebellion*, p. 238.

29. *Army Life in a Black Regiment*, p. 335.

30. *Major General Ambrose E. Burnside and the Ninth Army Corps*, pp. 420–21; *M.H.S.M. Papers*, Vol. V., p. 216.

31. *Battles and Leaders*, Vol. IV, p. 563; *Papers of the Kansas Commandery, Military Order of the Loyal Legion of the United States*, p. 16.

32. *Army Life in a Black Regiment*, p. 286.

LIKE THE NOISE OF GREAT THUNDERS

1. Humphreys, pp. 247–48; Grant's *Personal Memoirs*, Vol. II, p. 310; *History of the Second Army Corps*, p. 559.

2. *Letters of a War Correspondent*, p. 190.

3. *The Long Arm of Lee*, Vol. II, p. 846.

4. *R. E. Lee*, Vol. III, p. 466; *History of the Second Army Corps*, pp. 565–66.

5. Meade's orders are in the *Official Records*, Vol. XL, Part 1, pp. 43–44. His testimony at the court of inquiry, pp. 44–58, tells how he overruled Burnside on the use of the colored troops, and how Grant upheld him. The plan of attack, as finally approved, is well outlined in *M.H.S.M. Papers*, Vol. V, p. 229.

6. Burnside's testimony at the court of inquiry tells about the drawing of lots; *Official Records*, Vol. XL, Part 1, p. 61. There is a full account of his meeting with the division

commanders in *Major General Ambrose E. Burnside and the Ninth Army Corps*, pp. 432–34.

7. *Meade's Headquarters*, pp. 168, 199. It is interesting to note that during the fighting around Spotsylvania Court House, two and one-half months earlier, a IX Corps private was writing in his diary that "the regiment on our left, the 14th N. Y. Heavy Art., ran for life at the first fire, leaving our left flank entirely exposed." (Manuscript diary of Corporal S. O. Bryant, 20th Michigan Infantry.) This heavy artillery regiment was in the first assault wave at the Petersburg crater.

8. Brigadier General Stephen M. Weld, *M.H.S.M. Papers*, Vol. V, p. 218: "He was a drunkard and an arrant coward. In every fight we had been in under Ledlie he had been under the influence of liquor." See also the testimony of Surgeon H. E. Smith, 27th Michigan, at the court of inquiry; *Official Records*, Vol. XL, Part 1, p. 119. In his *Personal Memoirs* (Vol. II, p. 313), Grant remarked: "Ledlie, besides being otherwise inefficient, proved also to possess disqualification less common among soldiers."

9. *History of the 51st Regiment of Pennsylvania Volunteers*, p. 573; *History of the 36th Regiment Massachusetts Volunteers*, p. 233; *Papers of the Kansas Commandery, Military Order of the Loyal Legion of the United States*, pp. 16–17.

10. *Official Records*, Vol. XL, Part 1, pp. 600, 609.

11. *Ibid.*, p. 47.

12. *Ibid.*, p. 557; *Battles and Leaders*, Vol. IV, p. 551n.

13. *Major General Ambrose E. Burnside and the Ninth Army Corps*, p. 437; *History of the 36th Regiment Massachusetts Volunteers*, pp. 234–35; *Battles and Leaders*, Vol. IV, p. 564; *The Story of the 48th*, p. 230; *History of the 29th Regiment of Massachusetts Volunteer Infantry*, pp. 312–13; *Reminiscences of the War of the Rebellion, 1861–65*, p. 246; *M.H.S.M. Papers*, Vol. V, p. 246; *Official Records*, Vol. XL, Part 1, p. 323.

14. *Official Records*, Vol. XL, Part 1, p. 324; *Letters of a War Correspondent*, p. 195; *The Diary of a Line Officer*, p. 102.

15. *Battles and Leaders*, Vol. IV, p. 561; *The Story of the 48th*, p. 230; *M.H.S.M. Papers*, Vol. V, p. 208; *Musket and Sword*, p. 293.

16. *Battles and Leaders*, Vol. IV, p. 562; *Major General Ambrose E. Burnside and the Ninth Army Corps*, p. 438; *M.H.S.M. Papers*, Vol. V, p. 209; *The Story of the 48th*, p. 231.

17. Humphreys, p. 255. (General Humphreys declares flatly: "Had the division advanced in column of attack, led by a resolute, intelligent commander, it would have gained the crest in 15 minutes after the explosion, and before any serious opposition could have been made to it.")

18. *Official Records*, Vol. XL, Part 1, pp. 78, 84, 92, 121–22, 701.

19. Humphreys, pp. 256–57; *Major General Ambrose E. Burnside and the Ninth Army Corps*, pp. 439–40; *Official Records*, Vol. XL, Part 1, pp. 280–81, 567, 574. There is a good account of the work done by the Confederate artillery in *The Long Arm of Lee*, Vol. II, pp. 865–75.

20. For testimony on this point, see *Official Records*, Vol. XL, Part 1, p. 122.

21. *M.H.S.M. Papers*, Vol. V, pp. 214–15.

22. *Official Records*, Vol. XL, Part 1, pp. 48, 55, 80–81, 142–43.

23. *Ibid.*, p. 119.

24. *Personal Experiences of a Staff Officer*, pp. 18–19, 31; *Battles and Leaders*, Vol. IV, p. 564; *Official Records*, Vol. XL, Part 1, p. 104.

25. *Ibid.*, p. 105; *Battles and Leaders*, Vol. IV, p. 565.

26. *M.H.S.M. Papers*, Vol. V, pp. 210–11.

27. *Official Records*, Vol. XL, Part 1, pp. 49, 57, 144; *The Story of the 48th*, p. 239.

28. Report of Captain Theodore Gregg, 45th Pennsylvania, an unusually vivid picture of the situation in the crater, *Official Records*, Vol. XL, Part 1, pp. 554–56. See also *History of the 36th Regiment Massachusetts Volunteers*, p. 238; *Reminiscences of the War of the Rebellion*, p. 249.

29. Manuscript letters of Henry Clay Heisler.

30. Grant to Halleck, *Official Records*, Vol. XL, Part 1, p.

17; *History of the 36th Regiment Massachusetts Volunteers*, p. 240; manuscript letters of Henry Clay Heisler. Accurately enough, this young private remarked that the trouble was due to "a mismanage by some of the Brigadier Generals in our corps."

31. *The Iron-Hearted Regiment*, p. 154; *Battles and Leaders*, Vol. IV, p. 564.

Chapter Five: Away, You Rolling River

SPECIAL TRAIN FOR MONOCACY JUNCTION

1. Details as to Private Spink and his crew, the befuddled guard at Aqueduct Bridge, and the heavy growth of brush on the approaches to the defenses, are in the *Official Records*, Vol. XXXVII, Part 2, pp. 61, 83. For Lincoln's remark about Halleck, see *Fifty Years in Camp and Field: Diary of Maj. Gen. Ethan Allen Hitchcock*, edited by W. A. Croffut, pp. 463–64.

2. *Official Records*, Vol. XXXVII, Part 2, pp. 339–41, 365–67; *R. E. Lee*, Vol. IV, pp. 240–41.

3. *Official Records*, Vol. XXXVII, Part 1, pp. 555–56, 607; *I Rode with Stonewall*, by Henry Kyd Douglas, pp. 288, 290.

4. *Diary of Gideon Welles*, Vol. II, pp. 70–71, 73.

5. *Official Records*, Vol. XXXVII, Part 1, p. 259; *Diary of Gideon Welles*, Vol. II, p. 84.

6. *Official Records*, Vol. XXXVII, Part 1, pp. 231, 254–55.

7. *Ibid.*, pp. 346–47. Need it be remarked that any reader who has not yet allowed Douglas Southall Freeman to introduce him to Jubal Early, through the three volumes of *Lee's Lieutenants*, should get on with the ceremony at once?

8. *Personal Memoirs of John H. Brinton*, pp. 280–81. There is an artless story of the adventures of one of the 100-day militia outfits in *Record of Service of Company K, 150th Ohio Volunteer Infantry*, by James C. Cannon.

9. *Following the Greek Cross*, p. 222; *History of the 2nd Connecticut Volunteer Heavy Artillery*, p. 83; *Three Years in the Sixth Corps*, pp. 375-76.

10. *Following the Greek Cross*, pp. 222–23.

11. McCook's report, *Official Records*, Vol. XXXVII, Part 1, p. 231; *The Vermont Brigade in the Shenandoah Valley*, by Aldace F. Walker, p. 29.

12. Meigs' report, *Official Records*, Vol. XXXVII, Part 1, p. 259; *Diary of Gideon Welles*, Vol. II, p. 75.

13. Letter of General Wright, printed in *Three Years in the Sixth Corps*, p. 382.

14. *I Rode with Stonewall*, pp. 295–96. It should be noted that when Early made his remark about scaring Abe Lincoln he did not know that Lincoln had been present at Fort Stevens during the fighting.

15. *Following the Greek Cross*, p. 224; *The Vermont Brigade in the Shenandoah Valley*, p. 30; *Official Records*, Vol. XXXVII, Part 1, pp. 232–33, 247, 259–60, 276–77.

16. *The Vermont Brigade in the Shenandoah Valley*, p. 37; *History of the 2nd Connecticut Volunteer Heavy Artillery*, pp. 86–88.

17. *Three Years in the Sixth Corps*, pp. 383–87; *The Vermont Brigade in the Shenandoah Valley*, pp. 38–48; *Following the Greek Cross*, p. 228.

18. *History of the 2nd Connecticut Volunteer Heavy Artillery*, p. 90.

19. *History of the 19th Army Corps*, by Richard B. Irwin, p. 367.

20. Grant's *Personal Memoirs*, Vol. II, pp. 315, 317.

21. *Official Records*, Vol. XXXVII, Part 2, pp. 374, 408.

22. *Ibid.*, p. 558.

23. *Ibid.*, p. 582.

24. For Grant's move to Washington, his talk with Hunter, and his order moving the troops to Halltown, see his *Personal Memoirs*, Vol. II, pp. 318–20.

TO PEEL THIS LAND

1. *The Shenandoah Valley and Virginia, 1861 to 1865: a War Study*, by Sanford C. Kellogg, pp. 214–15; *History of*

the Shenandoah Valley, by William Couper, Vol. I, pp. 140–47, 217–26; *M.H.S.M. Papers,* Vol. VI, pp. 62, 156.

2. *Official Records,* Vol. XXXVII, Part 2, pp. 301, 329.

3. *Annals of the 6th Pennsylvania Cavalry,* p. 286.

4. *War Diary of Luman Harris Tenney, 1861–1865,* p. 136.

5. *Official Records,* Series 2, Vol. VII, pp. 1014–15.

6. *Ibid.,* pp. 976, 1012–13.

7. *Ibid.,* pp. 1092–93.

8. *Ibid.,* pp. 892–94, 997. As late as the winter of 1865, Senator Ben Wade was urging Congress to adopt a joint resolution prescribing retaliatory treatment on Confederate soldiers in Northern prisons. After much debate, the measure was watered down so that it simply condemned alleged mistreatment of captured Federals and enjoined humane measures on the men in charge of Northern prisons. (*Recollections of War Times,* by Albert Gallatin Riddle, p. 326.)

9. This particular estimate is from *The Vermont Brigade in the Shenandoah Valley,* p. 51. It can hardly be repeated too often that the numbers reported "present for duty" by Federal commanders seldom bore very much relationship to the number that would actually be put into action. Two examples may be cited. The morning report of one regiment in this summer of 1864 showed 708 enlisted men present for duty; but the regimental historian explains that only 472 would go into action. The other 236 would be accounted for by the infinity of details, and by the "present, sick." A less extreme case is shown by a Pennsylvania regiment which reported 343 "present for duty" at Gettysburg but which put only 300 into the fight there. (*History of the 2nd Connecticut Volunteer Heavy Artillery,* p. 118; *History of the 106th Regiment Pennsylvania Volunteers,* p. 169.)

10. *A Volunteer's Adventures,* by John W. De Forest, p. 163.

11. *Ibid.,* p. 165; *The Vermont Brigade in the Shenandoah Valley,* p. 23.

12. *The Vermont Brigade in the Shenandoah Valley,* p. 50; *Following the Greek Cross,* p. 228.

13. For the reaction to Sheridan, see *Three Years in the*

Sixth Corps, p. 391; *The Vermont Brigade in the Shenandoah Valley*, pp. 54–55; *History of the 19th Army Corps*, p. 367.

14. *History of the 17th Regiment Pennsylvania Volunteer Cavalry*, pp. 219–22; *Army Life; a Private's Reminiscences*, pp. 249–50.

15. *History of the 17th Regiment Pennsylvania Volunteer Cavalry*, p. 188.

16. Rosser to Lee, *Official Records*, Vol. XXXIII, p. 1081.

17. *Ibid.*, pp. 1082, 1120–21.

18. Telegram from General E. B. Tyler to Lew Wallace, *Official Records*, Vol. XXXVII, Part 2, p. 55.

19. *Memoirs of a Volunteer*, pp. 108–9.

20. *Sabres and Spurs: the First Regiment Rhode Island Cavalry in the Civil War*, by the Rev. Frederic Denison, p. 381.

21. *Ibid.*, p. 381.

22. *History of the 17th Regiment Pennsylvania Volunteer Cavalry*, pp. 211–12.

23. *Ibid.*, p. 212.

24. *Annals of the 6th Pennsylvania Cavalry*, pp. 286–87.

25. *Personal and Historical Sketches . . . of the 7th Regiment Michigan Volunteer Cavalry*, p. 263.

26. *History of the 17th Regiment Pennsylvania Volunteer Cavalry*, p. 228.

ON THE UPGRADE

1. *Lincoln's War Cabinet*, by Burton J. Hendrick, pp. 453–59; *Abraham Lincoln*, by Benjamin P. Thomas, pp. 441–42.

2. *Abraham Lincoln: the War Years*, Vol. III, p. 218.

3. There is a good account of this Confederate program in the North, and of Captain Hines's activities, in *Confederate Operations in Canada and New York*, by John W. Headley, pp. 214–20. See also *The Rebel Raider*, pp. 123–26, 132, 157–58, 167–73. The projected raid on the Johnson's Island prison camp is voluminously covered in the *Official Records*, Series 2, Vol. VII, pp. 842, 850, 864, 910–16.

4. Headley, *op. cit.*, p. 222.

5. *Ibid.*, pp. 223–28.

6. *Ibid.*, pp. 229–30. Swiggett (*The Rebel Raider*, p. 132) remarks that Hines was "by all odds one of the two or three most dangerous and competent men in the Confederacy."

7. *A Volunteer's Adventures*, p. 172.

8. *Battles and Leaders*, Vol. IV, pp. 506–7; *History of the 8th Regiment Vermont Volunteers*, by George N. Carpenter, p. 177.

9. *A Volunteer's Adventures*, p. 173; *Battles and Leaders*, Vol. IV, p. 507.

10. *Under the Old Flag*, Vol. I, p. 554; *Three Years in the Sixth Corps*, pp. 401–3; *Official Records*, Vol. XLIII, Part 1, pp. 173–74, 197, 222.

11. *A Volunteer's Adventures*, p. 186. This engaging book contains a first-rate account of the battle of Winchester by a Federal participant.

12. *History of the 8th Regiment Vermont Volunteers*, pp. 181, 255–56.

13. *Three Years in the Sixth Corps*, p. 404.

14. *History of the 8th Regiment Vermont Volunteers*, p. 183; *A Volunteer's Adventures*, pp. 187–90; *Battles and Leaders*, Vol. IV, pp. 509–10.

15. *A Volunteer's Adventures*, p. 189; *Official Records*, Vol. XLIII, Part 1, p. 189.

16. There is an odd similarity between Sheridan's handling of the battle of Winchester and Stonewall Jackson's conduct of the battle of Cedar Mountain. In each case a general of high reputation, enjoying a great numerical advantage over his opponent, put his troops in maladroitly, was rocked hard by an unexpected enemy attack, and for a time was in danger of outright defeat—winning out, finally, because his own driving energy at last made his numerical advantage effective. For a good critique of Sheridan's campaign in the Valley, see "The Valley Campaign of 1864: a Military Study," by Lieutenant L. W. V. Kennon, in the *M.H.S.M. Papers*, Vol. VI, pp. 39 *ff*.

17. *The Story of the First Massachusetts Light Battery*, p.

179; *The Vermont Brigade in the Shenandoah Valley*, p. 105.

18. *Under the Old Flag*, Vol. I, pp. 558–59.

NO MORE DOUBT

1. Thomas's *Abraham Lincoln*, p. 449; *Lincoln's War Cabinet*, by Burton J. Hendrick, pp. 45–47; *Diary of Gideon Welles*, Vol. II, p. 158; *Abraham Lincoln: the War Years*, Vol. III, pp. 237, 244, 246.

2. *Three Years in the Sixth Corps*, p. 413; *History of the 2nd Connecticut Volunteer Heavy Artillery*, p. 108.

3. *Three Years in the Sixth Corps*, p. 414; manuscript letters of Lewis Bissell; *History of the 2nd Connecticut Volunteer Heavy Artillery*, p. 108.

4. *M.H.S.M. Papers*, Vol. VI, pp. 48 *ff*.

5. *History of the 17th Regiment Pennsylvania Volunteer Cavalry*, pp. 135, 217–18; *History of the 2nd Connecticut Volunteer Heavy Artillery*, p. 109; *Sabres and Spurs*, p. 407; manuscript letters of Lewis Bissell.

6. *The Story of the First Massachusetts Light Battery*, p. 182; *Letters of a War Correspondent*, pp. 269–70.

7. *I Rode with Stonewall*, p. 315. Note that even the historian of the 17th Pennsylvania Cavalry, normally troubled by few qualms, wrote: "If ever troops found an incentive to strike vigorous blows for their 'homes and firesides' it was those who fought Sheridan's destructions from the 6th to the 9th of October, for we do not think the annals of civilized warfare furnishes a parallel to these destructive operations . . . the blackened face of the country from Port Republic to the neighborhood of Fisher's Hill bore frightful testimony to fire and sword." (*History of the 17th Regiment Pennsylvania Volunteer Cavalry*, p. 216.)

8. *History of the Shenandoah Valley*, Vol. II, p. 954.

9. *History of the 2nd Connecticut Volunteer Heavy Artillery*, p. 109; *The Story of the First Massachusetts Light Battery*, p. 182; *Three Years in the Sixth Corps*, pp. 415–16.

10. *I Rode with Stonewall*, p. 313.

11. *Battles and Leaders*, Vol. IV, p. 513; *Lee's Lieutenants*, Vol. III, p. 597.

12. *M.H.S.M. Papers*, Vol. VI, pp. 48, 97.

13. Early's narrative about all of this is in *Battles and Leaders*, Vol. IV, p. 526. There is a description of the Union position in *A Volunteer's Adventures*, pp. 205–6—whose author, incidentally, draws the parallel between Early's audacity at Cedar Creek and Washington's at Trenton.

14. *History of the 2nd Connecticut Volunteer Heavy Artillery*, pp. 119–20.

15. *Ibid.*, pp. 120–21.

16. *The Vermont Brigade in the Shenandoah Valley*, pp. 136–40.

17. *History of the 2nd Connecticut Volunteer Heavy Artillery*, pp. 121–23; *History of the 8th Regiment Vermont Volunteers*, pp. 215–18. For descriptions of the confused fighting in the heavy fog, and the unavailing attempt to stem the fugitives and their pursuers on the turnpike, see the *Official Records*, Vol. XLIII, Part 1, pp. 215, 233, 245, 267, 284. General Wright's report on the battle is in that volume, pp. 158–61.

18. *Personal Recollections of Distinguished Generals*, by William F. G. Shanks, pp. 340–41; *Battles and Leaders*, Vol. IV, p. 518; *A Volunteer's Adventures*, pp. 210–11, 213–14, 220. The latter work speaks of the flight as taking place "with curious deliberation." For accounts of the rallying of the soldiers who did not panic, see the *Official Records*, Vol. XLIII, Part 1, pp. 197, 209–11.

19. *Lee's Lieutenants*, Vol. III, pp. 603–4.

20. *History of the 17th Regiment Pennsylvania Volunteer Cavalry*, pp. 115–17; *Thrilling Days in Army Life*, by General George A. Forsyth, pp. 135–38.

21. *Thrilling Days in Army Life*, pp. 140–43; *Battles and Leaders*, Vol. IV, p. 519.

22. *The Story of the First Massachusetts Light Battery*, p. 189.

23. *The Vermont Brigade in the Shenandoah Valley*, pp. 147–48; *History of the 17th Regiment Pennsylvania Volun-*

teer Cavalry, pp. 117–18; *Official Records*, Vol. XLIII, Part 1, pp. 251, 309.

24. *Thrilling Days in Army Life*, pp. 155–56, 159–60.

25. *History of the 2nd Connecticut Volunteer Heavy Artillery*, pp. 126–27; *The Vermont Brigade in the Shenandoah Valley*, p. 152; *History of the 8th Regiment Vermont Volunteers*, p. 223; *A Volunteer's Adventures*, p. 227.

26. *A Volunteer's Adventures*, pp. 228–29. Sheridan probably got a better reputation out of Cedar Creek than he really deserved, and it has often been argued that Generals Wright and Getty would eventually have pulled the victory out of the fire even if Sheridan had not reappeared at all. Sheridan provided the dramatics and the spur, which had long been missing from the experience of men in the Army of the Potomac. The most unrestrained enthusiasm and admiration came to him from the VI Corps itself, which provided most of the casualties at Cedar Creek, lost the fewest men captured, did most of the fighting—and, all in all, seems to have been quite willing to give to Sheridan the credit which might well have been claimed for its own generals.

27. Manuscript letters of Lewis Bissell.

Chapter Six: Endless Road Ahead

EXCEPT BY THE SWORD

1. For a moving description of the autumn landscape at Petersburg, see *Letters of a War Correspondent*, pp. 275–76. The account of the fortified lines follows Humphreys, p. 310.

2. *History of the 10th Massachusetts Battery of Light Artillery*, p. 253.

3. *Official Records*, Vol. XL, Part 1, pp. 270–71; Series 3, Vol. V, pp. 70–71; *Letters of a War Correspondent*, pp. 155–59.

4. *Official Records*, Series 3, Vol. V, pp. 70, 72–73; *History of Durrell's Battery in the Civil War*, p. 209; *History of the 2nd Connecticut Volunteer Heavy Artillery*, p. 133; *Battles and Leaders*, Vol. IV, p. 708.

5. "Grant Before Appomattox: Notes of a Confederate Bishop," by the Right Rev. Henry C. Lay, in the *Atlantic Monthly*, March, 1932.

6. *South After Gettysburg*, p. 144.

7. *Recollections of a Private Soldier*, pp. 191–92; *Army Life: a Private's Reminiscences*, p. 209; *Service with the 6th Wisconsin Volunteers*, p. 309.

8. *The Passing of the Armies*, by Major General Joshua Chamberlain, p. 12; *Army Life: a Private's Reminiscences*, p. 209. Interestingly enough, one veteran wrote that it was the new regiments, plus the shirkers and bummers who never got on the firing line, who provided most of the vote for McClellan. (*History of the 150th Pennsylvania Volunteers*, p. 244.)

9. Report of Colonel Henry L. Abbot, *Official Records*, Vol. XL, Part 1, pp. 664–65.

10. Manuscript letters of Henry Clay Heisler; *History of the 12th Regiment New Hampshire Volunteers*, p. 427.

11. *History of Durrell's Battery in the Civil War*, p. 228; *History of the 36th Regiment Massachusetts Volunteers*, pp. 246, 277; manuscript letters of Henry Clay Heisler; *The Irish Brigade and Its Campaigns*, p. 510.

12. *Four Years Campaigning with the Army of the Potomac*, p. 160.

13. *The Story of the Regiment*, pp. 367–68.

14. *History of the 198th Pennsylvania Volunteers*, by Major E. M. Woodward, p. 25.

15. *Ibid.*, p. 27; *History of the Ninth Massachusetts Battery*, by Levi W. Baker, p. 155.

16. *History of the 24th Michigan*, p. 283.

17. *South After Gettysburg*, pp. 163, 165; *History of the 87th Regiment Pennsylvania Volunteers*, p. 218.

18. *My Life in the Army*, pp. 135–36; *Music on the March*, pp. 203–4; *History of the 7th Connecticut Volunteer Infantry*, p. 176; *M.H.S.M. Papers*, Vol. VI, p. 413; *In the Ranks from the Wilderness to Appomattox Courthouse*, p. 97; *The Passing of the Armies*, pp. 21, 23. For the recruiting and training of an entire new division of first-rate troops, see *Military*

History of the 3rd Division, Ninth Corps, Army of the Potomac, by Milton A. Embick, pp. 1–5.

19. *Following the Greek Cross,* p. 238.

20. *Ibid.,* p. 240; manuscript letters of Lewis Bissell; *History of the 2nd Connecticut Volunteer Heavy Artillery,* p. 144.

21. *Thirteenth Regiment of New Hampshire Volunteer Infantry in the War of the Rebellion,* pp. 533, 537–38.

22. Manuscript letters of Lewis Bissell; *Musket and Sword,* p. 303.

23. *Following the Greek Cross,* p. 240; *History of the 2nd Connecticut Volunteer Heavy Artillery,* p. 148.

24. *History of Durrell's Battery in the Civil War,* pp. 232–34; *History of the 51st Regiment of Pennsylvania Volunteers,* pp. 602–5. For early glimpses of Stephens and Lincoln, see *Abraham Lincoln: the Prairie Years,* by Carl Sandburg, Vol. I, pp. 378, 382 ff.

25. There is a good discussion of the peace mission and the Davis-Stephens relationship in "Alexander Stephens and Jefferson Davis," by James Z. Rabun, in the *American Historical Review,* Vol. LVIII, No. 2. See also *Abraham Lincoln: the War Years,* Vol. IV, pp. 39–46, 48, 58–60; *Jefferson Davis: the Unreal and the Real,* by Robert McElroy, Vol. II, pp. 435–40; *Diary of Gideon Welles,* Vol. II, p. 237. There is a mention of the return of Lieutenant Murray from his Southern prison in *Thirteenth Regiment of New Hampshire Volunteer Infantry in the War of the Rebellion,* p. 534.

26. *Ibid.,* pp. 447, 520, 542.

27. *History of the Ninth Massachusetts Battery,* p. 160.

GREAT LIGHT IN THE SKY

1. *History of the 1st Connecticut Artillery,* by John C. Taylor, p. 154; *Major General Ambrose E. Burnside and the Ninth Army Corps,* p. 476.

2. *Reminiscences of the War of the Rebellion,* p. 262.

3. *Memoirs of Chaplain Life,* p. 335.

4. *Military History of the 3rd Division, Ninth Army Corps, Army of the Potomac,* pp. 1–4, 14–16; *Battles and Leaders,*

Vol. IV, p. 584 *ff.* Hartranft's report on the fight is in the *Official Records*, Vol. XLVI, Part 1, pp. 345–49.

5. Grant's *Personal Memoirs*, Vol. II, pp. 433–34; Humphreys, pp. 320–21; *Official Records*, Vol. XLVI, Part 3, pp. 141–42, 171.

6. *Personal Memoirs of John H. Brinton*, p. 265.

7. Grant's *Personal Memoirs*, Vol. II, p. 425.

8. Manuscript letter of Sergeant George S. Hampton, 91st Pennsylvania Veteran Volunteers, in the possession of Mr. J. Frank Nicholson of Manassas, Virginia.

9. *Sherman, Fighting Prophet*, by Lloyd Lewis, p. 524.

10. Sheridan's report, reprinted in Moore's *Rebellion Record*, Vol. XI, p. 634 *ff.*

11. *Army Life: a Private's Reminiscences*, p. 251.

12. Humphreys, pp. 322–25; *Official Records*, Vol. XLVI, Part 1, pp. 50–51.

13. *The Passing of the Armies*, p. 34.

14. *The Story of the Regiment*, p. 381.

15. *Annals of the 6th Pennsylvania Cavalry*, p. 330; *Last Hours of Sheridan's Cavalry*, by Henry Edwin Tremain, pp. 19–24.

16. Grant's *Personal Memoirs*, Vol. II, p. 439; *Battles and Leaders*, Vol. IV, p. 709; Moore's *Rebellion Record*, Vol. XI, p. 644; *The Life of John A. Rawlins*, pp. 309–10.

17. Horace Porter describes the meeting between Grant and Sheridan in *Battles and Leaders*, Vol. IV, p. 710. See also *The Passing of the Armies*, p. 62; Grant's *Personal Memoirs*, Vol. II, p. 437.

18. There is an engaging description of Devin's movements, with particular reference to the difficulties of the horse holders on the retreat to Dinwiddie Courthouse, in *Last Hours of Sheridan's Cavalry*, pp. 37–45.

19. *Ibid.*, pp. 50–55; Sheridan's report, Moore's *Rebellion Record*, Vol. XI, p. 644; *Battles and Leaders*, Vol. IV, p. 711.

20. Grant's *Personal Memoirs*, Vol. II, p. 442; *Battles and Leaders*, Vol. IV, p. 711; *Official Records*, Vol. XLVI, Part 1, p. 380.

21. *Last Hours of Sheridan's Cavalry*, p. 56.

THE SOLDIERS SAW DAYLIGHT

1. *The Passing of the Armies*, pp. 65–78; *The Fifth Army Corps*, pp. 781–83; Humphreys, pp. 330–34; *Official Records*, Vol. XLVI, Part 1, pp. 337; 817–18.

2. *Campaigns of the 146th Regiment New York State Volunteers*, p. 292; *History of the Corn Exchange Regiment*, p. 574; Humphreys, pp. 337–40; *The Passing of the Armies*, pp. 90–96; *Official Records*, Vol. XLVI, Part 1, pp. 820, 822. In his report on Five Forks Warren explained that since his troops were so close to the enemy it was impossible to summon them out by drum or bugle; verbal orders had to pass down a long chain which began at corps headquarters and ended with non-coms arousing individual soldiers by shaking them. For the confusing series of orders Warren got that night, see the volume just cited, pp. 365–67, 410, 419–20.

3. *The Passing of the Armies*, pp. 104, 121.

4. Humphreys, p. 356; *Battles and Leaders*, Vol. IV, p. 723.

5. *The Passing of the Armies*, introduction, pp. xii-xiv.

6. Grant's *Personal Memoirs*, Vol. II, p. 445.

7. *In the Ranks from the Wilderness to Appomattox Courthouse*, pp. 193–94.

8. *The Fifth Army Corps*, pp. 800–4; Humphreys, pp. 346–48; *M.H.S.M. Papers*, Vol. VI, pp. 249–52.

9. *The Passing of the Armies*, pp. 129–30.

10. *Battles and Leaders*, Vol. IV, p. 714.

11. *Ibid.*, p. 713; *The Passing of the Armies*, pp. 133–34.

12. Very loyal to Warren but impressed by Sheridan in spite of himself, General Chamberlain describes all of these exchanges in *The Passing of the Armies*, p. 142. There are very extended descriptions of the battle of Five Forks, with particular reference to the movements of the V Corps, and with strong defense of Warren's actions, by Captain Charles H. Porter and Brevet Lieutenant Colonel William W. Swan, in *M.H.S.M. Papers*, Vol. VI, pp. 211–34, 237–55, 259–408.

13. Chamberlain, *op. cit.*, pp. 143–44, 151.

14. *Ibid.*, pp. 152–53.

15. *Battles and Leaders*, Vol. IV, pp. 714–15.

16. *Following the Greek Cross*, pp. 249–50; Humphreys, p. 364; "The Storming of the Lines at Petersburg," by Brevet Brigadier General Hazard Stevens, in Vol. VI, *M.H.S.M. Papers*, pp. 412–13, 418. The latter work has an exceptionally good description of the formidable Confederate defenses.

17. General Stevens, *M.H.S.M. Papers*, Vol. VI, p. 422; *Red, White and Blue Badge*, by Penrose G. Mark, p. 321.

18. *Following the Greek Cross*, p. 252; *History of Durrell's Battery in the Civil War*, pp. 241–42; manuscript letters of Lewis Bissell; *History of the Corn Exchange Regiment*, pp. 282–83.

19. *M.H.S.M. Papers*, Vol. VI, p. 423.

20. *Ibid.*, pp. 426–28; *History of the 5th Regiment Maine Volunteers*, p. 344; General Wright's report, *Official Records*, Vol. XLVI, Part 1, pp. 902–4.

21. *Following the Greek Cross*, p. 253; *History of the 5th Regiment Maine Volunteers*, p. 345; *Battles and Leaders*, Vol. IV, p. 717.

22. *History of the 2nd Connecticut Volunteer Heavy Artillery*, pp. 159–60. The break-through of the VI Corps was by no means inexpensive, the corps losing 1,100 men in fifteen minutes. The Confederate works at Petersburg were all but literally invulnerable, despite the extreme attenuation of Confederate manpower, and General Wright said later that the spot his corps attacked, which was the weakest place in the entire Confederate line, was the only place where an assault could possibly have succeeded. See Humphreys, p. 365.

THE ENORMOUS SILENCE

1. *Letters of a War Correspondent*, pp. 308–10; *Days and Events*, pp. 439–40.

2. *Music on the March*, p. 227.

3. *History of the 198th Pennsylvania Volunteers*, p. 53.

4. *The Story of the Regiment*, p. 394; *Last Hours of Sheridan's Cavalry*, p. 115; *Official Records*, Vol. XLVI, Part 1, p. 510.

5. *Army Life: a Private's Reminiscences*, pp. 247–48; *History of the Corn Exchange Regiment*, p. 583; Gibbon's *Personal Recollections*, p. 302; *The Story of the Regiment*, p. 395.

6. *Last Hours of Sheridan's Cavalry*, pp. 97–101.

7. *Meade's Headquarters*, pp. 345–46.

8. *Battles and Leaders*, Vol. IV, pp. 719–20; *The Generalship of Ulysses S. Grant*, p. 351.

9. "A Recruit Before Petersburg," by George B. Peck, Jr., from *Rhode Island Soldiers and Sailors Society, Personal Narratives*, Second Series, p. 52; *History of the 2nd Connecticut Volunteer Heavy Artillery*, p. 160.

10. *Last Hours of Sheridan's Cavalry*, pp. 133, 149–52.

11. *Four Years in the Army of the Potomac*, p. 199.

12. *Following the Greek Cross*, pp. 262–63. There is an unforgettable glimpse of what Lee himself saw of this disaster in *R. E. Lee*, Vol. IV, pp. 84–86. For Meade's anger at what he considered Sheridan's attempt to assume sole credit for this victory, see *Meade's Headquarters*, p. 351.

13. *Days and Events*, p. 449; manuscript letters of Lewis Bissell.

14. *Battles and Leaders*, Vol. IV, pp. 729–30; *History of the Second Army Corps*, pp. 681–83.

15. *Army Life: a Private's Reminiscences*, pp. 251–52; *In the Ranks from the Wilderness to Appomattox Courthouse*, p. 212; *History of the Corn Exchange Regiment*, p. 587. Looking back from his old age, Grant wrote glowingly that "straggling had entirely ceased" (*Personal Memoirs*, Vol. II, p. 481), but the men who did the marching made no such claim.

16. *Army Life: a Private's Reminiscences*, p. 253. This unpretentious book has a very good description of the march to Appomattox, the final scene there, and the surrender ceremonies. The artillery-infantry fight on the dark road is also depicted in *History of the Corn Exchange Regiment*, p. 587.

17. *Last Hours of Sheridan's Cavalry*, pp. 214–18, 228 ff.; *History of the 17th Regiment Pennsylvania Volunteer Cavalry*, p. 315.

18. *Army Life: a Private's Reminiscences*, p. 254; *The*

Fifth Army Corps, p. 849; *In the Ranks from the Wilderness to Appomattox Courthouse*, p. 213.

19. *The Sunset of the Confederacy*, by Morris Schaff, p. 214; Gibbon's *Personal Recollections*, p. 315.

20. *Ibid.*, pp. 316–17; *Sabres and Spurs*, p. 456.

21. *Army Life: a Private's Reminiscences*, pp. 255–56.

22. *The Sunset of the Confederacy*, p. 215.

23. *Army Life: a Private's Reminiscences*, p. 257. The author of *Last Hours of Sheridan's Cavalry* says (p. 427): "We were too sleepy to move rapidly. We were too cross to be shoved by bullets."

24. *The Sunset of the Confederacy*, pp. 219–20; *History of the 198th Pennsylvania Volunteers*, p. 57; *Last Hours of Sheridan's Cavalry*, pp. 252–53.

25. *Thirteenth Regiment of New Hampshire Volunteer Infantry in the War of the Rebellion*, p. 587; manuscript letter of Sergeant George S. Hampton, of the 91st Pennsylvania. For an interesting account of the presentation of the flag of truce, and a postwar letter from the Confederate officer who carried it, see *History of the Corn Exchange Regiment*, pp. 589–91.

26. *Thrilling Days in Army Life*, p. 187. The reference to the playing of "Auld Lang Syne" is from *History of the 198th Pennsylvania Volunteers*, p. 58.

Index

Index